THE CREATIVE CURRICULUM®

for Infants & Toddlers

Amy Laura Dombro

Laura J. Colker

Diane Trister Dodge

Teaching Strategies, Inc.
Washington, DC

Cover Art & Illustrations
Jennifer Barrett O'Connell

Editors
Emily Kohn
Diane Trister Dodge
Toni Bickart

Graphic Design
Margaret Pallas

Layout and Production
Debra Al-Salam
Margaret Pallas

Spanish Translator (Traducción del Ingles)
Claudia Caicedo Nuñez

Published by:

Teaching Strategies, Inc.
P.O. Box 42243
Washington, DC 20015

Distributed by:

Gryphon House
P.O. Box 207
Beltsville, MD 20704-0207

3rd printing: 1998
Printed and bound in the United States

ISBN: 1-879537-24-9

Library of Congress Catalog
Card Number: 97-060596

— �֍ —

Acknowledgments

Our decision to write *The Creative Curriculum for Infants & Toddlers* was not made lightly. For years, we had resisted the idea, telling colleagues who asked that we felt it wasn't necessary: "Caring for infants and toddlers is about building relationships and making the most of everyday experiences and routines," we said. "You don't need a curriculum to tell you how to do this."

While we still believe that caring for infants and toddlers is about building relationships, and agree that relationships must be at the core of any infant and toddler program, we now recognize that a comprehensive curriculum is as vital to this age group as it is for any other. It has, in fact, become increasingly important today as more and more children under three are being cared for outside the home. (With welfare reform, this number will continue to increase.) Knowing the critical importance of the first few years of life and the need for quality programs that promote children's healthy development, we also recognize how difficult it is for programs to achieve quality when they lack the resources to train and retain qualified staff. We have tried to address this need by developing a practical yet comprehensive approach for staff development that applies the latest research to everyday programming. We chose the format of a curriculum because we wanted to offer an alternative to resources that emphasize only activities without providing a framework for making decisions.

With the launching of Early Head Start, we formed partnerships that enabled us to begin our work. Our first words of appreciation must go to the three Early Head Start grantees who contracted with us for staff development support and served on a Design Team to assist us in conceptualizing our approach. We wish to thank and acknowledge our partners in this effort: Brattleboro Town School District, Brattleboro, Vermont; Project Chance, Brooklyn, New York; and Sacramento Employment and Training Agency, Sacramento, California. In 1996, United Cerebral Palsy of Washington and Northern Virginia joined our team.

Many individuals helped us to shape *The Creative Curriculum for Infants & Toddlers* into a product that conveys our best thinking on how to create and maintain a high-quality program for young children and their families. A very special acknowledgment goes to our editor, Emily Kohn, who was always supportive, but also willing to challenge our thinking and patiently helped us re-work many drafts of the book. When the first draft was complete, it was sent to a group of expert reviewers who gave us extremely constructive comments. We are very grateful for the feedback and recommendations we received from Cathy Gutierrez-Gomez, Dorothy Hartigan, Trudi Norman-Murch, Bart O'Connor, Peter Pizzolongo, Michele Plutro, Valerie Rhomberg, Sherrie Rudick, Sarah Minteer Semlak, Janice Stockman, Rachel Theilheimer, and Ruth Uhlmann. We also want to thank Dianne Itterly for reviewing and commenting on the health and safety chapters and Jean Racine for her suggestions on books.

Our words came to life during the production process when Jennifer Barrett O'Connell "introduced" us to our children, families, and caregivers/teachers through her illustrations. We felt we were truly meeting in person the people we had only known in our minds! And we are grateful for the expert support of Debra Al-Salam, who was part of this project from the beginning—organizing the process, inputting our changes to countless drafts, managing the review process, and collaborating with Maggie Pallas in the final production of the book.

Finally, we want to thank the entire staff at Teaching Strategies for their support and encouragement during the development of this *Curriculum*. Staff members assisted in so many ways as we refined, revised, re-designed, and at last finalized the book. We especially want to thank Toni Bickart who helped to edit and proof the final document, and Larry Bram who assisted us in describing strategies for including children with disabilities.

We hope our book will guide readers in visualizing and implementing a high-quality program that is developmentally, individually, and culturally appropriate for infants, toddlers, and families.

❖   ❖   ❖

Table of Contents

Why a Curriculum?

Why a Curriculum for Infants and Toddlers?

A s someone who cares for infants and toddlers in center-based programs and family child care settings, you have an awesome responsibility. We now know that the first three years of life are more critical to a child's development than we ever imagined. Research tells us that more rapid brain development takes place during these years than at any other time of life. During this period, children are discovering who they are, how others respond to them, and if they are competent. They are also learning how to relate to others, what it means to express their feelings, and whether they are loved. Their brains are being "wired" into patterns for emotional, social, physical, and cognitive development.

Your work is extremely important, for you are helping to build both a foundation and a future for each child and each family. Whether you call yourself a caregiver, teacher, provider, early childhood educator, "educarer," nanny, or child development specialist, we see your role as blending the abilities and ideals represented by all of these titles. In this *Curriculum*, we have chosen to use the title caregiver/teacher, because we feel that it comes closest to representing the full spectrum of what you do. Our *Curriculum* is addressed to you—the center–based staff and family child care providers who are committed to offering a high-quality program for infants and toddlers and their families.

What Is a High-Quality Program for Infants and Toddlers?

Every high-quality program whose mission is care and education shares certain characteristics. First and foremost, it meets the standards of the profession. These standards describe seven key indicators that identify an early childhood program of high quality.[1] As you read through this list of indicators, think of the role that you play to ensure that your program is a standard bearer for quality. Notice also that a developmentally appropriate program contains

---

[1] Based on Derry G. Koralek, Laura J. Colker, and Diane Trister Dodge, *The What, Why, and How of High-Quality Early Childhood Programs: A Guide for On-Site Supervision,* Revised Edition. Washington, DC: National Association for the Education of Young Children, 1995, Ch. 1.

three interwoven elements: age appropriateness, individual appropriateness, and cultural/social appropriateness.[2]

(1) The program is based on accepted theories of child development. We know that at each stage of life, children take on special developmental tasks and challenges related to their social, emotional, physical, and cognitive development. For infants and toddlers, development occurs in all of these areas as they use their senses to gain a sense of security and identity and to explore the people and objects in their world.

The key to meeting the developmental needs of infants and toddlers can be found in the responsive relationships children build with the important adults in their lives—including you. This is why it is so important to have small-sized groups and low adult-to-child ratios. For the same reason, it is also important for each child to have a primary caregiver, and, whenever possible, for that person to remain paired with the child throughout the first three years.

(2) The program is individualized to meet the needs of every child. A knowledge of child development tells you what is age appropriate—that is, what children, in general, are like at a given age. For example, most two-year-olds are energy in motion, testing limits as well as patience. However, what you don't know from child development theory, but learn through interactions and observations, is that a particular infant with colic can be soothed by laying him across your knees and gently rocking him from side to side, and that a certain toddler, who has limited manual dexterity but loves to paint, can do so with a special headband that holds a paint brush.

The information you gather from working with children and talking with their families enables you to make the program individually appropriate for each child. You do this by making changes to the environment, planning activities, and developing strategies that build on your intimate knowledge of each child's temperament, interests, culture, emerging capabilities, and preferred learning styles.

(3) Each family's culture is respected and family members are encouraged to participate in the program. Since the 1960s and the first days of Head Start, there has been a recognition that parents and early childhood professionals are natural partners in promoting children's growth and development. In programs for infants and toddlers, it is almost impossible to serve children without also serving their families.

(4) The physical environment is safe, healthy, and contains a variety of toys and materials that are both stimulating and familiar. Every high-quality early childhood program provides an environment where children can be safe and healthy, yet free to move around, explore, and experiment. Infant and toddler environments also need to be warm and engaging so that children and families feel welcome and comfortable. A soft, stuffed chair where you can curl up with a baby and read a book, or a covered fish tank at floor level are places that stir children's imaginations and are conducive to building trusting relationships.

---

[2] Sue Bredekamp and Carol Copple, Eds. *Developmentally Appropriate Practice in Early Childhood Programs*, Revised Edition. Washington, DC: National Association for the Education of Young Children, 1997.

To create this type of environment, you continually check indoors and out to remove hazards and prevent children from injuring themselves and others. You follow hygienic procedures for diapering, toileting, hand washing, food service, and management of illness. In addition, you arrange the indoor and outdoor environments to promote active exploration, and you include attractively displayed and accessible play materials and toys that reflect the children's culture, interests, and skill levels.

(5) Children select activities and materials that interest them, and they learn by being actively involved. During their earliest years, children are learning to trust the world, to actively explore their environment, and to do things for themselves. When you give a two-year-old a bottle to feed his doll while you feed his new baby sister, you recognize the child's need to understand this new relationship. Likewise, when you place a wedge-shaped pillow on the floor near the open shelf on which dolls are displayed, you enable a child with cerebral palsy, who lacks upper body strength, to reach for the dolls on her own, when she wishes. The more you allow children to follow their own interests, the more they learn from experience, and the greater the chances that they will continue to be successful learners throughout their lives.

(6) Adults show respect for children and interact with them in caring ways. We know from research that if any single factor defines quality in an early childhood education program, it is the caring nature of adult-child interactions. Children's healthy development depends on being cared for by adults who will respond immediately and appropriately to their needs and communications. This means not just talking with children in a soothing voice, but responding to a child's needs to be held, rocked, and comforted. It also means being a sensitive and responsive communicator, both verbally and non-verbally. Even children who are not yet able to talk need you to engage in meaningful conversations with them. Infants and toddlers are most likely to thrive when they have a primary caregiver who reflects their emotions, who is there to share the highs and lows of each and every day, and who experiences with them the excitement of new discoveries.[3]

(7) Staff and providers have specialized training in child development and appropriate programming. High-quality programs are planned, implemented, and continually revised by trained professionals who have the knowledge and skills to oversee a program that is developmentally appropriate. This training comes in many forms: through college courses, by obtaining a Child Development Associate (CDA) credential, by attending workshops and seminars, by being part of a network of colleagues such as a family child care providers' association, and from using a developmentally appropriate curriculum.

Where your program is located isn't as important as what you do in the program. If yours is a quality program, the seven characteristics highlighted above will be in evidence. What, why, and how you do things are far more important than anything else. High quality is high quality, and it takes many forms.

---

[3] This type of caregiving is described in the literature as "involved teaching." See Helen Raikes, "A Secure Base for Babies: Applying Attachment Concepts to the Infant Care Setting," *Young Children*, July 1996, pp. 59–67.

The Relationship of Curriculum to High-Quality Programming

What, why, and how you do things is the purpose of a curriculum. A curriculum guides you through the processes of planning, implementing, and evaluating a developmentally appropriate program. For this reason, every high-quality early childhood program should be guided by an appropriate curriculum.

While most would agree with this in theory, the idea of having a curriculum for children younger than three makes some people uncomfortable. Those who share this feeling frequently cite the fact that there are already guidelines for developmentally appropriate practice.[4] They rightly note that using the guidelines provides a clear definition of the components of a quality program and the roles of the key players who interact in ways that promote children's growth and development.

This book takes the position that the guidelines for developmentally appropriate practice alone are not enough. While a clear definition of developmentally appropriate practice is a vital part of quality programming, it is not a substitute for curriculum. Curriculum provides a framework for pulling all of the pieces of developmentally appropriate practice together. It provides the "big picture" of where you want to lead each child and family and how you can get there.

The Creative Curriculum for Infants & Toddlers

The Creative Curriculum for Infants & Toddlers provides a written vision of where developmentally appropriate practice will take you. It is your blueprint for action. Like all formal curriculum models, *The Creative Curriculum for Infants & Toddlers* outlines what children learn during the first three years, the experiences through which children achieve these learning goals, what staff and parents do to help children reach these goals, and the materials needed to support the implementation of the curriculum.[5]

Curriculum includes three key components:[6]

❖ **Content**—what emerges from the goals and objectives. The focus is on helping children to learn about themselves, about their feelings, about others, about communicating, about moving and doing, and to acquire thinking skills. In addition to goals for children, *The Creative Curriculum for Infants & Toddlers* includes goals and objectives for the other key players in the learning process: the children's families and you, yourself.

❖ **Processes**—what you do to help children learn. They include strategies for setting up the environment, selecting toys and materials, interacting with children, and planning activities. Most importantly, processes focus on decision

[4] J. Ronald Lally, Abbey Griffin, Emily Fenichel, Marilyn Segal, Eleanor Szanton, and Bernice Weissbourd. *Caring for Infants and Toddlers in Groups: Developmentally Appropriate Practice.* Arlington, VA: ZERO TO THREE/The National Center, 1995.

[5] Note that this definition of curriculum reflects the Revised Head Start Program Performance Standards (Federal Register, Vol. 61, No. 215, Tuesday, November 5, 1996, Rules and Regulations).

[6] Sue Bredekamp and Teresa Rosegrant, (Eds.), *Reaching Potentials: Appropriate Curriculum and Assessment for Young Children*, Vol. I. Washington, DC: National Association for the Education of Young Children, 1992, p. 10.

making. All day, every day, you use routines and provide activities to respond to children's growing abilities, interests, and needs. *The Creative Curriculum for Infants & Toddlers* provides a framework for making decisions that are developmentally, individually, and culturally appropriate for each child.

❖ **Context**—the setting in which learning takes place. For children under age three, relationships are the context. By building strong bonds with children and their families, you create a climate where learning flourishes. Using *The Creative Curriculum for Infants & Toddlers* to design and implement your program enables you to lay the groundwork for a lifetime of learning.

In graphic terms, the curriculum looks like this:

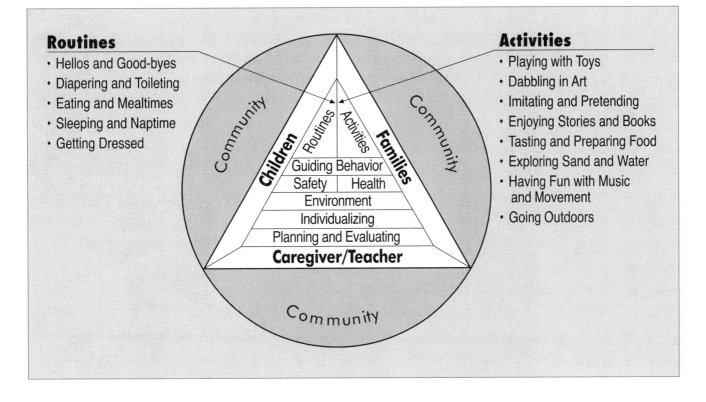

Routines
- Hellos and Good-byes
- Diapering and Toileting
- Eating and Mealtimes
- Sleeping and Naptime
- Getting Dressed

Activities
- Playing with Toys
- Dabbling in Art
- Imitating and Pretending
- Enjoying Stories and Books
- Tasting and Preparing Food
- Exploring Sand and Water
- Having Fun with Music and Movement
- Going Outdoors

Community
Children *Families*
Routines Activities
Guiding Behavior
Safety | Health
Environment
Individualizing
Planning and Evaluating
Caregiver/Teacher

As you can see, you are at the foundation of the curriculum. The children and families in your program are the focal points of your work. As shown in the graphic, they are also your equal partners. Your relationship with them is central to all that happens in your program.

Surrounding all of you is the community in which you live. The values and culture of your community are a constant, if less immediate, influence on your program. The community also symbolizes the interaction between the *Curriculum* and the larger society in which it exists: services are received from the community, but something is also given back.

By implementing *The Creative Curriculum for Infants & Toddlers,* you set the stage for children's learning. You do this by planning and continually evaluating your program. You individualize the program based on what you learn about each child and family from your observations and daily interactions. You create a warm, inviting environment, ensure that children are safe, and follow practices that promote children's health. You guide children's behavior in positive ways.

You use daily routines as opportunities to build relationships with children and promote learning. And you plan activities that respond to the growing interests and abilities of the children in your care.

Using This *Curriculum* to Make Decisions Each Day

While decision making occurs whether or not you have a formal curriculum, *The Creative Curriculum for Infants & Toddlers* gives you a framework for making decisions based on knowledge, your observations, and thoughtful reflection. How does this framework translate into practice? The best way to illustrate this process is to go back to the concept of decision making. Each day you make hundreds of decisions—both large and small—in your work with children and families. You think about questions such as the following:

❖ Should I hand the teething ring to the baby or let her reach for it?

❖ How can I personally greet each child and family if I'm in the middle of changing a diaper?

❖ How many books should I leave out for my toddlers to look at?

❖ Do the pretend play props reflect the children's home cultures?

❖ How can I be sure that the outdoor equipment is safe for the children to use?

❖ What is the best way for me to work with parents to help their child use more language?

To illustrate how you might use the *Curriculum* in your work, we take you through a typical day caring for infants and toddlers. On the following pages, we highlight some of the major responsibilities you have to juggle each day, and identify the chapters where they are addressed.

A Typical Day Caring for Infants and Toddlers

Review your plans for the day. As you walk into your center or make a cup of coffee before the first family arrives on your doorstep, think about the day ahead.

- ❖ Collect all the ingredients for playdough.

- ❖ Plan how you will give your special attention to a child who has seemed especially quiet and withdrawn for the past two days. Make a point of talking with the child's grandmother about what she has noticed at home.

> **Planning** ahead for an **art activity** gives you a mental picture of what to expect and frees you to be responsive to the individual needs of children and families. *(Chapters 5 and 17)*

> Knowing **infants and toddlers** and consulting with **family members** allows you to meet **individual needs.** *(Chapters 2, 3, and 6)*

Check over the environment. In the quiet of the morning, take a good look at the space.

- ❖ Hang a mobile over the changing table to give infants something interesting to see that they can touch or kick and make move.

- ❖ Note any toys that need to be repaired or replaced. Remove the broken fire truck with the sharp edge from the shelf.

- ❖ Replace a missing outlet cover immediately.

- ❖ Put a new picture book on the shelf to catch toddlers' interest. Remind yourself to sit down and read with children.

> Creating a **safe, welcoming environment** with interesting things to see and do encourages children to explore and learn. *(Chapters 7, 8, and 16)*

> **Reading** with children each day is critical to their development. *(Chapter 19)*

Greet children and their families. Welcome each child and family personally.

- ❖ Smile hello and explain you will be with an arriving family as soon as you finish changing a diaper.

- ❖ Ask parents questions about what has happened since you last saw their child. "When did she last eat?" "How did she sleep last night?"

- ❖ Share some of your plans for the day. "We will walk to the park later."

- ❖ Encourage a father to have a cup of juice or to read a book with his daughter as she settles in for the day.

> **Building relationships** with children's families forms a bridge for the child between home and child care. *(Chapter 1)*

> **Knowing families** helps you to better understand their needs and concerns. *(Chapter 3)*

Help children and families say good-bye to one another. Be there to assist with separations.

- ❖ Encourage parents to say good-bye, no matter how tempting it is to sneak out while their child is occupied.

- ❖ Suggest a good-bye ritual, such as walking with you to the door.

- ❖ Invite a child's grandmother to call later in the day to see how the child is doing.

- ❖ Reassure a toddler that mommy will come back just like she always does. Help him join in an activity you know he will like.

> Helping parents say **good-bye** instead of sneaking out promotes trust and strengthens the relationship between parents and their children. *(Chapter 11)*

> Listening to children and responding to their feelings helps you build **relationships.** *(Chapter 1)*

Change diapers and help toddlers learn to use the toilet. Changing a diaper or helping a child use the toilet can be much more than a simple mechanical task.

> Diapering and toileting provide excellent opportunities for one-on-one time with children. *(Chapter 12)*

❖ Help children feel good about themselves and their bodies through your language and attitude. "Let's change that diaper so you will be comfortable." "Accidents happen. Let's find a pair of dry pants."

> Taking **safety** and **health** precautions reduces the chances of accidents and guards against the spread of disease. *(Chapters 8 and 9)*

❖ Observe safety practices, such as never leaving a child on the changing table unattended and wiping up spills to avoid falls.

❖ Wash your hands—and children's—and disinfect the changing table after each diaper change.

> You **individualize** by observing so you know when a child is ready to begin working on a new skill, such as using the toilet. *(Chapter 6)*

❖ Play "Where Is Your Tummy?" as you change a child's diaper.

❖ Look for signs that indicate a toddler is getting ready to be a toilet-user—staying dry for long periods, saying when she has to urinate, or showing a real interest in sitting on the potty.

Encourage children to explore and play. Allow time for exploration.

> Offering children a range of appropriate **activities** helps them feel competent as learners. *(Chapters 16 through 23)*

❖ Provide materials that encourage infants and toddlers to use all their senses—rattles, unbreakable mirrors, squeeze toys, texture balls, finger foods to taste and smell, fill and dump toys, simple rhythm instruments, playdough, books, and simple puzzles.

> Making changes to the **environment** keeps it stimulating and challenging. *(Chapter 7)*

❖ Give the mobile a push as you change an infant's diaper.

❖ Surprise children—cover a table with a blanket to create a tent.

❖ Give a child with a disability who uses a walker the extra time needed to move to and explore different areas of the room.

❖ Share your enthusiasm and pleasure in children's discoveries. "You found our new puzzle!"

Observe children. Watch and ask yourself, "What is each child experiencing?"

> Observing helps you get to know each child so that you can **individualize** your program. Being aware of your own cultural beliefs helps assure that your observations are as objective as possible. *(Chapter 6)*

❖ Use a system for recording your observations, such as jotting notes in a notebook or on index cards.

❖ Observe and take notes on three children during activity time.

❖ Conduct both formal and informal observations.

> Making daily observations allows you to **evaluate** the program and make needed changes. *(Chapter 5)*

❖ Talk with your director or colleagues about an infant who doesn't respond to loud noises.

❖ Put away the push toys that children have been ignoring and take out some new toys to attract children's interest.

> Observing children gives you insight on their **health** and development and indicates whether screening for special needs is indicated. *(Chapter 9)*

❖ Talk with families about what a child is like at home to help you get a picture of the whole child.

❖ Be aware that your beliefs may interfere with objective observations.

Respond to children as individuals. Your challenge is to provide enough variety to meet the needs and interests of each child.

❖ Give children choices by offering a variety of activities each day.

❖ Share a book about dogs with a child who is fearful of real dogs.

❖ Be sure that each child has a "special" relationship with you— or with another adult in your setting.

❖ Use your observations and what you have learned from talking with parents to help you better understand each child's needs, interests, temperament, and learning style.

❖ Plan ways to respond to a child with special needs. For example, a child who is easily overstimulated may need to be encouraged to seek out a quiet, calming activity.

> Children learn best when they are given the opportunity to select their own play **activities.** (Chapters 16 through 23)

> Using observations gives you objective insights about a child's development, interests, and needs, which are the basis for **individualizing** your program. (Chapter 6)

> Sharing **stories and books** is important for children's language and literacy skills and is pleasurable as well. (Chapter 19)

Prepare and serve snacks and meals. Appreciate the many learning opportunities and nurturing feelings that are associated with food.

❖ Serve a variety of healthy foods.

❖ Communicate with families. Ask about cultural or dietary considerations. Learn about children's allergies, their special nutritional requirements, and food preferences. Post menus so parents know what their children eat each day.

❖ Involve older infants and toddlers in food preparation activities.

❖ Hold an infant on your lap during snack so he can enjoy all the activity. Invite toddlers to help put out plates and napkins, spread apple butter on their crackers, and pour their own juice from small plastic pitchers.

❖ Feed babies when they are hungry, not according to a preplanned schedule, and hold them on your lap when feeding them a bottle.

❖ Sit with older infants and toddlers while they eat. Talk about what they are eating and doing.

> Serving nutritious foods helps assure children's good **health** today—and tomorrow. Food habits begin at birth. (Chapter 9)

> Communicating with **families** about **mealtimes** helps you work together to build bridges between children's worlds of home and child care. (Chapters 3 and 20)

> **Tasting and preparing food** and **mealtimes** are wonderful learning opportunities for infants and toddlers. (Chapters 13 and 20)

Encourage children to sleep and take naps. The younger the child, the more individualized the schedule for sleeping and naptime.

❖ Allow children to nap when they feel the need, while you play with those who are awake.

❖ Play quiet music or dim the lights to signal that naptime is approaching.

❖ Base rituals to encourage sleep on each child's temperament and preferences. Sit with one child in a rocking chair; place another in his crib and talk quietly to him for a few minutes.

❖ Observe health and safety precautions. Be sure each child has his or her own space for sleeping and that pillows, heavy blankets, and large stuffed animals are not placed in cribs.

> Allowing children to **sleep and nap** as needed ensures they get enough rest. (Chapter 14)

> **Music** can be used as a transition from one activity to another. (Chapter 22)

> Creating a **safe, healthy** environment allows children to thrive. (Chapters 8 and 9)

Individualizing activities ensures that children get the most out of them. *(Chapter 6)*	**Offer planned activities.** Let children choose from activities that you plan and introduce.

Offer planned activities. Let children choose from activities that you plan and introduce.

❖ Think through activities appropriate to the developmental stages of the children in your care. Are the toddlers ready for five-piece puzzles? Is it a good day for fingerpainting?

Art, pretend play, sand and water, and music and movement can be particularly soothing activities. *(Chapters 17, 18, 21, and 22)*

❖ Repeat an activity from the day before that children especially liked.

❖ Choose the right time to introduce an activity. If the morning has been especially loud and hectic, bring out the playdough or puppets, or let children play at the sand box.

Sharing activities with families enables them to extend children's learning at home. *(Letters to Families)*

❖ Be aware that what children take from an experience may be different from what you had planned. Don't be disappointed if a walk to the corner turns into watching an earthworm right outside your door.

❖ Share ideas for activities and tips for doing them with families, so they can try planned activities at home. "This is the playdough recipe we made today. The children loved it."

Clearing away the clutter in the environment helps children see what is there so they can make choices. It also makes your job easier. *(Chapter 7)*

Clean up. Children learn from being involved in cleaning up.

❖ Encourage children to join you as you put things away.

❖ Be sure shelves and containers have picture labels so mobile infants and toddlers can help put their toys away on their own.

Low, open shelves that are labeled allow children to use and return toys on their own. *(Chapter 16)*

Going outdoors allows children to use their rapidly developing motor skills and explore a new environment. *(Chapter 23)*

Take children outdoors. Take children—even young infants—outdoors every day, when weather allows.

❖ Set aside a shaded soft area for young infants and quiet activities, an area with a small climber and swings, and an area for riding toys and for sand and water play in your play yard.

Encouraging children's explorations, while at the same time ensuring children's safety outdoors, requires your ongoing attention. *(Chapter 8)*

❖ Offer infants the opportunity to sleep, watch what other children are doing, and enjoy the fresh air—in a carriage, on a blanket, or in a baby carrier.

❖ Create safe places where mobile infants can crawl, cruise, climb, run, ride wheel toys, kick and throw balls, garden, and play with sand and water.

❖ Secure the straps on a stroller and insist that toddlers hold your hand when crossing the street during a neighborhood walk.

Guide children's behavior. By helping children learn how to control their behavior, you encourage inner control and the beginning of self-discipline.

❖ Guide children's behavior in ways that show respect and help them feel good about themselves: "I am going to help you stop kicking. We'll find something else for you to do."

❖ Have realistic expectations of children's behavior. An infant is not misbehaving when he cries—he is communicating with you. Toddlers are not being selfish when they fight over the ball—they are not yet ready to share.

❖ Consult with families about challenging behaviors, and together develop an approach to handling the problem.

❖ Pay close attention to a child who has a tendency to hit and bite when he becomes frustrated. Help him to express his feelings in acceptable ways.

❖ Use the environment to promote positive behavior: provide duplicates of popular toys; store pencils and other sharp objects up high and out of children's reach; use pillows to create a safe space for infants that keeps them out of toddler traffic.

> Developing positive relationships with children allows you to **guide their behavior** and helps them take their first steps toward self-discipline. *(Chapter 10)*

> Understanding child development enables you to have realistic expectations for **children's behavior** that can be shared with families. *(Chapters 2 and 3)*

> Reorganizing the **environment** can help address and prevent potential problems. *(Chapter 7)*

Help children and families reunite and head for home at the end of the day. Parents and children may need you to help them say hello to one another and good-bye to you.

❖ Invite family members to come a few minutes early and spend some time playing with their child before they have to leave.

❖ Help parents understand their son's confusing end-of-the-day behavior. When he has a tantrum about putting on his coat, explain he may have saved his deepest feelings for them—the people he loves and trusts most of all.

❖ Share news of the day with each child's family: "She finished her whole bottle at 3:30." "He helped feed the fish today." "She made it all the way to the top of the climber outside."

❖ Be available to help children gather their belongings, put on their coats, and say good-bye as they leave.

> Helping families look at **hellos and good-byes** through their children's eyes can be very reassuring. Departures are also an important time for building a bond with families. *(Chapter 11)*

> How you say good-bye to children and families is key to a strong **relationship.** *(Chapter 1)*

> **Dressing** children can be a time to build relationships and promote learning. *(Chapter 15)*

Reflect on your day. Take a moment to think about your day and what you learned, so that you can note any changes for the future.

❖ Identify an activity that went well and note who participated.

❖ Make notes about why the fingerpainting activity got out of control.

❖ Review your notes on individual children and think about new experiences you can plan for them.

> Reviewing your day enables you to **evaluate** what worked well and what aspects of your program need to be changed. *(Chapter 5)*

> Observation is the basis for **individualizing** your program goals and objectives. *(Chapter 6)*

Taking good care of yourself enables you to do your job. **You are your most important resource.** *(Chapter 1)*

When you model **healthy** behaviors, you teach children to value them, too. *(Chapter 9)*

Take care of yourself. Only by taking care of yourself will you have the resources and energy to care for the children and families in your program.

❖ Learn to lift children by bending your knees to protect your back.

❖ Display artwork or a special poster where you can see and enjoy it.

❖ Eat a nutritious breakfast and get a good night's sleep each day.

❖ Invite toddlers to join you in a few exercises each afternoon.

❖ Talk with a friend during a break or in the evening, when something is bothering you.

Being aware of and using **community** resources helps to strengthen families and enhances the quality of your program. *(Chapters 4 and 9)*

Being a **professional** means respecting the privacy of children and families and treating them honestly and ethically. *(Chapter 1)*

Meet and talk regularly with colleagues in child care and your community. Remind yourself that caring for infants and toddlers and working with families is both rewarding and demanding work. This work is easier and better done with the support of colleagues.

❖ Think about all the people who could help you with the daily questions and concerns about children and their families. This list might include your director, co-workers, members of your provider association, someone from the Child and Adult Care Food Program, and people from various social service agencies in your community.

❖ Call on community resources as issues arise. Discuss your concerns about typically developing children and those with special needs, always maintaining the confidentiality of individual children and families.

❖ Talk with colleagues regularly—at staff meetings, family child care association meetings, or even monthly pot-luck dinners.

❖ Be aware that sometimes the best way to support a family is to refer them to someone with the specific knowledge and skills needed.

The order and types of activities described in "A Typical Day" may vary from those in your program. There is, however, one important constant: being aware of *why* you do *what* you do will help ensure that your daily decisions add up to a high-quality program. Throughout this book, we will explore the ideas, strategies, and practices introduced in "A Typical Day."

Your Journey Through This Book

Depending on your experience and needs, you can use this book in different ways. You can read it chapter by chapter. You may choose to select chapters according to a prioritized need—health and safety first, for example. Or, you may wish to begin by consulting the routines and activities chapters first. However you begin, it is important to keep in mind that creating and maintaining a quality program is an ongoing journey, not a task that one can accomplish and cross off as "done."

For many of you, *The Creative Curriculum for Infants & Toddlers* will confirm the excellent practices you are already carrying out. For some, this will be your first introduction to caring for infants and toddlers. For all readers, we hope that the *Curriculum* will enhance what you do well and give you new ideas and strategies for improving your program.

Goals and Objectives for Caregivers/Teachers

To help you keep track of where you have been and where you are going as you journey through this book, we begin the *Curriculum* with goals and objectives for you, the caregiver/teacher.

Goal 1: To build responsive relationships

- ❖ To form positive, trusting relationships with children
- ❖ To form positive relationships with families to support children's growth and development
- ❖ To work with colleagues and community representatives to support children and families

Goal 2: To plan and manage a developmentally appropriate program

- ❖ To plan and evaluate a program that meets the needs of the children and families served
- ❖ To observe children regularly and individualize the program based on these observations
- ❖ To create a warm and welcoming environment that supports children's growth and development
- ❖ To ensure the safety of children in the program
- ❖ To ensure the health of children in the program
- ❖ To guide children's behavior in positive ways

Goal 3: To promote children's development and learning

- ❖ To use routines as opportunities for growth and learning
- ❖ To provide activities that will facilitate children's growth and development

Goal 4: To continue learning about children, families, and the field of early childhood education

- ❖ To participate in training to expand skills and knowledge
- ❖ To participate in professional early childhood education organizations
- ❖ To observe colleagues to learn new successful techniques and approaches

Goal 5: To maintain professional standards

- ❖ To be ethical in all dealings with children, families, and community representatives
- ❖ To respect the privacy and confidentiality of children and parents
- ❖ To demonstrate respect for all children and families

Goal 6: To be an advocate in support of children and families

- ❖ To educate others about the need for high standards and quality programs
- ❖ To work with community agencies in support of children and families

The *Goals and Objectives for Caregivers/Teachers* are presented in the form of a self-assessment tool in Appendix A. You can use this form to help you track your own professional development, to indicate those parts of your job you do well, and to identify areas you want to work on.

Other Goals and Objectives

As you begin reading through *The Creative Curriculum for Infants & Toddlers* and applying it to your own program, you will note that we have grouped children into three categories to highlight developmental differences that will influence the decisions you make. These categories are:

- ❖ young infants (birth through 8 months);
- ❖ mobile infants (8 months to 18 months); and
- ❖ toddlers (18 to 36 months).

A listing of goals and objectives for each of the age groups can be found in Chapter 5, Planning and Evaluating the Program. Forms to help you individualize your program are based on these goals and objectives. These forms, entitled *Individualizing Goals and Objectives for Young Infants, Individualizing Goals and Objectives for Mobile Infants,* and *Individualizing Goals and Objectives for Toddlers* can be found in Appendix B. In Chapter 6, Individualizing for Children and Families, we have modeled the process of individualizing by using the forms for toddlers to plan for 35 month-old Valisha Curtis.

Because families are your partners in creating a quality program, Chapter 5 also includes a list of goals and objectives for your work in building relationships with families. A form, entitled *Goals for Working with Families* can also be found in Appendix B. You can use it to plan and track your work with each family in your program.

Introducing Our Children, Families, and Caregivers/Teachers

We would like to introduce our cast of characters—the infants and toddlers, families, and caregivers/teachers you will meet as you journey through *The Creative Curriculum for Infants & Toddlers.* Though each child and family is distinct in culture, interests, temperament, and background, as a group they typify all of the children and families you serve. The programs described highlight the range of settings in which infants and toddlers can receive quality care, and the varied backgrounds of the caregivers/teachers who ensure that the care is of the highest quality.

Julio Gonzales, 4 months, lives in Florida with his parents Marta and José, and his 15-month-old sister, Maria. His parents speak both English and Spanish at home.
Linda Marquez has a two-year degree in early childhood education. She is bilingual and works at a center that serves a migrant community.

Jasmine Jones, 8 months, lives on a U.S. military base in Germany with her mother, Charmaine Jones, a Master Sergeant in the Air Force. Jasmine frequently spends nights with her caregiver's family when her mother is on travel duty.
Janet Walker became a family child care provider so she could stay at home with her own five children.

Willard O'Keith, 11 months, is the only child of Kevin and Monica who are graduate students in Iowa. **Grace Lincoln** is a college student majoring in child development who interns at the university-sponsored child care center.

Abby Kennedy, 16 months, was adopted from Korea when she was one week old. She lives with her parents, Robin and Edward, and her older sister, Talia, age nine. **Dr. Brooks Peterson,** a family child care provider, is a retired psychologist who provides infant and toddler care for two or three children at a time.

Leo New, 20 months, lives on a reservation in Arizona with his parents, Virginia and Elmer. **Barbara Yellowcloud,** a center-based teacher, earned her CDA credential and is currently taking distance learning courses by satellite.

Matthew Gerry, 26 months, lives with his parents, Nancy and Pete, and a newborn sister, Kara, in a Chicago suburb. **Mercedes de Jesus** has been a family child care provider for three years. She works weekends as a caterer.

Gena Domenica, 30 months, lives in Rhode Island with her parents, Neal and Rebecca and eight siblings ranging in age from 11 months to 21 years. Born with cerebral palsy, Gena has limited mobility. **Ivan Powell,** a center-based teacher, is very comfortable working with children who have special needs. He is taking courses leading to a CDA credential.

Valisha and Jonisha Curtis, identical twins, 35 months, live in Los Angeles with their parents, Yvonne and Johnny. Jonisha wears eye glasses as a result of an injury. **La Toya Thompkins** cares for six children in her home.

Part I Who's Who

Who's Who in a Quality Program

A quality program begins with the key players and the trusting, responsive relationships that exist among them. It evolves and changes as a result of interactions between the caregiver/teacher, the children, their families, and the community.

You play a central role in nurturing these relationships. The infants and toddlers you care for are learning who they are as people. How you relate to them affects how they will feel about themselves and others. As you model, guide, listen, and respond, you help children feel good about who they are and you help them learn how to relate to people and to objects in their world. As the children grow and change, you adapt your interactions to promote greater independence, more complex use of their skills, and further learning. Knowledge of patterns of child development and the individual characteristics of each child with whom you work forms the basis of the many decisions you make each day.

Children are part of families, and you interact daily with family members. Because research shows that effective programs require the joint efforts of families and teachers, good relationships with families are critical to the success of your program. Equally important, they help build strong families. You build relationships with parents as you establish an atmosphere of trust and respect. In this kind of atmosphere, you and family members each can contribute your own expertise to benefit and support the children in your lives.

Because families may look to you to guide them to other resources in the community, you need to be familiar with the services your community provides. To increase your awareness of available resources, you begin to build relationships with colleagues, professional groups, and with people who work in various community agencies. As you reach out, you'll discover how much you have to offer your community, based on your commitment to and knowledge of children and families. Building community relationships takes time, but once built, they can enrich your program, your community, and you, yourself.

No one can tell you that creating and maintaining a quality program for infants and toddlers is easy. It's not. But everyone can tell you that this work is valuable and worth your best efforts. By working with families and others in your community, you can give children the most valuable gifts possible—a positive sense of themselves and their abilities, a desire to relate positively to others, and a strong interest in learning. In so doing, you are building the foundation for their future success and happiness in school and in life.

❖   ❖   ❖

Building Relationships: The Focus of Your Work

Whether you work in your home or a center, building relationships with infants, toddlers, and their families is the focus of your work. You are the one who can make sure that your program meets the needs of the children and families you serve. For this reason, we place you at the foundation of our curriculum.

People who work with infants and toddlers don't always appreciate the critical importance of their work, as they face the fourteenth diaper change of the day. Or reach for the tissue box once again. Or explain to an upset mother that one of her child's socks is missing. While these tasks may at times seem unimportant or dull, it's important to keep in mind that every interaction is an opportunity to build the relationships that are at the heart of a quality program.

Building Relationships with Children

During the first three years of life, infants and toddlers are learning who they are. Through their interactions with you and their families, they gain answers to questions such as:

- ❖ Do people respond to me?
- ❖ Can I depend on other people when I need them?
- ❖ Am I important to others?
- ❖ Am I competent?
- ❖ How should I behave?
- ❖ Do people enjoy being with me?
- ❖ What should I be afraid of?
- ❖ Is it safe for me to show how I feel?
- ❖ What things interest me?

The daily interactions you have with children help shape their sense of themselves and how they will relate to other people. When you respond to infants' needs consistently, promptly, and lovingly, you help them learn to trust and show them what it means to be in a caring relationship with another person. When you guide toddlers' behavior in respectful, positive ways, you promote self-discipline and help children learn to express their feelings in acceptable ways. As you listen to children, create a safe environment filled with interesting things to do and opportunities to be competent, and share your pleasure in their discoveries, you help children feel good about themselves and their growing skills.

Each child in your program will benefit from a relationship with a **primary caregiver.** This person has the major responsibility for the child's daily care. The child-primary caregiver relationship serves as a child's "home base." In a family child care setting, you are likely to be each child's primary caregiver. In some larger child care homes and center-based programs, the owner or director may assign a primary caregiver for each child, or let chemistry determine special relationships. Regardless of how they are formed, special one-on-one relationships are key to a child's feelings of security in child care and to development of a positive sense of self.

Strategies for Building Relationships with Children

How do you build relationships with children? As in all aspects of your work, knowing yourself is a good place to start. The more aware you are of your own feelings, attitudes, and values, the more aware you can be of those of others. To be self-aware requires a willingness to ask questions such as, "Why am I acting this way?" as you find yourself, for example, becoming overly involved with one child, or shying away from another. Recognizing that your feelings shape your interactions will help you form relationships and respond to children individually. Here are some ways to build relationships with children as you care for them each day.

Allow time. Often, the demands of caring for a group of children can keep you so busy that you feel you have no time simply to be with an individual child and get to know one another. To help you slow down, remind yourself that building relationships is a central part of your work.

Be dependable. Let children know they can count on you. Be there to greet them at the door each morning. Respond promptly to a child who is crying. Keep your promises: "Yesterday we said you could help make playdough today. Are you ready?"

Handle children's bodies with respect. Explain to an infant, "I'm going to pick you up now so I can change your diaper." Ask a toddler, "Could you please help me take off your wet shirt?"

Listen and respond to what children tell you. Give children your full attention when you respond to them. Learn to distinguish an infant's cries, so you'll know whether to offer him something to eat, comfort him, or change his diaper. Sit down and listen to a toddler's story about helping to make pancakes over the weekend.

Use caring words to let children know they are respected and understood. Think about what you say and also how you say it. Even infants who can't talk yet and don't know the meaning of the words you say are sensitive to the sound of your voice. Use the child's home language whenever possible. Practice using caring words and a caring tone. For example, when comforting an upset child, you might say, "You are having a hard time. I can tell by your tears you're feeling sad. Let's sit here in the rocking chair together and see how we can help you feel better."

Adapt daily routines to meet individual needs. Offer an infant a bottle when she is hungry, regardless of whether it is snacktime or mealtime. Give a toddler time to finish his puzzle before you change his diaper.

Offer children opportunities to make decisions, whenever possible. Give children clear alternatives when the choice is theirs to make. At snacktime, asking children to choose among slices of banana, peach, or pear shows you respect their tastes and their growing decision-making skills.

Have realistic expectations of children's behavior. Knowing about child development means you won't be surprised, for example, if two toddlers fight over the same toy. Instead of getting upset or blaming the children, you'll know to provide duplicates of favorite items, and also to show children how they can use a toy together.

Tell children when you leave the room. Let children know that you are going into the kitchen or upstairs to a meeting. This tells them you won't suddenly disappear. Rather than keeping tabs on you, they can focus on what they are doing.

Attend to your own needs. To build and maintain relationships, you need to focus on children and not be distracted by your own concerns. Take a few minutes each day to take care of yourself so that you will have the energy you need for the children.

What If You Don't Like a Child

Have you ever worked with a child you didn't really like? If so, you are not alone. Though it can be a hard thing to admit, especially when talking about an infant or toddler, owning up to your feelings is part of being a professional. In rare cases, you may decide that things are not going to work out and that it is time to part ways with a child and family. More often, acknowledging your negative feelings is a signal to call on your professional self to figure out why this child is bothering you. Try to find something positive that will help you to be more open to building a relationship. It may help to share your feelings with a colleague, or even to ask a colleague to observe you and this child together. Consider this story, shared by Barbara.

"I worked with a toddler once who, to be honest, bugged me. It took me a long time until I could admit that. He seemed to be in constant motion and made lots of noise. It wasn't until I stopped to observe him that I found he liked looking at the fish in our tank. Feeding the fish together each morning was the way our relationship began."

All relationships have their ups and downs. Some are clearly easier than others. We believe, however, that the extra effort you put into building positive relationships with every child will be repaid many times over.

Building Relationships with Families

Children need you and their families to work together. By working together, you can both get to know a child better than either of you could on your own. Your relationship builds a bridge between a child's two worlds: home and child care.

Parents are specialists about their child. For example, Jasmine's mother, Charmaine, is able to share with Janet, Jasmine's family child care provider, that Jasmine cries for a bottle as soon as she wakes up from her morning nap, and that lately she has been afraid of dogs. Janet is a specialist, too. From her training and experience, she knows how children develop. She knows, for example, that babies' needs should be met quickly. She also knows that fears are common, and that with support, they usually pass. Sharing knowledge with one another helps both gain a more complete picture of Jasmine and how to respond to her needs.

Beginning a Relationship

When a family member comes to visit your program, take time to share a little about yourself—your background, training, and why you have chosen to work with infants and toddlers. Take them on a tour of your space. Describe your program and curriculum. Most important, assure families of your belief that they are—and will remain—the most important people in their children's lives. Let them know that your goal is to work with them to help their children grow and thrive.

Take time to listen to parents and answer their questions. Ask them about their hopes and dreams for their child. What concerns do they have? What do they want from you and from your program for their child? Discuss the program's hours, calendar, and what happens in case of illness (children's and yours). Clarify your program policies and outline business procedures. Make sure families know what responsibilities you and they have to each other and to the program. You'll probably want to provide printed copies of policies and procedures.

We strongly recommend making home visits as a way to get to know and build relationships with families. A home visit also provides a unique opportunity to see a child and his or her family in their natural environment, which builds mutual understanding. Your willingness to visit families at home sends a strong message that you want to reach out to them. But be aware that not all families feel comfortable about inviting you into their homes. For this reason, we suggest that you first visit those families with whom you feel welcome. It may take a little selling on your part to help other families understand the purpose of your visit. Assure them that you are not there to check up on them, but rather to reinforce the connection between home and child care for their child.

Sharing Information Daily

Sharing information about the basics of daily living—sleeping, eating, and toileting—can help everyone be more responsive to children's needs. For example, when a parent tells you that his child was up most of the night, you'll know that the child might need a nap earlier than usual. If you tell a child's grandmother that her grandchild didn't eat lunch, she may decide to offer him a snack before going home. Sharing information about a child's skills and interests may lead you both to give the child more opportunities to practice and explore. For example, when you tell a father how his toddler poured her own juice from a small pitcher, he may allow extra time for waterplay in the bathtub at home.

In addition, sharing information about events in a child's life can also help you understand a child's feelings. For example, knowing that a child's grandfather is very ill may explain why she has been more clingy and whiny than usual. With this information in mind, you may decide to spend extra one-on-one time with her and to talk about her grandfather.

Communication can take many forms. Little conversations at the beginning and end of the day are good ways to share news of a child's day and to tell families what will be happening in the near future. Some programs use a clipboard with a standard form on which they jot down notes about each child's day.

Occasional social events are another way to communicate with children's families. A pot-luck supper or a weekend picnic can give families an opportunity to know you better and to meet and talk with other families. Conversations that start with sharing a recipe or during a game in the park can continue long after the event is over.

Sometimes, sharing information can bring up feelings of self-doubt and worry. For example, a mother may be afraid to tell you that her child doesn't sleep through the night. Perhaps she fears this information makes her seem incompetent. You may worry about admitting that you haven't been successful in stopping a child in your program from biting. When these kinds of feelings arise, remember that no one knows all the answers when it comes to caring for children. Even when there is a clear-cut answer, it often changes as a child moves to a new stage of development. Only by sharing your questions can you and a child's family pool your ideas, seek information on ways to handle a situation, and build the kind of working relationship that benefits children.

While sharing information with families is very important, always be careful to respect confidentiality. Letting families know that your conversations will go no farther will help them feel more comfortable about sharing their concerns.

Holding Conferences with Parents

Conferences are another way to build relationships with families. These conferences can serve many purposes. They can help you and parents feel more comfortable working together. They can give you all a chance to learn more about a child. They can also provide an uninterrupted time to talk about the child's development, set new goals, and discuss how you might deal with a particular issue a child or family may be facing.

Planning in advance helps to ensure a successful conference.

❖ **Arrange a time that is convenient for families**. Make a special effort to invite fathers and other males who are important in a child's life.

❖ **Let families know what to expect.** When you set up the conference, explain how long it will take and the kinds of things you will discuss. Ask what other topics families want to talk about.

❖ **Think carefully about the points you want to cover.** Review your observation records and ask co-workers if they have any information or insights to contribute. Sharing stories and observations will help families get a clear picture of their child and of your program as well.

❖ **If language differences are a barrier, invite someone to help interpret.** Many families have someone they know who can serve as an interpreter and may feel more comfortable having that person help them to communicate with you. If such a person is not available, try to arrange for someone else to interpret.

❖ **Give some thought to where you will meet.** Find a comfortable place with adult-size furniture. Be sure the area is private and separate from the children.

Because conferences are not everyday events, think about ways to put everyone at ease. Here are some suggestions for making everyone comfortable during a conference.

❖ **Begin by welcoming parents.** Like Brooks, offer an observation that says you know and enjoy their child: "Abby just makes my day. She's always so eager to try new things. You should have seen the delight on her face when she tasted the kiwi yesterday."

❖ **Discuss the purpose of your time together.** Follow Mercedes's example: "Today we have the chance to think about how Matthew is doing. You said you wanted to know more about how he spends his days here. I thought we could begin there, then talk about the new skills he is learning. Are there some other topics you wish to discuss?"

❖ **Be sure there are many opportunities for parents to make comments and ask questions.** Grace does this by being sensitive to nonverbal cues: "Kevin, you have a puzzled look on your face. Did you want to ask me something else about Willard's progress?"

❖ **If a family speaks a language you are not familiar with, ask for some help.** Show an interest in learning some basic words in their language.

❖ **At the end of the conference, summarize the main ideas you've talked about.** Review any actions you've all agreed to take. Here's how Ivan does this: "Why don't we go over to the library right now. I can recommend some books that Gena might enjoy having you read to her."

Resolving Differences

There will be times you and the children's families will disagree about something. Many of the differences come from the fact that you both care deeply about a child and want the best for him or her. However, you each may have different ideas about what is "the best." Sometimes these conflicts are due to lack of understanding about cultural differences or appropriate practice.

When you and parents disagree, there are usually three courses of action you can take. You can choose to face the problem and work it out. (This is where we recommend you start.) You can let an issue go—that is, ignore it. Or you can decide things are unworkable and end your relationship. Which option you choose will depend on the way you usually handle conflicts, the conflict itself, and its importance to you.

Work together to find a solution. If an issue is bothering you and you don't try to resolve it, you will probably become annoyed. Even when you try to hide your feelings, children will sense that something is not quite right. It's worth taking time to find a resolution, as Linda did in the following example.

> Julio had been at the Shane Center for just one month, but each week his parents had been coming later and later to pick him up. The Center closed at 6:00 P.M., and Linda had to leave on time to attend a class. Linda was annoyed at Julio's parents because her reminders had not made a difference. Finally, she arranged a conference to explain to them how difficult it was for her when they were late. Julio's father said they didn't know they were causing a problem. If they had to be late from now on, the parents agreed to have a cousin pick up Julio.

Here are some steps you might try to resolve a difference:

❖ Identify the problem or issue.
❖ Work together to make a plan for dealing with the issue.
❖ Try your plan for a particular length of time.
❖ Check in with each other to see how things are going.
❖ Make changes as needed.

Let an issue go. Sometimes an issue really isn't all that important. If you decide on this option, however, be sure your reason is not merely to avoid a conflict. The example below shows how this option can be effective if, like Barbara, you really let the issue go.

> Barbara felt annoyed when Leo's parents kept forgetting to bring a blanket for him to use at nap time. Yet, when she considered all the problems and stresses in their lives, she realized it was quite amazing they even got Leo to child care. Barbara decided to let the issue go. She brought in one of her son's old blankets—and took it home each week to wash. For her, the situation was resolved.

End your relationship. Sometimes, it's impossible to resolve a difference in a way that will allow you to continue working comfortably. Under these conditions, your decision may be to part ways. The following example shows how Mercedes made this difficult choice.

> Sarah's parents insisted that she was toilet trained. Although she had several accidents each day and showed no interest in using the potty, her parents refused to let Mercedes put her in diapers during the day. Mercedes and the family had many discussions about toilet training. However, further discussion only led to arguments and Sarah was showing signs of increasing tension. For these reasons, Mercedes decided it was best to part ways.

Remember, this decision should only be considered as a last resort. When following this course of action, try to help families find alternative child care arrangements, for example, by suggesting they contact a child care resource and referral agency.

Differences can often stir up feelings of frustration and anger. These feelings can make it difficult to resolve problems. Sometimes, talking with co-workers who have had similar experiences can help you understand a problem and may give you ideas of how to work with families toward a resolution.

Here are some principles that may help guide you through the process of attempting to resolve conflicts.

Keep the children's best interests in mind. Children need you and their families to deal with your differences in ways that don't interfere with their care.

Let parents know you understand their feelings. Often the issues that come up generate strong feelings. Just acknowledging that you understand can put parents at ease.

Build on your history together. A disagreement doesn't have to mean that one of you is doing something wrong. Instead, a disagreement can be a point from which both you and families can learn and grow.

Have realistic expectations. Resolving differences often takes much time and discussion. And some differences may never be resolved. However, as long as you both are willing to discuss an issue, your relationship with families and your support of the child can continue.

When you know that conflicts are a normal part of sharing the care of a young child, you can look at them as opportunities to better understand a family's point of view. The more you know about children and families, the more likely you will be able to determine the best approach to handling conflicts. The next two chapters will help you to get to know children and families.

Knowing Infants and Toddlers

A ll curriculum planning begins with knowing the children—how they grow and develop; what makes them unique; and the cultural context or family environment in which they develop. All the decisions you make to create a quality program stem from this knowledge. The more you know about children, the more effectively you can meet their needs.

Generally, all infants and toddlers in your program follow a similar path of development, though in their own ways and at their own pace. In less than 36 months, the children in your program will change from being totally dependent on others to care for them to being able to choose which shirt they want to wear and proudly pouring their own juice.

This chapter provides information on child development—how children three and younger grow and develop and learn. We discuss how infants and toddlers learn:

- ❖ about themselves—self-concept development;
- ❖ about their feelings—emotional development;
- ❖ about other people—social development;
- ❖ to communicate—language development.;
- ❖ to move and do—physical development; and
- ❖ to think—cognitive development.

In addition to knowing about child development in general, you must take time to get to know each child in your program. This chapter, therefore, also explores how children differ in terms of individual temperaments and special needs. (In the chapter that follows, Knowing Families, we discuss the influence of culture.)

Learning About Themselves

In the first three years of life, infants and toddlers begin creating a picture of who they are, what they can do, and what they think and feel. It is a picture that will affect every area of their development. How you respond to children helps shape this picture. When you are respectful, share your pleasure in children's accomplishments and discoveries, and create an environment in which they can participate in daily routines and activities, you show children they are important, interesting, and competent. Your attitudes and actions help give children a good beginning during these important early years.

Building a Sense of Self

According to child psychiatrist Margaret Mahler, children go through a process that she calls a psychological birth.[1] Physically separated from their mothers at birth, they spend the next three years developing a sense of themselves as individuals who are attached to, but separate from, their parents.

Around the age of four to five months, young infants begin to discover that they are separate human beings. By about eight months, they have become emotionally attached to their parents and to other primary caregivers. You can often recognize this stage by observing the way an infant responds to strangers. It's typical for infants this age to hide their faces and shriek when they see someone unfamiliar. At this stage also, children often protest separating from their families. They may cry and cling when a family member says good-bye in the mornings.

By the time children are 10 to 16 months old, they act like explorers in love with the world. They are often so busy walking and practicing other new skills that their parents sometimes have to literally stand in front of them and wave good-bye to catch their attention. At this stage, parents sometimes worry their children don't care if they stay or go. This is not the case at all. If you observe carefully, you'll notice that children often seem a bit subdued or quiet when members of their family are not present. Quite the reverse is true at the end of the day. When a family member walks in the door, it's as if the children's emotional temperature rises. It is very important to understand this behavior, particularly for children who spend many hours each day in child care.

At around 18 months, the same toddlers who were so busy they didn't seem to notice when their parents were leaving often become upset and cling again when it's time to say good-bye. Having "seen the world," it's as if they gain a new awareness of how small and vulnerable they are. However, as toddlers move towards 24 months and beyond, they are better able to carry the image of their parents in their minds, when these adults are not physically present. Toddlers this age can also hold the memory that their parents will return. By the age of three, most children are "psychologically born"— though separations can still be difficult at times.

Building Trust and Autonomy

How children feel about themselves as they relate to others and learn who they are affects every area of their development. The psychologist Erik Erikson has identified eight stages through which each person passes in the lifelong process of developing a sense of self. Infants and toddlers are working on the first two stages.[2]

---

[1] Margaret S. Mahler, Fred Pine, and Anni Bergman. *The Psychological Birth of the Human Infant: Symbiosis and Individuation.* New York: Basic Books, Inc., 1975.

[2] Erik Erikson. *Childhood and Society.* New York: W.W. Norton & Company, Inc., 1950.

Infants are at the first stage: developing trust. Young infants have physical needs: to be fed when they are hungry; changed when soiled or wet; and allowed to sleep when they are tired. They also have emotional needs: to be comforted when upset; to have someone to talk with and interesting things to explore; and to be held and loved. When you meet their needs consistently, promptly, and lovingly, you help infants learn to trust themselves and their world.

Sometimes adults worry they will spoil infants by always responding to their needs. The reality is that infants need what they need when they need it. When you hold an infant securely in your arms and take time to sing a song or play "Where is your nose?" when you change a child's diaper, you are helping to build a sense of trust.

Toddlers are at the second stage: developing autonomy. According to Erikson, toddlers need to stretch their wings and assert themselves. At the same time, though, they need you to set clear and firm limits.

The world can be an exciting place to toddlers. Sometimes, it can feel so big that it's overwhelming. As a result, toddlers typically find themselves wanting the impossible: to be big and to stay little at the same time. As toddlers struggle with these feelings, you may find it difficult to know how best to respond to them. The most caring and knowledgeable adult can find herself at wit's end when a two-year-old screams, "No!" as she tries to help him put on his coat. Then she finds the same child five minutes later, dissolved in tears of frustration and wanting to be cuddled like a baby.

For toddlers, *no* is a favorite word. Saying *no* plays an important role in developing a sense of self. This powerful word helps children block out the often overpowering voice of adults and assert, "This is me."

You can help the toddlers in your program develop their independence and a positive sense of themselves. One way is to look at the world through their eyes so you can better understand what they may be experiencing. Using this approach can help you recognize that they aren't out to "get you"—even though it may feel that way sometimes. Rather, they are grappling with growing up. This understanding can help you respond to their often challenging behaviors with respect, appreciation, and with much needed humor.

Learning About Their Feelings

Day after day, your interactions with infants and toddlers help shape their emotional life. According to psychiatrist Daniel Stern, when there is **attunement**, a child learns that other people can understand and share his feelings.[3] For instance, Linda is attuned to Julio when she smiles and mirrors his pleasure in making a sound with his rattle. As she does this, she is reinforcing the pathways in his brain that create emotions. When an attuned adult such as Linda mirrors back an emotion and an infant responds, the adult is helping to reinforce the signals in the child's brain that produced that emotion.

---

[3] Based on Daniel Stern, *The Interpersonal World of the Infant.* New York: Basic Books, 1987.

However, when an infant and adult are not in emotional "sync" with one another most of the time, the child's brain circuits and emotions may become confused. Examples of being emotionally "out-of-sync" would be the adult who usually responds angrily when an infant feels sad, or responds to a toddler's joy with a resigned sigh.

Milestones of Emotional Development

Stanley Greenspan, a psychiatrist and pioneer in the field of emotional development, has charted milestones in children's emotional growth.[4] The following paragraphs describe each milestone briefly.

Self regulation and interest in the world (birth+). During this first stage, young infants have their own ways of dealing with sensations, taking in and acting on information, and finding ways to calm and soothe themselves. They need you and their parents to take note of these individual differences and respond to them in appropriate ways.

Falling in love (4 months+). By four months, some infants eagerly reach out for relationships. Others need to be gently sold on them. More hesitant infants need you and their parents to continue to woo them, even when some attempts are ignored or rejected.

Developing intentional communication (8 months+). By this stage, infants need to know that their families and caregivers can understand and respond appropriately to the signals they communicate. For example, they need adults to read their cues that signal the need for calm and when they are ready for more active play.

Emergence of an organized sense of self (10 months+). By 10–18 months, infants and toddlers need adults to recognize and show appreciation of all the new abilities they have mastered. When you follow a child's lead during play, help her shift from one activity to another, and extend her play, you help her see herself as a complex, organized individual.

Creating emotional ideas (18 months+). By 18–24 months, children use pretend play to act out their feelings and to put into words their curiosity about sexuality, aggression, rejection, and separation. When you help children express their feelings through words and gestures, you promote their emotional development. If children's emotions make you uncomfortable, you may find yourself cutting off play that includes anger and aggression. Rather than limit children's exploration of these emotions, acknowledge their feelings and model or suggest an appropriate way to express them.

Emotional thinking: the basis for fantasy, reality, and self-esteem (30 months+). By about 30 months, children begin to move from acting out their emotions to using reasoning. For example, rather than simply hugging a doll, a child might explain that the doll is sad because she fell down and hurt her knee. During this stage, children need you to set limits and guide their behavior in positive ways that take their feelings into account.

---

[4]Based on Stanley Greenspan and Nancy Thorndike Greenspan. *First Feelings: Milestones in The Emotional Development of Your Baby and Child From Birth to Age 4.* New York: Viking Penguin Inc., 1985.

Learning About Other People

A child's social development begins at birth. Infants and toddlers learn about how to relate to other people through daily interactions with their families and other important adults. They learn how to treat others by noticing how they are treated. Developing a supportive, loving relationship with each infant and toddler in your care is the most important way for you to promote positive social development.

Typically, during the third month of life, a special moment occurs: an infant smiles directly and purposefully at an important adult. Over the next month or two, there are further signs of recognition: infants respond more strongly by kicking or cooing and by protesting when an important adult moves out of sight. This is the time when, according to Greenspan, infants first "fall in love" with another person. It is also the time when, as Mahler noted, they begin to recognize that they are separate people and that being with other people is an enjoyable experience.

Mobile infants enjoy watching other children and may imitate what they see others do. They can crawl or walk to you and climb on your lap for a hug or a story. By noticing infants' cues, playing peek-a-boo, and rolling a ball back and forth, you help infants learn the give and take of responding to others. They discover that relating to another person is interesting, fun, and rewarding.

Toddlers, too, are naturally curious and interested in other people. By providing simple props and encouraging pretend play, you invite children to explore the roles and activities of the important people in their lives and, as a result, to feel closer to them. Toddlers are also very observant of one another. In a group setting, they quickly learn whose mommy and daddy, bottle, and shoes belong to whom. Have you ever been amazed at the ways toddlers can attend to and care for each other? They may, for example, hold a cup to a child's mouth who cannot do this independently, or gently pat another child who is crying.

At the same time, the reverse of this caring attention is equally common. You may have observed how often biting, hitting, and pinching occur, and how difficult it is for toddlers to share. Toddlers tend to have strong feelings and often don't know how to express them. Sharing is a developmental task that develops over time and requires considerable practice. As you set behavioral limits and respond to toddlers with respect and understanding, you lay the groundwork for their future relationships with others.

Learning About Communicating

Language development is one of the major accomplishments that occurs during the first three years of life. In this brief time, a child moves from communicating needs only through crying to understanding language and communicating through words or sign language. During these years, children learn hundreds of words, their meanings, and the rules for using them. They learn all this simply by being around adults who communicate with them and encourage their efforts to communicate.

The Development of Language in Infants

The development of language goes through predictable stages that are evident in all children, regardless of the language they speak. Crying is the first step in communicating. Then, during their first few months, infants begin making other sounds. They gurgle, coo, and squeal, using sounds to establish contact with adults. By about six to nine months, infants begin to babble sounds in their home language. In addition to making sounds, infants also listen and respond. Observers have videotaped infants as young as 12 hours making tiny movements in sync with someone's voice.

As they get older, infants may respond by smiling, kicking, and turning their heads to look at someone talking. They may also cry, turn away, or withdraw, should their surroundings become too noisy. Children this age understand more than they can say. Before they are able to talk, they look at objects we name and make gestures such as waving good-bye during leave-taking, or blowing on their carrots when you caution they are hot.

At about one year, some infants say a few recognizable words, usually the names of people and things that are important to them. In English-speaking families, favorite words often include *mama, dada, bottle, cat,* or *ball.* Soon, children start to use a mix of words and babble, forming sentences spoken with great expression. The language an infant hears determines the "language connections" that are formed in her brain as well as the sounds she makes and can distinguish. This is why children exposed to two languages from infancy can become truly bilingual.

The Development of Language in Toddlers

By the time they are about eighteen months old, many toddlers have at least 20 words in their oral vocabulary. They can use language to express a need, for they have learned that words can help them "get" something. They may begin putting words together to express a thought such as "Daddy go" or "me do." By the age of two, many children's vocabularies have expanded to as many as 50 to 60 words. Between the ages of two and three, they may be able to say anywhere from 200 to 1,000 words or more and use simple sentences to tell you about their needs, feelings, and experiences.

As in all aspects of development, young children develop language at their own rates. Some say their first words at eight months. Others hardly speak at all until they are almost two. Many factors influence how and when language develops. Some are individual differences present from birth. Others depend on a child's experiences with communication. One of your important tasks is to respect individual differences in language development.

Remember that learning to talk takes much practice. By sharing your pleasure in children's communication rather than rushing in to correct their mistakes, you help children build on their natural desire to communicate.

Learning to Move and Do

Physical development refers to gradually gaining control over gross (large) and fine (small) muscles. It includes acquiring gross motor skills that, over time, allow a child to roll over, sit, crawl, walk, run, and throw a ball. It also includes developing fine motor skills such as holding, pinching, and flexing fingers. As children develop these skills, they can use them to draw, write, eat with a spoon, and cut with scissors.

The exciting result of developing new motor skills is that it leads infants and toddlers to make other new discoveries. As they explore, they begin to make sense of their environment. For example, as Julio gains control of his head, he can use his eyes and ears to locate a sound. As Jasmine learns to use her fingers, hands, and wrists, she can touch, taste, and smell the slice of pear on her high chair tray. And as Jonisha turns the pages of her book one at a time, she is able to identify pictures of familiar objects and animals and recall a familiar story.

Motor Development in Infants

Most beginning movements of young infants are actually reflexes. That is, they happen automatically as the infant's muscles react to various stimuli. Some reflexes help assure that infants will get what they need. For example, when you touch the cheek of a newborn, she starts moving her mouth in search of a nipple. When you touch her mouth, or when her mouth touches the nipple of a breast or bottle, she begins sucking. Young infants have other reflexes, too. For example, one—called **reciprocal kicking**—occurs when an infant kicks first one foot, then the other. This reflex suggests skills yet to be developed, such as walking.

Over time and bit by bit, infants gain control of their muscles. Although they develop at different rates, infants learn to control their bodies in the same general way—from head to toe and from the center of their bodies out through their arms and legs to their fingers and toes. You can see this as you watch a child learn to lift his head, then sit, crawl, and walk.

During their first 18 months, infants make a remarkable journey. They change from having little control over their muscles to developing distinctive motor skills such as sitting, walking, and eye-hand coordination. These skills form the foundation of moving and doing throughout their lives.

Motor Development of Toddlers

Toddlers have a wide range of gross and fine motor skills. They can walk and run well and are developing new skills such as throwing and catching a ball and hopping. They can use their fingers and hands to turn the pages of a book, make strokes with a crayon, roll, pound and squeeze playdough, paint, and begin to cut with scissors. They need many opportunities and a safe environment to practice, refine, and build on these skills. You can promote motor development by encouraging children to try new skills, or by helping them to slow down a little so they can gain more control.

Using the toilet—an achievement welcomed by caregivers and parents alike—requires that children be aware of and able to control their bladder and bowel muscles. Every child develops at his or her own pace, but typically children are physically mature enough to begin using the toilet between 24 and 30 months.

Learning to Think

The psychologist Jean Piaget spent more than 60 years observing, studying, and writing about how children think. According to his ideas, children actively construct their own understanding of the world by interacting with people and objects. They use their entire bodies to explore actively. Children learn when they roll over, crawl around and over everything in their path, run, jump, knock things over, and lift them up. They learn as they grasp a rattle, pound playdough, and smell the grilled cheese sandwiches you make for lunch. They learn as they live their everyday lives with their parents and with you. As they eat, get dressed, have their diapers changed, sit on a potty, or move a chair across the room, they collect information and learn to think. They also learn as they play. When Jasmine discovers she can pull herself up on the sofa and see things she couldn't see when she was sitting on the floor, and when Willard crawls around pretending to be a tiger, they increase their understanding of the world and their place in it.

Piaget also found that children approach learning very differently than adults do. It is not just that they have less information, it's that they see the world differently. He noticed that at different ages, children answer questions in certain special ways. Piaget found that toddlers would usually explain things in terms of their appearance. For example, they describe a cracker broken into many pieces as more food than the same cracker when it is whole. Piaget also noted that toddlers seem to believe that everyone sees things from the same viewpoint they do, and that they alone are the cause of events: "I fell down because I was naughty."

Stages of Intellectual Development

According to Piaget, children pass through four stages of intellectual development. Infants and toddlers go through the first stage and into the beginning of the second.[5]

The first stage, which Piaget calls the **sensorimotor stage,** begins at birth. It lasts until a child is about one-and-a-half or two years old. At this stage, infants and toddlers learn as they move and use their senses of touch, taste, hearing, sight, and smell. For example, when Julio sucks on a toy, Jasmine squeezes, smells, and tastes the slice of banana, or Abby notices the sounds of birds and airplanes, they are using their senses to learn about their world. They are beginning to understand **object permanence**—that something or someone continues to exist even when out of sight. When a child who used to forget the spoon that she dropped from her highchair tray now drops the spoon and signals with a smile that she expects you to pick it up, you know she has learned about object permanence. "Peek-a-boo," a favorite game of most young children, reinforces this concept.

During this stage, children also begin to think more like adults. For example, they learn how to use tools and begin to understand cause and effect. When Abby wants the pull toy on the other side of the table, she gets it by pulling the string. She has learned that certain actions (pulling the string) have certain results (the toy attached to the string will move). Jasmine, on the other hand, would let an adult know she needs help, not realizing she could pull on the string to get the toy herself.

Piaget calls the second stage the **preoperational period.** The preoperational period begins at about age two and lasts until about age seven. During this stage, children learn to use language and mental images in their thinking. For example, toddlers can separate from their families more easily because they can create mental images of family members to hold onto throughout the day. They do lots of make-believe play, exploring daily events and activities, roles, and feelings. They begin to understand that time exists and to recognize that there is order to the day. Toddlers, for example, may find a book to read after lunch, knowing that quiet time comes before naps.

Children in the preoperational stage tend to be egocentric. This means they believe everyone thinks like they do and that they have the power to control the world. A toddler, for example, may believe he can make the traffic on a busy street come to a standstill simply by yelling, "Stop!"

[5] Jean Piaget. *The Origins of Intelligence.* New York: International Universities Press, 1952.

Little by little, as they explore and play, children collect new information to add to what they already know. The way they think begins to change as they realize that the moon does not follow them and that a broken cracker is actually the same amount as an unbroken one.

Recognizing a Child's Individuality

Knowledge of child development helps us to predict how children—in general—will behave at different stages of development. However, each child is an individual with particular characteristics. In addition to a general understanding of child development, you must take the time to learn about the special characteristics of each child.

Think of two infants you know well. What are they like? From the minute they are born, infants differ in terms of:

 * their activity level;
 * the regularity of when they eat, sleep or toilet;
 * how they approach (or withdraw) from people and things;
 * how often they display happy or sad moods and how frequently their moods shift;
 * the intensity of their reactions;
 * their sensitivity to stimuli such as bright lights, loud noises, and touch;
 * whether or not they like to be cuddled;
 * the amount of time it takes them to adapt to a new situation or routine;
 * how easily they can be distracted from activities; and
 * their persistence.

Yet because infants are so small and appealing, people often make assumptions about what they need, how they should be treated, and how they will respond. Do you?

Imagine an infant crying in his crib. How would you comfort him? Most adults would naturally pick him up and hold him closely. Yet, some infants don't enjoy being cuddled. They find it uncomfortable—even painful. They are better comforted by being placed on their stomach over your knees and gently rocked. Some infants are born cuddlers, others are born as non-cuddlers.

Try to understand what each child needs. For example, an infant who tenses in your arms isn't rejecting you. She may be asking you to try a different way of comforting her. She may respond better if you start by massaging and rubbing her back. Ask family members how they comfort the child. A toddler who tests limits isn't out to test your patience. He may be simply trying to figure out who he is. Looking through a child's eyes can help you get to know a child and appreciate his or her special characteristics.

Understanding Different Temperaments

Children are born with unique personalities and temperaments.[6] When you are aware of a child's temperament, you can sometimes predict how that child may react and behave in certain types of situations. You may also be able to do a better job of understanding and interpreting particular behavior. When your predictions are correct, you can respond appropriately. Yet, it's always important to remember that children don't fall into neat categories. While you may see general patterns in their behavior and your responses, you'll need to keep on your toes and be ready to respond to them in different ways at different times.

Abby may be described as a *flexible* child. She eats and naps regularly, is typically cheerful, and adapts easily to changes. When she is upset, she usually cries quietly and looks at her parents or Brooks for support. Abby is generally an easy child to live with, but she does have her challenging moments; last week she had a tantrum in the supermarket. Although she tends to be less demanding than other children, she needs the adults in her life to observe her regularly, read her signals, and offer support, encouragement, or comfort when necessary.

Gena can be described as generally *cautious* or *fearful*. She often needs time to warm up to new situations or new people—though she took a liking to Ivan within a few days of starting at the Crane School. Gena tends to watch things from the sidelines. Ivan has learned that his presence and encouragement can sometimes help draw Gena into activities. He has learned to respect Gena's style and give her the time she needs to open up to new experiences.

Willard could be described as *feisty, active,* or *intense*—take your pick. When he is happy or needs something, he lets his parents and Grace know. When he wants a toy another child is playing with, he may yell or cry loudly, even hit or push. Grace—who used to think Willard was a real handful, and even looked forward to the occasional days he wasn't at the Kendrick Center—has been surprised lately at how much she enjoys his spirited style. She has also discovered that Willard loves looking at pictures of children and their families in the program's photo album. Grace and Willard spend some quiet time doing this together each day.

Understanding children means appreciating their unique ways of interacting with the world and with people. It means taking time to learn about children's strengths, interests, challenges they like, challenges that frustrate them, and ways they are comforted. With this knowledge, you can respond in ways that address each child's needs.

---

[6] Infant researchers Alexander Thomas and Stella Chess have identified three basic types of temperaments. *The Program for Infant/Toddler Caregivers,* developed by West Ed/Far West Laboratory for Educational Research and Development, in collaboration with the California Department of Education, has named these *flexible, fearful,* and *feisty.*

Children with Special Needs

All infants and toddlers have needs to be met. Some needs are probably more familiar to you than others. You may have several suggestions for helping a child who has difficulty saying good-bye to his parents in the morning, or for another who has temper tantrums. At the same time, you may feel hesitant about working with a child who has cerebral palsy or who is visually impaired. You may wonder, "How can I ever meet the needs of these children?" Children with disabilities often have special difficulties seeing themselves as competent, valuable, independent individuals. Therefore, they can present special challenges. Experts believe, however, that all children can benefit when children with disabilities are included in early childhood programs.

The Creative Curriculum for Infants & Toddlers can help you in your work with all children, including those with disabilities. It provides a framework for assessing where each child is developmentally. It also gives you ideas of how children with very different interests and abilities can be included and feel successful in open-ended activities and daily routines. Experts believe that children with disabilities should have the same experiences as all children. You are in a position to bring this idea to life for the children and families in your program.

The Creative Curriculum's emphasis on building relationships is extremely important for young children with disabilities—who may be isolated—and for their families—who may fear bringing their child out into the real world. Some of the children may receive special services, such as occupational, physical, or speech/language therapy. It is helpful and important to invite specialists in these fields to your program to share ideas about common goals and strategies.

In 1975, federal legislation mandated a free, appropriate public education for all children with disabilities and special needs. Since 1986, states have offered services to three-to five-year-old children.[7] Beginning in 1990, states have been able to use federal funds to offer **early intervention services** for infants and toddlers with disabilities and their families. These services are designed to minimize the effects of developmental delays or diagnosed disabilities. The important provision in the law which applies to children from birth to age three is called Part C (formerly known as Part H).

Understanding Part C

Children are identified and become part of the program in many ways. Each state is required to have a "child find system" which identifies children in need of services and makes referrals to service providers. A child may be identified at birth as having a disability, during a check-up at the pediatrician's office, by a specialist such as a physical therapist, or by someone providing care and education, such as yourself.

Under Part C, state or community teams—which may include speech and physical therapists, physicians, social workers, public health nurses, and educators—work

---

[7] *Education for All Handicapped Children Act,* P.L. 94-142, 1975. *Early Intervention Amendments,* P.L. 99-457, 1986. Part H is part of this legislation. *The Individuals with Disabilities Education Act,* P.L. 101-476, 1990. P.L. 102-119, Reauthorized Part H, 1991. The 1997 reauthorization reclassified it as Part C. P.L. 105-17.

with family members to create an individualized family service plan (IFSP). IFSPs contain the following information:

❖ current developmental information, including a detailed picture of a child's abilities and emerging skills;

❖ desired developmental outcomes for the child and family on which team members agree; and

❖ specific developmental objectives that allow team members to see what progress is being made.

Your involvement with your local early intervention program may come about in a variety of ways. You may be the person who suspected a developmental delay and got the whole process started by suggesting to the family that they call the state's Part C Coordinator, who helped them make a local contact. You may know about a family's IFSP because you were contacted as the family's primary entry point into the system and have been involved from the beginning. Alternately, you may have been overlooked. If this is the case, talk with the child's family about requesting a review of their IFSP and adding your name to the team. In any case, you are an important member of the early intervention team, as you have the opportunity to work with the child each day to achieve developmental goals.

The new legislation requires each state to have one agency with central responsibility and a central directory of services. To help you learn more about Part C and how it can support the children and families in your program, there is a directory of Part C Coordinators and Lead Agencies in each state in Appendix E. You can also research the topic directly on the Internet through the ERIC (Educational Resources Information Center) Clearinghouse on Disabilities and Gifted Education (http://www.cec.sped.org/ericec.htm) or by contacting the ERIC Web Site (http://www.aspensys.com/eric). Your local school district office is another good resource.

Strategies for Addressing Special Needs

The suggestions that follow apply to all infants and toddlers. You'll find them particularly useful in your work with children who have diagnosed disabilities or other special needs.

See children as children first. Learn about each child's strengths and interests first, then consider the child's special needs. Indeed, this attitude can be, in the words of Gena's father, Neal, "the greatest gift anyone could have given us." He explains, "Sometimes as a parent of a child with a disability, you struggle so hard to overcome problems that you forget to enjoy your child. The first day we took Gena to the Crane School, we didn't know what to expect. When Ivan asked Gena about her stuffed lamb, Franklin—before talking with us about her impaired speech and dexterity—we knew we were in the right place."

The goal for all children is to feel included and successful. For this to happen, you must look beyond the specific diagnosis to see what effects it has on a particular child. You must be careful not to generalize about children on the basis of their diagnoses.

Learn about the effects of a specific disability. Consider how a specific disability may or may not affect the child's daily life in your program. Use this information to help you decide what, if any, adjustments you need to make. For example, you may need another adult to help you during certain parts of the day. Or you may need to move furniture so a child's wheelchair can fit into every part of the room.

Work closely with children's families. Parents of a child with a disability are your greatest sources of support and information. Ask them to share what they know about their child's condition. Invite them also to share tips and strategies they use at home. For example, Gena's parents, Neal and Rebecca, helped Ivan learn to position Gena in ways that give her the best possible control over her body. Also, ask parents about their involvement with the local early intervention program. If they are unaware of local services, give them the necessary information.

Set goals and work with a specialist. Use the goals and objectives from a child's IFSP to guide your work with that child. Many objectives will be the same as those you've set for all children and will fit easily into your regular planning and daily schedule. Others may mean adding special toys, adapting equipment, or changing routines (such as blinking lights to catch the attention of a deaf child). These strategies should be included in the child's plan. As with all children, you should observe continually and assess the goals you have set, adapting them as necessary. With parental permission, work with the child's therapist(s) to come up with strategies that will work in your program.

Encourage, but do not force independence. Some children may need extra support to develop skills as well as self-confidence. Feeling competent is important for all children.

Recognize, however, that children may have needs beyond your experience and expertise. If this is the case, seek the help of specialists in your community. Your openness to learn about various disabilities and reach out to experts will set a good model for the children—and adults—in your program.

Getting to know infants and toddlers can sometimes be challenging—and is always interesting and exciting. In the next chapter, we focus on families—your partners in getting to know children.

Knowing Families

The families you work with each day are at a very exciting but vulnerable stage in their lives. Parenting an infant or toddler can be wonderful. It is a chance to watch a brand new human being unfold. So much change takes place in the first three years that parents constantly marvel as their child explores and joyfully discovers new things about himself and his world. But parenting can also be demanding and overwhelming. As one parent put it, "I love my baby. But taking care of him is harder than I ever imagined. I feel so lost."

When you made the decision to work with infants and toddlers, you may not have considered how much you would also be working with children's families. It probably wasn't long before you realized, however, that to help children develop, you must also create a partnership with their families. Therefore, the more you know about families, the more responsive and supportive you can be of their needs. In turn, families who feel you understand and respect the central role they play in their child's life will be your greatest supporters.

This chapter can help you to get to know families by recognizing:

❖ the stages of parenthood that apply to families with children younger than three;
❖ the special concerns of families with children under three;
❖ the influence of culture in children's lives and the need to appreciate cultural differences; and
❖ the importance of involving the men in children's lives in your program.

Stages of Parenthood

The birth of a new baby means not only the birth of a new person, but also the birth of parents in a newly arranged family. According to pediatrician T. Berry Brazelton, "Falling in love with a baby may well happen at birth, but staying in love is a learning process—learning to love oneself as well as the baby."[1]

---

[1] T. Berry Brazelton. *On Becoming A Family: The Growth of Attachment.* New York: Delacorte Press, 1981, p. xiv.

Just as children follow certain stages in their development, so do parents. According to Ellen Galinsky, parents pass through six stages, each based on children's development. In each stage, parents reorganize the ways they think about themselves and their world and the way they respond to the child's changing behavior.[2]

Parents of infants and toddlers pass through three of these stages of parenthood: image-making (the way they think their new life with a child will be), nurturing (the way they care for and protect their children), and authority (the way they place limits on their children's behavior).

Recognizing these stages can help you understand what parents may experience as they learn about themselves and their children. This can help you decide how best to respond. As you read about each of these stages, keep in mind that your task is not to move parents from one stage to another. This will happen naturally as their children grow. Rather, it is to be aware of their interests and needs at certain stages so that you can support them as necessary. Your support can help them feel competent as they face new challenges.

If you are a parent yourself, you may find it helpful to reflect on your own feelings and experiences to better understand the parents with whom you work. If you are not a parent, observe and try to look through the eyes of parents. Ask yourself, "What are they experiencing?" Regardless of your background, remember that parents are often glad to share their feelings and stories with someone they trust—someone they can count on to listen carefully and respectfully.

The Image-Making Stage

This first stage of parenthood begins before a child is born. Parents-to-be start preparing and rehearsing for the great change that is about to take place in their lives—even if it is with a second or third child. Part of how they do this is to imagine their new life.

At this stage, expectant parents spend much time dreaming about what their child will be like. They also think about what kind of parents they will be and how being a parent will change their relationships with each other and their own parents. This is a time of roller coaster feelings. Parents may often feel "ready" and then "not ready" to deal with these changes in their lives.

Expectant parents (regardless of whether they have other children) will often appreciate your listening to their hopes, dreams, and fears—if and when they want to share them with you. They may also welcome your introducing them to other parents in your program who are awaiting the birth or adoption of a child.

The Nurturing Stage

The next stage begins with the birth of the infant. During this stage, parents bring together the picture of the child they imagined with the real child they hold in their arms. Many new parents report feeling a deep love and caring for their infant, while others experience this bonding as a more gradual process. They also report the challenge

---

[2] Ellen Galinsky. *The Six Stages of Parenthood.* Reading, MA: Addison-Wesley Publishing Company, 1987.

that occurs when the imagined picture of joyful parents and a smiling infant does not always match the reality. In fact, accepting these differences causes growth in parenthood. As Leo's mother said, "I thought my baby would be a smiler. Instead, he cried a lot. So did I during those first months!" Particularly when an infant is born with a disability, parents may feel as if their entire world has come apart.

In addition to getting to know a new infant, parents are redefining their relationship to each other, to their other children (if they have them), and to their own parents. At the same time, their immediate task is to become attached to their new infant, just as the infant's task is to become attached to them. Attachment creates possessive feelings in everyone who cares for a child—parents, grandparents, and child care providers alike. As a result, one of your jobs is to recognize these possessive and competitive feelings. You can turn them into cooperative feelings by supporting the parents in their primary roles.

It's easy to understand why parents with a new infant often feel overwhelmed. Everything they thought they knew and felt gets called into question: Am I feeding too much or too little? Is the baby sleeping enough? For employed mothers—should I really be working? It's a big relief when they can depend on you to keep their child (the new infant or an older brother or sister) safe in a quality program. You can help parents by listening to them and reminding them they are handling a great deal. A supportive word can sometimes make a world of difference to an unsure parent.

The Authority Stage

The third stage sets in slowly and gradually as children become more mobile and begin exploring the larger world around them. Parents who put aside many of their own needs during the Nurturing Stage now realize that there are times when they must say "No" to their children. What parents should control and what can be left up to the child become important decisions that must be resolved almost every day.

During this stage, both parents and children face the challenge of limits. As children explore, test, and accept limits, parents also explore and struggle with establishing and enforcing these limits. While it may appear that parents are often ambivalent or wishy-washy, this is the normal fumbling state that parents go through as they learn to be authorities.

Because setting limits is difficult and complicated, parents may look to you for direction. There are two things you can do. First, you can model or demonstrate how you set clear, realistic limits with their child and the other children in your program. Second, you can share your knowledge about infant and child development with parents. For example, understanding that Matthew is declaring his independence when he protests, "No!" as his parents try to put on his boots at the end of the day can help lessen the stress that often occurs when adults feel tested and not in control.

Parents also often look to other parents as they move from trying to be perfect to being "good enough." When you help parents of toddlers connect with one another, you open the way for them to encourage and learn from one another. They can also share the delights of watching their children develop.

Special Concerns of Families with Children Younger Than Three

Although each family has its own culture, values, strengths, and needs, most families of young children share some characteristics. These include:

- ❖ the stress of parenting an infant, including lack of sleep;
- ❖ conflicting feelings about how to share the care of the baby;
- ❖ confusion over who is who in their child's life; and
- ❖ the need to feel that they are part of their child's day, even when they are not physically with their child.

The Stress of Parenting an Infant

Being the parent of an infant takes a great deal of energy. It can be very demanding and stressful at times. Not only are new parents often confused by a child's behavior and unsure of what to do, but they are also very, very tired. Lack of sleep makes it easy for new parents to lose perspective and to despair that they will never learn as much as they need to know. When a parent is very young, single, or worried about having enough money to buy food or medical services, the stress is even greater.

What's more, many parents find child care centers or homes to be scary, no matter how welcoming your setting is or how warm and friendly you are. Are you surprised? Many caregivers who feel nervous around parents are often amazed to learn that parents see them as "all-knowing professionals." Kevin tells about being afraid to pick up Willard that first day: "I'd never been in a child care setting before. I didn't know who was in charge or what was allowed."

Why is this information important to you? It's because some families will feel comfortable asking you for the support they need. Others will not. They may be too overwhelmed with the changes in their lives. They may not yet trust you or they may view asking for help as a sign of failure. But you are in a good position to be helpful because you see parents every day. It's up to you to listen carefully and figure out how best to offer help. Sometimes that help can be a cup of juice or the way you assure a hassled parent that, based on your experience, a child's behavior is absolutely typical and nothing to worry about.

Conflicting Feelings About Sharing Care

Sharing the care of young children by placing them in a child care program often may stir up conflicting feelings. Some parents may feel sorrow, guilt, or some fear about leaving their child with you, no matter how professional you are and how highly rated your program.

Once a child is enrolled in the program, parents want you to be competent and want their child to like you. They may worry, however, that their child will like you better than he or she likes them. These feelings can be stressful for parents. Sometimes the stress is reflected in their children.

You also might have feelings about sharing care. As you become attached to a child, you may feel a bit competitive with a parent. You may resent having to work with parents when you really want to work with children. You may also have feelings about parents who choose to work instead of staying home to care for a very young infant.

How can you deal with these conflicting feelings? First, be aware that parents' feelings—and yours—go hand-in-hand with sharing care. Help parents see that their mixed feelings are normal and should not be cause for embarrassment. Raising and caring for infants and toddlers is passionate work. As for you, it is natural to feel deeply protective and attached to young children. You'll need to recognize these feelings for what they are, so they won't get in the way of working together with parents in the best interests of the child.

Confusion Over Who Is Who

Parents and caregivers each play an important but different role in a child's life. Infants and toddlers know who is who. Yet the adults in their lives sometimes don't feel so sure.

The difference, though, should be very clear. Parents are the most important people in their child's life. Their relationship is forever. It is built upon a deep trust and a love unlike any other. No matter how skilled and experienced you are, you can never take a parent's place.

However, the emotional bond you build with each child is also important, even though your relationship is temporary. As you develop these relationships, you show children that they can trust people outside their families. Because you are more objective than parents, you can more easily give children the time and space they need to get through a bumpy stage of development or to master a new skill.

With these differences in mind, you can understand how helpful it is to reassure parents who have young children in child care that they are the most important people in their child's life. You may also want to remind parents that you are aware of who is who, too.

Wanting to Feel a Part of Their Child's Day

Parents depend on you to fill them in on what has happened in their children's lives during the hours when they are apart. You may do this in many ways. For example, when parents come to pick up their children in the evening, you may share stories of the day. You may take photos of the children, write notes to send home, or hang a calendar of the day's highlights on the wall. In general, families will be very glad to hear the news you share.

There is one major exception, however. No one wants to miss one of their child's "firsts." For example, if you see the first time a child sits up or takes first steps, you may not want to share this information fully. Instead, consider saying something like this: "Willard's been pulling himself up a lot today! I'll be curious to know what his evening is like. I'm going to remember to ask you tomorrow morning."

Understanding the Influence of Culture

All people learn about their own culture simply by living it. Families have beliefs and practices associated with every aspect of life that they pass on to their children. Like the children with whom you are now working, your belief system was influenced by your family, specifically by your parents or whoever was directly responsible for raising you. As a caregiver, it is important that you have a clear understanding about your culture and how its influences affect your work.

For example, most people and many cultures have strong beliefs about names and how names should be treated. Being aware of these beliefs allows you to honor them as much as possible. Avoid changing or shortening a child's name because you feel it is hard to pronounce or is difficult to spell. If necessary, ask someone for a correct pronunciation and to help you practice saying it.

Learning from Families

It is easy to misinterpret what families do or say if you do not understand something about their culture. However, you also must avoid assigning cultural labels to families. Rather than making assumptions about cultural influences, it is better to ask questions and consider the values behind each family's beliefs.

Children's families can teach you a great deal about their cultural beliefs and traditions. Invite parents to spend time in your program whenever possible. Observe how they interact with their children. Arrange for a home visit. As your relationship grows, talk about culture. Ask questions. Think together about how your culture(s) shape each of you and how you respond to children.

Use these questions and any others you want to add to guide your efforts to understand families whose cultures are different from yours.

- ❖ How does the family define who is in their family? What gives them a sense of family?
- ❖ How do families select a child's name?
- ❖ How does the family balance children's independence with doing things for them?
- ❖ When should toilet training begin and how should it be handled?
- ❖ What, when, and how are children fed?
- ❖ How is discipline handled?
- ❖ Do family members have different and distinct roles in raising children?
- ❖ Are boys and girls treated differently?
- ❖ Is it acceptable for children to be noisy and to get dirty?
- ❖ What kinds of questions are children asked?
- ❖ How do people interact with one another? Do they look each other in the eye? Are they taught to pause and think carefully about a response before giving it? Do they touch each other as they communicate?
- ❖ How do families show respect for elders?

Incorporating Children's Cultures Into Your Program

By including experiences that are consistent with those the children have at home, you provide children with cultural continuity. This is especially important for infants and toddlers, because they are developing a sense of identity. Here are several ways you can achieve cultural continuity, even if your cultural background is different from that of the families in your program.

Use children's home language(s) as much as possible. In the best of all worlds, there would be an adult from the same culture(s) who spoke the same language(s) as the children in your program to build a bridge for children between home and child care. Because this is often not the case, you'll need to think creatively about how to bring children's language(s) into your setting. For example, encourage family members to speak in their home language when they visit and to teach you some important words. Ask families to make tapes of stories and music their children know from home. Get help, as necessary, to translate written communications. Identify someone a family trusts who would be willing to serve as a language resource, especially for conferences, home visits, and in emergency situations.

Reflect children's cultures in daily routines. Knowing how daily routines are handled at home can help you make children feel at home in child care. For example, a child who is expected to eat neatly at home may need extra reassurance when she spills her juice at lunch.

Reflect children's families in the environment. Display photographs of children's families which they have chosen to share. Incorporate foods, activities, toys, and songs that children know from home into their daily lives in child care.

Working Towards Understanding

When the adults in their lives share a consistent approach, children gain a sense of continuity that helps them feel safe and secure in child care. This doesn't mean you have to agree about everything. More likely, there will be times when you and a child's parents will have different points of view about caring for their child. The question is, "How can you achieve mutual understanding?"

> Gena's parents often sent her to child care in her best clothes. They became upset when the clothes were soiled with dirt and paint at the end of the day. Ivan felt it was very important for Gena to have many hands-on experiences. He explained this to the Domenicas and found they agreed. Together they worked out a solution. Ivan would keep a set of "play clothes" that Gena could change into on the days her parents dressed her in good clothes. That way she could participate in all activities without fear of getting dirty. At the same time, she could protect her good clothes.

When there are differences, a good policy is to problem-solve together and work at a compromise, as long as you feel the compromise will not harm the child. (See Chapter 1 for a discussion on resolving conflicts.)

Involving the Men in Children's Lives[3]

A quality program needs to involve everyone who is important in a child's life. Too often, however, men in children's lives are overlooked. Why is this? Primarily it's because our culture defines caring for children—in our homes and in child care programs—as "women's work." Perhaps it is also because most people who work with infants and toddlers are women who may feel more comfortable with other women. And some may not want to share child care with men, preferring to hold onto raising children as their special area of expertise. In addition, some people may think men are not good caregivers, especially for infants and toddlers.

Men themselves may be uncomfortable walking into a setting that is largely female. A society that values toughness for males rather than gentleness and caring doesn't encourage comfort in a child care setting. If a man has grown up without a caring father or other man in his own life, he may find it even more difficult to become involved with his own young children.

At the same time, more and more men are seeing how much their fathers missed and are taking a more active parenting role. Our culture increasingly supports men as nurturing influences in children's lives. Courts, too, are more willing to grant fathers custody of children. The number of single fathers is increasing. If men aren't involved in your program, you need to think about reversing the situation. Here are some suggestions to help you get started.

Examine your attitudes about men (even if you are a man). You may especially want to think about these questions.

> ❖ What kinds of experiences have you had with the men in your life—your father, brother, husband, or partner?
> ❖ Do you think men really care about children as much as women do? Why?
> ❖ Do you think men can contribute to your program? How?

Expect that men will participate. Ask for the name and address of a child's father if he doesn't live with the child. If possible, try to arrange for home visits when fathers will be there. It's helpful to assume that men are interested, that they care and want to do their best for their children.

Create a welcoming environment. First of all, let fathers (and other men who come to the program) know that you recognize that being in a child care setting can be a somewhat uncomfortable experience. Offer suggestions of things that men can do, as Barbara does

[3] Based on James A. Levine, Dennis T. Murphy, and Sherill Wilson. *Getting Men Involved: Strategies for Early Childhood Programs.* New York: Scholastic, 1993.

when she says to Elmer, "Do you want to go over and read with Leo? I'm sure he would love it." Other ways to make men feel at home at the program may include:

❖ sharing an observation that shows how well the child is doing;

❖ adding selections such as *The Father's Almanac* to your parent library; and

❖ including men in the photographs you display.

Provide meaningful ways for men to be involved. Men can do many different things in your program. They can nurture and play with children. They can help with routines, such as serving meals and snacks. They can help with maintenance and repair work. But even more important, having men involved in your program helps everyone. Children benefit by seeing male role models. Fathers and other men in children's lives benefit by developing stronger relationships with children. You and your program benefit as men bring new kinds of knowledge and interests that enrich children's lives.

As you think about the families in your program and get to know them better, you will learn about their many strengths and want to give them all the support they need. As much as you want to help, you are only one person and you represent only one program. However, you all—families, children, and programs—exist within a community that not only benefits from the services you offer, but can provide needed services. This is the topic of the next chapter.

Community: Building a Network of Support

Y our program is a part of your larger community. On the one hand, you give your community or neighborhood a valuable service that helps make it a better place for all families and children. On the other hand, your community gives you and the families you serve resources, including libraries, well-baby clinics, parks, and the support of neighbors and colleagues that can enrich your program. As a result, the relationship between your program and your community is a two-way street.

This chapter focuses on the community's role in your program. We discuss how you can work within the community to build a network of support for children and families by:

❖ recognizing why your program needs support;
❖ being aware of what other communities are doing;
❖ appreciating what you have to contribute to the community; and
❖ becoming involved in efforts to make your community a better place
  for children and families.

The Need for Support

Clearly, families today are under tremendous stress for a wide variety of reasons. These reasons include poverty; the break-up of the basic family unit; lack of affordable, quality health care; and widespread violence. Indeed, we need to redefine the term *family* in light of the current realities. Today, half of America's children live with only one parent at some point in their lives. In the past, more parents were part of an extended family in which elders helped out and provided advice. Today, families are often isolated. One significant result of these and other complications is that infants and toddlers—and their families—are at risk. In *The State of America's Children Yearbook 1997*, the Children's Defense Fund alerts us to the problems that face American children and families every day.[1]

---

[1] *The State of America's Children Yearbook 1997*. Washington, DC: Children's Defense Fund, 1997, pp. x and xi.

Risks Facing American Children and Families	
Every 10 seconds	a child is reported abused or neglected.
Every 24 seconds	a child is born to an unmarried mother.
Every 34 seconds	a child is born into poverty.
Every 1 minute	a child is born to a teen mother.
Every 2 minutes	a child is born at low birthweight.
Every 17 minutes	an infant dies.
Every 2 hours	a child is a homicide victim.
Every 4 hours	a child commits suicide.

In view of these sobering statistics, families may need many different kinds of support—including dental and medical services, family counseling, public housing, special education services, assistance in paying for food and eye glasses—and not know where to turn for help. You may be the first support person who really gets to know a family—their strengths as well as their needs. As a result, many families may look to you not only to provide quality child care, but also to guide them to other resources in the community.

Why You Need Support

As families' needs become more complex, so do the demands on you. Everyone working with infants and toddlers can benefit from the ongoing support of others who do the same kind of work. Whether you work with colleagues every day or see each other regularly at association meetings or training sessions, you'll find that ongoing professional connections can help you in many ways. You can share experiences and challenges and brainstorm solutions. When you feel supported, you can be more open to exploring new ideas. You will probably enjoy your work more, and as a result, you will be more likely to do a better job.

It is very likely you will also need to call on other people to help families address issues outside your area of expertise, such as physical or mental health concerns, or the need for job training. The better you know your community, the more likely it is you will know who offers which services and how to help families connect with the resources they need. How to provide this help depends largely on your community. In some communities, services for families are well coordinated. In other communities, service providers and services are fragmented.

If the latter is the case in your community, be persistent. Talk with everyone you know. Call your mayor's office. Contact organizations such as your city's health department and your local child care resource and referral agency. Only by persisting will you be able to find the services needed by the children and families in your care.

What Communities Are Doing

People all across the country are working together to make their communities more family-friendly. Generally, since funding for social services is often the first budget item to be cut, communities must find new and creative ways to make the most out of available resources. As communities recognize the need for coordinated, accessible services that build on families' strengths and focus on prevention, groups of people are coming together to try to meet this need.

Professionals in a wide variety of fields—education, health and mental health, social services, and business—are joining with parents to identify services that already exist and those that families still want and need. Knowing what others are doing can allow your community to build on their successes and lessons learned. Here are some examples of what communities are doing.[2]

❖ In Hampton, Virginia, a group of community partners launched the Healthy Families Partnership (formerly known as the Hampton Family Resource Project). Its goal is to ensure that every child in Hampton is born healthy and enters school ready to learn. The Partnership offers the following services: home visiting, parent education, young family centers in libraries, *The Healthy Stages* newsletter available to all families with children under 18, and Healthy Teen, a pregnancy prevention program.

❖ The KCMC Child Development Corporation in Kansas City is combining its Head Start funds with resources of other non-profit agencies and businesses. The Corporation aims to provide all children with comprehensive services that meet the Head Start Program Performance Standards.

❖ In Dover, New Hampshire, a community survey identified the needs of parents with young children. Results revealed that new mothers wanted a place that offered child care and other services, to which they could go at least weekly. The community responded by opening a center staffed by early childhood professionals. The Center is now open daily and provides information that parents say they need.

❖ In North Carolina, Family Ties is a state-wide community-based outreach initiative designed to identify low-income families with children under six who need child care or child development services. Its aim is to share information with families about existing community resources and programs, to obtain information about families' needs, and to build local leadership.

❖ In Indiana, Step Ahead Councils in 92 counties have completed needs assessments and are working to create plans of action for addressing families' needs.

---

[2] Based on Amy Laura Dombro, Nina Sazer O'Donnell, Ellen Galinsky, Sarah Gilkeson Melcher, and Abby Farber. *Community Mobilization: Strategies to Support Young Children and Their Families.* New York: Families and Work Institute, 1996.

❖ The Parent Voices Project, conceived by the California Child Care Resource and Referral Network, is currently working with local child care resource and referral agencies to examine how to identify and support parent advocates for child care.

❖ In West Virginia, Family Resource Networks (FRNs) in local communities are bringing together major parties that have an interest in children and families, including families themselves. These groups assess and determine the priority of community needs and create strategies to address those needs. For example, the Cabell-Wayne FRN found that families wanted more accessible services and a more helpful, respectful attitude from service providers. In response, the FRN is working to create services that are family-friendly, community based, and that focus on preventing problems—such as violence in the schools— before they occur.

❖ In Hawaii, Healthy Start, a home-based intervention program targeted to pregnant women and mothers with children up to the age of three months, attempts to provide support to families that may be at risk for child abuse. The participants are identified by screening hospital birth records, interviewing new mothers, and following up on referrals from physicians and public health agencies. The program has been so successful that today there are more than 100 Healthy Families America programs in 20 states, all based on Hawaii's Healthy Start model.

What You Have to Offer

You offer your community a valuable service. You have an in-depth view of the strengths and needs of its children and families, based on your knowledge of child development and your daily experiences running a program. Your insights, combined with your commitment to support families, can contribute to the well-being of your community, as well as to its individual members. You can also contribute by sharing your interests and skills from the "personal" side of your life, be they writing, illustrating, home repair, or speaking another language.

In addition, you can help parents become lifetime advocates for their children, working with other support people in their lives as well as on a community-wide level. When you work with families, you help them feel competent and fully involved in their children's child care experience. A positive experience with you can lead family members to feel more empowered in their relationship with, for example, their child's health care provider, and eventually, with their child's school. Such experiences often lead to participation in other community efforts to improve children's lives.

Getting Involved

Your community may be at the forefront in addressing the needs of children and families. Alternatively, it may not put a high priority on these issues and activities. If this alternative is the case, you will need to lobby for changes. Either way, getting involved is a positive step. Here are some suggestions to help you build relationships with community partners and to become involved in efforts that will benefit children and families in your program.

Identify community partners. A community partner can be just about anyone: the family child caregiver down the street; your physician or pediatrician; your local Part C coordinator; a teacher, principal, or guidance counselor at your local school; the priest, minister, or rabbi where you worship; a business owner; a librarian; or your neighbor who volunteers at the food bank. Some of these people may have information or offer services that families in your program can use. Each of them can probably introduce you to other people and programs.

Reach out. Each week, talk with one new person who shares your commitment to improving the lives of children and families.

Introduce yourself and your program. Let people know what you do and the types of things you know about. Describe your program. Share your goals for children and families. Invite new partners to come and visit.

Learn about what your new partners do. Find out about any special terms they may use in talking about their work. Ask questions. Read the literature from partners' organizations. Try to visit when possible. Learn to speak their "language."

Figure out ways to begin working together. For example, if you care for a child with a disability, invite specialists working with that child to participate in your program. Attend therapy (occupational, physical, speech/language) with a child and family to see what kinds of goals and strategies are addressed and to offer your perspective.

Stay in touch. Keep up to date on the services your community offers. Put your name on their mailing lists. Mark a time on your calendar to call community partners each month.

Find out about ongoing efforts—big and small—in your community. You may hear about a project or meeting from a neighbor, co-worker or community partner, or on the radio or TV. You may see a notice in the newspaper or find one posted on the bulletin board of a community center, school, or place of worship. You may even call the local paper, your local resource and referral agency, or the mayor's office.

Learn more. Attend a meeting. Join a community work group. Talk with people who are already involved. Try to get a picture of what is happening.

Think realistically about *when* to get involved and *how*. You may decide that for the time being, your focus needs to be on your program. However, if you want to become involved in a community effort and aren't sure how to go about it, explore various options for your involvement until you find one that fits.

Be patient. Remember, and remind others if necessary, that creating change takes time. Acknowledge accomplishments and celebrate small successes. This will help you keep going when the going is slow.

Because all these suggestions sound very time consuming, you may think you can't possibly handle more than your day-to-day work. Why not try just one suggestion as a start? Who knows? You may end up being president of your local professional organization, or a member of your city council!

Part
II The Big Picture

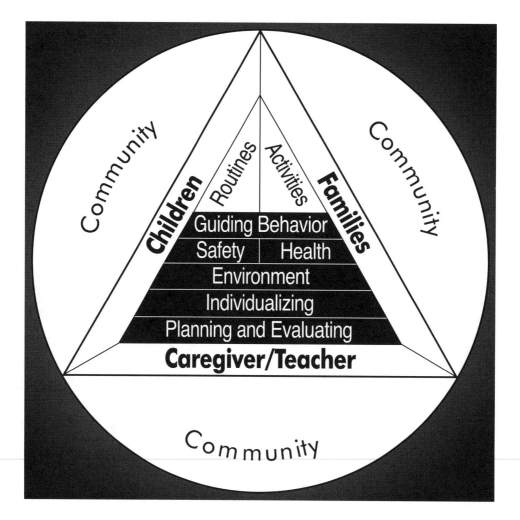

Putting Quality Into Action: The Big Picture

Often when people think about curriculum, they focus on the routines and activities that consume a child's day. But before any routine or activity takes place, you must set the stage and provide a context for learning. In Part II we discuss six components of quality—what we call "The Big Picture."

Planning and evaluating. Quality programs are well thought out. You define program goals and objectives for your work with children and families. Long-term and short-term plans follow taking into consideration the changing needs, interests, and special characteristics of the children and families you serve. Then you develop a schedule that is adaptable and responsive to children's changing needs. As you continually assess what is working and what isn't, you use what you learn from evaluation to guide your decisions and take steps that improve your program.

Individualizing. The more organized you are, the more time you have to observe children regularly. Observation enables you to learn about each child and individualize your program. It also helps you to follow their growth and development—one of the most interesting and rewarding aspects of working with young children. Using specific strategies for observing, you will be able to set goals for each child and plan your work with families.

Creating a welcoming environment. To implement the program you have planned, you begin by creating a welcoming and warm environment. Such an environment can help children feel more comfortable in child care and can also put parents more at ease about leaving their children. Equally important, a well-designed environment enables you to work efficiently so you have the time and energy you need to care for infants and toddlers in an unhurried and nurturing way.

Ensuring children's safety. Safety is a number one priority for parents and for anyone working with infants and toddlers. You ensure children's safety by routinely checking your indoor and outdoor environments for potential problems. You prepare yourself for possible emergencies and practice safety habits yourself to provide a model for children. And day in and day out, you work to balance your concerns for children's safety with children's need to take "reasonable risks" as they explore.

Promoting children's health. Healthy children are ready to learn. You promote children's health by informing yourself of health requirements, taking preventive measures, and constantly checking your program for practices that promote and maintain good health. Each day you model health practices that children can make part of their own lives. In addition, knowing you may be the first to recognize and report suspected cases, you learn the signs of child abuse and neglect and your legal responsibilities.

Guiding children's behavior. Young children learn from adults what behavior is acceptable what is not. When adults take a positive approach to guiding behavior, they help children learn how to relate positively to others. Then children can develop self-discipline and learn to make good decisions for themselves. Working with infants and toddlers also means that adults must have strategies for handling the challenging behaviors—such as biting and temper tantrums—that are sure to come up.

When all of these elements are in place, you will have created an appropriate setting and you will possess the information you need to promote children's learning through daily routines and activities.

Planning and Evaluating Your Program

Many people believe that caring for children younger than three means following the children's lead each day. While this is certainly a part of responsive caregiving, it is not the whole story. To create a quality program, you must have plans in place.

A plan shows you where you are going. Even when you change your plans to respond to children's needs, you will still have an overall picture of what you hope to accomplish. Because planning gives you a sense of what to expect, it actually enables you to be more flexible and responsive in your daily work.

To illustrate, think about what's different when you plan ahead to offer fingerpainting as a play choice versus what happens when you spontaneously decide to let children fingerpaint. When you plan, you can select a time of day when children can paint without interruption, you can assemble the materials ahead of time, and you can prepare the environment to reduce messes. As a result, you can focus your attention on the children rather than the activity. Not only does the fingerpainting itself become more manageable, but your time and energy are now devoted to making the experience meaningful for the children.

Evaluation goes hand in hand with good planning. To continue with the fingerpainting example, your observations tell you if the activity is successful. When this is the case, you may decide to prepare for and carry out fingerpainting again in much the same way. If you observe problems, you consider whether your plans were appropriate or whether they need adjustment.

This chapter focuses on two aspects of creating a quality program: planning and evaluation. You will learn about:

- ❖ making evaluation a regular part of the planning process;
- ❖ defining your program's goals for children and families;
- ❖ long-term planning and evaluation;
- ❖ short-term planning and evaluation; and
- ❖ creating a daily schedule.

Making Evaluation a Regular Part of the Planning Process

The needs, interests, and special characteristics of the children and families you serve are continually changing. As a result, your response to these needs, interests, and characteristics must continually change, too.

Evaluation allows you to judge how successfully you have targeted goals and strategies and implemented your plans. When you informally observe children at play, you are evaluating. When you administer a standardized observational instrument, you are also evaluating. So too, when you consult your colleagues and the children's families for their opinions, you are evaluating. Through these different types of evaluation, you gather the information you need to make informed decisions to answer questions, such as the following:

❖ Are all of the children engaged?

❖ Are the materials appropriate for the ages and stages of the children?

❖ Is each child getting individual attention?

Evaluation, as defined here, is a process that helps you in your work. It is not the threatening concept so many of us tend to fear. Evaluation helps you determine if you're "on target"—and if not, how to get there. It is the flip side of the planning process. If you believe in planning, then you are already a believer in evaluation.

Here is what the planning and evaluation process looks like in action.

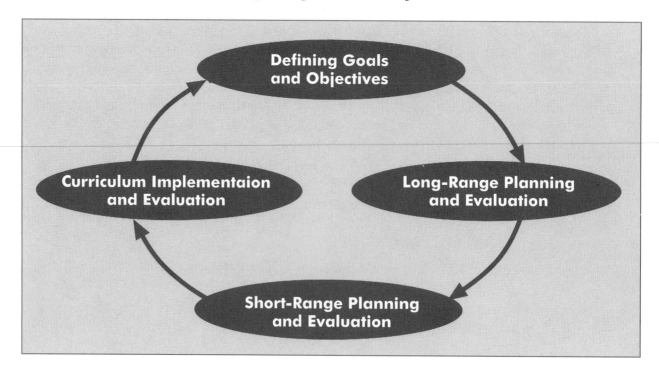

The remainder of this chapter explores how you can plan and evaluate your program to achieve your desired goals.

Defining Program Goals and Objectives

The ultimate goal of planning and evaluation is to achieve a high-quality program. Leading organizations, such as ZERO TO THREE/The National Center and the National Association for the Education of Young Children, have identified standards of quality for programs serving infants and toddlers.[1] These standards are reflected in the two sets of goals which form the framework for this *Creative Curriculum*: (1) Goals and Objectives for Children; and (2) Goals and Objectives for Working With Families.

Goals and Objectives for Children

Goal 1: To learn about themselves
- To feel valued and attached to others
- To feel competent and proud about what they can do
- To assert their independence

Goal 2: To learn about their feelings
- To communicate a broad range of emotions through gestures, sounds, and—over time—words
- To express their feelings in appropriate ways

Goal 3: To learn about others
- To develop trusting relationships with nurturing adults
- To show interest in peers
- To demonstrate caring and cooperation
- To try roles and relationships through imitation and pretend play

Goal 4: To learn about communicating
- To express needs and thoughts without using words
- To identify with a home language
- To respond to verbal and nonverbal commands
- To communicate through language

Goal 5: To learn about moving and doing
- To develop gross motor skills
- To develop fine motor skills
- To coordinate eye and hand movements
- To develop self-help skills

Goal 6: To acquire thinking skills
- To gain an understanding of basic concepts and relationships
- To apply knowledge to new situations
- To develop strategies for solving problems

[1] J. Ronald Lally, Abbey Griffin, et al. *Caring for Infants and Toddlers in Groups: Developmentally Appropriate Practice.* Washington, DC: ZERO TO THREE/The National Center, 1995.

Sue Bredekamp and Carol Copple, Eds. *Developmentally Appropriate Practice in Early Childhood Programs,* Revised Edition. Washington, DC: National Association for the Education of Young Children, 1997.

Goals and Objectives for Working with Families

Goal 1: To build a partnership with families

- ❖ To involve families in the program's planning and evaluation process
- ❖ To listen to and discuss families' questions, concerns, observations, and insights about their children
- ❖ To communicate regularly with families at arrival and departure times about how things are going for their child at home and at the program
- ❖ To schedule regular conferences and/or home visits
- ❖ To discuss with families ways to handle children's challenging behaviors
- ❖ To resolve differences with families in a respectful way
- ❖ To help families gain access to community resources

Goal 2: To support families in their parenting role

- ❖ To demonstrate respect for a family's approach to childrearing and their feelings about sharing the care of their child
- ❖ To celebrate with families each new milestone in their child's development
- ❖ To incorporate family rituals and preferences into the daily life of the program
- ❖ To offer workshops/training on child development and other topics of interest to families
- ❖ To help families network with one another for information and support

Goal 3: To support families in their role as primary educators of their child

- ❖ To encourage family involvement and participation in program activities
- ❖ To provide families with strategies to support children's learning at home

Goal 4: To ensure that the home cultures of the children's families are reflected in the program

- ❖ To support children's use of their home language
- ❖ To encourage children's awareness of and interest in home languages spoken at the program
- ❖ To seek families' assistance in learning about the children's home culture
- ❖ To include objects and customs from the children's home cultures in the program's environment, routines, and activities
- ❖ To interact with children in a style that is respectful of their home culture

Choosing Your Target Goals and Objectives

Taken together, these two sets of goals and objectives may be viewed as a master list. Your ultimate aim is, of course, to realize all of these goals. In reality though, achieving desired results occurs in small steps rather than leaps. For most programs, it is helpful to start out by pinpointing goals and objectives that most need your attention and to add other goals and objectives over time.

Therefore, to implement *The Creative Curriculum,* your first step is to review these two sets of goals and objectives. Consider how they relate to your program by responding to these questions:

- ❖ Are there certain goals you've already achieved and need only to continue doing what you're doing to maintain them?

- ❖ Are there other goals you haven't been as successful in reaching as you'd like to be?

- ❖ Are there goals you haven't focused on but think you should?

- ❖ Are there goals that need your attention as a result of your program's special circumstances?

There are several informal methods you can use to determine your focus. First of all, your own observations (see Chapter 6), will give you a firm idea of what children need, which parts of *The Creative Curriculum* work well, and which parts of your program need strengthening. You can also interview colleagues, families, and consultants, to ask their opinions about your program's needs. Then, as a team, you can decide which goals need your attention.

Alternatively, you can conduct a more formal standardized evaluation of your program. Instruments, such as *The Assessment Profile—Infant/Toddler Version* or *Family Day Care Version* (Abbott-Shim & Sibley) and the *Infant/Toddler Environmental Rating Scale* (ITERS) or *Family Day Care Rating Scale* (FDCRS) (Harms & Clifford), can describe how well your program meets recognized standards for environment, scheduling, health, safety, programming, and adult-child interactions.[2] With the information collected, you can decide on which goals to focus your energies.

At the same time that you decide to concentrate your energies on specific goals, it's important to remember two things:

- ❖ **If you use** *The Creative Curriculum for Infants &Toddlers,* **you won't be neglecting other goals while you concentrate on those you've selected**. This is especially true of the goals for children, since the areas of child development are so interrelated. For example, suppose you target the goal of helping children learn about themselves. As you help a child develop a sense of self, you can help the child develop social, emotional, physical, and thinking skills.

- ❖ **Although you may have chosen goals with specific children or families in mind, your efforts benefit all the children and/or families in the program**. Suppose, for example, you want to address some parents' unrealistic expectations about their children's development. You offer a workshop, and in so doing, all families benefit.

Thus, you can recognize that the purpose of targeting two or three specific goals is to give them the extra attention they need. It does not mean neglecting other goals.

---

[2] Both versions of *The Assessment Profile* can be obtained by contacting Quality Assist, 368 Moreland Avenue, Atlanta, GA 30307. Copies of the *ITERS* and *FDCRS* can be ordered from Teacher's College Press, Columbia University, New York, NY, 10027-6694.

Long-Range Planning and Evaluation

Once you and your colleagues have identified specific goals and objectives, you've begun the long-range planning and evaluation process. Long-range planning requires thinking ahead—typically for a month or more—about how to meet these targeted goals and objectives. There are five steps to follow when planning for the long term.

1. Identify the goals and objectives for children and families.
2. Identify specific strategies to reach each goal and objective. Develop a plan.
3. Implement your plan.
4. Evaluate your plan. How is it working?
5. Based on your findings, make a plan for the following month. It may focus on the same goal(s) and objective(s) or new ones.

To give you an idea of how to apply these steps, here are two examples that demonstrate how La Toya and Grace developed long-range plans for their programs.

La Toya's Long-Range Planning Process

Step 1: Identify Target Goals and Objectives

I feel good about all the interesting activities I offer children in my family child care program. I also feel good about how much children help with daily routines, such as setting the table. One thing I don't feel good about is that there's a great deal of hitting among the children. The children's parents are concerned that they've been hitting and having tantrums at home, too. I reviewed the goals and objectives for children in the Curriculum and I've decided to spend extra time to help the children learn about their feelings and how to express them in appropriate ways.

Step 2: Identify Strategies and Develop a Plan

I know toddlers have a wide range of feelings and that their feelings can be very intense. I plan to introduce a variety of activities which let children express their feelings in positive ways.

Step 3: Implement the Plan

I am talking more with the children about their feelings and reactions. I offer activities such as playing with dough and dancing to music, which let them express their emotions in positive ways. And today the children and I made up a song about things to do when they are happy, sad, and angry.

Step 4: Evaluate the Plan

The children were very interested in all these activities. On Tuesday I heard Valisha say, "I'm mad at you, Eddie!" She stomped her foot—a big improvement over smacking him the way she used to! I think children want and need more chances to talk about feelings and express themselves in positive ways.

Step 5: Review and Revise Plan

Because this is such an important topic and because we've had some obvious improvements, I plan to continue focusing on feelings as one of my target goals for children. Next month I'll ask colleagues at our provider association meeting to share their ideas for dealing with children's hitting and for helping children express feelings positively. I'll also pay more attention to ways I guide children's behavior.

Grace's Long-Range Planning Process

Step 1: Identify Target Goals and Objectives

I feel good about the way I relate to the children, but it bothers me that I don't know much about their families' backgrounds. Since our center serves the whole university community, there are many different cultures represented. To be perfectly honest, I sometimes feel uncomfortable working with families that are so different from mine. I've decided to make a real effort to focus on the goal of helping to reflect the children's home cultures into our program.

Step 2: Identify Strategies and Develop a Plan

As a first step, I plan to explore how my own background influences my views on child rearing and how I might learn more about the children's families' backgrounds.

Step 3: Implement the Plan

Last week, I attended a workshop on culture and child rearing. I've also talked with some of my professors about the subject. Most importantly, I have been talking with my own parents and siblings about our family beliefs. I'm starting to talk openly with the families in my program about their beliefs and values.

Step 4: Evaluate the Plan

To my surprise, I discovered how much my past influences my work. I realize now that growing up in a home where we were encouraged to be quiet makes it particularly challenging for me to deal with children like Willard, who are very active and noisy.

Step 5: Review and Revise Plan

Next month, I am going to invite members of the children's families to tape songs they sing at home with the children. I also plan to continue our discussions about what we want for the infants and toddlers in our lives. This is a goal I think I should continue to focus on for some time.

Short-Range Planning and Evaluation

Short-range planning is a way to make long-range plans materialize. As you think ahead about what you are going to do each day with children—what supplies you will need, which special events are coming up, and who is going to do what—you set your long-range plans in motion. The following suggestions can help you to begin:

> ❖ **Set aside a regular time to plan each week.** Can you use the time just before children arrive, after they leave, or during naptime? Remember, planning doesn't have to take long—especially when you do it regularly. But it does have to take place.

> ❖ **Look back at the previous week as you think about the week ahead.** Ask yourself (and colleagues, if any) what went well and what changes would make things run more smoothly. Include input from the children's families as well as support personnel, such as the bus driver or cook.

> ❖ **See how your last few weeks fit into your long-range plans.** What would you like to do that you haven't yet gotten to do?

The *Weekly Planning Form* we designed for this *Curriculum* asks you to consider seven aspects of weekly planning.

Goals for the week. Which goal(s) and objective(s) are you going to focus on this week with children? How do you plan to work with their families? For example, if you are focusing on helping children learn to express their feelings in appropriate ways, you may note that you will offer comforting and expressive activities, such as water play, pretend play, and fingerpainting, and that you will plan to sing songs about feelings, and consult with parents.

Changes to the physical environment. Are there changes to make? Do you need duplicates of materials to keep children from fighting over toys? Do materials reflect the children's cultural backgrounds? Does the fact that puzzle pieces end up scattered on the floor mean that the puzzles are too difficult and should be put away for now? That they aren't stored so that children can use them independently? That children aren't encouraged to clean up after themselves?

Activities for the week. Are there special activities you want to plan for the children, indoors and outdoors? Did you try an activity previously that you want to offer again? Are children ready for something new?

Changes to daily routines. How are daily routines and transitions going? Are children getting cranky because they are spending too much time waiting? Or do they feel proud as they help with "real work," such as feeding the fish or wiping the table after snack? Are any changes needed?

Working with families. What are some different ways to involve parents in implementing *The Creative Curriculum*? These may include asking for their ideas, making materials, inviting parents to participate in an activity or in daily routines.

Responsibilities. Who is going to do what to carry out the plans for the week? If you care for children alone in your home, you may consider asking an older child or another adult to help with a special activity. Think ahead about what you have to do and when you will do it.

After reviewing how La Toya filled out the *Weekly Planning Form* (on the following page), try using this form to plan your program over the next week or two. Then evaluate how it works for you and change it to suit your needs. (See Appendix B for a blank form.)

Adapting Your Plans

When you work with infants and toddlers, the one thing you can expect is the unexpected. Each infant has a uniquely personal schedule. As you zip up the last jacket and head for the door, an infant may begin crying to tell you he is tired or hungry or needs his diaper changed. Toddlers, too, have an amazing ability to capsize the best laid plans. You can't predict when a toddler may decide to flush her socks down the toilet or try out a balancing act on the back of the sofa.

You'll need to be able to adapt your plans if you're to respond to the children's changing needs and interests. Here are some steps you can follow.

Review your weekly planning form. Visualize your day first in the morning. Try to imagine how all the parts of the day will fit together.

Assess the realities of the day. Is there an infant who is going to need extra time and attention because she is teething, or for some other reason? Did a family bring in a bag of freshly picked apples tempting you to replace your plans to make French toast for snack with making applesauce? Are you feeling a little worn down and not up to organizing the fingerpainting activity you planned?

Adapt your plans as necessary. Consult Chapters 16–22 on activities for ideas you can use. Decide, for example, that because it is raining outside, that you will set up an obstacle course for some active indoor play.

Throughout the day, keep these two points in mind.

- ❖ **Remain flexible.** There is no way to predict that a toddler will throw a tantrum and require some extra attention. As a result, you won't be able to introduce the special gluing activity you had planned. Nor can you foresee that a bulldozer will begin working at the end of your road, giving you a new destination for neighborhood walks.

- ❖ **Be responsive to individual children's needs and interests.** If you know a child needs you to be ready to step in and keep her from biting another child, you may decide to postpone your plans for making playdough with the children. Instead, you might bring out the playdough you made a few days ago or spend extra time singing and reading with the children. You can make playdough tomorrow or next week.

Weekly Planning Form

Target goals/objectives: *To learn about their feelings/To be able to express their feelings in appropriate ways*

Week of: *10/18*

Changes to the Environment

Post the new article about positive guidance that I got from my last providers' association meeting.

Changes to Play/Activity Areas

Add more blocks so several children can build without fighting over who has the most blocks. Add doctor props to pretend play area because Eddie has a series of doctor appointments coming up.

Activities for the Week

	Monday	Tuesday	Wednesday	Thursday	Friday
Indoor Activities Planned	*Spreading apple butter on crackers*	*Make playdough. Take a trip to library to check out books for the week*	*Making French toast*	*Fingerpainting Sing songs about feelings*	*Making grilled cheese sandwiches*
Outdoor Activities Planned	*Walk to maple tree to collect leaves*	*Blow bubbles*	*Tell stories*	*Take a texture walk*	*Bring a magnifying stool outside*

Changes to Daily Routines *Make a point of inviting children to help me prepare snacks and lunch and to set the table. See if this cuts down on waiting, pushing, and hitting when children are bored and hungry.*

Working with Families *Talk with the Curtises who are concerned about Valisha hitting other children. Ask them what they do to help Jonisha when her sister hurts her. Share the new article about positive guidance with all families.*

Responsibilities *Borrow a set of blocks from provider association's toy lending library. Copy article on guiding behavior for all families.*

Creating a Daily Schedule

While almost everyone recognizes that creating the daily schedule is a part of the short-range planning process, not everyone agrees on what form it should take. Some people who work with infants and toddlers place great value on being spontaneous. They know that because they can't predict what young children will need and do, they must remain open to follow children's moods and cues. Others feel more comfortable following a timed schedule. They like knowing what they are going to do and when they should be doing it.

The best approach probably lies somewhere in the middle of these two extremes. Infants and toddlers need a schedule that is regular enough to be predictable, yet flexible enough to meet their individual needs and to take advantage of learning opportunities that can appear with no warning.

When an infant like Julio falls asleep soon after arriving at child care, he needs a nap even though the other children are awake and playing. When the wind begins swirling leaves in the backyard, toddlers like Jonisha and Valisha need some time to dance with the leaves, even though the schedule says it is time to come inside and get ready for lunch.

A daily schedule is important for children, families, and you. A schedule offers infants and toddlers a feeling of predictability that helps them develop a sense of trust about the world. It offers parents a sense of what their child is doing during the day. Finally, a schedule gives you a picture of the day that can be adapted as necessary to meet the needs of individual children.

Components of a Daily Schedule

A good daily schedule contains the same basic components day after day. Depending on the length of your program day and the ages of the children you serve, your daily schedule will probably include time for the following:

- ❖ arrivals and departures;
- ❖ feeding/preparing and eating snacks and meals;
- ❖ diaper changing/toileting;
- ❖ dressing;
- ❖ indoor and outdoor play (including clean-up and transitions for older children); and
- ❖ sleeping/naptime.

A good schedule offers children a balance between the following types of activities:

- ❖ time with others, time alone, and one-on-one time with a "special" adult;
- ❖ quiet times and active times; and
- ❖ activities children choose and those offered by adults.

The chart on the next page shows how you can adapt your daily schedule to meet the needs of children as they grow.

Adapting the Schedule to Meet Children's Needs

Young Infants	How You Can Adapt Your Daily Schedule
They depend on you to meet their basic needs—to be fed, kept dry and comfortable, and picked up and held.	Create a daily schedule that is flexible so you can respond to individual biological needs.
They like to spend time with familiar adults seeing and doing interesting things.	Allow plenty of unhurried time throughout the day to spend with individual children.
They are learning to trust themselves and other people.	Respond to children when they need you, regardless of your scheduled plans.

Mobile Infants	How You Can Adapt Your Daily Schedule
They begin to remember more from one day to the next.	Follow your schedule consistently so that children will learn to predict what happens next.
They sense how you feel about them.	Organize your plans so that you'll have time to enjoy children and demonstrate your pleasure in what they do.
They like doing things for themselves.	Allow enough time for children to participate as fully as possible at mealtimes and in other daily routines.

Toddlers	How You Can Adapt Your Daily Schedule
They rely on familiar routines to organize their picture of the world.	Follow your daily schedule consistently, but allow for flexibility.
They can often become overwhelmed if things get too hectic.	Plan the day to eliminate unnecessary confusion. Use transitions to help children move from one part of the day to another.
They can concentrate for longer periods of time.	Allow time for children to play and pursue their interests unhurriedly.

Individualizing the Schedule for Infants

You will discover, if you haven't already, that each child in your care has a unique schedule for eating, diapering and toileting, playing, and sleeping. The younger the children in your care, the more likely you'll need to juggle your schedule to meet these individual needs. Just as one child finishes a bottle and falls asleep, another may wake up hungry.

Here's how one particular day went for two infants, Julio and Abby. Notice that although they do many of the same kinds of activities, the timing and specific content of what they do differs. The difference results, in large part, because of their different ages, abilities, and temperaments.

Julio's Schedule (4-month old)	Abby's Schedule (16-month old)
Morning	**Morning**
Arrival: Julio arrives at the Shane Center with his mother, Marta. Marta says a long good-bye and hands Julio to Linda.	**Arrival:** Abby arrives at Brooks's home with her father, Edward. She cries as he says good-bye. Brooks comforts her by reading a book to her.
Mealtime: Julio sits in a rocking chair with Linda. She cradles him in her arm as she gives him a bottle.	**Handwashing:** Abby and Mollie wash their hands so they can help Brooks prepare their breakfast.
Diaper change: Julio gazes at Linda as she changes his diaper and talks to him. He begins rubbing his eyes.	**Food preparation/Mealtime:** Abby helps Brooks and Mollie set the table and make scrambled eggs. They eat breakfast together, then clean up and wash their hands.
Naptime: Julio falls asleep in his crib as Linda pats him gently and sings a lullaby.	**Indoor play:** Abby squeezes, pounds, pokes, and rolls playdough. She notices new photos hanging on the wall and looks at them with Brooks.
Diaper change: Julio's diaper is dry when Linda checks it.	
Indoor play: Julio lies on a mat with two other babies near a low, shatterproof mirror. Linda sits at the edge of the mat and talks with the children about what they are doing and seeing.	**Diaper change:** Abby plays a game touching her nose, tummy, and so forth with Brooks.
	Indoor play: She sings songs with Brooks and Mollie. Mollie and Abby pretend to be lions. They eat from a bowl of small wooden blocks and roar as they crawl through a cloth tunnel.
Mealtime: Julio drinks part of a bottle sitting in Linda's lap, then burps as Linda pats him on the back.	**Clean up:** Abby and Mollie help put the blocks away and fold up the tunnel.
Diaper change: Julio kicks his legs as Linda changes his diaper. She pushes the overhead mobile. He tracks it with his eyes as it turns.	**Diaper change:** Abby protests as Brooks picks her up to change her diaper. Brooks assures her it will only take a minute and then she can get down and go outdoors.
Dressing: Linda puts on Julio's jacket. She sings to him as she dresses him.	**Dressing:** Abby takes her jacket off her hook. Brooks helps her put it on. Mollie proudly helps with the Velcro™ tab.
Outdoor play: Julio goes outdoors in a Snugli™ Linda is wearing. He closes his eyes when a gust of wind blows across his face. Linda describes what it might feel like.	**Outdoor play:** Abby takes a walk around the block with Brooks and Mollie. She notices sounds of birds and cars. She points out three different dogs.
Midday	**Midday**
Diaper change: Linda changes Julio gently but quickly, knowing the other children need her attention.	**Diaper change/Handwashing:** Abby's diaper is dry when Brooks checks it. She washes her hands for lunch, taking time to splash a bit.
Mealtime: Julio refuses the bottle Linda offers. He sits in an infant seat and watches the children eat. Linda tries again in 10 minutes, and he's hungry.	**Mealtime:** Abby carries napkins and paper cups to the table. She eats most of her grilled cheese sandwich and several carrot sticks. She uses a spoon and her fingers to eat and drinks some milk from a cup. Then she cleans up and washes her hands.
Naptime: Julio begins dozing off. Linda places him in his crib.	

continued on next page

Julio's Schedule (4-month old)	Abby's Schedule (16-month old)
Diaper change: Linda talks quietly to Julio as she changes his diaper and plays a peek-a-boo type game with him.	**Brushing teeth:** Brooks finishes drying Abby's hands with a towel and gets down the toothbrushes. Abby and Mollie brush their teeth.
Mealtime: Julio drinks part of a bottle sitting in Linda's lap.	**Transition:** Brooks reads the girls a story and plays some quiet music to set the mood for naptime.
	Diaper change: Abby yawns and lies quietly as Brooks changes her diaper.
	Naptime: Abby falls asleep on her cot in the living room as Brooks rubs her tummy.
	Diaper change: Brooks changes Abby's diaper and sings her favorite song.
	Snacktime: Abby and Mollie spoon some cottage cheese on crackers and eat them. Abby also scoops some of the cottage cheese onto the table. They each drink a cup of milk and wash their hands when done.

Afternoon

Indoor play: Julio sits in Linda's lap as she sings with older infants.

Diaper change: Linda notices Julio is wet and changes his diaper. He squirms and she finishes promptly.

Indoor play: Linda places Julio on a mat on the floor under a low hanging mobile. Julio can bat the mobile with his fists.

Departure: Julio sits in a rocking chair with his mother, Marta, while she relaxes and talks with Linda. After about 20 minutes, Marta puts on Julio's jacket, says good-bye, and they leave for home.

Afternoon

Indoor play: Abby carries five large cardboard blocks, one by one, into the middle of the living room. She carefully places each one on the floor. When Brooks brings over a bin of rubber farm animals, Abby puts some animals on top of the blocks.

Clean up: Abby watches as Mollie and Brooks start to put away the blocks. When Brooks hands Abby a block and asks her to help, Abby puts it on the shelf.

Diaper change: Abby and Brooks talk about farm animals. They "moo" together as Brooks changes Abby's diaper.

Dressing: Abby gets her jacket and takes it over to Mollie, who is busy putting on her own jacket. Brooks helps Abby and explains that Mollie can help her tomorrow.

Outdoor play: Abby and Mollie play in the sandbox in Brooks's backyard. Abby watches the sand fall through a sieve.

Departure: Robin picks up Abby. She explains they have to hurry to go pick up Talia at a friend's. Brooks helps Abby put on her coat as Robin gathers her things. Robin and Abby say good-bye and leave.

A Schedule for Toddlers

By the time children are toddlers, their day is a little more consistent and predictable. For example, toddlers typically eat and sleep as a group and have a designated time for play. A consistent daily schedule helps toddlers feel more in control, and thus more competent and secure. Of course, it is still important to be flexible about responding to individual children's needs.

Here is a sample schedule for toddlers.[1] Notice that frequently several activities take place at the same time.

Sample Toddler Schedule	
Early Morning	Greet parents and children.
	Help children and parents say good-bye.
	Encourage children to explore the environment and materials in their own way.
	Set up and invite children to participate in adult-directed activity, such as playing a simple lotto game.
	Clean up and wash hands.
	Prepare and eat snack.
	Discuss plans and news of the day.
	Clean up and wash hands.
Late Morning	Change diapers and use toilet, wash hands.
	Help children get ready to go outside.
	Take small group walks (to the park, to mail a letter, to the playground).
	Come inside, take off coats, and hang on hooks.
	Wash hands, read stories.
Midday	Help prepare and eat lunch.
	Clean up and wash hands.
	Change diapers and use toilet, wash hands.
	Brush teeth.
	Read stories, play music.
	Help children prepare for naps.
	Wake up and cuddle time.
	Change diapers and use toilet, wash hands.
	Prepare and eat snack, wash hands.
Late Afternoon	Play indoors and outside.
	Offer option of free choice or adult-directed activities.
	Read stories or do quiet play, such as table art or toys.
	Help parents and children reunite and leave for home.

The schedule you develop for your program may vary from the ones we have outlined. However, they will give you a starting point for planning a schedule that meets the needs of your children and your program.

---

[1] K. Modigliani, M. Reiff, and S. Jones. *Opening Your Door to Children*. Washington, DC: National Association for the Education of Young Children, 1986.

Planning for Transitions

Every day is filled with transitions—the periods of time between one activity and the next. With toddlers, who have a more structured schedule, transitions are more apparent. The most important transitions, and often most difficult, are at the beginning and end of the day. These are the times when infants and toddlers say good-bye and then hello to their families. (This will be discussed in detail in Chapter 11.) However, any transition can become a problem if children don't know what to do or if they are required to wait for long periods of time. Young children can't wait. When they are made to do so while adults get organized, then disruptions (restlessness, pushing, hitting) are bound to occur.

Here are some suggestions of ways you can avoid making infants and toddlers wait by preparing for transitions and involving children in the process.

Plan ahead. Then you'll know what you'll be doing and can feel prepared for each new activity.

Be organized. Have the supplies for the next activity ready so you don't have to search for them while the children wait.

Give children a warning. Before a change takes place, say something like, "It's almost time to clean up. Think about finishing what you are doing."

Divide the group so children won't have to wait. For example, while some toddlers are brushing their teeth, the others might be listening to a story or helping you set up cots.

Guide children through a transition. You can do this by describing what you are doing or singing songs or chants. For example, you can have a special song for clean up time or for getting ready for lunch.

Planned transitions help children build a sense of order about their world. They feel competent when they know what is expected and are engaged. From your point of view, a well-organized day means that you feel more calm and can take the time you need to observe children and enjoy their development. In the next chapter, we will explore in detail how you can go about doing this.

Individualizing for Children and Families

I n the last chapter, we discussed planning and evaluating your program. In this chapter, we look at how you can plan and adapt your program's goals and objectives for each individual child and family. Because children and families come to your program with distinct needs, strengths, and values, your challenge is to customize the program's goals to fit the *particular* circumstances of *each* child. One of the hallmarks of a high quality program is this ability to individualize.

To individualize for children, you begin by identifying goals and objectives on which to focus, then determine how you can best support children's mastery of them. In addition to your work with children, you can customize your work with families to meet their individual needs and interests.

As you read through this chapter, you will learn about:

❖ using the forms for *Individualizing the Goals and Objectives for Children;*
❖ observing children systematically to get to know them as individuals;
❖ organizing your observations;
❖ putting it all together into the *Planning Form for Individualizing;* and
❖ using the *Goals for Working with Families* form.

Individualizing Goals and Objectives for Children

The goals and objectives for children listed in Chapter 5 identify social, emotional, physical, and cognitive skills for all children. However, as everyone who works with infants and toddlers knows, no two children are alike in their development. One nine-month-old may be crawling while another is already starting to walk. One 18-month-old may be expressing her thoughts in words, while another relies on grunts and gestures. Development in all areas follows its own timetable.

To truly meet the needs of every child in your care, you'll need to find out where each one is in terms of development. Then you can meet that child at a wholly appropriate level and help him or her to reach the next step.

To do this in a systematic way, we have created forms for *Individualizing the Goals and Objectives.* There are three versions of the form: one each for young infants, mobile infants, and toddlers. Each version lists the six goals, identifies the objectives within each goal, and provides three examples of behaviors that indicate a child has mastered the objective. There is space for you to record your observations right on the form.

Objectives. The examples for illustrating mastery of an objective are age-specific and are based on child growth and development over time. For this reason, Linda would select the checklist for young infants when observing Julio, Grace would use the mobile infant checklist with Willard, and La Toya would use the toddler checklist for Valisha and Jonisha. The examples only suggest some of the behaviors reflecting a child's mastery of the given objective. They are not intended to be a complete list, but rather to give you an idea of types of behaviors to look for.

Evidence. For each objective, you have space to record examples of behaviors you've observed that illustrate beginning, developing, or consistent mastery. By all means, list as many examples as you you think you need. Again, you do not have to observe the exact same behaviors as those in the examples provided.

Progress. Next to each objective you can check the child's progress toward mastery: has not yet (or only rarely) shown evidence of mastery; shown evidence sometimes; or shown evidence consistently. By checking the appropriate boxes, you can quickly see whether the child has mastered the objective, or whether it is one you need to target.

We recommend you use the *Individualizing the Goals and Objectives* forms in an ongoing way, whenever you need to reassess your plans for children. At a minimum, you'll probably want to observe children at the start of the program year and then at a midpoint, so that you can determine where children are in their development and plan accordingly. (Most people find that it takes about a month to conduct observations of this depth.)

You might also wish to use the observation form at the end of the program year, so that you can see how the child has progressed. You can share this information with families or—if a child is transitioning to a new program—the next caregiver or teacher.

A reminder, however: these forms are meant to serve as planning tools for individualizing your program. They are *not* intended to be a list of skills or milestones children should acquire by a certain age. Most certainly, they should not be used to compare the progress of one child with that of another.

Here is a sample form La Toya completed on Valisha at the start of the year. Notice that La Toya has checked "Not Yet/Rarely" next to some of the objectives. This is perfectly fine, since it reflects the course of Valisha's development. When La Toya next observes Valisha, she may find evidence of mastery of some of these objectives.

Individualizing Goals and Objectives for Toddlers

Name of child: _Valisha Curtis_   **Caregiver/Teacher:** _La Toya Thompkins_

Date of birth: _12/1/93 (35 months)_   **Date completed:** _10/29/96_

Goal 1: To learn about themselves

Progress	Objectives	Evidence
☐ Not Yet/ Rarely ☐ Sometimes ☒ Consistently	**To feel valued and attached to others** **Examples:** ❖ points out family picture in a scrapbook ❖ knows which child is out for the day after seeing who is there ❖ looks to caregivers for comfort and at times may comfort caregiver	V sat on my lap after her parents left and snuggled close to me. She proudly tells me her name is Valisha Renée Curtis.
☐ Not Yet/ Rarely ☐ Sometimes ☒ Consistently	**To feel competent and proud about what they can do** **Examples:** ❖ pours own juice at snack time and says, "I did it!" ❖ helps another child find the crayons ❖ stands on one foot and calls, "Look at me!"	V called me over to see her painting of a giant red cat. V told me girls can play the steel drums.
☐ Not Yet/ Rarely ☒ Sometimes ☐ Consistently	**To assert their independence** **Examples:** ❖ insists on putting on own jacket ❖ willingly joins in a new activity ❖ cheerfully says "good-bye" to parents and goes to play	V insisted on putting all the prunes and raisins to be soaked for a holiday black cake into the bowl by herself.

Goal 2: To learn about their feelings

Progress	Objectives	Evidence
☐ Not Yet/ Rarely ☒ Sometimes ☐ Consistently	**To communicate a broad range of emotions through gestures, sounds, and—eventually—words** **Examples:** ❖ says "I did it!" after using the potty successfully ❖ hugs a doll and lovingly feeds it a bottle ❖ raises hand to make a "high five"	V made Fluffy breakfast, then gave Fluffy a hug and told her, "You are a good cat."
☒ Not Yet/ Rarely ☐ Sometimes ☐ Consistently	**To express their feelings in appropriate ways** **Examples:** ❖ roars like a lion when angry instead of biting ❖ recognizes feelings in others (e.g., "Camilo sad.") ❖ bites on a bagel when has urge to bite	

Goal 3: To learn about others

Progress	Objectives	Evidence
☐ Not Yet/ Rarely ☐ Sometimes ☒ Consistently	**To develop trusting relationships with nurturing adults** **Examples:** ❖ imitates adult activities (e.g., reading a newspaper, setting the table) ❖ eager to help with chores (e.g., preparing meals, feeding the fish) ❖ calls adult over to show an accomplishment (e.g., a painting, block structure)	V told me, "I can help" as she came into the kitchen, climbed up on the chair, and reached for a spoon to help me make French toast for breakfast. V came right over to fingerpaint—something she had never done before.
☐ Not Yet/ Rarely ☒ Sometimes ☐ Consistently	**To show interest in peers** **Examples:** ❖ enjoys including other children in pretend play (e.g., driving in a car or going food shopping) ❖ refers to other children by name ❖ comments on who is a girl and who is a boy	V noticed when Vivian was absent. She asked when Vivian will feel better.
☐ Not Yet/ Rarely ☒ Sometimes ☐ Consistently	**To demonstrate caring and cooperation** **Examples:** ❖ responds to emotions of other children (e.g., helps adult pat a crying child) ❖ works with another child to complete a task (e.g., putting away a puzzle) ❖ feeds and puts doll to bed	V gave Janice a hug when Janice fell and scraped her knee.
☐ Not Yet/ Rarely ☒ Sometimes ☐ Consistently	**To try out roles and relationships through imitation and pretend play** **Examples:** ❖ acts out simple life scenes (e.g., making dinner, going to the doctor) ❖ puts hat on and says, "I'm going to work" ❖ uses object to represent something else (e.g., box as car, block as phone)	V played "going to the grocery store" with Jonisha and Eddie.

Goal 4: To learn about communicating

Progress	Objectives	Evidence
☐ Not Yet/ Rarely ☒ Sometimes ☐ Consistently	**To express needs and thoughts without using words** **Examples:** ❖ uses facial expressions to show excitement ❖ catches adult's eye for attention and reassurance when needed ❖ tugs on pants to indicate need to go to bathroom	V brought her <u>Millions of Cats</u> book over and held it out to me to read.
☐ Not Yet/ Rarely ☐ Sometimes ☒ Consistently	**To identify with a home language** **Examples:** ❖ speaks in home language with family members and others ❖ uses main language spoken in child care with those who don't speak home language ❖ recognizes tapes of stories and songs from home culture	V uses West Indian phrases with her family.

Goal 4: To learn about communicating (continued)

Progress	Objectives	Evidence
☐ Not Yet/ Rarely ☒ Sometimes ☐ Consistently	**To respond to verbal and nonverbal commands** Examples: ❖ follows directions such as, "Bring the book to me, please" ❖ responds to adult's facial expression (e.g., stops throwing blocks after a stern look) ❖ goes over to cot when lights are dimmed for naptime	V followed my directions about how to crack an egg when we made French toast.
☐ Not Yet/ Rarely ☐ Sometimes ☒ Consistently	**To communicate through language** Examples: ❖ tells a story ❖ tells about what happened over the weekend ❖ talks with other children while playing together	V told me about going to a street fair over the weekend and playing steel drums. She engages adults and children in conversation. She can recite nursery rhymes by heart.

Goal 5: To learn about moving and doing

Progress	Objectives	Evidence
☐ Not Yet/ Rarely ☐ Sometimes ☒ Consistently	**To develop gross motor skills** Examples: ❖ walks up stairs ❖ throws a ball ❖ runs	V is very comfortable climbing stairs holding onto the railing. She can balance on one foot.
☐ Not Yet/ Rarely ☒ Sometimes ☐ Consistently	**To develop fine motor skills** Examples: ❖ threads large beads ❖ scribbles with marker or crayons ❖ pastes papers together	V tries to use scissors but ends up frustrated and tearing the paper because cutting is so hard for her. She draws with crayons and uses fingerpaints.
☐ Not Yet/ Rarely ☐ Sometimes ☒ Consistently	**To coordinate eye and hand movements** Examples: ❖ places pieces in a simple puzzle ❖ closes Velcro™ fasteners on shoes ❖ stirs ingredients in bowl when helping to cook	V can do the cat puzzle that has six pieces. She mixes paints together to form new colors.
☐ Not Yet/ Rarely ☐ Sometimes ☒ Consistently	**To develop self-help skills** Examples: ❖ uses the potty and washes hands ❖ pours own milk and juice from small plastic pitcher ❖ puts on own jacket and hat when going outside	V can button her sweater with help. She uses the toilet by herself though I had to remind her to wash her hands. She helps me set and clean the table.

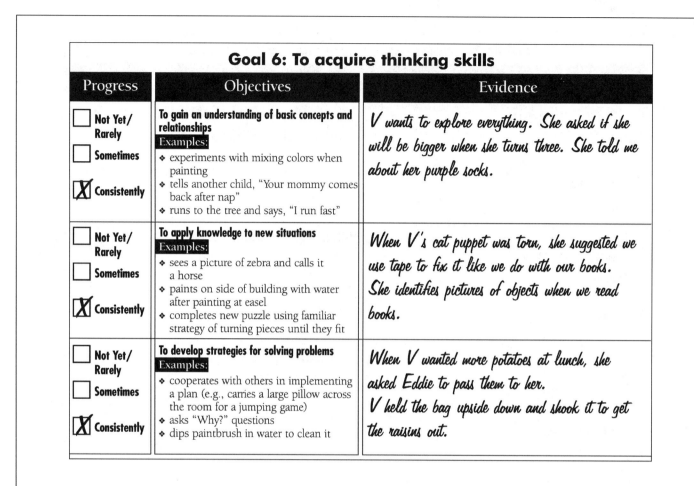

Goal 6: To acquire thinking skills

Progress	Objectives	Evidence
☐ Not Yet/ Rarely ☐ Sometimes ☒ Consistently	**To gain an understanding of basic concepts and relationships** Examples: ❖ experiments with mixing colors when painting ❖ tells another child, "Your mommy comes back after nap" ❖ runs to the tree and says, "I run fast"	V wants to explore everything. She asked if she will be bigger when she turns three. She told me about her purple socks.
☐ Not Yet/ Rarely ☐ Sometimes ☒ Consistently	**To apply knowledge to new situations** Examples: ❖ sees a picture of zebra and calls it a horse ❖ paints on side of building with water after painting at easel ❖ completes new puzzle using familiar strategy of turning pieces until they fit	When V's cat puppet was torn, she suggested we use tape to fix it like we do with our books. She identifies pictures of objects when we read books.
☐ Not Yet/ Rarely ☐ Sometimes ☒ Consistently	**To develop strategies for solving problems** Examples: ❖ cooperates with others in implementing a plan (e.g., carries a large pillow across the room for a jumping game) ❖ asks "Why?" questions ❖ dips paintbrush in water to clean it	When V wanted more potatoes at lunch, she asked Eddie to pass them to her. V held the bag upside down and shook it to get the raisins out.

Systematically Observing Children to Get to Know Them as Individuals

In addition to identifying the content goals and objectives for individual children, you also need to know how to best help children acquire these targeted objectives. When you understand what motivates a child, how the child approaches new tasks, and what his or her preferred learning style is, you can plan for that child.

You can gather this type of information in many ways. One of the most effective is to use systematic, focused observations, as Brooks did with Abby.

> Several months ago Brooks first observed Abby reaching for the spoon with which she was being fed. Brooks then decided to give Abby her own spoon to hold. A few days later, knowing that things would get messy but deciding it was worth it, Brooks gave Abby a small bowl of applesauce to eat with her spoon. Since then, Abby has become quite skilled at using a spoon to feed herself. She has also moved on to other self-help skills, such as wiping up spills and throwing away her napkin.

When Brooks observes, she uses a two-step process: she describes what she sees, then asks herself what it means. This type of careful observation is like watching children from the outside to understand what they are experiencing on the inside. Brooks figured out that in grabbing the spoon, Abby was asserting her independence and her desire to be in charge of feeding herself.

Through focused observations, you can gather information about children's

- ❖ family, culture, and home life;
- ❖ temperament;
- ❖ special interests;
- ❖ likes and dislikes;
- ❖ behavioral challenges; and
- ❖ learning styles.

Making a Commitment to Observe

There's no doubt that you already know a great deal about the children in your program. Why, then, are we now asking you to devote time regularly to observing in a focused way? Aren't informal observations—that one child has a cold, another isn't being very social, and that a third is spending most of the day playing dress-up—enough?

While informal observations certainly have their place, they don't provide enough information to make informed decisions about children. For this you need observations that are typical of the child, objectively reported, and accurately recorded. You'll need to plan and make a commitment to observe children routinely.

Although you may appreciate the value of observing, you may still wonder how you will fit observation time into your routine and activity-packed day. With only so many minutes in the day, something has to give. All too often that something is the time for focused observation.

The chart that follows identifies some of the main reasons people give to explain why they don't observe regularly and suggests strategies to overcome these obstacles.

Obstacles to Observing	Strategies to Overcome Them
"I don't have time in my schedule for observing."	Make observation a priority. Be aware that you are always observing as you care for children. However, when you observe in a purposeful way, you gain additional and valuable insights.
"I don't speak a child's home language."	Even a child who is not yet talking will have body language unique to a culture you might not understand. Consider asking someone who does speak the child's home language to observe with you.
"I can't observe and adequately supervise other children at the same time."	Schedule planned observations at times when children won't need constant supervision. If your program allows, you might make arrangements to have substitute staff, parent volunteers, or back-up providers on hand during scheduled observation times. Figure out a place where you can observe from the sidelines but still see and hear everything.
"There are too many things that need to be observed. I don't know where to begin."	Begin slowly. Choose one or two children to observe. Then, over time, gradually widen the scope until you are observing all children regularly.
"I miss what is happening when I have to go get a pen and paper."	Keep a pad of paper, notebook, index cards, and a pen in your pocket or in a convenient place. That way, you will always be ready to note something of interest.
"I'm afraid of breaching children's (and families') confidentiality."	You'll want to keep all your written observations in a secure place, such as filing cabinet you can lock.
"I don't know how to be objective."	Practice writing only what you see and hear. Keep a list of "red-flag" terms to avoid (such as active, quiet, bright, good, fussy, or happy) as a reminder. Request that your program provide training and assistance on becoming a better observer.

Recording Your Observations

Doing a focused observation implies having a purpose in mind. It also implies that you are systematic and use specific skills to make observations that are both accurate and objective. Focused observations can take many forms.

Anecdotal observations are recorded information about one specific event or behavior. They range from notations of developmental milestones (Jasmine pulled herself up on the sofa) to descriptions of children's behavior (Jonisha asked Eddie to join her at the sand box). Anecdotal records are often jotted down on index cards, large-sized adhesive labels, or Post-its,™ and can be as rich in detail as you want.

Running records are a narrative sample of what you see and hear during a specified period of time—usually between 2 and 20 minutes. How long you spend doing a running record depends on the time available, the presence of another adult who can watch the children while you observe, and the purpose of the observation. (Remember, lots can happen in even 2 to 3 minutes.) For example, seeing how children build with blocks might require more time than observing the effectiveness of your morning drop-off procedures.

Checklists are observations of a specific list of items, skills, or behaviors. Checking off an item indicates that the observed child performed the skill or behavior.

Rating scales require you to use a scale to judge the degree to which a child exhibits a specific behavior. Rating scales usually are numerical (on a scale of 1 to 5) or use descriptive phrases to cover a range of behaviors.

Sampling observations record behavior over a period of time or during a particular event. In time sampling, you record what children are doing at set intervals, such as every 10 or 15 minutes. In event sampling, you tally the number of times that children engage in a specific behavior, such as using the outdoor play equipment.

Videotaped observations allow you to study children in their natural setting with no exaggeration or distortion. Because videotapes are capable of instant replay and freeze framing, you can use them for in-depth investigation.

As you become a more skilled observer, you will probably make use of all these forms. However, you may want to begin with only one or two types of observations, and then progress to other approaches. We suggest that a good way to begin is by keeping anecdotal and running records. These methods are straightforward, do not require use of any standardized forms, and provide rich data.

On the following pages are sample anecdotal and running records that La Toya recorded as she observed Valisha. As you read through them, think about how this information can help La Toya in planning for Valisha.

Sample Anecdotal Records

Date	Observations
9/12	I spent 20 minutes with Valisha today reading every book I have about cats! She must have asked me to read <u>Millions of Cats</u> a million times. She held onto the books and pointed to the pictures when I asked questions. She's got most of our cat books memorized.
9/23	Valisha got very angry when I wouldn't let her bring Iris, the cat from next door, into the house. Nothing I said to her made any difference. When I firmly said "No," she had a real temper tantrum.
10/2	Valisha spent almost 30 minutes today stacking blocks. This caught my attention, because she's not usually very interested in blocks. I noticed that she watched Eddie making a tower and then went over to build next to him.
10/7	Valisha asked if I would help her write a letter to her siblings Jewel, Michael, and Patrice, who are in Port-of-Spain visiting their Granny and aunts and uncles. I suggested we do a tape recording so that she could send them a letter they could hear. Valisha's face lit up at the suggestion, and she immediately went to fetch Jonisha to join in. She then suggested we tape her and Jonisha playing the steel drums.
10/8	Valisha napped for two full hours today. This seems to have become her pattern.

Sample Running Records

Child: Valisha Curtis

Age: 35 months

Date: 10/15

Observer: La Toya Thompkins

Time: Began: 10:10 AM Ended: 10:20 AM

Setting: Kitchen. Mrs. Cruickshank (Eddie's mother) is helping Valisha, Jonisha, and Eddie soak fruit for a holiday black cake

Mrs. C. entered the kitchen. V. ran to her, hugged her leg. Mrs. C. greeted each child by name and turned toward Valisha, who was pulling at her pant leg. "Mrs. C., Mrs. C.," said Valisha, "did you see my Granny when you went home? Did you see Auntie Janice and Uncle Vic? Did Granny send anything for me?"

Mrs. C. stooped over to hug Valisha and told her that she didn't get to see her relatives because she had been in San Fernando where her own relatives lived, not Port-of-Spain. Valisha nodded. Mrs. C. started explaining how they were going to make the black cake.

"Can I help? Can I help?" asked Valisha, flashing a big smile to Mrs. C. Mrs. C. said she could help by soaking the prunes and the raisins. "Let's go," said Valisha, leading Mrs. C. to the table where the fruit was sitting in bags.

Child: Valisha Curtis

Age: 35 months

Date: 10/24

Observer: La Toya Thompkins (tape recorded)

Time: Began: 4:15 PM Ended: 4:20 PM

Setting: Outdoors

"Please, please," Valisha kept repeating. "I want to play ball with the boys." "I know you do Valisha. But you're just getting over bronchitis, and you shouldn't be running around. Why don't you take this book over to the picnic table instead?" Valisha grabbed the book out of my hand, yelled "No," and threw the book on the ground. "That's not how we treat our books," I said. "Please pick it up." Scowling all the while, Valisha picked up the book and handed it to me. "I'm sorry, Valisha," I said. "I know you'd like to play with the boys, but it's not a good idea until you're feeling better. Can you think of something more quiet you'd like to do?" Valisha took a moment and then her face lit up as she said, "Fluffy." "That'd be fine," I said. "Why don't you get Fluffy and some of the other stuffed animals and bring them outside to play with us."

Organizing Your Observations

To make use of your observations, you need to have some method of organizing the information you've collected. A growing number of professionals use portfolios. Portfolios contain the children's actual work (artwork or tape recordings of their singing), photos of their work (making playdough, building with blocks, preparing snack), and written records (logs of books children have had read to them, comments by children on their work). They also can contain systematic observations.

To illustrate how a portfolio works, let's peek inside Valisha's portfolio. La Toya uses the portfolios to plan and individualize, to track children's progress, and to share information with families.

Here's a sampling of what's inside Valisha's portfolio:

- ❖ background information
- ❖ accident/incident reports
- ❖ dated artwork (fingerpainting, drawings, paintings, collage)
- ❖ dated printout of computer art made by Valisha, with dictated description
- ❖ photographs of Valisha cooking peas and rice, on a field trip to a farm, playing dress-up
- ❖ log of books that La Toya has read one-on-one with Valisha
- ❖ audiotape of Valisha and Jonisha singing a calypso song
- ❖ anecdotal records
- ❖ running records
- ❖ event sampling
- ❖ the *Individualizing the Goals and Objectives for Toddlers* form

Samples of background information and event sampling are shown on the next page.

Background Information

Child: Valisha Curtis   **Mother:** Yvonne Curtis

Ethnicity: African-American/Trinidadian   **Father:** Johnny Curtis

Home Language: English   **Date:** September 7th

Family History: Valisha and her sister Jonisha are identical twins, age 33 months. (Jonisha, unlike Valisha, wears eyeglasses due to a car accident when she was 21 months old.) The twins live with their parents and a brother Patrice (age 5) in an apartment complex in central Los Angeles, in a largely West Indian community. Valisha's mother is from Trinidad. She has a large, extended family living in Port-of-Spain. Valisha's father is originally from Oakland, California. Johnny and Yvonne have been married for four years. Johnny is a mechanic, taking courses to become an airline mechanic. Yvonne is a receptionist at Virgin Records. With her boss's encouragement, she recently enrolled at a local community college.

Johnny drops off the girls in the morning at 7:45 AM. Yvonne picks the children up at 6:30 PM.

Event Sampling:

A tally of times Valisha offered to be/was a HELPER* on October 2nd: Total—4 times

* helper = assisting me or another child in a task or chore at her initiative, not anyone else's

Putting It All Together: Using the Planning Form for Individualizing

Once you have observed and documented children's progress, you have a wealth of information you can use to individualize your program. The next step is to turn this information into a plan for action. This can best be done by summarizing what you have learned about an individual child on a form such as the *Planning Form for Individualizing* which appears in Appendix B.

To illustrate how this summary form helps in planning for a specific child, here's how La Toya uses the information she collected on the *Individualizing the Goals and Objectives for Toddlers* form and her ongoing observations to individualize for Valisha.

As you read the forms, remember that every child in your program should receive the same attention given Valisha. And each child will benefit from the knowledge you gain through careful observations and planning. In addition, you will have valuable information to share with children's families. They can often offer suggestions that will further strengthen your individualizing plans. Count on completing an individualizing plan for each child several times a year, or following a period of rapid growth or change in the child's circumstances.

Planning Form for Individualizing

Name of child: _Valisha Curtis_   **Caregiver/Teacher:** _La Toya Thompkins_

Date of birth: _12/1/93 (35 months)_   **Date completed:** _November 2nd, 1996_

This child's family background (use background information and observations):

Valisha's mother is from Port-of-Spain, Trinidad; her father is a native of California. English is the family's first language. Culturally they are involved with the West Indian community. In particular, calypso and soca music are a very important part of their heritage.

This child can (use the *Individualizing the Goals and Objectives for Children* form):

Solves problems readily, such as fitting puzzle pieces together, combining two paint colors to make a third, and figuring out missing body parts from pictures. She can undress and dress herself (except for buttons); wash and dry her own hands; help set and clear the table; climb steps holding on to the railing; jump; walk backwards; balance on one foot; draw and paint; identify objects in a book; speak in long sentences; tell you that she is a girl and what this means.

This child is learning to (use the *Individualizing the Goals and Objectives for Children* form):

Button her clothing; use the toilet by herself; hop on one foot; give her full name; recite nursery rhymes by heart; use a scissors.

This child likes (use observations):

Being a helper; soft, cuddly toys; anything having to do with cats, including her favorite book _Millions of Cats_ (by Wanda Gag).

This child's temperament is (use observations):

Outgoing; Like her twin sister Jonisha, Valisha is active and lively. She is very verbal and engages everyone in conversation; she is usually ready to join in new activities.

This child learns best by (use observations):

Observing and doing things for herself. She follows verbal directions well.

This child's special needs are (use observations and the *Individualizing the Goals and Objectives for Children* form):

Sometimes needs help to deal with her emotions when she begins feeling out of control; needs longer naps than other children her age.

Sometimes this child has these behavioral challenges (use observations):

Sometimes lashes out when angry or frustrated.

To individualize for this child, I intend to make these changes:

To the environment:

Since Valisha is so active, I might ask Reggie to build a climbing structure to go with the outdoor playhouse he already built for the children. Since Valisha is motivated by stuffed animals, I should provide more soft toys like Fluffy for her to cuddle during dramatic play.

To materials and equipment:

— I want to encourage Valisha to do sensory activities such as sand and water play, art, or dramatic play. These activities will provide outlets for expressing her emotions in safe, appropriate ways.

— I also need to make sure Valisha has time to run, jump, and play outdoors each day, since she has so much energy.

To routines, transitions, and planned activities:

Since Valisha enjoys demonstrating her self-help skills, I want to give her lots of opportunities to help do "real work." Her cooperation and enthusiasm for helping should be acknowledged. I can encourage Valisha's mastery of self-help skills such as buttoning her coat, using a scissors, and washing her hands after going to the toilet. I want to be careful, though, of not typecasting Valisha in the helper role—she's still a little girl and needs lots of opportunities to just have fun and act silly.

To the daily schedule:

I also want to be sure that I allow Valisha to nap as long as she needs to—even if the other children are up and ready for their snack. Valisha can have her snack when she gets up—it's more important for her to get the sleep she needs to function well.

To interactions:

— I need to help Valisha develop strategies for expressing her strong feelings in appropriate ways as she plays with others. For example, she might sing songs about feelings and learn to express her anger or frustration by stomping her foot, rather than hitting.

— When I work with Valisha on new skills such as climbing steps without holding on or using a scissors, I should give her lots of opportunities to do these things herself as that's how she learns best.

Using the Goals for Working with Families Form

Throughout this curriculum, we have emphasized the importance of family in a young child's life. It is for this reason that in Chapter 5 we included goals and objectives for your work with families in addition to goals and objectives for children.

We believe that to serve a child well, you must also individualize your program to serve that child's family. For this reason, we have developed the *Goals for Working With Families* form. You can use this form, which appears in Appendix B, to document your work with each family and to evaluate your progress in achieving each goal and objective. There are two different sections to complete.

Documentation of what was done. In this section, you record what you've done to meet a particular objective and indicate when that activity took place. You'll find that by implementing *The Creative Curriculum for Infants & Toddlers,* you will be addressing many of the objectives for working with families in the course of your everyday activities. For example, if you have sent home copies of the letters to families that are included in Chapters 7–23 of the *Curriculum,* you can list this activity under the Objective, "To provide families with strategies for supporting children's learning at home," which comes under Goal 3: To support families in their role as primary educators of their child. (You'll note in the example below that La Toya has done this.)

Next steps. This section asks you to reflect on what else you might do to further a particular objective. Your responses to this section should fit what you already know about this family's make-up and needs.

Again, using La Toya as an example, the following pages show what a completed form might look like. With this information, La Toya can make the accommodations to her program she's listed under "Next Steps." This will enable her to serve the Curtis family even more successfully. Like La Toya, when you individualize your program for children and families, you plan for high quality.

Goals for Working with Families

Name of family: _Yvonne and Johnny Curtis_   **Name of child:** _Valisha Curtis_
Completed by: _La Toya Thompkins_

Goal 1: To build a partnership with families		
Objectives	**Documentation of What Was Done**	**Date**
To involve families in the program's planning and evaluation process	During our initial meeting, I asked Yvonne and Johnny what their goals are for Valisha while she's in my care.	8/30
To listen to and discuss families' questions, concerns, observations, and insights about their children	Yvonne and I had tea together. She asked my advice about a number of topics—biting, when children should start reading, stalling at bedtime, etc.	9/12
To communicate regularly with families at arrival and departure times about how things are going for their child at home and at the program	I talk with Johnny every morning and Yvonne every evening about how the twins' day went.	Daily
To schedule regular conferences and/or home visits	Haven't done this on a formal basis.	
To discuss with families ways to handle children's challenging behaviors	Valisha has hit Jonisha both here and at home. We're all working on ways to redirect her anger. We've seen some progress.	9/12
To resolve differences with families in a respectful way	So far we haven't had any differences that need to be resolved. We've been a good team!	
To help families gain access to community resources	Nothing has been done here. I do know that Yvonne's taking night school classes that her job is paying for.	

Next steps:
I plan to share the Planning Form for Individualizing with the Curtises.
I intend to meet with the children's parents formally once a month—not just in the informal ways
I do now. I'll inquire if Yvonne needs any further support, now that she's going to school at night.

Goal 2: To support families in their parenting role

Objectives	Documentation of What Was Done	Date
To demonstrate respect for a family's approach to childrearing and their feelings about sharing the care of their child	I always talk with the Curtises about discipline matters. We think together about how best to handle things. I want to make sure Valisha gets consistent messages from me and her parents.	9/23 9/30
To celebrate with families each new milestone in their child's development	When Valisha became toilet trained (without accidents after naps), I bought her some "big girl" panties to wear at home. I always send home artwork and creations—such as her first fingerpainting.	9/20 10/6
To incorporate family rituals and preferences into the daily life of the program	Before naptime, I sing the children a Trinidadian lullaby Yvonne taught me. It's quite similar to the ones we sing in Jamaica.	Daily
To offer workshops/training on child development and other topics of interest to families	I haven't done this.	
To help families network with one another for information and support	I haven't done this.	

Next steps:

I need to ask parents if they'd like to have a workshop on any particular topics. If so, I'll coordinate with my providers' association. It might be fun to have an expert on twins come speak—since 2 other providers I know care for twins and one has a set of triplets!

I think I should sponsor a potluck supper so that everyone who has children in my program can get to know one another.

Goal 3: To support families in their role as primary educators of their child

Objectives	Documentation of What Was Done	Date
To encourage family involvement and participation in program activities	I've asked the Curtises to join us on field trips, but so far they haven't been able to because of their jobs.	9/27
To provide families with strategies to support children's learning at home	I've given the Curtises the Letters for Families on Health, Safety, Hellos and Good-byes, Art, and Books. We've discussed them and they've given me feedback on what they've tried.	9/5 9/8 9/15 9/21 10/1

Next steps:

Find a way for the Curtises to become involved in the program that won't interfere with their jobs.
Continue giving out Letters to Families and discussing them with the Curtises.

Goal 4: To ensure that the home cultures of the children's families are reflected in the program

Objectives	Documentation of What Was Done	Date
To support children's use of their home language	English is the first language for all of us.	
To encourage children's awareness of and interest in home languages spoken at the program	Not applicable.	
To seek the families' assistance in learning about the children's home culture	When Valisha's Uncle Ronnie was visiting, he came over to show the children how to play classical music on the steel drums. Ronnie's a semi-professional musician (he plays with the Amoco Renegades) and it was super.	9/6
To include objects and customs from the children's home culture in the program's environment, routines, and activities	We have a pan (steel drums) in the music area along with Carnival costumes. The children love to dance to calypso and soca. (I can occasionally get them to hear some reggae.) We prepare lots of West Indian foods at meal and snack (e.g., caloloo, pelau, peas and rice, macaroni pie).	Daily
To interact with children in a style that is respectful of their home culture	Being West Indian myself, this is no problem for me. I place great value on family and try never to undermine any relative.	Daily

Next steps:
  Continue doing the same types of activities. I'll ask the parents for any suggestions.

Creating a Welcoming Environment

One of the first steps in implementing the program you've planned is to set up your home or center. It should be both a welcoming place for children and families and a pleasant and efficient place in which you can work. The environment you create has a profound effect on the feelings and actions of the children in your care, their families, and on you, yourself.

Children will spend most of their waking hours in your program. A new environment, no matter how welcoming, can be unsettling for them. They will probably be most comfortable when they are in a place that feels "homelike." A familiar environment produces the same feelings of safety and security they experience when they are with their own families. Thus, the trust children have built at home needs to be transferred to this new environment.

A warm and friendly environment can also be very reassuring to families. Areas specifically designed with families in mind send the message that they, as well as children, are always welcome. Environments that reflect children's backgrounds and special needs offer further security to children and families. You want to be sure that your program's environment communicates a sense of trust and security to all children and families.

Finally, because you also spend most of your work time in this environment, it should be a place where you enjoy spending time. If you design your environment so that you can work efficiently, you will have the time and energy you need to relate to each child in a caring, unhurried, and nurturing way.

In this chapter you will learn about:

- ❖ planning a responsive environment for infants and toddlers;
- ❖ arranging the environment to convey positive messages;
- ❖ creating appropriate indoor spaces;
- ❖ defining play areas outdoors;
- ❖ selecting and organizing materials;
- ❖ adapting the environment for children with special needs; and
- ❖ including children's families and cultures in the environment.

Planning a Responsive Environment

Because infants and toddlers grow and change so quickly, the environment must be changed continually to provide new challenges and inspire new interests, as shown on the chart below.

Planning a Responsive Environment		
What Children Can Do	**Ways You Can Arrange the Environment**	**How This Supports Development**
Young Infants Notice and watch what goes on around them. Reach for, bat, and poke at objects. Respond to being held and rocked. Developing the ability to sit and crawl.	Place pictures on the wall at child's eye level. Hang mobiles where infants can see and kick them. Have comfortable places for holding infants, such as soft chairs and hammocks. Install soft carpet so infants can crawl comfortably.	Encourages infants to focus and attend to objects in their environment. Teaches infants they can have an impact on the world. Builds relationships and a sense of trust. Promotes physical development.
Mobile Infants Pull themselves up to a standing position. Push, pull, fill, and dump objects. Take comfort from familiar objects and reminders of home. Sometimes need to be alone.	Be sure furniture is sturdy, with protected edges. Use mats with a variety of surfaces. Offer a variety of playthings, including household objects. Display pictures of family members and invite families to make audiotapes. Create private spaces.	Allows mobile infants to explore in safety and builds large muscles. Builds motor skills as well as coordination. Helps children feel safe and secure. Reduces separation anxiety. Helps children develop a sense of self.
Toddlers Walk, run, climb, and play with objects and toys. Sometimes want to do more than they can do. Play alongside and also with others.	Arrange the space so toddlers can move around safely. Organize toys on low shelves and label them with pictures. Offer materials and activities that meet children's level of development. Define areas where two or three children can play. Provide duplicates of toys.	Allows toddlers to explore freely and independently. Provides a variety of appropriate challenges so toddlers experience a sense of their own competence. Promotes the ability to engage in sustained and purposeful play.

Arranging the Environment to Convey Positive Messages

Have you ever watched children when they first enter a new environment? They look around and try to decide what kind of place it is. If you could read their minds, they might be asking themselves:

❖ Do I feel comfortable here?

❖ Do people know who I am and do they like me?

❖ Is this a place I can trust and where I can feel safe?

❖ Can I explore and go wherever I want?

❖ Can I count on people to take care of me?

Your daily interactions with infants and toddlers—the caring way in which you hold them, meet their needs, and encourage them to explore their world—are the most important way you answer these very typical questions and concerns. However, how you organize the physical environment also sends powerful messages to children and their families. Listed below are five positive messages you can send children and examples of how the environment can convey these messages.

"This place is comfortable."

❖ Special blankets and toys from home are in each child's crib or cubby.

❖ Familiar household objects—aluminum pots and pans, utensils, plastic containers—are available as play materials.

❖ There are home-like touches—plants, curtains, pillows covered in attractive fabrics, a fish tank.

❖ Cuddling places are available—stuffed chairs, couches, rocking chairs, and hammocks.

❖ There are "nooks and crannies" in which children can snuggle and feel protected.

"We know who you are and we like you. You belong here."

❖ Pictures of children and their families are displayed at a child's eye level and are laminated so children can touch them.

❖ There are places for each child to store belongings from home.

❖ Pictures and materials reflect the ethnic and individual characteristics of children and families.

❖ A message board tells parents about each child's day.

"This is a place you can trust."

❖ Furniture is arranged so children can explore freely and not get hurt.

❖ Toys and books are consistently displayed in the same places so children know where to find them.

❖ There are soft places where children can crawl and walk without fear of being hurt if they fall.

❖ Sick children have a comfortable place where they can rest or wait until their parents come.

"You can explore on your own."

❖ Areas that are off limits are blocked so children can't get there.

❖ Walls are decorated with interesting pictures and textures children can touch.

❖ Electrical outlets are covered and the rooms have been "child-proofed."

❖ Toys are on low shelves with picture labels so children know where to find and return them.

"We will take care of you."

❖ Child-adult ratios are low, group sizes are small, and each child has a primary caregiver.

❖ Changing tables are comfortable and safe; everything needed is within reach.

❖ Each child has his or her own crib or cot for resting.

❖ Food preparation is efficient so children can be fed on their individual schedules.

Take a look around your program setting. What messages do children receive? Consider the examples listed above and think about whether there are any changes you want to make.

Creating Indoor Spaces

Most of your day with infants and toddlers is spent in routines and activities. The daily routines of saying hello and good-bye, preparing and eating food, napping, diapering and toileting, and dressing occupy much of a young child's day—and therefore much of yours. As infants become more mobile, they need places to explore safely. They are ready for activities such as playing with toys and blocks, exploring sand and water and art materials, cooking, music and movement, and exploring books. These routines and activities translate into the following types of spaces you may want for your indoor environment:

- ❖ a greeting area;
- ❖ a food preparation and eating area;
- ❖ a sleeping area;
- ❖ a changing area and bathroom; and
- ❖ play areas with spaces for both active and quiet play; individual and group play.

If you work in a center-based program, you will need to create the areas described above. A counter-top with a bottle warmer and small refrigerator may serve as your kitchen, and you may define a play area with movable, low shelves or furniture. In a family child care home, these places exist naturally. Your own family members may feel less intruded upon if you ask them to help you figure out how to arrange your home for child care—and still preserve their sense of privacy. In either setting, arrange the indoor space to be inviting to children and an easy place to work. Here are some guidelines to keep in mind.

Include special touches. Think about places you enjoy. What makes them special? Is it the decorative touches, such as plants and pictures? Is it the soft furniture and reading materials that invite you to sit down and relax? These same features can make a family child care home or center just as welcoming to children and families.

Avoid overstimulating children. Even if you have all the toys and materials anyone could want, resist the temptation to put everything out. Think how overwhelming a warehouse store filled with merchandise can be. Displaying a few carefully selected toys on low shelves is more likely to lead to purposeful play than shelves with many playthings.

Allow for movement. Movement, as we discussed in Chapter 2, is essential for a child's healthy development. Children who are in an environment where they are free to move safely will develop the physical skills that help them feel competent.

Be aware of how space affects behavior. Large open spaces encourage children to run and use their large muscles. Small, enclosed areas promote social interaction and make it easier to concentrate. Your environment should offer both types of spaces.

Make each space easy-to-maintain. Ideally, you'll use washable area rugs to cover areas where children will crawl or move. You'll have children eat and do messy activities in spaces with washable flooring. If your environment includes spaces that aren't washable, you can use an old shower curtain to cover the floor during messy activities.

Organize and label storage space. Take the time to assess what you need so you'll know where to put things. Place shelves, bins, and hooks where you can reach them easily. Make picture labels to show where children's toys and belongings belong. Good storage allows you full use of your resources, and makes it easy for a substitute caregiver/teacher.

Minimize the physical strain on your body. Take care to avoid back problems that may result from lifting and holding infants and toddlers. Be sure there are comfortable places with good support for you to sit with children. Install sturdy steps so toddlers can climb up to a changing area.

Continually evaluate how the environment is working. Observe how children use the space and how they react to changes you make. Be prepared to make adjustments to meet the changing needs and growing abilities of infants and toddlers.

The chart on the facing page shows how indoor areas can meet the needs of infants, toddlers, and adults. In addition to the spaces identified on the chart, mobile infants and toddlers will benefit from defined spaces for a variety of play activities.

- ❖ **Imitating and pretending.** Items such as simple dress-up clothes (hats, assorted bags), a toddler-sized table, chairs, cooking utensils, and dolls inspire dramatic play. Prop boxes can be used anywhere.

- ❖ **Playing with toys.** This area might have a carpeted platform, rug, or low table. You can store small toys such as pop beads, puzzles, sorting games, and small blocks in labeled dishpans. Cardboard or plastic blocks, and a few props are all toddlers need for construction and building activities.

- ❖ **Enjoying stories and books.** You can display books in see-through holders hung on the wall, or stand the books on a low shelf. Soft places to sit, such as a covered mattress or a pillow invite children to settle in with a book.

- ❖ **Dabbling in art.** This area should be set up on washable floors and located near a sink. It might include a table, low easels, and shelves with paper, colored markers, crayons, and playdough.

- ❖ **Tasting and preparing food.** Utensils and ingredients for a cooking activity can be brought out and used on a low table so that mobile infants and toddlers can easily participate.

- ❖ **Exploring sand and water.** Outdoors, sand and water play can take place in tubs, sand boxes, or wading pools. Indoors, children can use a low sink, shallow dish pans placed on low tables, or a sand and water table. Props may include basters, plastic containers, rubber animals, funnels, and scoops.

- ❖ **Having fun with music and movement.** You'll probably want to locate a tape player and tapes in a place that is convenient for you. Musical instruments might be stored in a box and brought out when needed.

How Indoor Areas Can Meet the Needs of Infants, Toddlers, and Adults

Area	Infants	Toddlers	Adults
Greeting Area	Bulletin board for parent notices; cubbies or individual storage tubs; photos of children at play and with their families; children's artwork; bench or adult-height counter to make dressing and undressing children easier		
Sleeping Area	Cribs, bassinets, or cradles set apart to accommodate different sleep schedules; mobiles to look at; restful colors	Mats/cots; special toys and blankets from home; restful colors	Chairs/hammocks to sit in and cuddle children or to watch them nap or play quietly
Eating Area	Infant seats, high chairs, and tables with support chairs in an area with a washable floor; supply of bottles and child-size eating utensils	Low tables and chairs in an area with a washable floor; plastic dishes and cups; child-sized utensils; small pitchers; paper towels for spills	Sink and counter storage for food, trays, utensils; serving and clean-up equipment; some places to sit and feed babies, such as rocking chairs
Diapering/ Toileting	Wall-mounted, large unbreakable mirror; soft toys to hold and watch; changing table with raised lip and strap for safety	Changing table with steps; potty chairs or low toilets; steps up to a sink to wash hands; soap and paper towels where children can reach them; waste baskets conveniently placed	Convenient location near sink or bathrooms; covered diaper pail; changing tables at 36"; shelves with supplies easily accessible; spray bottle with bleach solution
Gross Motor Play	Mats and protected areas in which to roll over, crawl, sit, pull up	Open spaces for active play; furniture to encourage climbing, sliding, stepping up and down; large cubes/blocks; riding toys; tumble mats; large cardboard boxes to crawl into	Movable, low dividers to define spaces
Quiet Play	Places for watching the action—two infant seats, side by side, suspended at adult eye level; backpack; or someone's lap	Lofts/platforms on which to sit; soft chairs; a stocked aquarium with cover on a bottom shelf; tape player and tapes	Comfortable places to sit, cuddle, and read

Learning from Others

Many people find it helpful to visit other programs to see different ways of organizing space. You can join a tour of homes run by your local family child care association, or exchange visits with another provider or with the staff from a nearby center. During your visit, ask yourself questions such as the following.

❖ What areas can I identify?

❖ Is each area inviting for children and adults? In what ways could each space be made more inviting?

❖ Can adults easily reach the materials they need to carry out routines and activities efficiently?

❖ Are there clear pathways so children and adults can get to and around the various areas?

❖ How does the space make it easy for adults to supervise and take care of children? Are any improvements needed?

❖ Are there places for children to be alone—away from the "crowd"—when they desire?

When you return, ask yourself the same questions about your environment. A few changes can really make a difference to you and to the children.

Defining Play Areas Outdoors

Time outdoors each day is important for children's physical health and emotional well-being. Children love to be outdoors, even when the weather isn't perfect. A change of scenery and fresh air is also beneficial for you.

Think about what you enjoyed doing most outdoors when you were a child. Do you recall rolling down a grassy hill? Looking up at the sky and watching the clouds change shape? Jumping from curbs and low walls? Running as fast as you could? Picking bouquets of flowers? Collecting leaves? Watching bugs? The outdoor environment offers many different kinds of experiences for children—it truly doubles the learning environment.

Going Outdoors Must Be Manageable

To make the time spent outdoors fun for the children and enjoyable for you takes some planning. As always, children's developmental abilities can guide your decisions.

Young infants want to look around and take in the action. To spend time outdoors with young infants, you need:

- a way to transport them outside;
- enclosed spaces where infants can reach, grasp, roll, and kick freely;
- soft places such as grass, colorful blankets, or mats; and
- elevated swings in which infants can safely take in the sights.

Mobile infants are going to crawl and cruise as they explore the outdoors. Think about these additions to your outdoor space:

- mats, cardboard boxes, and tunnels;
- plastic railings children can hold onto;
- logs and tree stumps children can pull up on and straddle;
- containers children can fill and dump;
- seat swings, low to the ground; and
- tires embedded in the sand.

Toddlers will run, climb, jump, push, pull, haul, and dump when they get outside. An outdoor space for toddlers should include a variety of surfaces (soft and hard) and a range of equipment. Here are some ideas that will delight most toddlers:

- balls of all sizes and textures;
- wagons, buckets, and baskets that children can fill, haul, and dump;
- riding toys, carts, and push and pull toys;
- hollow blocks, plastic crates, ladders, and planks with which children can create new structures;
- low easels with chalk, paint, or colored markers;
- brushes and buckets for painting with water;
- sand boxes (that can be covered when not in use) and props for digging and pouring;
- sling swings, hung low so children can swing on their tummies;
- small slides and rocking toys children can use on their own;

❖ water play containers and materials, finger paints, and playdough; and
❖ musical instruments.

Don't forget to consider your own comfort outdoors. Benches, a porch swing, soft mats, or logs can be good perches from which to keep a watchful eye on the children and engage them in activities as you cuddle others on your lap.

Evaluate your outdoor space and think about whether it offers children age-appropriate challenges and experiences. Consider activities you offer children indoors that they could do outdoors equally well. You will find many suggestions of indoor activities you can take outside in the activity chapters.

Selecting and Organizing Materials

The materials you select make your environment an interesting place for infants and toddlers to investigate and explore. Safety—which is addressed in detail in the next chapter—is always the first concern. Check every day to be sure that toys and play equipment are in good condition—that is, they have no broken parts, chipping paint, or splinters. Remove anything with parts that are small enough for a child to swallow. (If an object can fit into an empty film container, it is too small for infants and toddlers.)

Materials Should Reflect Children's Interests and Abilities

For very **young infants,** you are by far the most interesting part of the environment. An adult who responds to their sounds, expressions, and actions is better than any "busy box." Infants enjoy seeing and hearing interesting things even before they can reach for and hold on to objects. They are attracted to bright colors, simple designs, patterns such as a bull's-eye, and human faces, especially eyes. They will track and respond to the movements of a mobile, particularly if it makes noise. Once infants begin to hold on to objects and explore more actively, their toys and materials must be chewable, washable, and easy to grasp. Anything that responds to their actions by making a noise or moving will encourage infants to continue exploring—and learning.

Mobile infants who can crawl, climb, or walk to get what they want will be attracted to toys and materials that are displayed at their eye level. Everyday objects such as wooden spoons, buckets, pots and pans, hats, and telephones are as fascinating as anything you can purchase in a toy store. Mobile infants are ready for new challenges that allow them to test out their new skills: stacking, filling and dumping, pushing and pulling, and fitting objects together. As they get older and more mobile, they will enjoy ride-on toys, low climbing structures, and materials that promote pretend play. Dolls, cars and trucks, balls, and push and pull toys are very popular with this age group.

Toddlers, with their strong drive to be independent and increasing gross and fine motor skills, benefit from an environment that offers them opportunities to manipulate and explore objects for a purpose. Toddlers especially like materials they can sort, match, fit together, or arrange in an interesting way. Providing duplicates of popular materials minimizes the need to share and makes it easier for toddlers to relate in positive ways to one another. With their increased fine motor skills, toddlers enjoy exploring and creating with art materials such as playdough, paint, and crayons. They increasingly engage in pretend play: a block can become a car; a toy telephone can inspire a lengthy phone conversation; a variety of hats, props, and dolls can lead to dramatic play.

In deciding which toys and materials to put out and when, ask yourself the following questions.

❖ Will the toy interest infants and toddlers?

❖ Will they be able to use these materials safely?

❖ Do children have the skills to handle the toy?

❖ Will this toy help children learn?

The list that follows offers some suggested toys and materials. You will find more detailed lists for young infants, mobile infants, and toddlers in each of the activity chapters in Part IV.

To promote fine motor skills:

Rattles	Clutch balls	Containers to fill and dump
Bean bags	Busy boxes	Cardboard boxes with lids
Stacking rings	Interlocking blocks	Large wooden beads and shoelaces
Nesting cups	Shape sorting boxes	Wooden and rubber puzzles (3 to 8 pieces)

To promote gross motor skills:

Riding toys	Large cardboard boxes	Balls of all sizes
Climber and slide	Push and pull toys	Low steps covered with carpet
Wagons	Tumbling mats	Foam furniture covered with vinyl
Tractor tires	Cars and trucks	

To encourage children to use their senses:

Playdough	Large nontoxic crayons	Paper for coloring and tearing
Finger paint	Sand and water table with containers, scoops	Ribbons, scarves, and fabrics

To inspire dramatic play:

Dolls	Suitcases	Doll beds or shoe-box beds
Telephones	Plastic dishes	Full length mirrors
Dress-up clothes	Pots and pans	Hats and simple dress-up clothes

To encourage children to explore shape, size, and balance:

Sponge blocks	Hollow or unit blocks	Rubber animals
People props	Large cardboard blocks	Small cars and trucks

To invite quiet, peaceful play:

Tape recorder	Cardboard and cloth books	Picture books for toddlers
Bean bag chairs	Soft cushions	Music and story tapes

To engage children in cooking:

Potato mashers	Metal or plastic bowls	Utensils
Wooden spoons	Plastic knives	Plastic measuring cups and spoons

The Value of "Beautiful Junk"

How many times have you heard about a child ignoring a new toy and playing with a cardboard box instead? Toys don't have to be expensive and new to be good. With the help of children's parents, you can collect many materials—for example, an empty appliance box to crawl through and dramatic play props such as pots and pans, hats, and telephones. You can make toys, too. An oatmeal box and wooden spools make a great "drop-in and dump-out" toy. The lid of a used "wipes" box can be cut out to fit shape blocks. Magazine pictures can be mounted on cardboard, laminated, and cut into three pieces to make simple puzzles. Keep in mind, too, that garage sales or second-hand stores often have many inexpensive resources.

How You Display Materials Is Important

The way children use and care for materials may depend, in large part, on the way the materials are organized and displayed. Here are some suggestions for organizing and displaying toys and materials.

❖ **Display toys that children can safely play with on their own.** Arrange toys neatly on low shelves so children can reach them safely.

❖ **Remember that less can be more.** Young children are easily overwhelmed. Display a few carefully selected toys.

❖ **Display toys on a surface painted in a neutral color.** Leave space between materials so children can see what is available and choose exactly what they want.

❖ **Store toys with small pieces in clear plastic containers.** You may want to store some toys with many pieces on higher shelves to avoid chaos.

❖ **Place picture labels on containers and shelves.** This shows that everything has a place and helps children participate in cleaning up. Make labels from photographs, pictures in catalogs, or draw them on cardboard.

Adapting the Environment for Children with Special Needs

To fully include children with special needs in your program, you may need to make some changes to the physical environment. The changes or additions will depend on the type of disability and the severity. Your objective is to enable the child with special needs to participate and interact as fully as possible—to be part of the action!

Physical Challenges

Most of the furniture and equipment described in this chapter and in the activity chapters in Part IV is appropriate for children with physical disabilities. For example, swing seats, a pool of balls, soft mats to crawl on, tumble forms to climb over are all usable. In some instances, though, you may need to modify the arrangement of furniture and obtain adaptive equipment.

If you have a child who is in a wheel chair or who uses a walker to get from one area to another, take a careful look at your space to see where barriers exist. You may need to increase the size of a doorway, rearrange tables or play areas, and install ramps and grab bars in the bathroom, so that a child (or family member) in a wheelchair can have access to the program environment.

Outdoor time is important for all children. Hammock swings can provide the support and stability a child needs to feel comfortable and view the changing scenes. A therapy ball is a large ball that can be used to sit or lie on to challenge a child's balancing skills or to provide various forms of sensorimotor experiences. It can be used to stimulate a child's motor reactions, or to relax a child with hypertonic reactions (spasms). Children who have seizure disorders or problems with balance may need to wear a helmet to protect their head in case they fall. These are just a few examples of ways you can ensure access to outdoor play for all children.

To participate fully in some activities and during small group times, children with physical disabilities may need assistance in order to sit. A beanbag chair or a large pillow can be molded to provide the support needed. In addition, there are a variety of specialized chairs available as described below.

- ❖ **Educube chair** is a hard chair with a raised back and sides that provides stability and support for a child who cannot maintain balance to sit.

- ❖ **Tumbleform chair** is a semi-hard foam chair that comes in various sizes and is used for children who cannot sit independently.

- ❖ **Pummel chair** is a hard chair designed for a child's specific needs and contains a pummel that is placed between the legs to separate the legs (typically seen with children who have cerebral palsy).

Children can learn to use materials and toys independently with the addition of bolsters and wedges. **Bolsters** are used to position a child either straddling or sitting to keep the child's legs apart, or, if the child lies prone across the bolster, to prop the

arms forward and keep the head up. They come in various sizes to accommodate the size and special needs of a child. **Wedges** are used to lay a child prone (as with the bolster) or to position a child on his or her side. This frees the child's hands for play.

For activities where a child needs to stand in order to take part in an activity, a **prone stander** provides support at the hips, waist, trunk, and/or legs. This helps a toddler who cannot stand independently (such as a child with spina bifida) at a water table or easel.

Some simple adaptations can make it possible for a child with a disability to explore and learn from sensory activities such as art, cooking, and sand and water play. Some children with special needs are "tactily defensive"—they may not enjoy touching or using sensory materials such as paint, water, or playdough. Provide gloves, sticks, or paint brushes to allow these children to participate in the activity. Have on hand large markers and crayons for children who have a weak grasp, and attach Velcro™ straps to paint brushes or writing utensils to help a child who cannot maintain a grasp.

Sensory Impairments

If you have a child who is hearing impaired or who is blind, examine your environment from the child's perspective. Children with sensory impairments need clear sensory cues. An environment that has too many sights, sounds, smells, and textures can be overwhelming.

Children who are hearing impaired will use visual cues, touch, and vibration to interpret what is happening around them. Good room acoustics and a minimum of conflicting noises will help them to use what hearing they do have.

Children who are visually impaired learn to tune into the sounds and textures in their environment. The sounds of music, bubbles in a fish tank, and familiar voices are reassuring. A piece of felt or fur can help them identify their cubby. Clear pathways and well-defined areas, as well as textural cues, such as a defined line between the carpet and tile, help children know they have entered a new area.

Involving Specialists

It's important to keep in mind that you are not expected to be an expert. As in most situations, the best experts are the children's families. Additionally, there are resources to help you identify changes you can make so that your environment maximizes the opportunities for all children to participate as fully as possible.

If you have a child with a disability in your program, chances are he or she is receiving services from one or more specialists (for example, an occupational or physical therapist or an early childhood special educator). With parental permission, invite these individuals to come observe (and work with) the child in your environment. Specialists know a great deal about the particular challenges a child faces and how best to help that child meet those challenges. (See the discussion in Chapter 2 on Part C.) Ask for suggestions of ways to help the child be fully included and successful. Often the simplest suggestion can turn frustration and failure into an opportunity for success.

Including Children's Families and Cultures in the Environment

Family members are more likely to feel welcome if your environment conveys the message that you want and value their input and participation. Look around your home or center. In what ways does the physical environment suggest to families that they are welcome and considered important to your program?

During home visits, you can learn a great deal about how culture influences a family's environment. Think about what seems to be important to each family and find ways to incorporate some of these items into your environment. For example, a colored weaving from Bolivia might make a decorative wall hanging, and family photographs reinforce the connection between home and the program.

Listed below are messages that invite families to feel a part of the program, and some ways these messages can be conveyed by the environment.

"You are always welcome here."

- ❖ Make the entrance way attractive with decorative touches such as plants and pictures.
- ❖ Provide places for parents to hang their coats and safely store belongings.
- ❖ Hang a sign that conveys a welcoming message.
- ❖ Set up a schedule for parent volunteering and post a calendar.

"Transitions can be difficult; take your time."

- ❖ Allow space near children's cubbies where parents can linger with their children.
- ❖ Have adult-sized chairs for parents.
- ❖ Offer private spaces where mothers can nurse.
- ❖ Display photographs of children with their families in the entrance way.

"Make yourself at home; observe your child at play."

- ❖ Place a few adult-size chairs in the room where parents can sit and observe the program or join in a snack or meal.
- ❖ Display signs on room dividers or walls that explain what children are learning in each area of the room.

"Your interests, ideas, and help can enrich our program."

❖ Display and acknowledge examples of contributions families have made to the program.

❖ Create a suggestion box and invite parents to contribute ideas for the program.

❖ Select books and pictures that reflect the cultures of all families.

❖ Post a schedule of work days or "fix-it nights" to encourage family members to work together to improve the environment—such as building a sandbox for the outdoor play area, repairing toys, bringing fresh flowers, or painting a room.

"We are all learners."

❖ Create a bulletin board where you can display articles and information of interest to parents.

❖ Set aside a place where parents can sit and look through books and magazines on parenting and child development.

❖ Post information on adult education, GED classes, and conferences.

There are many ways to set up your environment so that it is warm and welcoming to children, family members, and to you. A primary consideration must be ensuring children's safety so that they are free to play and explore without fear of hurting themselves. This topic is covered in detail in the next chapter.

Sharing Thoughts About Our Program Environment

Dear Families:

When you visit our program, the first thing you'll notice is how we've arranged our space. This is also what children notice. Therefore, we want our setting to be as welcoming, comfortable, and interesting as possible.

Our space for young infants (birth–8 months) has comfortable places where we can sit and hold them, soft carpet and mats for infants to lie on and crawl over, and places where they can safely watch the action. Because we know infants are learning all the time, we provide interesting objects for them to watch and to explore.

Our mobile infants (8–18 months) are eager to pull up on anything available, so we make sure all furniture is sturdy. Because they're interested in things that remind them of home, we've posted family pictures on the walls at their eye level.

Toddlers (18–36 months), as you well know, are constantly on the move. Therefore, we've arranged the space so they can explore freely and safely. You'll see lots of toys and materials that encourage toddlers to build, pretend, look at books, draw and mold, respond to and make music, and even cook.

How We Can Work Together

Your child will feel most comfortable if the program environment feels familiar. We need your help to build this connection between child care and home. Here are some suggestions to consider:

- *Bring us a few pictures of your child with family members.* After we cover them with clear Contact™ paper to protect them, we'll display them where your child can see them every day. Children love to have this connection with the most important people in their lives.
- *Make a tape for your child.* Record yourself reading your child's favorite stories or favorite songs that you sing together. We'll play these tapes during quiet periods of the day to remind children of their parents.
- *Tell us about your child's favorite things.* If you have some favorite books your child likes to read with you, or some music that you play on special holidays or events, we'd love to include it in our program, too. We believe it is very important for children to see aspects of their culture in the child care setting
- *Bring "loveys" from home.* If your child has a favorite toy or blanket that provides comfort for those times when he or she might miss family members, please feel free to bring it to the program.

We welcome your ideas and contributions to making our program a place where your child will be comfortable and happy.

Sincerely,

Algunas ideas acerca del ambiente de aprendizaje de nuestro programa

Estimadas familias:

Cuando ustedes visiten nuestro programa, lo primero que notarán será cómo hemos organizado nuestro espacio. Para los niños más pequeños (recién nacidos – 8 meses) hay lugares cómodos en los que nos podemos sentar y sostenerlos, una alfombra suave y colchones para que los pequeños se acuesten o gateén, y lugares en los que pueden observar lo que ocurre sin ningún peligro. Porque sabemos que los infantes aprenden todo el tiempo, les ofrecemos objetos de su interés para observar y explorar.

Nuestros infantes ya se mueven por doquiera (8 – 18 meses) y están deseosos de asirse de lo que puedan. Además, como a ellos les interesan las cosas que les recuerdan su hogar, hemos pegado en las paredes a la altura de su vista, fotografías de sus familias.

Los mayorcitos (18 – 36 meses), como ustedes lo saben, se mueven constantemente. Por eso, hemos organizado el espacio de tal manera que puedan explorar libremente y sin peligro. En el mismo, hay una gran diversidad de juguetes y de materiales que los estimulan a construir, pretender, observar libros, dibujar y moldear, responder a la música y producirla, e incluso, a cocinar.

Cómo podemos trabajar juntos

Sus hijos se sentirán más a gusto si el ambiente del programa les resulta familiar. Pero, para lograr establecer el vínculo entre el hogar y el programa de cuidado infantil, necesitamos de su ayuda. Las siguientes son unas cuantas sugerencias:

❖ *Traigan al programa unas cuantas fotografías de sus hijos con miembros de su familia.* Después de recubrirlas, las colocaremos a la vista de los niños.

❖ *Graben una cinta para sus pequeños.* Grábense leyéndole a sus hijos sus historias preferidas o cantando juntos sus canciones favoritas.

❖ *Menciónennos cuáles son sus objetos preferidos.* Si sus hijos tienen libros preferidos, o alguna música que toquen en fechas o eventos especiales, nos encantaría incluirlas en nuestro programa. Estamos convencidos de que es muy importante que los niños vean aspectos de su propia cultura en el ambiente del programa de cuidado infantil.

❖ *Traigan algunos de los objetos preferidos de los niños.* Si su hijo(a) tiene algún juguete o una manta que le ofrezca seguridad en los momentos en que pudiera extrañar a los miembros de su familia, siéntanse en libertad de traerlos a nuestro programa.

Nosotros le damos la bienvenida a sus ideas y contribuciones para convertir nuestro programa en un espacio en el que sus hijos se sientan cómodos y felices.

Les saluda atentamente,

Ensuring Children's Safety

A sk parents to tell you their chief priority when looking for child care, and most will reply, "A place where my child is safe." No matter what else a program does, if it does not keep children safe from harm, it is not doing its job. Safety is a basic requirement of any quality program.

In this chapter you will learn about:

❖ carrying out safety procedures that meet the changing developmental needs of children;

❖ preventing accidents;

❖ planning for and responding to emergencies;

❖ helping children become aware of safety; and

❖ balancing concerns for children's safety with their need to explore and take risks.

Ensuring children's safety takes both commitment and knowledge. In this chapter, we provide information that will help you make decisions about how best to keep infants and toddlers safe.

Safety Procedures and the Developmental Needs of Children

As children grow, their needs change. For example, many of your safety concerns with infants involve the routines that take up so much of their everyday experience—sleeping, diapering, and feeding. As infants become more mobile, you must shift your attention to making the environment safe for them to explore. What was once of little concern may now pose a major safety hazard.

Because maintaining children's safety can be a huge job, taking a developmental approach helps you focus your energy and resources. Remember that you don't have to implement every safety procedure. You need only concern yourself with safety measures that make sense for the ages and stages of the children in your care. Suppose, for example, that all the children in your program rest on cots or beds. If this is the case, you don't need to deal with safety precautions about cribs.

The following chart offers guidelines to help you respond to infants and toddlers at different developmental stages. As you read through this chart, think about how this information applies to the children in your program.

Young Infants		
What Children Are Doing Developmentally	**What You Can Do to Keep Them Safe**	**How This Supports Their Development**
Put everything in their mouths.	Provide sanitized non-toxic toys that have no breakable parts and cannot be easily swallowed.	Providing infants with safe playthings allows them to use all their senses (including their mouths) to explore and learn.
Use their whole bodies to learn—they wiggle, squirm, and roll over.	Place infants in areas where they can safely view the world from different viewpoints. Be especially watchful when changing a baby.	Providing safe spaces encourages movement and exploration. Infants learn as they move and explore.
Learn to sit.	Make sure high chairs, changing tables, strollers, and swings have safety buckles.	Sitting without fear of falling gives infants a new point of view for exploring the world.
Hold a bottle.	Give each child his own bottle. Hold infants while they feed themselves. Do not prop bottles for infants who can't yet feed themselves.	Holding infants provides security and encourages them to want to feed themselves. Propped bottles discourage learning this skill and are also a choking hazard.

Mobile Infants

What Children Are Doing Developmentally	What You Can Do to Keep Them Safe	How This Supports Their Development
Crawl and pull themselves up by grabbing onto furniture.	Provide protected areas for crawling. Make sure furniture won't tip over from an infant's weight or roll away.	Crawling and pulling themselves up encourages infants to explore their world.
Enjoy getting into things.	Provide safe playthings and play space. Cover outlets and hide electrical wires. Always keep children in sight.	Playing without always having to be told, "No," encourages exploration and learning.
Understand many words, but not rules.	Set boundaries with furniture. Explain rules but don't expect children to fully understand or obey them.	Reinforcing your words with actions ("We need to play in front of the bookcase, where your toys are.") helps children learn to understand language and to begin to understand what rules mean.
Begin walking.	Provide carpeted surfaces. Remove objects that might trip a child.	Practicing in a safe environment helps children master the skill.

Toddlers

Walk, run, climb, and get into things.	Provide open space for active play both indoors and outdoors.	Recognizing that they can fall without being injured encourages exploration and active learning.
Master self-help skills: toileting, dressing, nose blowing, teeth brushing, and hand washing.	Keep tissues, paper towels, and soap where children can reach them. Make sure faucet water does not burn and that stools for reaching the sink are steady.	Maintaining a safe environment encourages children to develop and use self-help skills. Mastering these skills makes children feel independent and competent.
Begin to understand rules but need to test limits.	Latch doors and gates to enclose play areas. Be ready to explain rules many times.	Using fences or furniture to enclose play areas helps children understand what rules and limits mean.

Preventing Accidents

Prevention aims to stop possible problems before they occur. By anticipating the causes of accidents, you can take measures to keep them from happening.

Probably the most important prevention measure you can take is to check indoor and outdoor environments routinely for potential problems. Begin by making sure that these *policy-related* measures are in place.

❖ A stocked first aid kit is kept at the program, in any vehicles used for transporting children, and in a fanny pack or book bag that can be taken on walks and field trips.

❖ Smoke detectors are located outside all sleeping areas and at the top of any stairway.

❖ ABC-type fire extinguishers are located on every floor and near the kitchen stove.

❖ Evacuation plans are posted and up-to-date safety contingency plans are readily accessible.

❖ All paint is non-toxic and lead-free.

❖ Furniture is the appropriate size for the ages of the children.

❖ Cribs (if in use) have no more than 2⅜ inches of space between slats (to prevent head entrapment).

❖ Cribs (if in use) have mattresses that come within "two fingers" of the sides of the crib (to prevent suffocation).

❖ Furnishings, cloth toys and books, bedding, and carpeting are flame resistant.

❖ Stairs and hallways are well lighted.

❖ Stairs have child height handrails; steps have non-slip treads; bathtubs (if used) contain skid-proof mats or stickers.

❖ Outdoor play areas are enclosed by fences or natural barriers at least 4 feet in height (the bottom edge of which is no more than 3½ inches above the ground).

❖ Outdoor play equipment is no higher than 3 feet (unless play area is used by older children, in which case maximum height can be 5½ feet).

❖ Outdoor play equipment is securely anchored with 9 feet of clearance space for the use of each item (15 feet for any equipment with moving parts, such as swings).

❖ All outdoor play equipment is surrounded by resilient surface material such as wood mulch, loose sand, or rubber mattings, all specifically made to absorb shock.

❖ Tool sheds, garages, workbenches, and balconies are locked and off-limits to children.

❖ Adult sporting and hobby equipment is stored out of children's reach.

❖ Any glass doors are made of safety glass and have decals at child's eye level (to alert child to their presence).

❖ All visitors are required to sign in.

❖ Children are released only to authorized individuals.

❖ Appropriate adult-to-child ratios are maintained.

The following equipment, materials, and toys should <u>not</u> be used by your program.

• Walkers, unless indicated by a child's IFSP, Individual Family Service Plan (may cause falls and injuries)

• Trampolines (may cause falls and injuries)

• Toys or objects having a diameter of less than 1¼ inches (choking hazard)

• Toys or objects with detachable parts (choking hazard)

• Toys or objects with attached cords or strings longer than 12 inches (strangulation hazard)

• Unused refrigerators (suffocation hazard)

• Plastic bags (suffocation hazard)

• Styrofoam packing material (choking hazard)

• Uninflated or underinflated balloons (choking hazard)

• Marbles (choking hazard)

• Straight or safety pins (internal injuries)

• Talcum powder (gets in children's lungs)

• Foods such as whole grapes, cough drops, hot dogs, olives, hard candies, gum, and peanuts (choking hazards)

• Plants poisonous to children such as azaleas, daffodils, diffenbachia, ivy, and mistletoe (A complete listing is available from your Regional Poison Control Center or Cooperative Extension Service.)

• Art materials that are harmful if swallowed by young children: powdered clay, powdered paint, glazes with lead, oil-based paint, cold-water dyes, permanent markers, instant pâpier maché, epoxy, and instant glues

You'll also need to check regularly to be sure that you're carrying out accident-prevention practices. To assist you in monitoring your program, Appendix C contains a safety checklist you can use to identify and address potential problems.

Planning for and Responding to Emergencies

Emergencies are facts of life. While prevention goes a long way to make your program safe, you can't eliminate every danger. At some time, a toddler may fall off a climber and hurt herself, or an infant may choke on a piece of fruit. You may smell gas in the kitchen or find yourself without electrical power during a sudden storm.

If you've ever experienced an emergency, you know just how difficult it is to think clearly. Even if you've had some prior training, it is not at all easy to remain calm and do what you are supposed to do. Things happen quickly. If others around you are upset, it's hard not to feel this way too.

Because many of us tend to panic or freeze up when an emergency arises, we need to prepare ourselves thoroughly ahead of time. When we're prepared, we don't have to worry about reacting properly, because we're on "automatic pilot."

Preparing Yourself

There are three basic steps to follow if you're to feel prepared for an emergency situation: participate in training; maintain a well-stocked first aid kit; and have up-to-date emergency plans readily available.

Training

Everyone who works with infants and toddlers ought to be certified in pediatric first aid. Pediatric first aid, which includes first aid for choking and rescue breathing (blowing air from your lungs into a child's) are your first lines of defense in saving a child's life.

Knowing what to do immediately is the most important step you can take. In fact, a recent study of injuries at a child care center showed that 85% of the children needed no further treatment than first aid.

If you are not certified in pediatric first aid or need refresher training, call your local Red Cross chapter to find out where and when such courses are offered. You can get the same information by writing to:

American Red Cross National Headquarters
Health and Safety
18th & F Streets, NW
Washington, DC 20006

Experts recommend that every adult who works with young children—whether in a family child care home or part of a center-based team—be trained in emergency management of these conditions:[1]

1. bleeding	6. shock	10. head injuries
2. burns	7. convulsions or noncon-	11. allergic reactions
3. poisoning	vulsive seizures	12. eye injuries
4. choking	8. musculoskeletal injury	13. loss of consciousness
5. injuries, including insect,	(such as sprains, fractures)	14. electric shock
animal, and human bites	9. dental emergencies	15. drowning

Although what you do for a child varies according to the type of injury, there are some basic common sense procedures that apply across the board.[2] Consider posting this *Emergency Procedures List*.

1. **Find out what happened.** Discover who was injured, if the scene is safe, and if there are bystanders who might be of assistance.

2. **Check for life-threatening problems.** These are known as the ABCs:
   A = open the airway;
   B = check for breathing;
   C = check for circulation (pulse and bleeding).

3. **Call your local emergency medical services—911 or an ambulance—if you have any doubts about the seriousness of the problem.** In situations that are life-threatening, it may be advisable to call the emergency medical service before administering any first aid, so that the ambulance can be dispatched and on its way while you are tending to the child. Use your judgment and good common sense to decide if the child has a better chance of survival if you call for an ambulance before or after you administer emergency first aid.

4. **Check for injuries, starting at the head and working down.** You will need to give this information to medical personnel.

5. **Regroup. Calm the other children.** If the injured child needs your attention, ask a co-worker or back-up provider for assistance.

6. **Contact the child's parents or guardian** as soon as possible.

7. **Follow local procedures for filing an accident report.** Be sure families get a copy.

Above all, experts in safety recommend the following:

- **Do not move a child,** unless it is to save the child's life. Movement may make injuries worse; and,

- **Do no harm.** *Harm* means failing to do anything or making things worse.

---

[1]American Public Health Association and American Academy of Pediatrics. *National Health and Safety Performance Standards: Guidelines for Out-of-Home Child Care Programs.* Arlington, VA: National Center for Education in Maternal and Child Health, 1992, p. 23.

[2] Abby Shapiro Kendrick, Roxanne Kaufmann, and Katherine P. Messenger, Eds. *Healthy Young Children: A Manual for Programs.* Washington, DC: National Association for the Education of Young Children, 1995, pp. 93–102.

Maintaining a First Aid Kit

Your first aid kits ought to contain everything you need, should any type of safety-related emergency arise. Store kits where you can get at them easily, but the children cannot.

Make a point of checking your program's first aid kits several times a year to ensure that they are always fully stocked. You will find a checklist in Appendix C to help you make sure your first aid kit is fully equipped.

Emergency Plans

As the name suggests, emergency plans tell you what to do in a crisis: who to call (parents, doctors); what to do for a child (administer first aid, not move the child); and the order in which procedures should be followed. Plans also should include procedures to follow if you have to leave your home or center. Fires, gas leaks, and other natural disasters are the usual reasons to evacuate a building.

You should have on hand written plans to cover each type of medical emergency cited earlier. In developing plans, be aware that first aid procedures for opening airways, rescue breathing, and treating choking require different responses for children younger than 12 months than they do for children older than 12 months.

Many people who work with children like to develop symptom-based plans. These plans describe, for example, what to do for a child who has convulsions, faints, or starts to vomit uncontrollably. To the left is one such plan for responding to a child who has fainted.

Sample Emergency Plan

Type of Emergency: FAINTING

What I Need To Do:
1. Place the child in a flat position.
2. Loosen clothing around the neck area.
3. Turn the child's head to one side.
4. Keep the child warm and the mouth clear.
5. Make sure the child has nothing to swallow.
6. Call for medical assistance **immediately.**
7. Notify the child's parent or guardian.
8. Complete an accident/incident report. Make sure parent/guardian has a copy.

In developing your emergency plans, there are several resources you can consult. Chapter 8 of *Healthy Young Children: A Manual for Programs* (Kendrick, Kaufmann, and Messenger, Eds. and *American Red Cross Child Care Course Health and Safety Units* (American Red Cross and American Academy of Pediatrics) are two excellent manuals that outline medically-approved procedures. Experts in your community are another resource. The Red Cross, hospitals, and military installations often have staff eager to help.

Evacuation Plans

Evacuation plans should state the procedures you will follow to get children out of your house or building and to a safe place. For example, you may need to have a special evacuation crib positioned near an exit door which could hold several infants in case of fire or smoke. Your first and only priority must be to save lives, not property. Evacuation plans should be approved by a fire marshal and shared with families. These plans also need to be posted as a reminder. When volunteers or other staff have a first language other than English, it's a good idea to have plans translated into all applicable languages. During an emergency, quick comprehension may be vital.

On the next page is a sample evacuation plan Mercedes developed for Matthew and his seven-week-old sister, Kara. Mercedes's family child care home is housed on the ground floor of an apartment building.

Sample Evacuation Plan

1. Sound the alarm.
2. Grab the outdoors first aid kit (black book bag), which contains list of emergency contacts. Place the kit over my left shoulder.
3. Brace Kara on my right hip.
4. Take hold of Matthew with my left hand.
5. If we need to exit from the front door, unlock the door and lead the children outside.
6. If we need to exit from the back door, unlock the sliding door, and lead the children to the picnic area.
7. If we need to exit by a window, open the window, climb out with Kara and then place her on the grass. Go back to window and help Matthew climb through.
8. When the children are in a safe area, double check they both are with me.
9. Take the children to a neighbor's apartment and notify the fire department.
10. Calm the children down, if need be.
11. Notify the children's parents to let them know what happened and that everyone is safe.

Practice evacuation procedures once a month so that they become automatic for both you and the children. Document your efforts.

In addition, you'll want to develop plans for any natural disasters likely to occur in your area. If you live in a hurricane, earthquake, or tornado zone, you'll need to know what to do if one strikes. If your home or program is in an area where flooding occurs, you should know how to manage during this type of disaster. The Federal Emergency Management Agency (202-646-2400) or your local Red Cross can give you guidance in developing an appropriate emergency plan.

Once the plans are developed, review them with supervisors, colleagues, and volunteers. Keep these suggestions in mind.

❖ **Share your emergency plans with families.** Knowing your plans gives the children's parents peace of mind. In addition, parents often have information you can use as you develop these plans. For example, a child may have specific health concerns that would affect how you administer first aid. Or parents might wish to indicate which emergency contact to call first.

❖ **Make sure that you have all emergency-related forms on file.** These might include emergency transportation permission forms, permission to administer medication, and a Power of Attorney should hospitalization or surgery be immediately required. Together with the children's parents or guardians, you can decide which forms make sense for you to maintain. In addition, you will want to have updated emergency contact forms as well as accident/incident reports on hand. In family child care, you'll also want to have a designated back-up provider who has been pre-approved by the children's parents.

❖ **File your plans so that you can get at them as quickly as possible.** You need to be able to use your plans at a moment's notice.

Helping Children to Become Aware of Safety

Throughout this chapter, we've underscored the idea that adults must take responsibility for young children's safety. Yet ultimately, children need to become responsible for their own safety. This transfer of responsibility is not something that happens overnight or occurs magically when children reach a certain age. Safe practices are learned gradually throughout life.

You may be surprised to know that a significant part of this process takes place without any concentrated effort on your part. By attending to children's safety needs in the ways we've discussed thus far, you create a "culture of safety." Children become aware of the importance that safety plays in their lives by spending day after day in a safe setting with you.

Infants learn about safety first hand. When you secure them to the changing table by fastening a strap, or when you check their toys for jagged edges, they learn that safety is important.

Toddlers, too, learn that safety is valued by watching you. When they observe you removing a nail that has started to work its way out of a toy shelf, they learn about safety measures. At the same time, they also begin to realize that they can do things to keep themselves and others safe. For example, when Barbara invites Leo to help pick up toys someone might trip over, she encourages him to take an active role in promoting his own safety. He also learns that safety is something over which he can have some control.

Here are some strategies you can try to further encourage children to practice safety-related behaviors.

- ❖ **Model good safety practices.** This is probably the best way to help young children learn about safety. Young children are great imitators.

- ❖ **Make children informed partners in your safety routines.** As you practice good safety habits, let children know what you are doing and why. Explain why you are testing the batteries in the smoke alarms. Go over the procedures for using knives safely, and explain why they are stored in the kitchen.

- ❖ **Talk with children about safety rules.** Help them understand that there are things that they can do to keep themselves safe: "Chairs are for sitting. If you want to climb, use the climber."

- ❖ **Involve the children's families in your safety efforts.** Share the things you do with families, so that they can extend these activities at home. You can also learn about families' safety practices at home. When children observe both you and their families practicing safety measures, they recognize more strongly the importance of safety in their lives.

Of course, your use of these strategies will vary with the developmental level of each child. Very young infants won't be able to understand all of what you are telling them. But even the youngest children will get the message that safety is important, since you take the time to talk to them about it. Your interest and attention to safety are what is most important at the early ages.

Older toddlers can begin to understand safety messages and rules. However, they don't always grasp the consequences of a rule, because they are just beginning to understand cause and effect. That is why Matthew might one day proudly follow a "walk when inside" rule and another day stare at you in defiance when you remind him of the rule.

Try to remember that children Matthew's age are testing limits—not your patience. You may find it helps children to learn safety rules by stating them simply in positive language with a few short reasons. Then, by repeating these rules often and enforcing them with consistency, children gradually learn that "We throw balls. Blocks are for building."

By making children active partners in safety awareness, you set the stage for future self-responsibility.

Balancing Concerns for Children's Safety with Their Need for Exploration

Everyone agrees that safety plays an important role in a quality program. At the same time, everyone also agrees that children should have opportunities to experiment and take reasonable risks. Children need to be free to explore their surroundings. Learning can only take place when children use all of their senses to interact with the people and objects in their environment.

Can there be such a thing as too much attention to safety? Aren't cuts and scrapes an inevitable part of growing up? Where is the line between precaution and freedom? How do you balance your obligation to protect children with the need to let them "be children?" These are important questions. They deserve a thoughtful response.

Clearly, you don't want to be so cautious and watchful that you overprotect children. To make children fearful of their environment is to do them a disservice. Jim Greenman makes this observation in strong language: "Children are cheated if we sacrifice challenge and experience before the altar of ostensible safety."[3]

Children need to be able to take risks. For one thing, we know from research that if children are kept under too close supervision, they are likely to postpone their risk-taking to another time and place—when things may not be as safe as they are at your program.

Risk-taking, too, is tied up with creativity. Creative people are those who are willing to risk failure. If we cut off children's risk-taking ability, we may very well eliminate creativity as well.

Your task is to somehow find a balance—to create a safe environment where children can explore and learn.

---

[3] Jim Greenman. *Caring Spaces, Learning Places: Children's Environments That Work.* Redmond, WA: Exchange Press, 1988, p. 78.

Making Decisions About Balancing Safety and Exploration

Take a few minutes to explore your feelings about this issue by reflecting on the following questions.

- ❖ Do children feel free to explore the indoor and outdoor environments in my program?
- ❖ Do children find the environment sufficiently challenging?
- ❖ Am I preoccupied with safety concerns?
- ❖ Am I always saying "No" to children in an effort to protect them?
- ❖ Do I encourage children to take reasonable risks?

Your answers to these questions should give you an idea of your thinking on this issue.

After asking himself these questions, Ivan felt confident that he had a good balance in his program at Crane School. While he did a daily safety check and closely supervised children, he did not feel he was overprotecting them. Rather, Ivan believed that he went out of his way to encourage children to solve problems, resolve conflicts, and be creative in their play. Because he was working with children with special needs like Gena, Ivan thought it was especially important to make sure they did not become fearful, but were encouraged to take reasonable risks.

La Toya, on the other hand, had to admit that she was somewhat obsessed with safety. She recognized she had become increasingly watchful ever since the time a toddler in her family child care program seriously injured himself trying to climb a jungle gym. While she is aware that she might be overprotecting all children as an overreaction to this one incident, she is afraid to let up on her caution.

If, like La Toya, you don't feel comfortable about the balance in your program, discuss the issue with the children's families and some colleagues whose teaching and advice you respect. Ask for their responses to these same questions. They may have observed these same things. You may, however, be surprised to learn that they view things differently.

After talking with families and colleagues, take a second look at your practices. Think about ways you can best find a balanced approach that serves your children and their families, as well as yourself. For example, would it be helpful to devote more attention to prevention and less to monitoring?

Periodically review your approach to safety. Always bear in mind, though, that freedom to explore does not mean that you should lower your standards. Children's safety should never be compromised.

❖ ❖ ❖

Sharing Thoughts About Children's Safety

Dear Families:

Your child's safety is just as important to us as it is to you. Preventing accidents and preparing for emergencies is basic to our program.

For children, a safe program meets many needs. First and foremost, a safe program keeps children free from harm. A safe program also makes children feel secure. When an infant picks up a rattle without fearing being cut or bruised, she learns to trust her world. When an older infant holds on to a steady shelf to pull himself up, he, too, gains confidence that he is in a safe place. Once he realizes that he won't be hurt, he doesn't mind pulling himself up and falling back down over and over again! It is through explorations such as these that children learn.

How We Can Work Together

Safety efforts will be most successful if we join forces to protect your child. Here are some thoughts.

❖ *Look at our evacuation and emergency plans.* Perhaps you'd like to take part in one of our monthly fire drills. This will give you a first-hand demonstration of our safety preparations.

❖ *Make it a point to review your child's records regularly.* Once a month or so we can look at your child's file together and see if anything needs to be added or changed. For example, has your child developed an allergic reaction to a particular food or medicine? In what order should we contact people in an emergency? Whatever works best for your family is what we should do.

❖ *Remember that you are a "safety role model" to your child.* When you arrive here in the morning and help your child wipe up mud that he brought in on his boots, you show him how to prevent accidents. We can plan ways together to present positive safety messages to your child.

❖ *Be a second pair of eyes and ears.* You can be a great help by looking out for safety details and sharing your observations. If you see an area that needs improvement, let's make sure it gets the attention it needs.

We welcome your suggestions of ways to keep your child safe. That way, we all gain peace of mind.

Sincerely,

Algunas ideas acerca de la seguridad de sus hijos

Estimadas familias:

Para nosotros, la seguridad de sus hijos es tan importante como lo es para ustedes. Por consiguiente, prevenir los accidentes y estar preparados para las emergencias, es básico para nuestro programa.

Un programa seguro, satisface muchas de las necesidades de los niños. En primer lugar, lo más importante es que, con un programa seguro los niños viven libres de peligro. También, que ellos se sienten seguros. Cuando un(a) niño(a) agarra un sonajero sin temor a cortarse o a golpearse, aprende a confiar en su mundo. Cuando uno mayorcito se agarra de un anaquel para ponerse de pie, también adquiere confianza con respecto a encontrarse en un lugar seguro. Una vez que se dan cuenta de que no se harán daño, a los niños no les importa ponerse de pie y volver a tirarse al suelo, una y otra vez. Mediante esta clase de experiencias es que los niños aprenden.

Cómo podemos trabajar juntos

Nuestros esfuerzos en pro de la seguridad de sus hijos tendrán éxito si combinamos nuestras fuerzas. Las siguientes son unas cuantas sugerencias:

❖ *Observen nuestros planes de evacuación y emergencia.* Quizá ustedes deseen participar en alguno de nuestros simulacros mensuales. Así, presenciarían una demostración directa de nuestra preparación.

❖ *Háganse el propósito de revisar con regularidad los registros de sus hijos.* Por lo menos una vez al mes, podríamos revisar la carpeta de sus hijos y ver si es necesario cambiar o añadir algo. Por ejemplo, ¿su hijo(a) ha tenido alguna reacción alérgica a algún alimento o medicamento específico? En caso de emergencia, ¿en qué orden y a quién debemos contactar? Lo que sea que funcione mejor para su familia, es lo que debemos hacer.

❖ *Recuerden que ustedes son un "modelo de seguridad" para su hijo(a).* Al ustedes llegar en la mañana, y ayudarle a sus hijos a limpiar el lodo que pudieran traer en sus botas, les están demostrando cómo prevenir accidentes. Juntos, podremos planear formas de presentarle mensajes positivos y seguros a sus hijos.

❖ *Sean un segundo par de ojos y de oídos.* Ustedes pueden ser de gran ayuda al notar detalles de la seguridad y al compartir con nosotros sus observaciones. Si ustedes notan que un área necesita mejoras, les garantizaremos darle la atención necesaria.

Les agradecemos sus sugerencias para mantener seguros a sus hijos. De esa forma, todos podremos estar tranquilos.

Les saluda atentamente,

Promoting Children's Health

To be healthy is to be more than disease-free. Good health is a state of well-being. It includes emotional and social wellness, as well as physical vigor. Children who get the sleep they need and who eat nutritious foods are ready for learning. A healthy child is a strong child, in every sense of the word.

This chapter focuses on ways to promote children's total well-being. As you read through the chapter, you will learn about:

- ❖ meeting children's health requirements from birth to age three;
- ❖ preventing health problems;
- ❖ responding to child abuse and neglect;
- ❖ responding to sick children;
- ❖ helping children develop good nutrition and other health habits; and
- ❖ using partnerships to promote children's health.

Meeting Children's Health Requirements from Birth to Age Three

At every stage of development, children have health needs common to all children and some that are particular to children at a given developmental stage. Young infants, for example, need to be fed and changed when they need it, not when some prearranged schedule permits it. Their health and well-being depend on your responsiveness to their biological needs. Mobile infants, who are hard at work exploring every aspect of their environment, need space and opportunities for active play. Your challenge is to create play spaces that are free of germs—but not sterile in warmth and charm. Toddlers are busy finding out who they are and what they can do. When you teach them self-help skills that will keep them healthy, they become confident of their own capabilities.

While your approach to children's health adjusts to each child's needs at a particular stage of development, all young children need an environment as germ free as possible. This is particularly important since young children tend to put everything in their mouths, regardless of where that object has been before.

While it takes time and effort to sanitize the changing area after each use, to clean table tops, toys, and equipment with a bleach solution daily, or to take moist towelettes with you outdoors, it's necessary to do these things. Becoming lax about sanitation can be fatal, as the following real-life story illustrates.

Several young children in Washington State became gravely ill and others died from eating hamburgers infected with *E. coli* bacteria. In addition, two other toddlers who had not even eaten the infected food, got sick and died. Public health investigators discovered that these two toddlers who became sick were in day care with the infected children, and the bacteria had spread to them.

The National Health and Safety Standards: Guidelines for Out-Of-Home Child Care Programs, developed by the American Public Health Association and the American Academy of Pediatrics, provides detailed guidance on sanitizing and disinfecting infant and toddler environments in both center-based programs and family child care homes.[1] This reference book can help you to follow safe procedures. (See Resources in Appendix F for a list of some other useful references.)

As you reflect on the chart that follows, think about the children in your care and their stage of development.

Young Infants

What Children Are Doing Developmentally	What You Can Do to Keep Them Healthy	How This Supports Their Growth
They put everything in their mouths.	Sanitize toys, diaper changing surfaces, table tops, and eating utensils with a solution of ¼ cup bleach to one gallon of water.	Children learn by using all of their senses. By making it safe to put objects in their mouths, they can learn without becoming sick.
They get hungry and thirsty according to their own individual time clocks.	Give infants expressed breast milk (if parents so desire and local health regulations permit), formula, or warmed milk in bottles on demand. Use water rather than milk or juice when giving infants a bottle before sleeping. Label bottles with children's names. Formula and expressed milk should be dated.	To help infants develop a sense of trust, feed them when they are hungry or thirsty. Juice or milk that stays in a baby's mouth during sleep can lead to tooth decay. Labeling bottles prevents the spread of germs. Dating milk guards against spoilage. Expressed milk can be kept safely for 24 hours in the refrigerator and for 4 weeks in the freezer.

continued on next page

---

[1] American Public Health Association and the American Academy of Pediatrics. *National Health and Safety Standards: Guidelines for Out-Of-Home Child Care Programs.* Arlington, VA: National Center for Education in Maternal and Child Health, 1992.

Young Infants (continued)

What Children Are Doing Developmentally	What You Can Do to Keep Them Healthy	How This Supports Their Growth
They soil or wet their diapers and their clothes.	Change babies who are awake as soon as they have soiled themselves. Change diapers in an area removed from food preparation and eating. Place disposable diapers in covered, lined containers; soak soiled clothing and linens. Wash your hands and the child's hands when finished. Wash and disinfect the changing table after each use. Seal soiled clothes in plastic bags to be sent home daily. Record each diaper change.	Diapering children on demand meets their physical needs. Because germs are present, careful sanitation procedures need to be followed. Tracking the infant's bathroom habits (and noting anything unusual) provides a health record for each child.

Mobile Infants

They use their fingers to feed themselves.	Offer children a healthy range of foods, such as bananas, crackers, or cheese. Give them plastic drinking cups filled halfway with milk or juice.	When children try a variety of foods, they lay the groundwork for healthy nutrition practices. When they can feed themselves, the children feel competent.
They begin to undress themselves and often cooperate in letting you dress them.	Encourage children to let you know when their diapers need changing but discourage them from removing them themselves. Wash children's hands if they touch soiled clothing. Also, encourage children to keep coats and jackets on when playing outdoors in chilly weather.	Children can learn self-help skills, without exposing themselves to health dangers.
They crawl and pull themselves up with the aid of furniture.	Sanitize floors, table tops, and toys daily with bleach solution (¼ cup bleach to one gallon of water). Keep cleaning supplies in locked cupboards. Keep room temperature in the 65°–72°F range and be sure play areas are well ventilated.	Crawling and standing help children explore the world around them. Sanitizing surfaces reduces children's exposure to germs.

Toddlers

What Children Are Doing Developmentally	What You Can Do to Keep Them Healthy	How This Supports Their Growth
They are beginning to understand rules, but need to test limits.	Be prepared to discuss health rules with toddlers many times. These rules may include wiping up spills, throwing dirty tissues in the trash, washing hands before touching food, and so forth.	Children need encouragement as well as positive feedback to follow rules.
They are learning self-help skills such as toileting, dressing themselves, blowing their noses, brushing their teeth, and washing their hands.	Give children opportunities, time, and praise for mastering these skills. Keep tissues, paper towels, soap, and outdoor clothing where children can get at them on their own. Provide covered trash cans where children can throw away used tissues and paper towels.	Mastering these skills begins with teaching children to be responsible for their own health. Setting up experiences for success reinforces skill mastery.
They begin learning about healthy foods from the foods you serve. In addition, they begin to associate food and nutrition with pleasant experiences by participating in mealtime conversations.	Serve toddlers family style lunches and snacks. Encourage children to serve themselves and to try a variety of foods. Discuss in simple terms how foods keep our bodies healthy.	Serving family style meals will promote self-help skills and encourage children to begin taking responsibility for their own nutrition. Offering children a wide variety of food sets a pattern for lifelong eating habits.

Preventing Health Problems

The best way to promote children's health is to prevent problems before they occur. Consider this example. Leo, who is highly allergic to citrus fruits, broke out in hives after a parent volunteer, unaware of his allergy, offered him some orange juice for snack. Both the parent volunteer and Leo panicked as welts began to appear all over his upper body. Luckily, Barbara was nearby and able to calm them both. She also knew what to do, because she had an emergency plan on file for responding to Leo's allergy.

Had better preventive steps been in place, however, the volunteer never would have offered Leo orange juice. From now on, Barbara will be sure to alert all staff—including classroom visitors—to any allergies the children have. Moreover, she will post this information in the eating area, where it will be a constant reminder.

Prevention puts staff in charge—not the crisis. It lessens the chances that neither the children nor you will become sick or injured. It also helps to create a calm and comfortable atmosphere.

Prevention involves three basic strategies: screening children for potential health problems; checking children regularly for signs of child abuse or neglect; and checking daily to be sure that preventive health measures are in place. All of these practices are important.

Screening for Health Problems

Prevention begins with screening. Screening involves taking a complete look at a child's health so that problem areas can be identified at the earliest possible point. Often, many problems can be corrected on the spot. Others can be minimized through treatment and follow up, or at least can receive the attention they need. All children, including seemingly healthy ones, should be screened on a regular basis.

Screening children for health-related problems allows health professionals to determine whether a child is healthy and has no apparent problems, is possibly at risk and in need of further assessment, or is definitely at risk and in need of follow-up treatment.

Infants and toddlers, as a group, are potentially at risk for a number of health problems, including developmental delays and vision and hearing difficulties. Individual children may be at further risk of developing diseases based on heredity, family health habits, and environmental factors, such as the presence of lead paint in the home or contaminants in drinking water.

Your job is to work as a part of a team with families and health professionals to make sure that the children in your care are screened. Screening may already be a part of your program, as it is in Early Head Start, for example. However, if your program does not conduct screening, we urge you to work with families to obtain these services. (See the last section of this chapter for further guidance on this issue.)

In conducting screenings, it's very important that you continue using a team approach. This may mean doing something as simple as maintaining a "tickler" file to help you remember to remind families when immunizations are due. It may also mean taking on more complicated tasks, such as helping families find assistance for the medical costs of the screenings and immunizations.

When should children be screened? The American Academy of Pediatrics recommends that infants and toddlers receive complete physical examinations when they are 1 month, 2 months, 4 months, 6 months, 9 months, 12 months, 15 months, 18 months, 24 months, and 36 months old.[2]

Each of these visits should include a family history, height and weight measurements, and a vision, hearing, and a developmental assessment. Metabolic screenings should be conducted at the first office visit, and thereafter according to state laws. Head circumference measurements should be recorded during visits in the child's first year of life. In addition, the Academy recommends these tests/readings:

- ❖ yearly tuberculin tests;
- ❖ hematocrit or hemoglobin tests at the 9-month examination and yearly thereafter;
- ❖ urinalysis at the 6-month and 24-month check-ups; and
- ❖ blood pressure readings at the 36-month check-up.

[2] American Academy of Pediatrics Committee on Practice and Ambulatory Care. *Recommendations for Preventive Health Care*, Elk Grove, IL: American Academy of Pediatrics, September 1995.

At three months, an infant should have an initial dental exam. A second dental exam should be scheduled when a child has all 20 baby teeth showing, at approximately 36 months.

In addition to physical screenings, all children need to be immunized against preventable diseases such as measles, chicken pox, and mumps. The Centers for Disease Control and the American Academy of Pediatrics regularly revise and set a schedule for what and when infants and toddlers should receive immunizations. Appendix D includes the schedule published in January, 1995 for children under age three.[3] Be sure to check for updates, as recommendations are subject to change.

It's important that you work with families whose children have not yet had immunizations and check-ups. For example, if a child comes into your care who did not receive the medical attention he should have, you'll need to work with the family to get the child the immunizations and other care he needs. The American Academy of Pediatrics has developed an immunization schedule for children who received no vaccinations during their first year of life. You can order this free reference from:

National Maternal and Child Health Clearinghouse
2070 Chain Bridge Road
Suite 450
Vienna, VA 22182-2536
Tel.: (703) 821-8955 X254
Fax: (703) 821-2098

In addition to medical screenings for health problems, children also need to be screened for developmental problems in any of these areas:

- gross and fine motor skills;
- perceptual discrimination;
- cognition;
- attention skills;
- self-help skills;
- social skills; and
- receptive and expressive language skills (for older children).

Although these screenings increase the chances of identifying and addressing problems, a word of caution is in order. There is always the danger of missing a problem or of diagnosing a problem that really isn't there. Diagnosing a disability when it is not there happens most frequently when the screening and assessment tools do not accurately reflect the development of children from certain cultural or linguistic backgrounds. Clearly, we don't want children to be considered at risk for a disability or developmental delay because they come from a cultural or linguistic background different from the mainstream. We also don't want their disabilities or delays to go undetected for the very same reason.

---

[3] *Recommended Childhood Immunization Schedule: United States January, 1995.* Approved by the Advisory Committee on Immunization Practices, the American Academy of Pediatrics, and the American Academy of Family Physicians.

The best way to deal with this issue is to become **culturally responsive**. In theory, to be culturally responsive is to honor the beliefs, interpersonal styles, attitudes, and behaviors of the multicultural families you serve.[4] In practice, it means working with health professionals to ensure that the screening instruments and practices used are accurate. That is, they measure what the test is supposed to measure for the cultures of the children being tested.

Of course, screening should always be supplemented with your own ongoing assessments of the children in your care. Information you contribute is just as important as that collected by health professionals. Furthermore, you should regularly review your observations of the children at play, resting, eating, and toileting—plus the anecdotal information you have gathered from families and staff about each child's health. You can be effective in uncovering potential health problems only if you make assessment an ongoing process.

Finally, remember that the screening process doesn't end once children have been tested. Follow-up, if indicated, involves both you and the children's families at every step.

Checking for Good Health Practices In Your Program

An important part of prevention is maintenance. Every day you take steps to keep children well when you keep these health concerns in mind.

- ❖ The environment needs to support children's total well-being.
- ❖ Children should be able to play with toys and equipment that are as germ-free as possible.
- ❖ Diapering and toileting practices need to be hygienic and should also be opportunities for learning.
- ❖ Personal hygiene practices should serve as models for the development of self-help skills.
- ❖ Sleeping and rest periods should take place in healthy environments. Infants should be placed on their backs or sides to sleep to reduce the risk of Sudden Infant Death Syndrome (SIDS).[5]
- ❖ Feeding and eating should provide children with appropriate nutrition and should support the development of self-help skills.
- ❖ Illnesses that do occur need to be managed so as to support the sick child and prevent the spread of disease to others.

By being conscientious about procedures that promote wellness, you dedicate your program to keeping children healthy. In Appendix C you will find a checklist that can help you make sure your program promotes good health.

---

[4] Maria Anderson and Paula F. Goldberg. *Cultural Competence in Screening and Assessment: Implications for Services to Young Children with Special Needs Ages Birth through Five.* Minneapolis: National Early Childhood Technical Assistance System, December 1991, p.4.

[5] Countries where infants are placed on their backs or sides to sleep have found a 50 percent reduction in the rate of SIDS. It would be wise for each program to have a policy in place on this issue.

Responding to Child Abuse and Neglect

We all know that child abuse and neglect are facts of life today. We also know that abuse can occur in any family, regardless of income or background.

Because your legal responsibilities and the possible repercussions of your actions are so significant, you need to know exactly what child abuse and neglect are. The Child Abuse, Domestic Violence, Adoption, and Family Service Act of 1992 (Public Law 102-295) defines child abuse and neglect as:

> ". . .Physical or mental injury, sexual abuse or exploitation, negligent treatment, or maltreatment of a child under the age of 18 (except in the case of sexual abuse) or by the age specified by the child protection law of the State by a person who is responsible for the child's welfare, under circumstances which indicated that the child's health or welfare is harmed or threatened . . . ."

What does all this mean? Most experts agree that there are four types of abuse:

* **physical abuse**, including burning, kicking, biting, pinching, or hitting a child;

* **sexual abuse**, including using a child for another's sexual gratification through such activities as fondling, rape, sodomy, and using a child for pornographic pictures or film;

* **emotional abuse or maltreatment**, including blaming, belittling, ridiculing, and constantly ignoring a child's needs; and

* **neglect**, including failing to provide a child with food, clothing, medical attention, or supervision.

Following is a list of physical and behavioral indicators of child abuse. Remember, though, that there is no single sign or cue that can tell you with certainty that a child is abused. Repeated or multiple signs, however, should be regarded as "red flags."

You should check children daily for any of the following **physical signs:**

* bruises and welts (especially on the face, back, back of legs, or buttocks; unusual patterns that might indicate use of a buckle or other object; clusters that might indicate repeated contact; wounds in various stages of healing);

* burns (glove or donut-shaped marks that might result from immersion; cigarette or rope marks; dry burns that might indicate application of a hot surface);

* cuts, scrapes (especially on the face or genitalia);

* broken bones (especially in various stages of healing);

* head injuries (black or bruised eyes or jaw; bleeding beneath the scalp);

* bleeding or discharge (in genitalia or anal area; in urine, throat, or mouth);

* pain (difficulty walking, sitting, or urinating);

* constant hunger or abnormal weight loss/drowsiness; and

* vomiting (without signs of flu or other illness).

Check also for these **behavioral signs**:

❖ unhappiness (seldom smiles; has deep fear of adults; reacts with emotion to unpleasantness; flinches in the presence of others; has excessive tantrums);

❖ aggression (is disruptive; exhibits angry behavior; has poor peer relationships);

❖ withdrawal (is unwilling to participate in activities; hugs self; refuses to have clothes or diapers changed; shows loss of appetite);

❖ acts inappropriately for age, either as one who is considerably older or younger (shows keen interest in sexual matters; excessively seeks or shuns affection from adults; has delayed growth/development);

❖ is frequently absent or late (parents habitually arrive early/late to drop off and/or pick up);

❖ lacks adequate/appropriate clothing/hygiene;

❖ hurts self or others; and

❖ touches others in a sexual way or masturbates excessively.

Observing any of these signs should lead you to wonder whether a child may be a victim of abuse or neglect. If you know the family well, you can often determine if the observed signs come from probable abuse or from something else. Some problems may be temporary and readily handled by families; others may be chronic and require your intervention. Consider, too, that the risks of child abuse increase when families are under stress from marital, economic, or social pressures.

If you believe that a child in your care is indeed being abused, you must do something about it. We say this not on moral or ethical grounds—although these surely apply—but for legal reasons. Every one of the 50 states has laws governing the reporting of suspected child abuse. Your own program should have a written policy in place.

This means that if you have any reason to suspect that a child is being abused or neglected, you are obliged to report your suspicions to the appropriate authority (e.g., Department of Social Services, the Department of Human Resources, the Division of Family and Children's Services, or Child Protective Services of your local city, county, or state government). You need to check your state laws for exact reporting requirements.

You'll notice that in this discussion we keep mentioning the word *suspect*. Even though you'd be far more comfortable in making your report if you had proof, the law is very clear that you must report your suspicions—even if your suspicions should later prove to be wrong.

Undoubtedly, this is an uneasy position for you. You might think, "What if I'm wrong? What if there is a logical explanation for the symptoms I've observed? I might be ruining a family's reputation. In all likelihood, I'll never regain that family's trust. And what about the child? Might I not, through a false accusation, be making matters worse?"

No one can know whether all or none of these "worst case" scenarios will come true. The fact is, though, that you can't afford to risk that your suspicions might be correct. There is no greater responsibility you have as a professional and as a member of society than to pledge yourself to protect children from harm.

Responding to Sick Children

Although prevention goes a long way in keeping children well, it's impossible to prevent childhood illnesses from occurring. When children are sick, they need your comfort, concern, and—above all—your knowledge of good health practices. This section examines ways to respond to children who are temporarily ill; children who have long-term illnesses; and children experiencing health emergencies.

Caring for Children Who Are Temporarily Ill

Despite every effort on your part, young children typically get sick five to twelve times a year. One recent study found that on any given day, 17% of the children in care arrive feeling ill. Fortunately, most instances are not serious.

Much of your approach to dealing with sick children is a management issue. You need to have a policy in place that outlines step-by-step procedures to follow when a child becomes ill. Your first move is to decide which illnesses require you to send children home and which illnesses you can deal with in your daily routine. Some programs have neither the staff nor the space to care for a child who is too ill to participate fully. Generally, however, most programs try to allow mildly sick children to stay. Keeping them with you is often the most compassionate choice for the child and the family.

The American Academy of Pediatrics takes the position that there are very few illnesses for which children should be sent home. Their stand is based on the fact that many common childhood diseases, such as earaches, are not contagious. Still other diseases—such as the so-called common cold—are spread before symptoms first appear. By the time you know a child has a cold, the other children will already have been exposed to it. Sending the sick child home does nothing to prevent the further spread of the illness.

Your best strategy for stopping the spread of a cold or other disease is to be especially sure to carry out the sanitation and hygiene practices described earlier in this chapter. As long as you wash your hands every time you attend to a sick child and make sure tissues and wipes are disposed of carefully—as long as you are sure that dirty clothing and linens are appropriately handled and washed, and that the sick child's hands, crib or bed, and playthings are kept clean—you can prevent the spread of germs.

When then, is a child too sick or too contagious to remain at your program? Your state licensing program has specific "sick child" policies that identify diseases that require you to send children home. The list also identifies those diseases that must be reported to your state department of public health. In general, these include highly contagious diseases such as bacterial meningitis, Hepatitis A, measles, salmonella, and the like. Infestations of scabies, head lice, and ringworm also typically require that children stay home 24 hours after treatment has started. Check your local health department requirements.

Most health authorities—including the Centers for Disease Control and the American Academy of Pediatrics—recommend that children be excluded from care if any of these symptoms are present:

❖ fever (oral temperature of 101°F or higher, rectal temperature of 102°F or higher, armpit [axillary] temperature of 100°F or higher), accompanied by behavioral changes and other signs of illness;

❖ uncontrolled diarrhea;

❖ uncontrolled coughing;

❖ difficult or rapid breathing;

❖ vomiting two or more times within the past 24 hours;

❖ mouth sores with drooling;

❖ rash with fever or behavior change;

❖ pinkeye (purulent conjunctivitis); and

❖ behavioral changes (lethargy, irritability, persistent crying).

Sick children who remain in care need adequate rest, an appropriate diet (usually including increased liquids to prevent dehydration), medication as ordered (with written instructions from the child's physician on dispensing the medicine, as well as written permission from the parent to do so), and both physical and emotional support. Your chief role is to make the sick child as comfortable as possible without neglecting the other children in your program.

Caring for Children with Long-Term Illnesses

Long-term conditions can range from mild allergies to terminal illnesses. Chronic health problems may include cancer, asthma, diabetes, anemia, sickle cell disease, epilepsy, heart-related problems, and kidney or liver-related problems.

If you have a child with a long-term health problem in your care, talk to the child's parents and doctor to find out as much as you can about the child's condition. Read up on the disease. Send for information from a professional organization, such as the American Diabetes Association. Do a literature search on the Internet (use MEDLINE or another medical database). Ask your local librarian for help.

As with all children, sick children long to be a part of the group. And for the most part, children with chronic health conditions can participate fully. It's important that you and everyone in your program make the sick child feel as "normal" as possible. Try to avoid making a child feel as if he or she is constantly being "sanitized." In most cases, children with chronic conditions are not contagious. Sick care management demands only the same everyday sanitation precautions you would follow anyway.

The obvious exceptions are AIDS and other diseases caused by "blood-borne pathogens," such as Hepatitis B. We know that exposure to blood and certain other bodily fluids of infected persons can spread these diseases. For this reason, it is critical to have appropriate health practices in place and to follow them diligently.

Health care professionals recommend that anyone who is exposed to blood— whether it is in an infant's stool, a toddler's nosebleed, a skinned knee, or under any conditions at all—adopt the universal precautions developed by the Centers for Disease Control and the Occupational, Safety, and Health Administration (OSHA). These include wearing gloves, disinfecting blood-contaminated areas and cleaning supplies, disposing of blood-contaminated materials and diapers properly, and washing hands with antibacterial soap after exposure.[5] The reasoning behind making these precautions universal is that practicing appropriate hygiene and sanitation on a regular basis prevents infection at all times, not only when the circumstances are life-threatening. It also does not isolate or discriminate against a child with a disease.

In cases when the child's illness becomes debilitating, it may be classified as a health impairment disability. If you have a child with a health-related disability in your program, you'll need to consult with specialists.

Responding to Emergencies

One of the chief concerns you may have about caring for children who are chronically ill is what to do if a crisis occurs. Nearly every chronic condition can bring on a crisis. A child with asthma might have a wheezing attack, a child with allergies can break out in hives, a child with epilepsy may have a seizure, or a child with diabetes whose sugar level gets too low may lapse into unconsciousness. Days may pass without incident, and then, without warning, an emergency arises.

What do you do? As with safety emergencies, your best strategy is to be prepared. Health experts recommend having emergency plans in place and accessible. If you care for infants and toddlers who are chronically sick, you must be ready at the first sign of distress to swing into action.

For every child with a chronic health problem, you'll need to do the following.

❖ **Know what to expect.** Talk to the child's family and doctor about the types of crises that might occur.

❖ **Become knowledgeable about what causes these crises**, how often they are likely to occur, and how long each one is likely to last.

❖ **Learn the signs of an approaching crisis** and also how the child is likely to behave just prior to the crisis.

❖ **Get trained** by a family member, the child's doctor, or the American Red Cross on the procedures you should follow in a crisis.

❖ **Have a written plan for dealing with the crisis**, listing simple step-by-step directions that you would be able to follow, even under stress.

❖ **Train other staff, volunteers,** and children (if appropriate) in emergency procedures.

❖ **Identify—in the child's health record—activities that should be avoided** and/or dietary restrictions that might bring on an emergency. Post reminders prominently so that everyone knows, for example, that Leo should not eat citrus fruits because he is severely allergic.

In addition to having plans related to children's chronic conditions, you'll want to make sure that you have symptom-based plans that tell you what to do if any child in your program experiences an emergency. Contaminated food, for example, can make

---

[5] American Public Health Association and the American Academy of Pediatrics. *National Health and Safety Standards: Guidelines for Out-Of-Home Child Care Programs.* Arlington, VA: National Center for Education in Maternal and Child Health, 1992, pp. 75-76, HP38.

your entire group ill. You'll therefore want to know how to respond, should one or more children experience stomach cramps and diarrhea or vomiting. Likewise, you need to know what should be done for a child who faints, has convulsions, or chokes. You'll probably find it most efficient to combine this effort with the development of your plans for safety-related emergencies, since much of the information will be the same. You can consult Chapter 8 for further guidance on writing emergency plans. (As always, don't forget to share your plans with the children's families. Include their ideas and make sure they are comfortable with these plans.)

Helping Children Develop Good Nutrition and Other Health Habits

From the time an infant begins nursing or taking a bottle as she is lovingly held in her parent's arms, the child learns about nutrition. If these same feelings of warmth and comfort carry over to mealtimes at your program, children learn to associate nutrition with caring and pleasure. This association is the first step on the road to lifelong good nutrition.

The tone you set and the foods you offer children set the stage for permanent nutrition habits. As examples, think about the ways in which these staff are helping children develop positive habits through eating experiences.

Linda picks up four-month-old Julio and sits with him in the rocker. She nestles Julio in the crook of her left arm and holds the bottle for him with her right hand. As she feeds the baby, she looks him intently in the eyes and talks to him in a low, soothing tone, commenting in Spanish on how hungry he is. She rocks the chair and begins singing a Guatemalan folk song Julio's mother told her she sings to him.

Eight-month-old Jasmine has been eating mashed cooked fruits for three months now. Janet introduced Jasmine to orange slices several days ago. After an initial nasty expression, Jasmine has been screeching for orange slices at every meal, which Janet gladly gives her. Even though the child has had no physical reactions to the orange, Janet is going to wait a few more days before starting Jasmine on another raw fruit.

Willard (11 months) enjoys feeding himself cubes of cheese and eating applesauce with a spoon. Grace lets him spend unhurried time feeding himself and babbling to his food.

Matthew (26 months) is helping Mercedes place five plates on the table for lunch. They will eat lunch family style, joining Mercedes's great nieces who are visiting from Brazil. Mercedes offers the serving bowls to each child one at a time. The children use the small spatula and ladles to help themselves to chicken kabobs, mashed cassava, and carrots.

Matthew tries to pour milk from a small pitcher into his glass, with Mercedes's assistance. During lunch, they talk excitedly with one another. When Matthew is through eating, he clears his plate over the trash basket and carries it into the kitchen.

La Toya encourages Jonisha and Valisha (35 months) to prepare their own snack of cottage cheese and strawberries. She walks them through the steps of using an ice cream scoop to put cottage cheese on a plate and shows them how to pull out the strawberry leaves. If the children forget what to do, they can use the picture cards La Toya made on laminated cardboard. La Toya gives Jonisha and Valisha lots of encouragement as they attempt to do these tasks on their own.

Other Healthy Habits

In addition to helping children develop good nutrition habits, you can encourage children to learn and use lifelong self-help skills to promote their own good health. Chief among these skills are:

- **washing hands** before handling food and after sneezing, cleaning up, handling pets, and toileting (wiping hands with damp paper towel moistened with a liquid antibacterial soap, rinsing hands under running water while rubbing hands back and forth, drying hands with paper towel, turning off faucet with paper towel, and discarding towel in trash);
- **brushing teeth** after eating;
- **sneezing and coughing toward the floor** and away from people;
- **blowing one's nose into a tissue,** discarding the tissue, then washing hands;

❖ **disposing of trash correctly,** dropping used paper cups, paper towels, and tissues in a lined plastic receptacle with a pedal-operated lid or into a metal receptacle lined with plastic; and

❖ **putting on outerwear** for going outside in cool, cold, or rainy weather.

Young infants like Julio experience good health habits when someone takes care of their health needs. This builds a foundation for developing life-long self-help skills.

Mobile infants take pride in doing the same things that important adults in their lives do. When Abby, for instance, sees Brooks and her parents washing their own hands, brushing their teeth, or disposing of a used paper cup in the trash, she wants to copy their actions.

Toddlers can acquire self-help skills as part of their everyday routines. Valisha, for example, can help mash the potatoes for her lunch, pour juice from small pitchers for an afternoon snack, take off and hang up her coat when she comes inside from outdoor play, and throw away used paper towels and tissues.

Here are some strategies you can use to encourage the children in your care to develop self-help skills.

❖ **Model good practices.** Even infants can begin to learn health habits.

❖ **Involve children in healthy routines.** Ask children to wipe up spills or throw away used paper cups, napkins, and tissues. Eventually, children will take on responsibility for these actions.

❖ **Ask families to join you.** Involve parents in what you are doing, and ask them to be role models for their children. Children will soon learn that both you and their families value health habits.

❖ **Read books about healthy habits with children.** Many delightful picture books focus on healthy routines. Books such as *Teddy Bears Cure a Cold* (Suzanna Gretz), *The Philharmonic Gets Dressed* (Karla Kushin), or *Going to the Potty* (Fred Rogers) help children understand that everyone practices health habits.

❖ **Give children dramatic play opportunities.** As they dress a baby doll, feed it a bottle, or prepare a pretend meal, children practice self-help skills. Pretend experiences lay the groundwork for real life successes.

❖ **Encourage and praise children's efforts.** Sincere feedback lets children know that you appreciate their attempts at self-help skills. It contributes to both their confidence and competence.

Using strategies such as these, children are more likely to develop positive health habits and practices. Ultimately, children will become responsible for their own well being—which is a goal that you, families, and the children themselves most likely share.

Using Partnerships to Enhance Children's Health

You can see that keeping infants and toddlers healthy is a big, big job. In fact, to do this job well, you can't possibly do it alone. The responsibilities are too many and too great for any one person or any one program.

The solution rests in reaching out to other individuals and organizations in your community. There are many places to go for help. Here are some thoughts.

❖ Create links among child care programs, families, and resource and referral agencies to ensure communication about health issues.

❖ Conduct training for families on ways to use community resources.

❖ Contact your local and state health department and community resources (such as Child Find) about conducting screenings and identifying and helping children with health impairments.

❖ Obtain Spanish and English videos, stickers, and posters on Sudden Infant Death Syndrome (SIDS) by calling 800-505-CRIB for materials on "Back to Sleep" positions for infants.

❖ Contact local and state chapters of the American Academy of Pediatrics, the American Dental Association, the Association of Dental Hygienists, and the American Academy of Pediatric Dentists for informational material.

❖ Contact professional organizations (the American Academy of Pediatrics; American Public Health Association; the American Red Cross; the Association for the Care of Children's Health; the National Association for the Education of Young Children; the Children's Defense Fund) and government agencies (Maternal and Child Health; Medicaid/EPSDT; Food and Nutrition Service) for information on parent education and children's health issues.

❖ Contact local community health centers, mental health providers, hospitals, maternal and child health programs, and HMOs about serving as resources for families and the program.

❖ Link up with national health campaigns such as The Healthy Mothers, Healthy Babies Coalition, *Sesame Street*'s lead poisoning campaign, and the National SAFE KIDS Campaign.

❖ Use area health education centers, nursing schools, colleges, police and fire departments, health fairs, and public libraries as resources to educate families, colleagues, and yourself on health issues.

❖ Work with child care health consultants who offer training on health issues, ranging from the best placement of changing tables to sick child care policies.

You serve children best when you work as a team with their families and community agencies.

Sharing Thoughts About Children's Health

Dear Families:

As a parent, you have every right to assume that your child will be well and happy while in our care. And we want you to know that your child's health is very important to us, too. We work very hard to stop the spread of germs by following good health practices.

We believe that children's health is more than just their physical well-being. It also includes emotional and social wellness. A child who eats nutritious meals, gets plenty of rest, can explore in an environment that is relatively free of germs, and feels valued and secure, is one who can focus on the important job of learning.

How We Can Work Together

We do many things to promote your child's good health. And in everything we do, we welcome and need your support. Here are some examples.

❖ *We work with you to screen your child for possible health problems*, including those related to vision, hearing, and developmental delays. We would like to have your participation during screening so your child will feel comfortable.

❖ *We work with you to make sure your child gets all of his or her shots and other needed medical attention*. At these times, and at other times as well, we need to have the most current information about your child's health situation.

❖ *We practice and teach children personal hygiene*, including hand washing, toileting, tooth brushing, and other self-help skills, just as you do at home.

❖ *We feed your child nutritious meals and snacks*. If your child develops a food allergy, please let us know so we can post this information for everyone to see.

❖ *We make sure that children who are ill are supported,* and that others are not exposed to infection. We will, of course, let you know if a child in the program has a contagious disease (such as chicken pox).

❖ *If your child is supposed to take medication, we do need written permission*. If a health emergency arises, we also need to have a release form on file.

We regard you as our full partner in all of the health-related activities we do. We need to work together and be constantly watchful. Your child's health depends on it!

Sincerely,

Algunas ideas acerca de
la salud de los niños

Estimadas familias:

Como padres de familia, ustedes tienen el derecho a asumir que su hijo(a) sea feliz y esté bien mientras se encuentre en nuestro cuidado. Nosotros deseamos que sepan que la salud de su hijo(a) también nos es muy importante. Mediante unas buenas prácticas de salud, nosotros trabajamos fuertemente para evitar la propagación de gérmenes.

Nosotros creemos que la salud de los niños consiste en mucho más que el bienestar físico, pues el bienestar emocional y social también hacen parte de la salud. Un niño que consume alimentos nutritivos, descansa suficiente tiempo, puede explorar en un ambiente relativamente libre de gérmenes y se siente valorado y seguro, puede concentrarse en el importante trabajo de aprender.

Cómo podemos trabajar juntos

Nosotros hacemos mucho para promover la buena salud de sus hijos. Y, en todo lo que hacemos, les damos la bienvenida y les solicitamos su apoyo. Los siguientes son unos cuantos ejemplos:

❖ *Trabajamos con ustedes para detectar posibles problemas de salud de sus niños,* incluyendo aquellos relacionados con la visión, el oído y los retrasos en el desarrollo. Nos gustaría que durante dicha detección ustedes estuvieran presentes para que los niños se sientan cómodos.

❖ *Trabajamos con ustedes para garantizar que sus hijos reciban todas las vacunas y demás atención médica necesaria.* Hoy en día y, de hecho, en cualquier otro momento, necesitamos contar con la información más actualizada sobre el estado de salud de sus hijos.

❖ *Nosotros practicamos y les enseñamos a los niños higiene personal,* incluyendo lavarse las manos, ir al baño, lavarse los dientes y otras destrezas autónomas, tal como ustedes lo hacen en su hogar.

❖ *Nosotros les ofrecemos a sus hijos nutritivos alimentos y meriendas.* Si su hijo(a) es alérgico(a) a algún alimento, permítanos saberlo para anunciarlo y que todos lo sepan.

❖ *Nosotros confirmamos que a los niños enfermos se les apoya y que los demás no estén expuestos a infecciones.* Nosotros, por supuesto les haremos saber si algún niño del programa tiene alguna enfermedad contagiosa (como el sarampión).

❖ *Si su pequeño(a) debe tomar medicina, necesitamos la autorización por escrito.* Y, en caso de emergencia, también necesitamos contar con una autorización en nuestros archivos.

Nosotros les consideramos nuestros socios en todas las actividades de salud que realizamos. Necesitamos trabajar juntos y mantenernos alerta. ¡La salud de sus hijos depende de ello!

Les saluda atentamente,

Guiding Children's Behavior

Children need adults to guide them—to help them learn what is acceptable behavior and what is not. The fact is that getting infants and toddlers to stop doing something or to do something else is not difficult. Because we adults are so much bigger and more powerful than they are, we can actually make children behave. But is this all we want? Wouldn't we prefer that children behave because they have developed self-control and have learned to balance their own needs with the needs of others?

In *The Creative Curriculum,* we place great importance on helping young children develop inner controls and positive social skills. We believe that when young children begin learning how to control their own behavior, it is more likely they will grow into people who can make reasonable decisions. We also recognize that children who know how to relate to others in positive ways and can make friends tend to be happier and more successful in life.

In this chapter, you will learn about:

❖ taking a positive approach to guiding behavior;
❖ responding to challenging behaviors, such as temper tantrums and biting; and
❖ helping children relate positively to each other.

Taking a Positive Approach

When you have realistic expectations of children and gently guide their behavior in ways that show respect and help children feel good about themselves, you are taking a positive approach. Your positive approach can help young children learn for themselves what behavior is acceptable and what is not.

Positive guidance can take many forms. Sometimes you take steps to prevent dangerous or unacceptable behavior. You *prevent dangerous behavior* when, for example, you cover an electrical outlet so children cannot hurt themselves. You *prevent unacceptable behavior* when you plan your daily schedule so children have plenty of time outdoors to practice their gross motor skills and burn up energy. Other times you may intervene to *redirect children's behavior*. For example, you give an infant a rubber toy to chew on instead of the piece of paper that had been lying on the floor, or remind a toddler to climb on the climber instead of the table. At still other times, you intervene directly to *stop a dangerous behavior*, such as kicking or biting.

The first steps in providing positive guidance and promoting self-discipline are understanding child development and building trusting relationships. When you know what children (in general) are like at different ages, you can meet their needs in caring ways. Struggles often result from unrealistic expectations. For example, when La Toya organizes lunch so that everything is ready when the children sit down, she decreases the chances children will end up crying, climbing on the table, or pushing one another because they are hungry and frustrated. As a result, instead of focusing on maintaining order, she and the children can enjoy the smell of an orange and talk about the morning's events as they eat lunch together. Because children feel close to her, they will imitate her actions and look for her approval. La Toya's smile of encouragement when Valisha shares a piece of her orange will inspire Valisha to do it again another day.

How you guide a child's behavior depends in large part on the child's age and temperament. Because children grow and change so rapidly during their first three years, the strategies you use to guide their behavior must change, too.

Guiding the Behavior of Young Infants

Misbehaving is not an appropriate term to describe what young infants do. When infants cry to be held, they are not trying to manipulate you—even though it may at times feel that way to you. Rather, they are telling you what they need. Guiding the behavior of infants means keeping them safe. You can do this by anticipating dangerous situations. (For additional information, see Chapter 8, Ensuring Children's Safety.)

❖ **Stay nearby when babies are lying or sitting close to each other.** If they begin pulling each other's hair or hitting one another, separate them a bit and show them how to be gentle.

❖ **Offer an alternative when one child grabs for what another is holding.**

❖ **Limit the number of times you have to say, "No."** Be sure everything within reach is all right for children to play with and mouth.

❖ **Feed infants and help them nap according to their individual schedules.**

Guiding the Behavior of Mobile Infants

By about 10 months, mobile infants begin to understand that their actions affect others. Your challenge is to discourage certain behaviors in ways that help children feel good about themselves, even when you don't feel good about what they are doing. Here are some suggestions.

❖ **Use simple, clear language to communicate which behaviors are acceptable.** Let your expression and tone of voice emphasize your message as Grace did when she explained to Willard, "You may use the crayons on the paper."

❖ **Use "No" sparingly.** Save this for dangerous situations so it will be effective.

❖ **Give children many opportunities to move and be active throughout the day.** Eliminating frustration and boredom will reduce the likelihood that behavioral problems will occur.

❖ **Use familiar signals to let children know when it's time to move from one activity to another.** For example, give a two-minute warning when it's time to clean up. Dim the lights and play soft music when it's time for nap. When children have a sense of what to expect, they tend to feel secure and calm during transitions. With less confusion, the possibility of problems arising also decreases.

❖ **Plan the day so there are no long waits between activities.** If children have to wait for a few minutes, sing a song, do a fingerplay, or tell a story to help the time pass in an interesting, relaxed way.

❖ **Look at a situation through children's eyes before intervening.** Be aware, for example, that what looks like one child grabbing a toy from another may be a "taking away-giving back" game.

❖ **Give children the chance to work things out themselves**—if no one will be hurt. Children may briefly react and then decide they don't care when others pick up a toy they had been playing with.

Guiding the Behavior of Toddlers

Toddlers' behavior can, at times, stretch your patience. It can also be exciting, depending on your viewpoint. Remember, toddlers are testing limits to define themselves. With this thought in mind, here are some suggestions that can help you guide toddlers' behavior in positive ways.

❖ **Encourage toddlers' growing sense of independence.** Invite them to participate in daily routines. Give them many chances to make choices. Set up the environment so children can hang up their own coats and reach the sink to wash their own hands.

❖ **Set a few, simple clear rules**—knowing that children may need your help to follow them. Rules such as, "Sit at the table when you cut with scissors" give children a sense of order and security as well as the opportunity to develop self-discipline. Over time, and after many reminders, children will learn to take their scissors to the table.

❖ **Understand that toddlers are not yet ready to share.** When they don't share, they aren't being greedy or mean. They need time to develop a sense of ownership and to learn to share. Model and encourage sharing but do not insist on it. Have duplicates of favorite toys available to help avoid conflicts.

❖ **State rules positively rather than negatively.** Give children an alternative way to behave. For example, you might say, "Walk when you are inside" instead of "Don't run."

❖ **Share your feelings about certain behaviors.** "I know that you are angry and that's O.K. But I don't want people to hurt each other. I'm going to help you so you don't hit."

❖ **Give children alternative ways to express their anger.** "If you feel angry, tell us. Say, 'I'm mad!' so we will know how to help you."

❖ **Ask toddlers silly questions so they have lots of opportunities to say, "No."** Matthew loves Mercedes to ask questions such as, "Do we eat a shoe for dinner?" or "Is it time to go to sleep after breakfast?"

❖ **Pay close attention to a child who is likely to hit or bite.** Look for opportunities to help a child stop a behavior before another child gets hurt.

❖ **Acknowledge when children show self-discipline.** Barbara did this when she saw Leo—who was about to throw a block—catch her eye, and then put the block down on the floor. "That was good stopping, Leo."

❖ **Avoid talking with other adults about a toddler's challenging behavior in front of the child.** Toddlers are very aware when they are the topic of conversation. Being talked about can be uncomfortable.

When you take a positive approach to guiding children's behavior, you help children learn self-control and promote their self-esteem. But how do you do this when their behaviors challenge your patience or upset you? We address that question next.

Responding to Challenging Behaviors

When faced with an outbreak of crying, hitting, kicking, temper tantrums, or biting, all teachers of infants and toddlers have, at one time or another, found themselves thinking, "What do I do now?" Here are some ideas to consider.

Review your goals for children. Ask yourself, "What do I want to teach children about themselves and their feelings?" La Toya, for example, wants children to receive the message that their feelings are legitimate and respected. She also wants to help them understand what is acceptable behavior as well as what is not.

Be realistic. Base your expectations of behavior on what you know about child development. Infants and toddlers have immediate and intense feelings of joy and excitement, as well as feelings of anger and frustration. They have not yet learned to express their feelings in acceptable ways. Therefore, you can expect that sometimes children will lose control and display behavior that is difficult to handle.

Be aware of your own feelings. Young children's feelings are deep and raw. They have a way of reaching back and stirring up feelings such as happiness, anger, loneliness, sadness, and frustration from your own childhood. Before you can decide how to respond to a child's needs, you must first be aware of who is feeling what.

Maintain a calm atmosphere. Children are quick to sense adults' tension and may become more tense themselves. Increased tension often increases the likelihood of negative behavior. To help children, try to keep things in perspective. Remind yourself that this is a rough time and that it will pass.

Consider what the child is feeling. To help you figure out how to respond in a positive way, ask yourself, "What is this child saying?" When children cry, withdraw, hit, bite, or lie on the floor kicking and screaming, they may be telling you, "I am lonely," "I am scared," "I am overstimulated by too many exciting things to do," "I am angry," or, "I need you to set some limits for me."

When you intervene, do so in ways that acknowledge children's feelings and give them acceptable ways to behave when an incident does occur. Here is an example of what La Toya said and did after Valisha kicked Eddie (who had taken all the farm animals off the shelf and was playing with them).

- ❖ She acknowledged that Eddie was kicked. "That really hurts, Eddie, doesn't it?"
- ❖ She described what happened. "Valisha, you kicked Eddie and that hurts him."
- ❖ She acknowledged Valisha's feelings. "I think you're angry, Valisha, because Eddie has all the farm animals and you want some too."
- ❖ She stated what is not acceptable. "I can't let you kick because kicking people hurts."
- ❖ She stated what is acceptable. "You can kick the ball if you want to kick something. Or you can tell us in words how angry you are."
- ❖ Finally, she helped Valisha come up with a solution. "How can you let Eddie know that you want some of the animals? That's a good idea. You can ask him for some."

Talk with others. Colleagues and a child's parents can help you put together a picture of what is happening in a child's life. Events at home or in the neighborhood may be upsetting a child. Perhaps something has happened in child care—such as the absence of a primary provider—that may leave a child feeling sad or angry.

When a child's behavior is especially upsetting, talk about it with parents and colleagues. Review the steps you have taken. Indeed, it sometimes happens that after adults talk together about a child's behavior, the behavior disappears. It is as if the act of talking the subject through helps the adults relax and be more available to a child in a way they couldn't when tension was running high.

Since temper tantrums and biting are challenging behaviors among infants and toddlers, we discuss each of these separately.

Temper Tantrums

Temper tantrums are no fun for anyone. They can leave children feeling exhausted and frightened at their loss of control. They can also leave adults feeling angry, incompetent, and even embarrassed, if they occur in public.

If children could tell us what a tantrum feels like, they would probably describe it as a storm of frustration and rage that sweeps in and overwhelms them. It's important to remember that life can be very frustrating for toddlers. Developmental theory tells us that they are learning about limits. They often struggle to accept the limits you set for them as well as the limits of their own abilities. In addition, they frequently find themselves caught between wanting to be a "big kid" and to be a baby. One minute they want you to hold them in your arms. The next, they become upset because they can't tie their own shoes, carry a heavy bag of groceries home from the store, or tell you something because they don't have all the words they need.

Once a tantrum begins, there is often little you can do except keep a child from hurting himself or someone else, and assure the child that you are there. After he has calmed down, acknowledge his feelings in ways that show you accept him and his feelings. Do not shame him. "Not being able to finish that puzzle really frustrated you! It can be scary to be so angry." Suggest other ways to deal with the frustration: "Next time, maybe you should try the animal puzzle instead. Or you can ask me to help you."

It's best to focus your energies on prevention. Planning ahead to minimize temper tantrums will help avoid what can be a very stressful experience for children—and for you.

Minimize frustrations. Create an environment that is as frustration-free as possible. Set up an interesting, safe space that children can explore freely without constantly having you say, "No." Make sure the toys, games, and puzzles you offer match the abilities of the children in your care. Always have on hand familiar toys and puzzles that children have successfully played with in the past.

Give toddlers plenty of opportunities to feel competent. A child who frequently feels competent is less likely to have tantrums. Invite toddlers to help you with everyday chores, such as setting the table or folding the laundry. Offer them many opportunities to make choices about what to wear, eat, and play with. Label shelves with pictures so children can find what they want and help put toys away. Use children's cues to help you understand what they want to communicate.

Give toddlers a chance to be babies, too. Keep in mind that toddlers need hugs and cuddles. Be there to offer them when they are needed.

Anticipate children's physical needs. You can often turn the tide and ward off a tantrum by doing things such as serving lunch before children get too hungry, helping children take naps before they start falling apart, and giving them a chance to play outdoors when they are ready for active play.

Biting

Biting is very common in group settings of young children. Yet whenever it happens, it is always disturbing to parents and caregivers alike. As with tantrums, it's best to focus your energies on prevention. Understanding the reasons for biting will help you come up with effective strategies to prevent it.[1]

The chart that follows identifies some typical situations when children tend to bite and what you might do to prevent this behavior from happening.

Why Children May Bite	Strategies to Help Prevent Biting
They have a strong need for independence and control. The response to biting satisfies these needs and reinforces the behavior.	Give choices throughout the day and reinforce positive social behavior. If children get attention when they are not biting, they will not have to use this negative behavior to feel a sense of personal power.
Teething causes their mouths to hurt.	Offer children teething toys or frozen bagels to mouth.
They are experimenting. An infant or young child may take an experimental bite out of a mother's breast or caregiver's shoulder. They may simply want to touch, smell, and taste other people to learn more about them.	Provide a wide variety of sensory-motor experiences (such as fingerpainting, playing with dough, preparing and eating food, or engaging in water and sand play) to satisfy this need.
They are exploring cause and effect: "What will happen when I bite?"	Provide several different activities and toys that respond to children's actions and help them learn about cause and effect.
They are trying to approach or interact with another child.	Give children many opportunities to interact with one another. Guide their behavior as necessary, paying special attention to positive interactions.
They feel frustrated or angry. Some children lack skills to cope with situations and feelings such as wanting another child's toy or an adult's attention. When frustrated or angry, they bite.	Watch for signs of rising frustration and potential conflict. You can often intercept a potentially harmful incident by responding to children's needs promptly.
They are asking for attention.	Give children lots of attention throughout the day.
They are imitating behavior.	Model loving, supporting behavior. Offer children positive alternatives for negative behavior. Never bite a child to show how it feels to be bitten.
They feel threatened. When some children feel they are in danger, they may bite in self-defense. Other children may be overwhelmed by their surroundings and the events in their lives and bite as a means of gaining control.	Provide support and assurance so that the child recognizes that he and his possessions are safe.

---

[1] Based on Donna Witmer, "Children Who Bite," *Scholastic Pre-K Today,* March 1992; and Fact Sheet, *Biters: Why They Do It and What to Do About It.* National Association for the Education of Young Children, June 1996.

Unfortunately, no matter how attentive you are, it is likely that sooner or later a child in your program will bite another. Here's what you can do at that moment.

Respond to the situation promptly. As soon as an incident takes place, you must take immediate action.

❖ **Comfort the child who was bitten.**

❖ **Wash the wound.** Apply an ice pack to help keep bruising down. If the skin is broken, follow the universal precautions for handling blood, which include wearing nonporous disposable gloves, and recommend that parents notify their pediatrician and follow his or her advice.

❖ **State clearly that biting is not all right.** Speak firmly and seriously.

❖ **Invite the child who bit to help you care for the bitten child.** This gives the child the opportunity to be a helper and leave the role of aggressor. Use these moments to offer the biter support and to teach caring behavior. Remember that, from the biter's point of view, it's scary to be so out of control that you end up hurting someone.

❖ **Help the child who bit understand that there are other ways to express anger,** such as using words or growling like a tiger.

Document injuries due to biting. Include the name of the child bitten, as well as the date, time, and location of the incident. Describe how the injury occurred and the actions you took. This information will be helpful in identifying patterns. It will also help you keep the situation in perspective.

Acknowledge your own feelings so you don't add more tension to the situation. Children are quick to pick up your feelings. Biting can be particularly frustrating because it occurs in spite of many preventive measures. In addition, no one wants to see a child hurt. Talk with colleagues about biting and help each other maintain emotional balance.

Hold onto your positive vision of the whole child. When a child is biting, adults tend to focus solely on the negative behavior. They may refer to the child as "the problem" or even "the mouth." A child who is biting is a child in distress. He or she needs your care and support to get through a tough time, during and following an incident.

Make and carry out an ongoing prevention and intervention plan. Here are some positive steps you can take.

❖ **Observe to try to identify patterns of instances when biting occurs.** For example, is a child more likely to bite before lunch? Or when things get very loud and confusing?

❖ **Ask parents about what might be going on at home.** Find out if there have been any changes recently. Talk together about how you might help a child stop biting.

❖ **Decide on a plan.** For example, if you notice that a child tends to bite when things get hectic, plan to spend extra one-on-one time with her and make sure to include her on many small group walks.

❖ **If you work in a center, have someone focus on the child who is biting, ideally someone who knows and enjoys this child.** This person should be available to the child all day, to provide support, encourage positive behavior, and of course, to be ready to step in quickly and help the child stop biting. If you work on your own, you may need to adapt your plans for the day so you can give the biter the attention needed. You may, for example, decide not to offer fingerpainting—which requires your supervision—and instead provide colored markers that children can use more independently. Alternatively, you may decide to bring in an extra adult to help out for awhile.

❖ **Observe.** Keep track of how things are going. Adapt your plan as necessary.

Help parents understand the situation. Because biting can upset all parents in a program, it's often helpful to address this issue before it occurs. Discuss with parents the many reasons why children may bite and describe various preventive steps you can take. Share strategies to prevent and deal with biting that parents can use at home. Invite parents to share their strategies with you. Always remember that biting the child back "to see what it feels like" is never an option. If biting does occur, talk with parents directly and openly. Acknowledge their feelings. Consider inviting a community health specialist to meet with parents to address health concerns.

Seek help if biting continues or grows more vicious. Though most episodes of biting fade in a few weeks, there are times when biting signals that a child needs special assistance. If you become concerned, call in a community resource person, such as a developmental specialist, to help you explore interventions a child may need if the approaches we outlined do not help.

While guiding children's behavior may sometimes appear to be taking up too much of your time, it is an important part of your work with infants and toddlers. As you help children learn to control their behavior, you also build a solid foundation for their positive interactions with others.

Helping Children Relate Positively to Each Other

Children begin to learn about relationships from the time they are born. They learn about caring for others, using as models the way others care for them. When you treat children in loving and consistent ways and show how much you value and respect them, you promote positive attitudes toward others—what is also called **prosocial behavior**.

Day after day, you have many opportunities to teach children about getting along with each other. Here are examples of some of the things you can do.

Remember that children look to you as a model. The infants and toddlers you care for are very aware of what you do. How you interact with each child, with colleagues, and with parents teaches children more powerfully than any words you might say about how to get along with other people.

Mirror the behavior of infants and toddlers. When you smile at an infant who's smiling at you, or reflect back the funny expression on a toddler's face, you confirm a child's self-image and what he or she experiences. Because infants and toddlers are so aware of their special adults—including you—mirroring is a powerful way to support children as they create a sense of self and to show them the pleasure of relating to other people.

Respect each child's style of interacting. Some children jump immediately and enthusiastically into activities. Others need time to watch and may eventually need some gentle encouragement. You can respond in the most helpful way when you are aware of each child's style, and understand that it may be culturally based.

Arrange your environment so that children have opportunities to spend time alone or in small groups during the day. Living all day in a large group can be stressful for children and for you. Time away from the large group offers a chance for social interactions that may not take place when everyone is together. Examples of physical spaces that give children a break from group life and promote one-on-one interactions are a large cardboard box or a comfortable chair with room for two. Examples of activities during which you and one or two children can enjoy being together are taking short walks in the neighborhood or preparing a snack.

Acknowledge children's positive interactions. Comment when you see a child interact in cooperative and helpful ways. For example, when two six-month-olds are sitting on a blanket together, you might say, "You are getting to know each other. You touched her face very gently." When Jonisha draws a picture for Valisha, La Toya might comment, "That was very thoughtful. What good sisters you are."

Give children opportunities to help you. Children feel proud of themselves and begin to understand how to be contributing members of a community when you invite them to help you. When Mercedes asks Matthew to carry a letter to the mailbox or help set out his mat at naptime, he feels good about helping.

Encourage children to help one another. Throughout the day, offer children opportunities to assist each other. Invite one child to help look for another's missing sock. Acknowledge when a child uses words or gentle pats on the back to comfort another child.

Read books with themes of helpfulness and friendship. There are wonderful books such as *Grampa Can Fix It* and the *Max* books you can read to toddlers. Children also love homemade books about familiar events and people they know—for example, *Valisha Helps Jonisha Find Her Shoe*.

Include equipment and materials that promote interaction and cooperation in both your indoor and outdoor environments. To set the stage for children to interact with one another, you might provide a wooden rocking boat that two or more children can sit in and rock, set out large sheets of butcher paper for children to color or paint on together, or provide opportunities for water and sand play.

Allow children time to work out their differences—but be ready to step in if you are needed. When you wait a few minutes before stepping in, you give two toddlers a chance to discover there is room for both of them to sit on the sofa together. Keep your eye on them so you can be there if you see one or the other about to be pushed off.

Guiding behavior is something you do throughout the day when working with infants and toddlers. We discuss how you guide behavior as part of daily routines and activities in the remaining chapters of this book.

Sharing Thoughts About
Guiding Children's Behavior

Dear Families:

Young children need adults—to help them learn what is acceptable behavior and how to relate positively to others. We focus on social skills and self-discipline because we know that children who practice these behaviors are more successful in life. Researchers also tell us that children who learn to take personal responsibility for their actions are better able to make good choices in life.

We take a positive approach to guiding behavior. We try to prevent problems, for example, by giving children time outdoors each day to burn up energy. At other times, we try to redirect children's behavior, for example, by giving an infant a rubber toy to chew on instead of the piece of paper from the floor. And, when necessary, we intervene directly to stop hitting or biting.

How We Can Work Together

Guiding children's behavior is a very important responsibility we share. Here are some approaches we can both use.

❖ *Model how we want your child to relate to others.* When we treat your child with love and respect, we set the stage for future relationships. Watching us work together in respectful ways also teaches your child how people should behave towards one another.

❖ *Give your child every opportunity to develop a sense of responsibility.* Young children love to help with everyday chores such as putting napkins on the table. They also like to have choices such as: "Do you want milk or juice with your crackers?" or "Shall we read the book about the bear or the one about the train?"

❖ *Help your child express feelings in acceptable ways.* We can talk about what your child might be feeling to introduce the practice of expressing feelings in words. We can also offer activities like pounding playdough and playing with puppets. When we have to step in, we should always give a positive alternative—"I can't let you hit because someone will get hurt. If you are angry, growl like a lion or kick the ball."

Let's talk about any challenging behaviors, such as biting and temper tantrums. Together, we can figure out how best to deal with them. We can look for patterns in these behaviors to help us better understand what your child might be experiencing. This will help both of us respond in ways that strengthen your child's self-control and self-esteem.

By working together, we can help your child develop the social skills and self-control that are so essential for success in life.

Sincerely,

Algunas ideas sobre cómo guiar el comportamiento de los niños

Estimadas familias:

Los niños pequeños necesitan que los adultos guíen su comportamiento para aprender lo que es y no es aceptable, y para ayudarlos a relacionarse positivamente con los demás. Nosotros nos concentramos en las destrezas sociales y en el autocontrol, porque sabemos que aquellos niños que aprenden a relacionarse con otros en formas positivas y a hacer amigos, tienen más exito en la vida. Además, los niños que aprenden a asumir la responsabilidad de su comportamiento, están mucho más capacitados para hacer buenas elecciones en su vida.

En cuanto a la orientación del comportamiento infantil, nosotros asumimos un enfoque positivo, tratatando de prevenir los problemas. Otras veces, tratamos de reorientar el comportamiento infantil, y cuando es necesario, intervenimos directamente, para detener los golpes o los mordiscos.

Cómo podemos trabajar juntos

Guiar el comportamiento infantil es una importante responsabilidad que todos compartimos. Los siguientes son unos cuantos enfoques que, conjuntamente, podemos emplear.

* *Modelen la manera en que desean que sus hijos se relacionen con los demás.* Los niños aprenden sobre las relaciones sociales, a partir de de los adultos importantes en su vida. Al tratarlos con amor y respeto, creamos la base para las relaciones futuras. Además, cuando ellos observan esto, aprenden cómo deben comportarse unas personas con otras.

* *Bríndenle a sus hijos todas las oportunidades posibles de adquirir el sentido de responsabilidad.* A los pequeños les fascina colaborar con las tareas diarias y les encanta poder escoger entre opciones. Por ejemplo: "¿Deseas jugo o leche con las galletas?" o "¿Quieres leer el libro del osito o el del tren?".

* *Ayúdenle a sus hijos a expresar sus sentimientos en formas aceptables.* Podríamos hablar acerca de lo que pudieran estar sintiendo sus pequeños, con el fin de introducir la práctica de expresar los sentimientos oralmente. Cuando debamos intervenir, debemos hacerlo siempre ofreciéndoles una alternativa positiva: "No puedo permitirte que golpees, porque puedes herir a alguien. Si estás furioso(a), ruge como un león o patea la pelota".

* *Hablemos sobre los comportamientos desafiantes como morder o gritar con furia.* Juntos podremos establecer la mejor manera de manejarlos. Cuando dichos comportamientos ocurran, podemos intentar descubrir patrones, con el fin de comprender mejor lo que los niños sienten. De esta manera, conjuntamente, podremos responder en formas que fortalezcan el autocontrol y la autoestima de su hijo(a).

Trabajando juntos, podremos ayudarle a sus hijos a adquirir las destrezas sociales y el autocontrol esenciales para que tengan éxito en la vida.

Les saluda atentamente,

Part III Routines

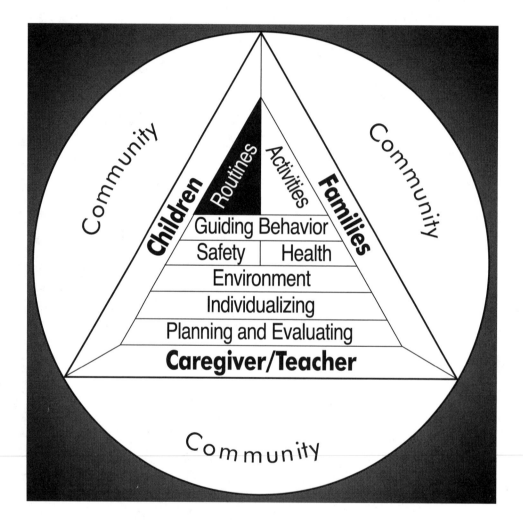

Routines

Hellos and Good-byes
Diapering and Toileting
Eating and Mealtimes
Sleeping and Naptime
Getting Dressed

Putting Quality
Into Action:
Routines Day By Day

T he best thing about routines, as seen through the eyes of infants and toddlers, is that they happen day after day, often several times a day. They are predictable, enabling children to learn what to expect. At the same time, they vary enough to hold children's attention and interest.

As infants grow into toddlers, daily routines take on new meaning and offer new challenges. It is also true that different children may experience the same routine in different ways. Leo, for example, may have a full-fledged temper tantrum to protest his mother's leaving, while Gena, who also doesn't want her mother to go, may quietly watch her walk out the door. Matthew may eye the potty seat in the bathroom curiously, while Jonisha proudly uses the toilet on her own, remembering to flush and to wash her hands. Julio may fall asleep as snack is being prepared, while Valisha intently practices using a plastic knife to cut slices of banana and pear. The decisions you make about how to respond to children and promote their learning through routines should be based on each child's developmental level, interests, and personality.

When we talk about promoting learning through routines, we are not talking about "teaching" in the traditional sense. Certainly there will be times when you need to give a child information about how to do something, such as how to place her jacket on the floor so she can "flip flop" it over her head. But, primarily, we are talking about how adults can nurture children's curiosity and guide them so they make increasing sense of the world through their own actions.

As children participate in daily routines, they learn to think, collect new information about themselves and their world, and develop skills. The discussions that follow point out key learnings for each routine. Bear in mind though, that for young children, all learning is integrated. Physical skills affect thinking skills and vice versa. Therefore, when Jasmine is asked if she wants "a cracker" or "yogurt," she not only learns the names of things, she also learns about making choices. Similarly, when Matthew learns to put on a jacket by himself, he develops fine motor skills, explores concepts such as *in* and *out*, learns about cooperation (when an older friend shows him the flip-flop method), and confirms his sense of independence. Everyday routines help children grow and learn in all areas.

In Part III, we look at five routines:

- ❖ hellos and good-byes;
- ❖ diapering and toileting;
- ❖ eating and mealtimes;
- ❖ sleeping and naptime; and
- ❖ getting dressed.

For each routine, we discuss its importance to children and families and offer suggestions under the following headings.

Questions to Consider

As you work everyday with children, you make decisions. Thoughtful decision making will help you make the most of each moment. Routines are not just something to get through; they are an integral part of the curriculum. In this section, we identify some of the questions that typically arise and offer suggestions for addressing them. These questions may relate to how to set up your environment, what supplies and materials you need and how to arrange them, what procedures will enable you to work efficiently, how to ensure children's health and safety, and how to involve children's families.

Helping Children Learn

Every routine offers opportunities to shape and extend children's learning. To highlight the range of possibilities, we consider how the routine might vary for young infants, mobile infants, and toddlers. We present this information in a series of charts that identify some typical behaviors you might observe. Then, we consider the following.

What the child might be experiencing. To respond appropriately, you must try to determine what is behind a child's behavior. You combine your knowledge of how infants and toddlers grow and learn with your observations of children in your program to help you determine what the child may be feeling or thinking.

How you can respond. There are many ways to respond to children's actions. When you decide to step back and observe as a child plays peek-a-boo, you give her the opportunity to explore hellos and good-byes at her own pace. During lunch time, when you ask a question such as, "What do you think we'll see when we peel this orange?" you stretch children's thinking. In this section we offer suggested responses based on what a child may be experiencing.

Sample letters to families. These letters explain why you focus on the routine in your program and invite families to be your partners in supporting children's learning. Letters are in English and Spanish.

Hellos and Good-byes

— ◈ —

Leo sits on the floor in front of his family pictures that Barbara has covered with clear Contact™ paper and hung at child-level on the wall. He runs his fingers over the pictures of Virginia, Elmer, Leo, and their dog Isabelle, all standing in front of their house. "What are you doing?" asks Barbara, as she comes over to join him. "Mommy and Daddy," he says, looking up at her with a smile.

— ◈ —

Infants and toddlers usually arrive at programs with their families. In some situations, however, they may come by themselves on a center-operated bus. No matter. Each day in your program begins with families and children saying hello to you and good-bye to one another. Each day ends as families and children reunite and say good-bye to you.

Learning to separate from and reunite with people we love is a life-long process. It is not a goal to be achieved in the first week or month or even year of child care.

Separations and reunions can bring out deep feelings in everyone involved. Some of these feelings can be uncomfortable, and it is natural to want to avoid them. It is not surprising that you and children's parents may often conspire to get through the beginning and end of the day as quickly as possible.

In part because hellos and good-byes arouse such strong feelings, they can provide valuable learning for infants and toddlers. Infants can learn about trusting others when the important adults in their lives say good-bye and return as promised. Toddlers can learn about what it means to be a separate person who has deep attachments to others. Caring adults can support this kind of learning.

Questions to Consider

How do you set the stage for hellos and good-byes in your program? Here are some questions and suggestions to guide your thinking as you make decisions.

"How can I support children and their families when it comes time to say hello and good-bye?"

Look at your program through the eyes of children and their families. What do you already do to ease their anxiety about separation and reuniting? What else might you do? Consider the following ideas.

Spend some time with each child and his or her family before the child is left in your care for the first time. Invite parents and other family members to visit your program with their child. Offer to conduct a home visit ahead of time so that they and their child can get to know you. As parents get to know you, they will feel more comfortable when it's time to say good-bye each day. Then too, children will feel more at ease when they see you spending time with their families.

Hang a welcome sign up at the beginning of the year with the names (and photos) of children and members of their families. It's a good idea to keep the sign up for a month or two. In addition to communicating the message of welcome, photos will help families get to know

one another's names and the names of each others' children. You can also make a list of names for families to take home. This will prove especially helpful when children enter your program during the year.

Plan a meeting at the beginning of the year in which you talk about hellos and good-byes with families. Give parents and other family members—who will regularly drop children off in the morning and pick them up later—a sense of what they might expect. Encourage them to allow a little extra time to help their child make the transition between home and child care. Point out that you'll work with them to make both transitions easier.

Encourage parents to leave their child for gradually increasing amounts of time, if at all possible, until the child is on his or her regular schedule. Some families may be able to arrange to ease their child into your program over the course of a week or two. They can spend time with their child in your setting, say good-bye, and return, but gradually increase the amount of time they are away. As a result, a child may experience less stress and feel more able to manage, knowing the parent will be back soon. When this type of gradual transition is not possible, be especially sure to spend time with a child and his or her family before the first good-bye.

Greet families each morning. Say "good-bye" each afternoon. If you are busy with another child or family, signal that you will be there as soon as you are finished. Give each family a warm hello and share news of something you will do that day. Be sure to say "good-bye" as each family departs.

Pay attention to and participate in rituals children and their families develop. Be available to hold an infant after a parent gives him or her a good-bye kiss. Walk a toddler to the door to wave good-bye. If families haven't developed a ritual, consider helping them do so. Rituals help children—and adults—feel more secure because they know what to expect.

Hang children's pictures in their cubbies, and label drawers so parents can find their children's belongings and whatever else they may need. Parents will probably feel more comfortable at your program if they can find a cup to get their child a drink of juice, or if they can find their child's belongings in a labeled cubby. When family members are comfortable, they'll be better able to help their children feel more comfortable, too.

Set out an interesting object or activity every morning. A flowering plant, photos you took during a neighborhood walk, or a new toy displayed where everyone can see it, can give parents and children something to explore together as children settle in for the day. Because these transition times often leave adults and children unsure of what to do next, having something to focus on is especially comforting.

Keep in touch with parents about how things are going for them and their children. Keeping the doors of communication open can help parents feel more at ease about sharing any questions or concerns they may have about hellos and good-byes.

"How can I help children feel connected to their families throughout the day?"

Learning how to express and deal with feelings about hellos and good-byes doesn't just happen in the morning and afternoon. When you offer opportunities for children to feel attached to their parents throughout the day, children can gain a sense of security and better understand that they are individuals—attached to, yet separate from their parents. Here are some ways you can help children feel in touch with their parents when they are apart.

Encourage families to bring a child's special blanket or stuffed animal from home. These items, sometimes called transitional objects or "loveys," help young children feel more secure when they are away from those they love. Respect a child's needs and wishes to hold onto her special object. Ivan did this when another child wanted Gena's toy lamb, Franklin: "I explained that Gena wanted to hold Franklin close and helped Tim find a toy to play with." Label these items to prevent them from getting lost. Identify a place to keep them when children aren't using them. Remind parents to take these objects home at night to avoid making a trip back or facing a miserably unhappy child.

Include pictures of children and their families in your environment. Ask parents to bring in photos, or photograph families yourself in your setting or during a home visit. Laminate the photos or cover them with clear Contact™ paper and display them on the wall at children's eye level. You can also fill a basket with family pictures so children can literally "carry" their families around with them. Make a photo album or book of family pictures. Better yet, try all of these ideas and your own, too.

Place toy phones or old real ones near family pictures. Invite children to make pretend calls to their parents. Make a call yourself, if you think it will be helpful.

Talk about children's parents throughout the day. Comments such as, "How did you and mommy get here today?" and, "Your daddy told me you helped wash the car over the weekend," can help children feel close to their parents.

Make daily routines an important part of each day. Invite children to participate in the kinds of activities they do at home with their parents, such as putting on their coats and carrying a letter to the mailbox. You can also invite parents to join their children for lunch or snack as often as possible.

Have parents record a favorite bedtime story or song that children can listen to, especially before a nap. Children will find these sounds of home soothing.

Photograph family members in your setting. Display pictures of family members playing and reading with their children. These photos can help make parents a constant part of your program. They also are a concrete way to help children feel connected to their parents during the day.

"How can I help children gain some sense of control over hellos and good-byes?"

Here are some suggestions of ways you can help children begin to feel more comfortable and competent as they experience hellos and good-byes.

Create an environment in which children can feel competent throughout the day. Children gain a sense of mastery when they can hang up their own coats, reach the sink to wash their hands, help spread cottage cheese on crackers, or find a paper towel to wipe up the juice they spilled. These feelings help them to feel capable of handling separations.

Offer activities that allow children to express their feelings about hellos and good-byes. You want to give children the message that it is okay to feel whatever they feel. Activities such as playing musical instruments, dancing, painting, and playing at the water table or with puppets provide acceptable ways children can explore and express their emotions.

Encourage play that helps children gain a sense of mastery over separating and reuniting. Encourage peek-a-boo games. Offer many opportunities for children to appear and disappear by playing in tunnels, cardboard boxes with doors that open and close, or tents made by draping a blanket over a table. Provide props such as hats, briefcases, cloth bags, and empty food boxes to encourage toddlers to pretend they are leaving for work or going shopping and coming home again.

Read books with children about comings and goings. Books such as *Are You My Mother?* by P.D. Eastman (*Eres tú mi mama?*) and *Goodnight Moon* by Margaret Wise Brown can help children understand separation as they hear about others saying hello and good-bye. (In the first book, a little bird falls from the nest and asks everyone, "Are you my mother?" until he finally finds her. In the second book, a bunny says goodnight to all the objects in the bedroom.) Consider writing your own books. *Jonisha and Valisha Say Good-bye* is the twins' favorite of all the books at La Toya's house.

Hold the vision of children as competent. Children can sense when you have confidence in their ability to handle hellos and good-byes. Your feelings about them help to shape their sense of themselves.

Helping Children Learn From Hellos and Good-byes

Young Infants		
What You Observe	**What the Child May Be Experiencing**	**How You Can Respond**
Seeming not to notice when her parents leave	This doesn't necessarily mean she won't notice they're gone at a later time. At this time, though, she may be distracted. For example, she may feel hungry or be listening to the sound of other children playing. Or she may not yet have a sense of her parents as separate people.	Encourage her parents to say good-bye. Over time, she will learn what the term means. This understanding should help make her feel more secure because she knows her parents won't disappear without warning.
Crying strongly when his parents leave	He may understand that his parents are separate people and he wants to be with them.	Show you understand his feelings: "You probably feel sad when Mommy leaves." By listening to him, you show respect. You also help him learn that, no matter what he feels, he can tell you.
Breaking into tears when she spots her parent(s) at the end of the day	She may be showing how deeply she trusts her parents. When they arrive, she feels safe to share any and all her feelings and to ask her parents to comfort her. She may also be hungry or tired. On the other hand, she may be relieved that they've returned.	Help parents understand this hard-to-take declaration of love and trust. Help them realize that crying doesn't mean their child doesn't want to see them. By helping parents feel more at ease, you encourage them to respond to their child in ways that tell her she is safe and loved.

Mobile Infants		
What You Observe	What the Child May Be Experiencing	How You Can Respond
Withdrawing and sucking her thumb after her grandfather leaves	She may feel very upset about her grandfather leaving. On the other hand, her behavior may be unrelated to separation. She may not feel well or she may be tired, and this is a way to let you know she needs a low-key morning or an early nap.	If you think that her behavior is related to separation, encourage her grandfather to develop a good-bye ritual. Knowing what to expect will help her feel more in control of partings.
So busy practicing climbing up and down the slide that he does not say good-bye	He may be feeling the joy of exploring a new skill.	Encourage his parents to say good-bye (because he may become more aware of their departure after they have left). Hearing a good-bye—even if he is busy on the slide—teaches him he can trust his parents to let him know they are going.
Ignoring her parents when they arrive at the end of the day	She may be happily and deeply involved in what she is doing. She may also be expressing feelings about being left or about something that happened earlier in the day. She may also be trying to gain a sense of control over the situation.	Assure parents that their being ignored doesn't mean she is happier in child care than with them at home. Encourage parents to spend a few minutes talking about what she is doing and about her day. This will help her reconnect in a way that gives her a sense of control and begins the transition to home.

Toddlers

What You Observe	What the Child May Be Experiencing	How You Can Respond
Clinging, kicking, and screaming as his parents begin to say good-bye	He may feel very sad about their leaving. He knows he needs his parents and may feel afraid when he is separated from them.	Encourage his parents to develop a good-bye ritual to help him feel more in control. Then help him find something comforting to do after his parents leave. Promote his sense of competence through-out the day by, for example, offering him realistic, manage-able choices and inviting him to help with "real work," such as watering the plants.
Crying and protesting when her aunt leaves, although she has taken comings and goings in stride for sometime now	She may be experiencing a normal, bumpy stage in dealing with separation. Perhaps she has just realized that this intriguing place with its toys and nice peo-ple will be an everyday thing. Now that its newness is gone, she misses those she loves. Also, she may have something else going on in her life that is upsetting her.	If you feel confident that she'll soon take hellos and good-byes in stride, she'll pick that up. Focus on being generally supportive and helping her feel good about herself. Remind yourself—and her aunt—that learning to deal with separation involves ups and downs. Talk with her aunt about whether something is happening at home or in child care that may be upsetting, and if so, make a plan to address it.
Saying good-bye to his parents cheerfully and going off to play with a friend; greeting his "Gam-ma" with a hug at the end of the day; waving good-bye to you and happily walking out the door	He can usually keep a picture of people in his mind, even when separated from them. This gives him a good sense of security and comfort.	Encourage his sense of compe-tence by continuing to provide reminders of his family through-out the day. Appreciate with his parents how—by working together—you have helped him feel good about his growing independence. Recognize, however, that on some days, he may still have difficulty saying good-bye.

Sharing Thoughts About Hellos and Good-byes

Dear Families:

Every day you and your child say good-bye to one another in the morning and hello again in the afternoon. These hellos and good-byes are children's first steps on a life-long journey of learning how to separate from and reunite with important people in their lives.

Learning to say hello and good-bye to people we love is a process, not a goal to be achieved in the first week or month or even year of child care. Indeed, after many years of experience, we adults sometimes find it difficult to separate and reunite.

We focus on hellos and good-byes in our program because they are such a major part of your child's life—today and always. Being able to separate is necessary if children are going to develop as independent, competent people. Being able to reunite is necessary to building and maintaining caring, long-term relationships.

How We Can Work Together

❖ *Try to spend some time each morning and afternoon here with your child.* Your presence will help make the transition between home and child care easier for your child.

❖ *Remember always to say good-bye.* By saying good-bye, you strengthen your child's trust in you. Your child can count on the fact you will not disappear without warning. When you let us know you are about to leave in the morning, we can help you and your child say good-bye.

❖ *We can work together to create a hello and good-bye ritual.* This may be as simple as walking to the door with your child or giving your child a giant hug before you leave. Having a ritual offers you both the comfort of knowing what to do.

❖ *Be aware that sometimes good-byes and hellos will be "bumpier" than others.* As we all know, good-byes and hellos can stir up many deep feelings. These feelings, combined with your child's stage of development and other factors such as being hungry or tired, can make saying good-bye and hello difficult at times.

❖ *Bring in family photos and other reminders of home that you want to share.* Seeing these special objects will help your child feel connected to you throughout the day.

By working together, we can help your child feel comfortable, secure, and competent in child care.

Sincerely,

Algunas ideas sobre
los saludos y las despedidas

Estimadas familias:

Diariamente, ustedes y sus hijos se despiden en la mañana y se saludan nuevamente en la tarde. Estos saludos y despedidas constituyen los primeros pasos de un viaje que dura toda la vida, de aprender a separarse y a reunirse con las personas importantes en nuestra vida.

Aprender a saludar y a despedirse de quienes amamos es un proceso, no un fin que deba lograrse durante la primera semana o el primer mes, ni siquiera durante el primer año del cuidado infantil. De hecho, después de varios años de experiencia, incluso los adultos encontramos dificultades para separarnos y reunirnos nuevamente.

En nuestro programa nos concentramos en los saludos y las despedidas por constituir —hoy y siempre— un aspecto primordial de la vida de su hijo(a). Poder separarse es necesario, si se desea que los niños sean independientes y competentes. Y, poder reunirse es necesario para construir y mantener relaciones afectivas a largo plazo.

Cómo podemos trabajar juntos

❖ *Traten de pasar un tiempo con su hijo(a) aquí, cada mañana y tarde.* Su presencia contribuirá a facilitarle a su niño(a) la transición entre el hogar y la guardería.

❖ *Recuerden despedirse siempre.* Al despedirse, ustedes fortalecen la confianza de sus hijos en ustedes, pues ellos podrán contar con que ustedes no desaparecerán sin avisarles. Si nos permiten saber que se encuentran próximos a irse en la mañana, podremos ayudarles a ustedes y a sus hijos a despedirse.

❖ *Podemos trabajar juntos para crear un ritual de saludos y despedidas.* Esto puede ser tan sencillo como caminar con su hijo(a) hasta la puerta, o darle un fuerte abrazo antes de marcharse. Un ritual les ofrece a ambos la comodidad de saber qué hacer.

❖ *Mantenga presente que algunos saludos y despedidas son más "difíciles" que otros.* Como es sabido, las despedidas y los saludos pueden revolver diversos sentimientos profundos. Estos sentimientos, combinados con el nivel de desarrollo del niño y con otra serie de factores, como el estar cansado o hambriento, pueden hacer más difícil en ciertas ocasiones despedirse y saludarse.

❖ *Traigan fotografías familiares u otro(s) objeto(s) que recuerden su hogar.* El ver estos objetos especiales le ayudarán a su hijo(a) a mantenerse conectado con ustedes durante el día.

Si trabajamos juntos, podremos ayudarle a su hijo(a) a sentirse a gusto, seguro(a) y competente en la guardería infantil.

Les saluda atentamente,

Diapering and Toileting

— ◆ —

"Let's change that wet diaper," says Grace as she picks Willard up and places him on the changing table." Those are bright blue pants you are wearing today. Did your Daddy put them on you this morning?" "Daddy," says Willard. "We're going to put those bright blue pants right back on as soon as we're finished, okay?" As Grace pulls off Willard's pants, he touches his tummy. "I see your tummy," she says. "Are you giving your tummy a little pat?"

— ◆ —

If a child is changed six times a day until he's thirty months old, he will have had his diaper changed more than 5,400 times. Anything a child experiences 5,400 times is an important part of his life—and of those who change him.

Diapering offers you a chance to focus all your attention on a single child. It is a time you can talk together, sing a song, or play a game of "Where are your toes?" When you can approach diapering as an activity to be experienced together rather than an unpleasant task to hurry through, you teach children an important lesson: that their body functions are a normal, healthy part of everyday life. You can also use diapering as an opportunity to help children learn about many other things, such as the names of parts of their bodies and clothes, and concepts such as up and down, wet and dry, and cool and warm.

Sooner or later, typically sometime in the last half of their second year, children reach the point when they are ready physically, cognitively, and psychologically to begin using the toilet. If you—and a child's parents—follow children's leads, are supportive, work together, and avoid getting into power struggles with toddlers, you can help make mastering the skill of using the toilet a pleasant and educational experience. Children will learn to feel good about their bodies and accept their body products as natural parts of themselves. They will develop new fine motor skills as they learn to buckle and button. They will also learn about the pleasure and sense of achievement that comes with wearing "big kid" underpants and gaining self-control.

Questions to Consider

Here are some questions to consider as you decide how best to make diapering and toileting in your program as efficient and pleasant as possible.

"How can I manage the group so that diapering is a time to focus on one child?"

Though of course there will be times when you will want or need to change a child quickly, in many instances, you can make diapering a special time by planning ahead. Here are some strategies to consider.

Coordinate with your co-workers so you can spend unhurried time with a child when changing his or her diaper. Assuming that each child has a primary caregiver, that person has the basic responsibility for changing one or more certain children. You'll need to cue one another when one of you is going to change a child so the other can keep an eye on all the remaining children, and also to let each other know when it's necessary to finish up quickly and return to the group.

Follow a set procedure for changing diapers to assure children's safety and health. As you follow these steps, remember to talk with the child and take advantage of this one-on-one time you have to be together.[1]

- ❖ Put a nonabsorbent, disposable cover on the diapering surface. Check to be sure the supplies you need are ready and within reach, so that you can always keep one hand on the child. If you plan to use diaper cream, put a dab on disposable paper. Put all containers away.
- ❖ If you use disposable latex gloves, put them on now.
- ❖ Pick up the child. If the diaper is soiled, hold the child away from you.
- ❖ Lay the child on the diapering surface. Never leave the child unattended.
- ❖ Remove the soiled diaper and clothes. Put them aside.
- ❖ Clean the child's bottom with a moist disposable wipe. Wipe from front to back, using the towelette only once. Repeat with fresh wipes, if necessary, until the child is completely clean. Pay particular attention to skin folds.
- ❖ Leave the wipes in the soiled disposable diaper.
- ❖ Do not use any kind of powder; inhaling it can be dangerous. Use cream or other skin care products only if parents request it.
- ❖ Fold the disposable diaper with the soiled wipes inward, reseal it with its own tape, and discard it into a lined, covered step can, using the foot pedal. Put cloth diapers in a sealed plastic bag or container to be taken home.
- ❖ If you used disposable gloves, discard them now into the step can.
- ❖ Wipe your hands with a moist, disposable wipe. Dispose of it in the step can.

---

[1] Caryl A. Haddock, Serena Dee, Abby S. Kendrick, and Yvette Yarchmink, Eds. *Health and Safety in Child Care: A Guide for Child Care Providers in Massachusetts,* 2nd Edition. Commonwealth of Massachusetts: Massachusetts Department of Health, 1995, p. 57. Reprinted with permission.

❖ Diaper and dress the child in clean dry clothing. Children should always wear outer clothing over a diaper to further contain urine or feces. Now you can hold the child close to you.

❖ Wash the child's hands with soap and water (or a disposable wipe). Help the child return to the group.

❖ Dispose of soiled items. Label and securely tie the bag for cloth diapers and put it out of children's reach for parents to take home. (Do not rinse diapers in a toilet; bulky stool in the cloth diaper, may, however, be emptied into the toilet.)

❖ Put soiled clothes in a labeled and securely tied plastic bag to be taken home. (Children should not handle soiled clothing.)

❖ Remove the disposable cover from the diapering surface and discard it into the lined, covered step can.

❖ Wash and rinse the diapering area with water (use soap if necessary), and then sanitize with bleach solution made fresh daily.

❖ Wash your own hands thoroughly with soap and running water.

❖ Record the diaper change. Report any concerns to parents (unusual color, odor, frequency, consistency, or rash).

Remain aware of the rest of the group as you change a diaper. Watch through the corner of your eye, listen, and use your sixth sense to recognize when you are needed. This is vital if you are the sole adult in a program.

Be sure your environment is safe. Use the checklist for safety in the changing area (see Chapter 8, Ensuring Children's Safety). Check each day to be sure that all children will be safe as they play while you change a diaper.

Schedule regular times to check children's diapers each day—of course, changing children in between as needed. *The National Health and Safety Performance Standards Guidelines for Out-of-Home Child Care Programs* recommends that diapers be checked at least hourly for wetness and feces.[2] Following this type of schedule will help you guide other children into activities that do not require your active participation, leaving you free to pay attention to the child you are changing.

---

[2] American Public Health Association and the American Academy of Pediatrics. *National Health and Safety Standards Guidelines for Out-of-Home Child Care Programs.* Arlington, VA: National Center for Education in Maternal and Child Health, 1992, p. 70.

"How can my space help children feel competent as they master the new skill of using the toilet?"

Think of the many ways you can arrange your bathroom space to encourage children to use the toilet and wash their hands. Here are are some ideas to consider.

Adapt your bathroom as necessary to help children feel more independent. If you have child-sized toilets and sinks, that's great. If not, offer children the option of using a potty chair that sits on the floor or a potty seat on the toilet. (*The National Health and Safety Performance Standards* recommend you provide child-sized toilets or safe and cleanable step aids and modified toilet seats secured to adult-sized toilets. *The Standards* discourage using potty chairs because they are difficult to maintain. If you use them, be sure you can clean and sanitize them easily.) There are many different types of potty seats designed to meet the needs of children with various disabilities. Families and therapists can advise you on selecting appropriate equipment. If you have a child in a wheelchair or using a walker, be sure to allow enough space in the bathroom. You'll also need handrails to make the transfer from a wheelchair to the toilet an easy one.

Provide steps so children can reach the sink, turn on the water, and wash their hands when they are through. Place paper towels close to the sink so children can dry their hands. Finally, display pictures of children doing a variety of activities, including using the toilet. (See Chapter 9, Promoting Children's Health, for more information about handwashing.)

Make the bathroom a pleasing place for you to be. Have a comfortable place to sit. Hang up a pretty picture. You will be spending lots of time there, and if you are relaxed, children will sense this and be more relaxed too.

Provide books about children using the toilet. Make your own books. Offer books such as *Going To The Potty* (Mr. Rogers). Children will enjoy and learn from reading about another child's feelings, successes, and accidents.

"How can I work with parents to support children as they learn to use the toilet?"

Be aware that parents—and you—are likely to have strong feelings about, and perhaps different strategies for toilet learning. One's approach to toilet learning is largely shaped by childhood experiences and culture. For example, many believe that teaching a child to use the toilet means the adult taking responsibility for getting the child to the bathroom at the right time. People with this idea begin toilet training a child around the child's first birthday. Others believe that learning to use the toilet should begin when a child is ready to assume responsibility for his or her own use of the toilet, typically around 30 months of age. Sometimes other issues are at stake. Ivan, for example, worked with a mother who toilet trained her son at 20 months—it was an area of his life where he could excel.

Ask parents how they are helping their child learn to use the toilet at home. Listen carefully, and try to understand families' perspectives when they do things differently than you do. Ask questions to help you understand what is going on.

Share your approach to toilet learning with "prospective families." Ask parents who are considering putting their child in your program what their approach to toilet learning is, or what they think it will be. Depending on the extent of your differences, parents may decide to look elsewhere for care or you may suggest they do so. More likely, though, your discussion will serve you both by alerting you to differences you will have to negotiate when the time comes.

Hold a parent meeting or offer a workshop about toilet learning. These activities usually are of interest to parents whose children are starting to use the toilet and to parents of soon-to-be users. Discuss the signs that indicate a child is ready to begin using the toilet. These signs include:

- ❖ staying dry for long periods of time;
- ❖ wanting to sit on the toilet with their clothes on;
- ❖ telling you they have urinated or had a bowel movement or are going to (though usually too late to get them to the bathroom in time);
- ❖ being able to remove their clothing by themselves or with a little assistance;
- ❖ being able to push when having a bowel movement; and
- ❖ saying they want to use the toilet and talking about their "pee" and "poop" or whatever words they have been taught at home.

Share with parents the steps you take to help a child learn to use the toilet. These steps generally include the items that follow.

- ❖ Watch for signs children are ready.
- ❖ Encourage children persistently and calmly, but without shame and undue pressure, to use the toilet.
- ❖ Remind children to go to the toilet frequently. That way they won't get so involved in what they are doing that they forget and have an accident. Take advantage of group potty time so children can see and learn from one another.
- ❖ Applaud children's success without overdoing it.
- ❖ Allow children to see what they have produced and invite them to help flush it away if they choose to.
- ❖ Treat accidents matter-of-factly.

Help families be realistic in their expectations of how toilet learning will go. Point out that accidents are par for the course and should be treated in a matter-of-fact way. Explain that even children who can use the toilet successfully may need to wear diapers at night for a time, or may temporarily regress in response to stresses in their lives. Explain that boys and girls differ in how readily they learn to use the toilet. Girls usually become successful "toilet users" at a younger age because they can more easily control voiding urine. Finally, remind parents that all children are different and that it is important not to expect one sibling's experience with toilet learning to be the same as another's.

Set a relaxed tone. Assure parents that over time, their children will learn to use the toilet. We all did.

Make resources available for parents who may be feeling a little confused or overwhelmed. Some parents will be easy-going about toilet learning, while others will want to learn everything about it that they can. Display books or articles you think would be helpful. Encourage parents to share their experiences with one another.

Negotiate differences in your approaches, if necessary. Keep in mind that, from a child's perspective, a sense of continuity is very helpful. Things don't have to be done exactly the same at home and in child care, but children need to know what to expect. For example, La Toya feels it is not realistic in a group setting for her to assume responsibility for getting a child to the toilet on time, even though parents may choose to do so at home. Usually she and parents decide together that a child will continue wearing diapers for a few more months at the program, even though the child goes diaperless during weekend days at home. La Toya's experience has been, "When I take time to work through differences with parents, children sense this and everything turns out just fine."

Discuss toilet learning with parents regularly. Exchange observations about what is happening at home and in child care. Share strategies that are particularly helpful to a child. Give parents encouragement as necessary. Above all, keep your sense of humor.

Post a chart or daily notes to back up your daily conversations. Include information about when a child last went to the toilet and whether he or she has had a bowel movement. Note any "accidents" that have occurred. Notes help create an awareness of patterns that may exist. They also serve as reminders to take home wet or soiled clothes and replace them with fresh items.

Helping Children Learn from Diapering and Toileting

In the charts that follow, we consider typical behaviors you may observe, what children may be experiencing, and how you might respond to promote learning.

Young Infants		
What You Observe	**What the Child May Be Experiencing**	**How You Can Respond**
Fussing or crying Squirming in your arms	He may be uncomfortable because his diaper is wet or soiled.	Check his diaper. If that is the problem, change it promptly to show him you are listening and care about his comfort. Promote a sense of self-respect and competence by inviting him to participate in the process. Explain: "I am going to pick you up now." Wait for him to look at you before doing so.
Looking at you as you change her diaper	She probably enjoys being with you. She may be curious about what you are doing. She may want to "talk" with you.	Look at her and smile. Talk with her about what you are doing. Explain: "I'm going to lay you down here. First, let's take off your purple socks." Reinforce the pleasure of interesting sounds and communicating with another person when you say to her: "Your snaps go pop, pop, pop."
Trying to roll over as you change his diaper	The paper covering the changing table may be scratchy. He may want to see something across the room. He may be protesting having to lie still.	Make the changing table's surface as comfortable as possible. Be sure there is a strap to keep the child from falling. Acknowledge his feelings: "I know it is hard for you to lie still." Offer him a job to hold his attention: "Will you please hold your clean diaper?"

Mobile Infants

What You Observe	What the Child May Be Experiencing	How You Can Respond
Resisting lying down on her back	As she begins to walk, she may be feeling so driven to be upright and explore that it is actually uncomfortable to be placed flat on her back.	Show that you understand how she feels by changing her in a standing position, if possible. Acknowledge her desire to be upright and exploring: "I know you want to keep moving, so we'll change you just as quickly as we can."
Reaching into his diaper to explore his bowel movement as you get ready to change him	He may be curious about what he has produced and is learning about it through his senses—the way he learns about everything else.	Explain that his "poop" is not for playing with, but for flushing away. Help him wash off his hands without making a big deal of it. Provide a variety of sensory experiences throughout the day, including some with smells.
Trying to fasten the buckles on her overalls after you change her	She may feel competent about her developing skills and want to participate in the changing process.	Acknowledge her efforts: "You just about have that buckle fastened." Offer help in a way that encourages her participation: "I'll hold this button part and you put the loop around it." If she is having trouble with the buckles, suggest that her parents dress her in clothes with easier closures, such as Velcro,™ so she can experience success. Offer her other opportunities to develop fine motor skills, such as turning the water off and on when she washes her hands and helping to open a new box of diapers.

Toddlers		
What You Observe	**What the Child May Be Experiencing**	**How You Can Respond**
Touching his genitals as he prepares to sit on the potty	He may be curious about his body and its various sensations. He may be exploring a new topic of interest—the difference between girls and boys—or just aiming!	Continue to help him accept and feel good about his body. Use the same words his family uses at home. Discuss with parents the words they use at home, and use the same words at your program.
Using the toilet successfully	She may be feeling pride and pleasure in being a "big girl."	Encourage a repeat performance by expressing your pleasure without overdoing it and adding unnecessary pressure. You might just say: "Good job!"
Wetting or soiling himself after using the toilet successfully	He may feel embarrassed or ashamed.	Take a matter-of fact approach: "Accidents happen. Let's clean you up." If they continue or occur with increasing frequency, talk with his parents about whether something at home or in child care is adding stress to his life. If possible, address the stress-producing situation.

Sharing Thoughts About
Diapering and Toileting

Dear Families:

If your child is changed six times a day for two-and-a-half years, he or she will have had a diaper change more than 5,400 times. Anything experienced 5,400 times is an important part of your child's life—and of yours. Over time, your child will be doing the growing and learning he or she needs to begin using the toilet—a milestone we will celebrate together!

We focus on diapering and toileting in our program because they are such rich opportunities for spending one-on-one time with your child in our group setting. Through these daily routines we can help your child learn to feel good about his or her body. We can also help your child feel proud and competent about using the toilet and about becoming more independent.

How We Can Work Together

❖ *Please provide us with fresh disposable diapers and dry clothes for your child.* This will free us to focus on your child's needs during diapering and toileting, rather than on searching for supplies.

❖ *Let's talk together about approaches to helping children learn to use the toilet.* How we each do this is, in large part, determined by our own childhood experiences and our culture. Talking together will let us build on the similarities in our approaches and work out any differences we may have.

❖ *Keep in touch with how things are going.* This will allow each of us to have a clear picture of how your child is doing. We can then make decisions about ways to give your child the support he or she needs.

❖ *Remember that accidents are to be expected.* Learning to use the toilet takes time. Even children who can use the toilet successfully may have accidents in response to stresses at home or in child care, such as the birth of a new sibling or the prolonged absence of the child's favorite caregiver. Having realistic expectations allows us to respond to accidents matter-of-factly and address issues causing stress, as necessary.

By keeping a sense of perspective and a sense of humor, we can give your child the time and support needed to learn to use the toilet.

Sincerely,

Algunas ideas sobre el cambio del pañal y sobre ir al baño

Estimadas familias:

Si a su hijo(a) se le cambia el pañal seis veces al día durante dos años y medio, quiere decir que a él/ella se le cambiará el pañal más de 5.400 veces. Cualquier clase de experiencia que tenga lugar 5.400 veces, constituye una parte importante de la vida tanto de su niño(a) como de la suya. En el debido tiempo, los niños crecen y aprenden lo que necesitan para comenzar a ir al baño. ¡Lo que celebraremos juntos!

En nuestro programa nos centramos en el cambio del pañal y el uso del baño por ser ricas oportunidades que tenemos en nuestro ambiente de grupo, de compartir tiempo en forma individual con su hijo(a). Mediante estas rutinas diarias podremos ayudarle a su niño(a), a aprender a sentirse a gusto con respecto a su propio cuerpo. También contribuiremos a que se sienta orgulloso(a) y competente para hacer uso del baño y con respecto a su mayor autonomía.

Cómo podemos trabajar juntos

* *Por favor traigan pañales desechables y una muda de ropa limpia para su niño(a).* Así, podremos centrarnos en las necesidades del niño, cuando necesite que se le cambie el pañal o ir al baño, en lugar de tener que buscar recursos.

* *Hablemos acerca de los enfoques para ayudar a los niños a utilizar el baño.* El enfoque de cada uno está, en gran parte, determinado por nuestras experiencias infantiles y nuestra cultura. Hablar de ello, nos permitirá trabajar con base en las similitudes de nuestros enfoques y resolver las posibles diferencias que tengamos.

* *Manténganse al tanto de cómo marchan las cosas.* Esto nos permitirá a todos, tener una idea clara de cómo le va a su niño(a). Luego, podremos tomar decisiones con respecto a las maneras en que podemos brindarle el apoyo que necesita.

* *Recuerden que pueden ocurrir accidentes.* Aprender a ir al baño toma tiempo. Incluso los niños que lo utilizan con éxito, pueden tener accidentes como reacción a las tensiones en el hogar o en la guardería, como en el caso del nacimiento de un hermano, o la ausencia prolongada de la persona preferida encargada del cuidado del niño. Tener expectativas realistas nos permitirá responder a los accidentes y ocuparnos de lo que pudiera causar tensión, en la medida en que sea necesario.

Al mantener tanto un sentido de perspectiva como sentido del humor, podremos ofrecerle a su niño(a) el tiempo y el apoyo necesario para aprender a ir al baño.

Les saluda atentamente,

Eating and Mealtimes

— ◈ —

"Here Matthew. Will you please carry these spoons over to the table?" asks Mercedes. "We need them to eat our lunch." Matthew takes two spoons from Mercedes and reaches up to put them on the edge of the kitchen table. He climbs up on a chair. "My like beans," says Matthew, as Mercedes spoons some rice and beans on his plate. "Me too," says Mercedes as she sits down next to him.

— ◈ —

Eating involves much more than providing fuel for our bodies. Mealtimes and related activities—such as setting the table, washing hands before sitting down to eat, carrying on a conversation with others, and brushing teeth—give children opportunities to develop self-help, communication, and social skills. Mealtimes are also times to practice fine motor skills and develop good nutrition and health habits.

When Linda holds Julio in her arms to give him his bottle, she is telling him, "You can trust me to take good care of you." When Janet puts a plastic dish of mashed sweet potato and a spoon on Jasmine's high chair tray, she is saying, "Go ahead. Here's a chance to practice feeding yourself." When La Toya talks with children about how the green beans are the same color as the playdough they made, reminds them that their chairs are for sitting on, and helps them to brush their teeth, she is teaching concepts, social skills, and supporting their development of healthy habits.

Eating and mealtimes also offer opportunities to build on your partnership with families. At home, the foods families eat reflect personal tastes as well as the family's culture or heritage. Parents need to know that in your program, the meals their children eat also stay within the family culture (and meet the children's nutritional needs, too). In addition, for children younger than three, there are special eating issues that you and parents must discuss together. These issues may include nursing, weaning, introducing solid foods, allergies, and what to bring to child care for a child's lunch.

Questions to Consider

You'll have to make many decisions about mealtimes and eating. Here are some questions and suggestions that can help you.

"How can I work with parents to be sure there is continuity between mealtimes in the program and what children are used to at home?"

Communicating with families is necessary to create familiar and pleasant mealtimes. Here are some suggestions for you to consider.

Recognize that certain topics can call up very deep feelings in parents and you. Depending on children's ages, discuss topics such as nursing, weaning, and introducing new foods at the very beginning of your relationship with families. Respect parents' wishes and follow them whenever possible. For example, do not give extra bottles to an infant whose mother wants to continue nursing. If differences arise, try to negotiate with parents. Welcome mothers to come to the program at any time to nurse their infants. Provide a comfortable place where they can be together without interruption.

Talk with each child's parents about what their child eats at home and in child care. When appropriate, discuss parents' plans for introducing solid foods. Ask parents about foods their toddlers eat at home. Share your program's menus. If parents provide their child's lunches, offer suggestions of safe and nutritious foods to bring. Respect and follow parents' special food requests as closely as possible, whether for health, cultural, or personal preference reasons.

Keep and post records of what and how much children eat during the day. Giving parents a brief note with this information will help them plan their children's meals and snacks for the rest of the afternoon and evening.

Work hand-in-hand with families when it comes to introducing foods to infants. With the knowledge and approval of parents, introduce new foods gradually. Children need time (usually five days) to be sure that they aren't showing signs of allergic reactions.

Experts recommend introducing semi-solid foods (such as rice cereal) first, when infants are at least four months old and their digestive tracts are able to break down solid foods. Then, at about six to eight months, you can offer fruits and vegetables. At about eight to nine months, most infants are ready to taste foods with lumps. You can give table foods at about nine months, and offer eight- to ten-month-olds finger foods so they can begin feeding themselves.

"What health and safety concerns do I need to consider?"

Be sure families know you take health and safety concerns seriously. Here are some points to consider and to share with families, whether you provide food for children in your program or parents prepare and bring food for their child.

Avoid serving foods that may cause choking. Children under three should not eat certain foods because they present choking hazards. Hot dogs and peanuts are the most frequent causes of choking in children younger than three. Other foods that can cause a young child to choke include: raw carrots, raisins (and similar dried fruit such as cherries or cranberries), popcorn, whole grapes, blueberries, whole olives, corn, uncooked peas, nuts, peanut butter, crumbly cookies or crackers, jelly beans, and hard candy.

Follow practices that promote good nutrition. Other food health precautions include the following.

- ❖ Avoid giving infants honey, because it may carry bacteria that can cause food poisoning in infants.
- ❖ Don't substitute low fat or skim milk for whole milk until children are 18–24 months old, because it has too much protein for younger children.
- ❖ For digestive reasons, avoid giving infants under 12 months white table sugar, artificial sweeteners, corn syrup, eggs, fried foods, shellfish, raw onions, and processed meats.
- ❖ Delay offering infants tomatoes and pineapple during the first year of life. The high acidity in these foods can harm delicate mouth tissues.

Be aware of any allergies that children may have. If you observe or learn from parents that a child is allergic to a particular food (chocolate, strawberries, peanut butter, and tofu are among the most common food allergies), make sure this information is circulated and posted where everyone—including volunteers—can see it.

"How can I organize mealtimes so that I can sit down and talk with the children instead of running around?"

An important part of children's mealtime experiences is being with you. You can model good manners and the pleasures of social interaction over food. For young infants, who need to be fed on demand and to be held when you give them a bottle, mealtime is one-on-one time with you. For a group of mobile infants, toddlers, or a mixed-age group, family-style dining is a good way to organize mealtimes. In this arrangement, everyone sits together around the table—on chairs, in high chairs, or on your lap, depending on children's ages—so they can see and interact with each other. In programs where food is provided, it can be served in plastic dishes. You help children, as necessary, allowing those who can to help themselves. Alternatively, when children bring their lunches from home, you all can sit together and eat. Here are some suggestions to help make family-style dining a positive experience for children—and for you.

Plan ahead. Think about how to arrange your tables to make mealtimes manageable, based on the number of tables you need, your staffing, and the age of the children. If you are in a setting with other adults and are caring for mobile infants and toddlers, you may want to serve meals at child-sized tables that seat three or four children and one adult. If you are the only adult in the setting, consider seating yourself and the children together at one large table so you can participate and oversee things. Be sure to have everything you need on hand—food, plates, spoons, and so forth. This way you won't have to leave the table to look for missing items.

Create a calm and pleasant atmosphere. Transitions that help set a quiet tone include reading a book or doing another quiet activity. Attractive placemats tell children that mealtimes are special.

Keep waiting time as brief as possible. Invite one or two children to help you set the table while others are playing. Have the food ready when the children get to the table. If hungry children have to wait, confusion and conflicts are bound to occur.

Model good manners. Say "please" and "thank-you," and encourage children to do the same to you and to one another. Ask children to wait to begin eating until everyone is served. Be flexible about this, however, since the younger the child, the harder it will be to wait.

Invite parents to join their children for snacks and meals whenever they can. With extra hands available to help, each child can get more attention. Having family members present can also ease separation and help children make the connection between eating at home and in child care.

Make cleaning up as easy as possible. Spills and messes are bound to occur. What can you do to focus on the children rather than on keeping everything neat and tidy? You can locate your eating space in an area with an easy-to-clean floor, have the children wear bibs, place extra napkins and paper towels nearby, and invite children to help clean up spills. These are simple solutions to help you remember what's really important.

Encourage relaxed, friendly conversation. Talk together during mealtimes about familiar topics of interest to the children, such as the taste and smells of the food you are eating, activities you did earlier in the day, or plans for the afternoon Encourage children to let you know what they want and need during mealtimes.

Create an after-meal ritual with mobile infants and toddlers. For example, encourage children to stay at the table and talk with each other until everyone has finished. If the children can't wait, let them leave the table to brush their teeth or work on a puzzle until all have finished the meal.

Consider the best time for you to eat. Although you want to be a good model for children, you may find that trying to eat at the same time you're supervising a group at the table is too much. You may prefer having your lunch during a more quiet time, which is certainly understandable. Janet has figured out a compromise that works for her. She eats some of her lunch with the children and saves the rest for later while the children are napping.

"How can I promote children's growing independence during snack and mealtimes?"

When children leave the table, they should have had enough to eat. They should also feel good about themselves and about their growing abilities. Here are some ways you can promote these positive feelings.

Use plates and eating utensils that are unbreakable, safe, and easy to handle. Small plastic pitchers for pouring juice or milk and plastic serving bowls encourage children to serve themselves. Special seats, utensils, deep-sided bowls, and mugs with two handles are adaptations that can help children with special needs to be independent, too.

Avoid struggling over food. Encourage children to try new foods, but don't force them to eat something they really do not want. Talk about new foods, serve them in attractive ways, and taste everything yourself. Don't worry if toddlers eat just one or two foods at a time. Research has shown that they will get the nutrients they need over the course of a week or even a month——if not in a single meal.

Encourage children to participate in whatever ways are appropriate for their level of development.
Place an infant seated on your lap so he can hear and see the other children. Offer a mobile infant a chance to use her fingers to feed herself. Invite toddlers to help you set the table and do other mealtime-related tasks.

Offer activities that promote new mealtime skills throughout the day. For example, include plates and eating utensils in the dramatic play area. Toddlers can role-play mealtime events. You can also provide small pitchers and cups for water play. Children can use these to practice pouring liquids.

Recognize children's skills and new accomplishments. Don't forget to make a positive comment when you see a child just learning to hold a bottle, drink from a cup, or spread cottage cheese on a cracker. Your praise can encourage children to improve their skills and learn new ones.

Helping Children Learn from Eating and Mealtimes

In the charts that follow, we consider typical behaviors you may observe, what children may be experiencing, and how you might respond to promote their learning.

Young Infants		
What You Observe	**What the Child May Be Experiencing**	**How You Can Respond**
Fussing	He may be hungry.	Set the infant on your lap as you give him a bottle. From that position, he can experience the sights, sounds, and smells of mealtime.
Cooing or babbling while eating a banana	She is expressing pleasure and interest in what is happening.	Talk with her about what's going on: "We're having some banana for snack today."
Reaching in his bowl to grab a handful of mashed sweet potatoes; tasting and smearing the food all over his high chair tray	He is exploring the taste and texture of this food.	Even if it makes a mess of face, hair, and high chair, you'll want to encourage touching and tasting as a way to learn. You may suggest he use a spoon, but don't be surprised if he continues to eat with his hands.

Mobile Infants

What You Observe	What the Child May Be Experiencing	How You Can Respond
Throwing the peach slice you hand him on the floor or turning his body away	He may be saying that he has had enough to eat or doesn't like peaches.	Ask if he has finished eating. Offer him another peach slice. If he still is not interested, wipe his hands and face and guide him to another activity.
Grabbing a piece of sandwich from another child	She may not know how to ask for something she wants or how to share.	Explain that the sandwich belongs to another child. "That's Eileen's sandwich. Here's one for you."
Getting up from the table	He has finished eating.	Help him think about what to do next. "I guess you're finished eating. Let's clean up and wipe your hands and face. Then you can play."

Toddlers

What You Observe	What the Child May Be Experiencing	How You Can Respond
Watching as you set the table	She is curious about what you are doing.	Give her a way to participate. "Let's wash your hands. Then you can help me put the napkins and plates on the table."
Pouring juice carefully and eating cooked vegetables with a spoon	He is proud of serving and feeding himself.	Build his confidence by commenting on his growing skills: "Good job! You ate all your vegetables with your spoon!"
Finishing her milk and the last bit of food on her plate	She has finished eating and may still be hungry.	Ask if she wants more food, and if so, provide it. If not, remind her of what to do: "Put your plate in the dirty plate bin. Then you can wash your hands and face and brush your teeth." Encourage her to do a quiet activity until everyone has finished eating.

— ❈ —

Sharing Thoughts About
Eating and Mealtimes

Dear Families:

Picture your child eating a meal or snack in child care. What is he or she experiencing? For one thing, your child is getting the kinds of foods he or she needs to be healthy and strong. But there is so much more. Eating snacks and meals—and for older children, doing related activities such as setting the table, cleaning up, and brushing their teeth after eating—give your child a chance to feel cared for, and to develop self-help, communication, and social skills. Mealtime is also a chance for children to begin practicing good nutrition and health habits.

Children's experiences and the attitudes they form today will help shape their eating habits in the future. By modeling healthy practices and making eating a pleasurable and social time, together we can lay the groundwork for nutritional and enjoyable eating for the rest of their lives.

How We Can Work Together

❖ *You are welcome to join us for a snack or meal whenever you can*. Your child will love having you with us. So will we! In addition, you'll have a chance to see how we do things so you can ask questions and make suggestions. Of course, if you are nursing your child, please come anytime. We will find a comfortable place where you can feed your baby without interruption.

❖ *Please share with us what your child experiences during mealtimes at home*. What does your child eat and drink? What kinds of things do you talk about? How does your child participate? This kind of information will help us give your child a sense of continuity by talking about family meals and serving some of the same foods.

❖ *Give us any information we need to keep your child healthy*. Let us know, for example, whether your child has any allergies or perhaps a tendency to choke. Keep us informed of any changes. Check to be sure we post this information so that any adult working in our program who may feed the children will know it, too.

❖ *Please ask us for menus and ideas for mealtimes*. Sometimes it's hard to come up with ideas for lunches. We'll be glad to give you some tips. We welcome your ideas as well.

Together, we can make mealtimes an enjoyable and valuable learning experience for your child.

Sincerely,

Algunas ideas acerca de
la comida y las horas de comer

Estimadas familias:

Imagine a su hijo en la guardería comiendo o merendando. ¿Qué es lo que experimenta? Para empezar, está recibiendo alimentos necesarios para mentenerse fuerte y saludable. Pero, se trata de mucho más. Comer y merendar —y para los niños mayorcitos, llevar a cabo otras actividades relacionadas como poner la mesa, recoger y limpiar, y lavarse los dientes después de comer— les brinda a los niños tanto la oportunidad de sentir que se les atiende, como de adquirir autonomía, desarrollar la comunicación y destrezas sociales. Las horas de comer, también les brindan a los niños la oportunidad de comenzar a practicar buenos hábitos de nutrición y salud.

Las experiencias de los niños y las actitudes que adopten hoy en día, les ayudarán a conformar sus hábitos alimenticios futuros. Al modelar prácticas saludables y convertir la hora de comer en un tiempo placentero y de socialización, juntos podremos darle los cimientos a una alimentación nutritiva y grata para el resto de sus vidas.

Cómo podemos trabajar juntos

❖ *Ustedes son bienvenidos a compartir con nosotros una merienda o comida cuando puedan hacerlo.* A sus hijos les encantará que ustedes estén con nosotros. ¡Y también a nosotros! Además, ustedes tendrán la oportunidad de ver lo que hacemos y cómo, y podrán hacernos preguntas y sugerencias. En nuestro salón, encontraremos un lugar en el que se pueda alimentar a su bebé sin interrupciones.

❖ *Por favor, compartan con nosotros las experiencias de los niños en el hogar a la hora de comer.* ¿Qué come y bebe su hijo(a)? ¿De qué hablan? ¿Cómo participa su hijo(a)? Esta clase de información nos permitirá ofrecerle a los niños un sentido de continuidad al hablar de las horas de comer familiares y servir algunas de las mismas comidas.

❖ *Proveánnos la información necesaria para mantener saludable a su hijo(a).* Déjennos saber si, por ejemplo, su niño(a) tiene alguna alergia o, quizá, tendencia a ahogarse, y manténgannos informados sobre cualquier cambio. Verifiquen, para estar seguros, que exhibimos esta información, de manera que cualquier adulto que trabaje en nuestro programa y que pudiera alimentar a su hijo(a), también esté al tanto.

❖ *Soliciten menús e ideas para las horas de comer.* A veces, es difícil imaginar qué almuerzos nutritivos disfrutará su hijo(a). Nos encantaría hacerle unas cuantas sugerencias, así como recibir sus ideas.

Juntos, podremos convertir las horas de comer en experiencias de aprendizaje gratas y valiosas para todos nosotros.

Les saluda atentamente,

Sleeping and Naptime

— ◼ —

Barbara notices Leo lying on the blue pillows in the reading corner rubbing his eyes. "Leo, you look a little sleepy. Your daddy told me you didn't sleep very well last night." Leo looks up at her. "I think maybe you could use an early nap today." Barbara checks in with Carol who is making playdough with three children. Carol says they are almost finished and that she will watch things while Barbara takes Leo into the nap room. Barbara goes over and picks Leo up. "Let's go sit together in the rocking chair."

— ◼ —

Sleeping and naptime ensure that children get the rest they need during their active day in child care. Even for those who do not sleep, naptime can serve as a break from group life. It gives children some relaxed time on their own to rest or look at a book. Naptime also provides a quiet time when you can relax, meet with colleagues, and refocus your attention and energy so you can be more available to children.

In addition to meeting children's physical needs, sleeping and naptime also give children of all ages an opportunity to experience trust in their world and in themselves. When Barbara rocks Leo to sleep, and Abby wakes up in the familiar setting of her own crib at Brooks's house with her blanket from home, they experience their world as safe and predictable. When you give individual children the support and time they need to fall asleep and wake up, they learn to trust themselves as they negotiate the path from being awake to asleep and back again.

Finally, discussing sleeping and naptime with families gives you the opportunity to strengthen your relationship. You can share information about a child's patterns of falling asleep and waking up, exchange strategies about helping a child fall asleep, or work through differences you may have on issues such as whether a child should be awakened if he or she sleeps past a certain time.

Questions to Consider

How will you set the stage for sleeping and naptime in your program? Here are some questions and suggestions to guide your thinking as you make decisions.

"How can I create an environment that encourages sleeping?"

An environment that is too stimulating can make it difficult for children to fall asleep. Here are some suggestions of ways to lessen stimulation and promote sleep.

Make space where children can sleep quietly and safely. If children sleep in a separate room, it should be quiet and well-ventilated. If children sleep in your main room, consider playing soft, soothing music to cover any background noise. Arrange cribs to create a sleeping space, rather than putting them around the room's edges. This arrangement will help protect children from over-stimulation and free more space for other activities. Set up cribs or mats three feet apart and place children head to foot to discourage the spread of germs. Check your state and local policies for further guidance, since some require a separate sleeping room. (See Chapters 8 and 9 for additional information about naptime safety and health concerns.)

Be sure each child sleeps in the same place each day. Infants will feel more secure when they are placed in the same crib day after day. Two-year-olds will be comforted by the routine of being on the same mat or cot in the same location.

Provide children with clean sheets and blankets. You may provide and launder these regularly or parents may do so, depending on your situation.

Encourage families to bring in comfort objects from home, such as a child's blanket or stuffed animal. Holding onto these reminders of home is soothing and can help children feel secure enough to fall asleep.

"When and for how long should children sleep each day?"

From birth, children differ in how much sleep they need, how soundly they sleep, and the regularity of their sleep patterns. They also differ in the length of time it takes them to wake up and in their moods upon awakening.

Typically, the younger a child is, the more sleep he or she needs. Infants such as Julio need more sleep than toddlers like Matthew. Children also need to be able to sleep according to their personal schedules. Sometime during their second year, children change from sleeping in the morning and afternoon to sleeping only during the afternoon. During this transition, two naps a day can be too many, while one isn't enough. This can be a challenging time when children can easily become overtired and adults frustrated. It is helpful if you can remain flexible and plan your day to give children the option of one or two sleep periods. Over time, most two year olds such as Gena and Valisha will typically sleep one time each day during regularly scheduled after-lunch naps.

"Why do some children find it so difficult to fall asleep?"

Do you know a child who fights sleep? The reasons for this are many and depend in large part on a child's temperament and stage of development. Here are some common reasons for resisting sleep.

Sleeping means being still. Infants on the verge of walking and those who are new walkers want very much to be upright and to move. Being picked up and placed in a crib to sleep is exactly what they do not want. You may find children at this stage standing in their cribs protesting sleep and sometimes moving their legs as if they are walking, even as they fall asleep.

Sleeping means "losing touch" with the world. The world is filled with many fascinating things to do. Some children find it hard at times to "disengage" and fall asleep.

Falling asleep can be experienced as a kind of separation. When children close their eyes and fall asleep they may feel as if they are saying "good-bye" to the people and things in their world. Children like Leo, who are struggling with separation, often fight sleep.

Toddlers may be asserting their independence and trying to act more grown up. Refusing to nap when you ask them to is one way toddlers can take charge and demonstrate their grow-ing independence. They may also be very aware of older siblings who no longer nap and may even say, "Napping is for babies."

Overstimulation, stress, and being overtired can make it hard to relax and fall asleep. Have you ever found it hard to unwind after a particularly busy or stressful day? Or when you are overtired? Children, too, can become so wound up that they find it difficult to slow down and sleep.

Stalling gives a child more one-on-one time with his or her special adult. Some children want or need extra attention. They learn that not cooperating at naptime is a way of engaging an adult.

Children may sense the tension of the adult who wants them to sleep. Have you ever noticed that the more you want children to nap, the less likely some of them will do so? As Barbara has discovered, "It's like they have radar. They can sense my worry that they won't fall asleep and this makes it hard for them to relax."

A child may not be tired. Some children need less sleep than others. Knowing this, you can offer alternative options to sleeping, such as playing quietly.

"What can I do to help assure children get the sleep they need?"

Here are some suggestions of strategies you can use to help children get the rest they need.

Take children outdoors each day. Daily exercise and time in the fresh air and sunshine help children relax enough to go to sleep.

Watch for cues throughout the day that tell you a child is tired. The better you know a child, the easier it will be to tell when that child needs a nap. Children's cues may include crying their "I am tired" cry, rubbing their eyes, or being more fussy, cranky, or easily frustrated than usual.

Establish a regular routine. Create a relaxed mood by planning a quiet activity—such as reading a story or playing soft music—before naptime. This will help toddlers quiet down and know that it will soon be time for a nap.

Develop naptime rituals that you do each day with individual children to help them fall asleep. Talk with families about what they do at home so you can offer similar routines. These may include singing a lullaby, playing a tape of a parent singing or reading, rocking with a child for a few minutes, or rubbing a child's back. For some children, the routines may be simply putting them in their cribs and saying, "Night night," or "Sleep well."

Be aware of children's individual styles as you plan naptime. Helping a group of children sleep is a bit like doing a juggling act. Knowing how individual children fall asleep and wake up can help you decide how best to manage this routine. Barbara and her co-workers at the Head Start Center find it works best to help the soundest sleepers get settled first and then focus on the children who need more attention and time.

"What do I do when a child cries at naptime?"

There really is no magic formula about how long to let a child cry before picking him or her up. How you respond to a child who cries depends in large part on what you know about that individual child. Here are some points to consider when faced with a crying child at naptime.

Look for patterns (with families' help) to understand why a child may cry at naptime. Is a child crying to release tension before he can fall asleep? Is he overtired? Is he fearful? Comparing notes on a child's behavior at bedtime and naptime can help you and families better understand the reasons for crying. As a result, you and they are more able to address the child's needs.

Listen to the intensity of the cry. Is the child letting off steam or merely protesting for a few minutes? Is the crying winding down? Does the child seem to be in serious distress? Does the child stop crying and settle down if you sit with him for a few minutes? Are things going along relatively smoothly, or has there been any upset at home? Also, consider the effect of crying on other children. Will it upset any children or start other children crying? Your answers will help you decide how long to let a child cry.

Avoid making naptime a battleground. When children associate naptime with tension and anger, it is only natural that they should cry.

"What do I do when a child doesn't sleep?"

Perhaps the most important thing you can do is to expect that there will be days when one or more children aren't going to fall asleep as planned. While it is perfectly natural to look forward to a break when children are sleeping and to feel frustrated when they don't easily fall asleep, your tension will make it more difficult for children to relax. By trying not to communicate your impatience, you make it more likely that children will relax and fall asleep.

Again, reflect on what a child might be experiencing to help you decide how to respond. Try to understand why a child is having trouble sleeping to help you decide how to help the child. For example, Grace is aware that Willard is just about to begin walking on his own. She knows it is hard for him to stop to sleep. She has been making an extra effort to do quiet, relaxing activities when she sees he is getting tired. Yesterday, when he didn't sleep at all and became very cranky, she talked to a colleague at the Kendrick Center who reminded her that he was going through a stage that wouldn't last forever. In another example, when Matthew recently had trouble sleeping, Mercedes realized that, because it had been cold and rainy for several days, he had been cooped up inside. The next day, with a cold rain falling, she got out the cloth tunnel and made up a jumping game which Matthew loved. After the exercise, sleep came easily.

Plan your day so you can do what's necessary and get a break, even if some of the children don't sleep. On days when you need to do something such as attend a staff meeting or meet with a parent, try to arrange for a substitute to watch the children at naptime. This can help you feel less pressure over naps and allow you to meet your other responsibilities. In center-based programs and family child care programs where there is more than one adult, rotating the times each adult goes for lunch permits everyone to get a break, even if some children stay awake. As some toddlers begin outgrowing naps, many programs make a rule that children should lie on their mats at least 10 to 15 minutes. Toddlers often will fall asleep once they are quiet. Children who do not sleep are encouraged to read or play quietly so they don't wake the other children.

Take a look at the big picture, if no one sleeps. If, day after day, none of the children are sleeping, there is usually something program wide that needs adjusting. Here are some questions to ask yourself: Are you giving children enough time for outdoor play and exercise each day? Have you planned your daily schedule so that naptime is too early? Do you give children ample wind-down time after lunch and a busy morning? If answering these questions still doesn't help the problem, try asking a colleague to observe. Often another pair of eyes can help you see things you may not be able to see on your own.

"How can I work with families around sleep issues?"

Here are some suggestions of ways to work together to make sleeping a positive experience for children.

Exchange information each day about children's sleep patterns. You and children's parents each need to know how long a child slept, when he or she last slept, and any changes in sleep patterns, so you can plan accordingly. Knowing Matthew had a restless night means Mercedes can be on the lookout for signs of tiredness and offer a quiet activity or an earlier-than-usual nap. Knowing Abby had a two-hour nap means her father might stop to do some food shopping on the way home, since Abby is well rested.

Ask families about how their child sleeps at home. In some families, children sleep on a schedule and always in their cribs. In other families, children may sleep whenever they fall asleep and wherever they are. Some children may sleep on a mat on the floor or in a hammock. Knowing children's habits can help you plan so that you can offer as much continuity and comfort as possible.

Work together to resolve differences. Some parents may ask you to limit the amount of time their child sleeps at the program so he or she will go to sleep easily at home. You may feel it is not right to awaken a sleeping child. Other parents may want their child to sleep a long time during the day so they can have time with him or her at night. You may feel that children need to go to bed early so they are rested when they arrive at your program. To avoid a power struggle, talk about your differences and come up with a plan that is workable for both of you—always considering the child's best interests.

Be available to support parents whose children have sleep problems. Assure parents that sleep problems are common—especially during the second year of life—and that they pass. Explain that parents need not worry that their child will suffer from lack of sleep; children do get the sleep they need. Encourage parents to talk with one another so they can share experiences and strategies and know they are not alone.

Helping Children Learn from Sleeping and Naptime

In the charts below, we consider typical behaviors you may observe, what children may be experiencing, and how you might decide to respond to promote their learning.

Young Infants		
What You Observe	**What the Child May Be Experiencing**	**How You Can Respond**
Rubbing his eyes	He may be sleepy.	Describe what you think he is feeling: "You look sleepy." Though he will not yet understand your words, when you respond to his needs he will learn that he can trust you. Then consider what this child needs to fall asleep. For example, does he want to sit in your lap in the rocking chair and rock? Or does he need to lie in his crib and cry for a few minutes to release tension before he sleeps?
Falling asleep in the stroller during a neighborhood walk	She is tired and needs to sleep.	Let her sleep. Even though she may not be learning as she sleeps, she will be more alert and better able to take advantage of other learning opportunities when she awakes and is rested.
Waking up crying	He may be hungry or uncomfortable because he is wet. Or he may need some comforting as he makes the transition between being asleep and awake.	Talk gently and pick him up. Check his diaper and offer him a bottle if you think he is hungry. Assure him that everything is all right: "You will be OK. Shall we read a book together while you wake up?"

Mobile Infants

What You Observe	What the Child May Be Experiencing	How You Can Respond
Protesting strongly when you put him in his crib—even though you know he should be tired	He may be so driven to be up and moving and doing that he is feeling uncomfortably restrained.	Describe what you think he is feeling: "It's hard to stop playing." Sing a soothing song or rub his back gently. Offer him his "lovey" from home if he has one. Explain: "Now it's time to rest. Later you can play some more." Let him cry for a brief time if he needs to do so to wind down. If his protests persist and he shows no sign of settling down, you may want to get him up and let him play. Offer him a nap later in the day. He will sleep when he needs to sleep.
Stirring and beginning to call for you after sleeping for only a short time	She may be rested and ready to get up. Or she may still need more sleep.	If you think she is ready to wake up, get her up and spend some quiet time with her until the others wake up. If you think her sleep has been interrupted and that she is still tired, help her fall back to sleep by gently laying her back down and patting her back.
Appearing to be very sleepy soon after arriving at child care	He may have a long commute to child care or he may not have slept well the night before. He may be in between needing one nap and two.	Adapt your plans to allow for his sleeping. For example, change your morning plans as necessary so you can offer him a nap. Be sure there is stroller space for him if he gets tired during a walk. If he can sleep when he is tired, he can enjoy and take advantage of various experiences when he is more rested.

Toddlers		
What You Observe	What the Child May Be Experiencing	How You Can Respond
Squirming on her mat and having trouble getting settled	She may need to go to the bathroom. Alternatively, she may be overstimulated by sounds and sights in the room.	Ask if she needs to go to the bathroom and let her go if necessary. Dim the lights and play quiet soothing music. Sit with her and talk quietly as you rub her back or cover her with a blanket. Be sure she has her "lovey" from home.
Moving off his cot and making a lot of noise that disturbs the other children	He may not feel tired or may need help settling down. He may be asserting his growing independence by testing to see how you will respond.	Step in immediately. Explain: "The other children are sleeping. Now it is time to be quiet and lie down on your cot so you don't wake them up." Help him relax and settle down.
Staying awake at naptime	She may have outgrown the need for a nap.	Encourage her to lie down on her cot for 10 to 15 minutes to see if she will fall asleep. If she remains awake, explain: "You can play quietly or read on your mat until the other children wake up."

Sharing Thoughts About
Sleeping and Naptime

Dear Families:

Having enough sleep makes it more likely that children will enjoy and benefit from learning opportunities throughout the day.

In addition, sleeping and naptime offer important lessons about trust and being competent as children learn to move from being awake to falling asleep and being awake again. As we—with your help—learn your child's individual style of preparing for sleep and waking up, we can offer the support he or she needs. For example, while some children like to be rocked or have their backs rubbed, others prefer to be left alone as they drift into sleep.

How We Can Work Together

❖ *We can communicate each day.* By keeping each other informed about the length of time your child sleeps and any changes in his or her sleeping patterns, we each can plan better. For example, if we know your child didn't sleep well the night before, we can offer an early nap, if necessary. If you know your child took a long nap and is well rested, you may decide it is all right to stop and buy groceries on the way home. Do you think your child is getting enough rest during the day? Let us know.

❖ *Please share with us ways that you help your child fall asleep.* If we know, for example, that you sing a certain song or rock your child for a few minutes before placing him or her in the crib, we can do the same thing. This will help your child experience some of the safe and secure feelings he or she has with you and make it easier to fall asleep.

❖ *Please bring your child's "lovey" from home.* Having a special blanket, stuffed animal, or other object from home can make falling asleep easier for a child. If your child has such an object, please label it with your child's name and bring it in. We'll take care it doesn't get lost and help you remember to take it home at night.

Together, we can help make sleeping and naptime a pleasant and restful experience for your child.

Sincerely,

Algunas ideas sobre el sueño y la siesta

Estimadas familias:

Dormir suficiente tiempo hace más probable que los niños disfruten y se beneficien de las oportunidades de aprendizaje diarias, pues además de satisfacer la necesidad de descansar, el sueño y la siesta les permiten a los niños sentirse confiados y competentes, a medida que aprenden a estar despiertos, a dormirse y a despertarse nuevamente. Con su ayuda, aprenderemos sobre el estilo individual en que su niño(a) se prepara para dormir y despertarse, y podremos brindarle el apoyo que necesita. Por ejemplo, mientras que a algunos niños les gusta que los mezan o que les acaricien la espalda, otros prefieren quedarse solos mientras se duermen.

Cómo podemos trabajar juntos

❖ *Podemos comunicarnos diariamente*. Al mantenernos informados sobre la cantidad de tiempo que duerme su hijo(a) y sobre cualquier cambio en sus patrones de sueño, tanto usted como nosotros podremos planificar mejor. Por ejemplo, si su niño(a) no durmió bien la noche anterior, podríamos ofrecerle una siesta más temprano. Si, en cambio, durmió una larga siesta, usted podría decidir ir al supermercado en su camino a casa, ya que su hijo(a) habrá descansado suficiente tiempo.

❖ *Por favor compartan con nosotros la manera en que usted le ayuda a su hijo(a) a dormir*. Si, por ejemplo, usted le canta cierta canción, o le mece por unos cuantos minutos antes de colocarlo en su cuna, podremos hacer lo mismo. Así, su niño (a) podrá experimentar la seguridad y tranquilidad que siente con ustedes y le será más fácil dormirse.

❖ *Le damos la bienvenida a su objeto "preferido"*. Si su niño(a) está apegado a algún objeto en especial, márquenlo con el nombre del niño y tráiganlo. Se lo cuidaremos para que no se pierda y se le recordaremos a la hora de irse a su hogar.

Juntos, podremos convertir el sueño y la siesta en una grata experiencia para su hijo(a).

Les saluda atentamente,

Getting Dressed

— ◈ —

As Brooks lifts Abby's wet shirt over her head, Abby breaks away and runs to the other side of the room. Brooks walks over and says firmly, "We need to put a dry shirt on you. It's cold in here." She leans over Abby and begins to put on her shirt. "This will only take a few seconds," she says as Abby tries to pull away. "Help me count one . . . two . . . three. There, we are done."

— ◈ —

Dressing offers pleasant—and sometimes challenging—moments to enjoy being with infants and toddlers. You can use these moments to promote cooperation, introduce names of body parts and colors, give children the chance to develop and practice self-help skills, and help them learn to make decisions.

Young infants often may lie on their changing tables as you do the work of pulling legs through pants and freeing an arm from a sleeve. However, they are making some important discoveries: about parts of their bodies; where their bodies begin and end; and even about trusting others. Over time, they will become more active partners in dressing.

Mobile infants like Willard and Abby, who love to move and do, may often protest having to stop and be dressed. How can you deal with their protests? Try to involve them in the process. If their protests continue, be firm, respectful, and finish dressing them as quickly as possible. Also, keep your sense of humor, even if you turn around to find a child pulling off the overalls you just struggled to pull on. (Undressing is easier than dressing for children. With practice, they will develop the fine motor skills they'll use one day to put their clothes on.)

Toddlers may also protest the restrictions of dressing. Yet, as they practice new skills—such as pulling on their socks and opening and closing Velcro™ fasteners—and learn names for parts of their bodies and colors of their clothes, they feel proud and competent. In addition, when you ask them to choose between changing their paint-spattered shirt now or after snack, they begin to see themselves as capable decision-makers.

Questions to Consider

Here are some questions and suggestions to guide your daily decision-making.

"How can I use dressing to promote children's sense of competence and independence?"

Your challenge is to promote children's confidence in their own abilities, while sometimes needing to dictate exactly how they will move their bodies as you dress them. Here are some strategies to help you meet this challenge.

Talk with children about what you are doing. As you describe what is going on, introduce vocabulary and concepts such as *sleeves, corduroy, red, in, out,* and *through.* Describing what is happening gives children some sense of control.

Let children participate in whatever way they can. The extent of children's participation will vary greatly, depending on their level of development. While Jasmine might lift her arm as Janet puts on her sweater, Valisha and Jonisha may be able to put on their shoes and secure the Velcro™ fasteners.

Step in to prevent frustration when children attempt a task that may be too difficult. Although children really try very hard to master new skills, sometimes they choose a skill that is way beyond them. For example, Jonisha insists on buttoning her sweater by herself, like her older brother Daniel does. When she can't do this, she becomes frustrated. At this point, she needs La Toya to step in, free her from the unrealistic pressure she has put on herself, button the sweater, and explain that when Jonisha gets older—like Daniel—she will be able to button her sweater herself.

Give children clear-cut choices whenever possible. Offering children choices they can manage serves two purposes. It provides a much-needed sense of control, and more importantly, it provides decision-making practice. Examples of choices you might offer include: "Do you want to get dressed here in the nap room or in the living room?" and "Do you want to wear your green socks with butterflies or the purple ones?"

Be aware that children's temperaments may shape the way they experience dressing. For example, intense children like Matthew sometimes respond very strongly to any change—even putting on a new pair of pants. When you work with this type of child, be sure to have an extra set of familiar clothes available. Other children may fuss because they are sensitive to touch and may find certain textures uncomfortable. You'll want to have soft, well-worn cotton clothing on hand for these children.

"How can I promote children's dressing skills throughout the day?"

Dressing oneself requires mastering many different motor skills. For example, to put on a sock or to slip their arms into the sleeves of a sweater, children need to be aware of their bodies and to be able to control their body movements. Eventually, children need to be able to manipulate snaps, buttons, zippers, and buckles with their fingers. All the motor experiences you offer children—such as threading beads (eye-hand coordination) or dancing (awareness of different body movements)—will help them master dressing. In addition, there are some activities specifically based on dressing that you might want to offer.

Select dress-up clothes and props with large, easy-to-manage fasteners. Children can practice snapping, buckling, zipping, and buttoning as they stretch their imaginations during pretend play.

Make practice boards. Mount a zipper, snaps, and Velcro™ fasteners on a board. Attach an old shoe with Velcro™ fasteners to a board.

Sing songs and do fingerplays about dressing. Children usually enjoy going through the motions while singing with you: "This is the way we snap our snaps, snap our snaps, snap our snaps" (or "zip our zippers," "button our buttons," and so forth).

"How do I handle a mobile infant or toddler who is protesting getting dressed?"

Though not all mobile infants and toddlers will protest getting dressed, you can count on the fact that some will. Here are some suggestions to help make a trying situation easier on you and on the child you are dressing.

Encourage children to help you. Give children a task as you dress them. For example, ask them to hold their shoes, or to reach up to the ceiling as you pull on their sweater. Children who are a year old can usually take off their own hats and pull off their socks and shoes. By 18 months, they usually can unzip their jackets.

Acknowledge children's feelings. For example, explain that you know a child wants to play some more with the farm animals, but that you need to change his wet shirt first so he doesn't get cold.

Be quick. In some situations, the faster dressing is over with, the better it will be for all concerned!

Talk with parents about strategies they use to make dressing easier. Don't forget that parents share the challenge of dressing active, protesting children. Ask for any ideas they use to make dressing easier and more pleasant for all.

Above all, avoid turning protests about dressing into a power struggle. Try to understand why children sometimes struggle against the restrictions that are part of getting dressed and undressed. Once you recognize that they are not trying to make your life difficult, you'll be better able to focus on the dressing process itself, rather than your frustration.

Helping Children Learn from Dressing

In the charts below, we consider typical behaviors you may observe, what children may be experiencing, and how you might decide to respond to promote their learning.

Young Infants		
What You Observe	**What the Child May Be Experiencing**	**How You Can Respond**
Looking up at you as you put on her pants	She may be interested in you. She may want to communicate with you.	Take time to explain what you are doing: "I'm snapping closed your bright red pants."
Fussing as you remove his shirt over his head	He may not like having his head covered, even temporarily.	Remove the shirt quickly. Soothe him by taking a few minutes to talk together, or play "Where is your tummy?" When you put a shirt back on, choose one with buttons or snaps down the front.
Moving her arms and kicking her legs in the air after you remove her clothes	She may be enjoying the sensations of air flowing over her exposed skin and the freedom to move without the restrictions of clothes.	Talk with her: "It feels good moving your arms and legs through the air, doesn't it?" Give her a few minutes to enjoy the freedom of movement. Hold her securely on the changing table to prevent her from rolling off.

Mobile Infants		
What You Observe	What the Child May Be Experiencing	How You Can Respond
Squirming as you try to dress him	He may be feeling restrained.	Finish as quickly as possible. Explain: "I know you want to play. Let's get this shirt on quickly so you can get going." Try to involve him by offering him a job, such as holding his shirt or singing a song with you to help make dressing go faster.
Giggling as you play "This Little Piggy Went to Market" with her toes	She may be enjoying having some one-on-one time with you.	Continue playing. Focus on enjoying a few minutes with her and knowing that you are doing an important part of your job.
Pulling off the overalls and socks you just struggled to put on	He may be declaring his independence. He may be practicing dressing skills.	Appreciate the humor in the scene. Give him time to enjoy his accomplishment before you dress him again. Provide opportunities to practice with snaps and other closures throughout the day.

	Toddlers	
What You Observe	**What the Child May Be Experiencing**	**How You Can Respond**
Insisting "Me do!" as you begin to dress her	She may be firming up her emerging sense of self by making her wishes known.	Talk with her parents about choosing clothes that encourage her independence, for example, shoes with Velcro™ fasteners and pants with elastic waists. Give her chances to undress and dress herself. Step in to offer guidance or to take over if she begins to get frustrated.
Turning dressing into a game of chase	He may be having fun playing with you. He may be asserting his independence by taking control over the activity.	Try to turn dressing into a game. Ask: "Let's see how fast we can get these pants on you." Respect his independence by allowing him to choose what he wants to wear (from two acceptable choices) and suggesting he do certain tasks himself. If necessary, insist firmly that it is time to get dressed and dress him as quickly as possible.
Pulling her shirt over her head and breaking out into a big laugh, while being changed into clean clothes.	She may be feeling proud and competent.	Acknowledge her accomplishment: "You put your shirt on. Good going!" Share your pleasure in her accomplishment with her parents.

Sharing Thoughts on Dressing

Dear Families:

Infants and toddlers are dressed and undressed throughout the day—every day—at home and in child care. And yet dressing is one routine that adults—and children—often want to get through as quickly as possible. Let's face it: dressing a squirming infant or a protesting toddler is no simple task. You can imagine that being an infant who must lie still or a toddler who must stop what he or she is doing to get dressed is no fun, either.

We focus on dressing in our program because we believe that by giving this routine some special attention, it can become a valuable learning experience. Equally important, dressing offers many opportunities just to spend time together with children.

How We Can Work Together

❖ *Please leave an extra set of your child's clothes with us.* Having spare clothes on hand makes it easier for us to dress your child and assure that he or she is always dry, warm, and relatively clean. When clothes are labeled, we can spend our time with your child instead of trying to figure out which clothes belong to whom. Wearing familiar clothes will help your child experience the safe and secure feelings of home here in child care.

❖ *Dress your child for active, sometimes messy play.* Clothes that need to be kept clean can interfere with children's enjoyment of activities such as climbing, food preparation, or painting. If you want to bring your child to child care in "good" clothes, we'll be happy to help your child change into clothes that will allow him or her to "move and do" throughout the day. Of course, we'll do our best to take care of your child's good clothes.

❖ *Choose clothes for your child that are easy to manage.* Pants with elastic waists, shoes with Velcro™ fasteners, and overalls with straps that stretch make it easier for your child to dress him or herself. This skill can make your child feel competent.

❖ *Communicate with us. How do you handle dressing at home?* Do you offer your child lots of help? Or do you encourage your child to learn to dress independently? By sharing our approaches, we can learn from one another and strengthen our partnership to benefit your child.

Together, we can make dressing a positive learning experience for your child.

Sincerely,

Algunas ideas acerca de vestirse

Estimadas familias:

A los niños pequeños se les viste y se les desviste varias veces al día —todos los días— en el hogar y en la guardería. Sin embargo, vestirse constituye una rutina que los adultos —y los niños— desean llevar a cabo lo más rápidamente posible. Veamos. Sin duda, vestir a un niño que se retuerce o a uno que protesta, no es tarea fácil. Y no es difícil imaginarse que, para un niño pequeño quedarse quieto, o dejar de hacer lo que esté haciendo por vestirse, tampoco sea agradable.

En nuestro programa nos centramos en vestirse, porque creemos que prestarle atención especial a esta rutina, puede convertirla en una valiosa experiencia de aprendizaje. De similar importancia es que, vestirse les ofrece a ustedes y a sus hijos múltiples oportunidades de estar juntos.

Cómo podemos trabajar juntos

❖ *Por favor, traigan una muda extra de ropa para su hijo(a).* Contar con ropa adicional a la mano, nos facilitará cambiar a su niño(a) y garantizar que siempre esté seco, no sienta frío y esté relativamente limpio. Si la ropa está marcada, podremos pasar más tiempo con su hijo(a), en lugar de estar tratando de averiguar qué ropa le pertenece. Usar ropa conocida le ayudará a su niño a experimentar en la guardería, la sensación de seguridad y de tranquilidad del hogar.

❖ *Vistan a sus hijos para el juego activo, en el que a veces se ensucian.* Usar ropa que no se pueda ensuciar puede interferir con el placer de actividades como escalar, preparar alimentos o pintar. Si desean traer al niño con ropa "buena", con gusto le ayudaremos a cambiarse y a ponerse ropa con la que se pueda "mover y actuar" todo el día. Por supuesto, también le cuidaremos su ropa buena.

❖ *Elijan ropa fácil de manejar.* Los pantalones de cintura de elástico, los zapatos de apuntar con "velcro" y los "overoles" con tirantes que se estiran, le facilitarán al niño vestirse solo(a). Esta destreza contribuye a que se sienta capaz.

❖ *Comuníquense con nosotros.* ¿Cómo manejan en su hogar el vestirse? ¿Le ofrecen al niño demasiada ayuda? O, ¿le animan a vestirse autónomamente? Al compartir nuestros enfoques podremos aprender mutuamente y fortalecer nuestra labor conjunta para beneficiar a su hijo(a).

Juntos, podremos convertir el vestirse en una grata experiencia de aprendizaje para su hijo(a).

Les saluda atentamente,

Part IV Activities

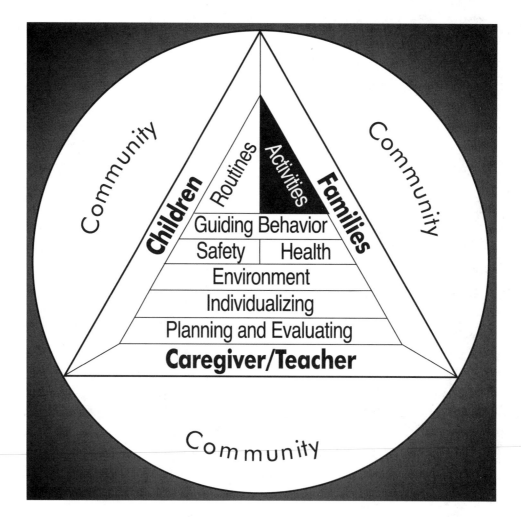

Activities

Playing with Toys
Dabbling in Art
Imitating and Pretending
Enjoying Stories and Books
Tasting and Preparing Food
Exploring Sand and Water
Having Fun with Music and Movement
Going Outdoors

Putting Quality Into Action: Activities Day By Day

Infants and toddlers are learning about their world. Each interaction and each exploration is an opportunity for learning. As we saw in Part III, much of children's learning takes place through the routines that occupy a young child's day. In his parents' morning good-byes, in diaper changes, bottle feedings, clothing changes, and naps, infants even as young as Julio learn about trust, pride, cause and effect, patterns, dealing with their emotions, and becoming competent, confident individuals.

Young infants do most of their learning in the context of routines—because most of the day is devoted to responding to their basic needs. The younger children are, the more their lives are subject to routines. As they grow, children begin to view the world around them as an interesting place that beckons them.

Take a few moments to think about this evolution of a child's day and what it means to you. Because you make decisions based on what you know about development and what you learn about each individual child, you probably realize that, as children mature and acquire new interests, you need to focus more of your planning time on activities.

When you focus on the word "activities" what are your first thoughts? Do you envision planning an activity for a specific time of day, gathering materials, introducing the activity to a group, and conducting the experience? When we think of activities for infants and toddlers, we envision a very different kind of experience. Activities are integrated into everything you do with infants and toddlers throughout the day. When you feed an infant, allowing him to mush the carrots on his tray, you are providing a "tasting and preparing food" activity. When you put on a tape, hold an infant in your arms, and march around the room with two toddlers, you are "having fun with music and movement." There will, of course, be times when you plan activities, especially as children get older and more capable. These planned activities will be one of many experiences available to children at any given time of the day.

The next eight chapters explore the following activities:

- Playing with Toys
- Dabbling in Art
- Imitating and Pretending
- Enjoying Stories and Books
- Tasting and Preparing Food
- Exploring Sand and Water
- Having Fun with Music and Movement
- Going Outdoors

Although activities can take place at any time of day, and often occur in the context of routines, we have chosen to present them in separate chapters. We do this in order to show the range of possibilities and to offer you practical ideas you can use with your children. We have presented ideas for each age group, though these categories are by no means rigid. A mobile infant, for example, may be able to do activities we suggest for toddlers or for young infants. Development is very individual and therefore, you plan based on decisions you make daily for each child.

Planning for activities involves two types of decisions:

Setting the Stage for the Activity

By addressing health and safety issues, examining what changes you need to make to your program's environment, and what an ideal inventory of materials would be for young infants, mobile infants, and toddlers, you can maximize the chances that the activity will be successful for both the children and you.

Promoting Children's Play and Learning

Here, we discuss how children are likely to respond to different activities depending on their stage of development and individual learning styles. We suggest ways that you can promote children's development by providing appropriate experiences and responding to children's actions.

Each activity chapter concludes with a sample Letter to Parents (in English and Spanish) which is intended to be shared with the children's families. The purposes of this letter are to inform families of what goes on in your program and to invite them to participate. By working together with parents, you further encourage children's learning through activities.

Playing with Toys

— ◈ —

As Julio lies on the changing table, Linda taps her finger against the mirror fastened to the table's side. Hearing the sound, Julio moves his head toward the mirror. Slowly, Linda swings her finger to and from the mirror's edge, while Julio tracks her moving finger intently with his eyes.

— ◈ —

Try to think of a world without toys. Can you? Probably not. That's because toys take many forms. Some toys, like hardwood blocks, are store-bought. Others, such as empty milk cartons covered with Contact™ paper, are home-made versions of their more expensive counterparts. For infants and toddlers, an empty box can be just as exciting as anything you can buy.

Some of the very best toys for young children are already in your home or program, serving other purposes. An unbreakable wall mirror, plastic measuring cups that nest together, and a wooden spoon that can be banged against a metal pot (like a drum) are all wonderful toys. In fact, any object that young children can explore, put together, take apart, push or pull, stack, and create with becomes a toy in a child's hands.

The best thing about toys is that they can teach children skills at the same time children are playing and having fun. Abby, for example, learns about size, shape, and sequence as she stacks rings on a peg. As Leo pulls the string on a wheeled toy, he learns about problem solving, cause and effect, balance, and eye and hand coordination. By rolling a ball back and forth with a friend, Matthew develops social skills. Toys are natural teachers.

Setting the Stage for Toys

Although you won't have to "prepare" children for playing with toys, you will have to make many decisions about toy selection, display, and arrangements. The key is to match toys to children's capabilities, interests, and needs.[1]

"What toys are appropriate for young infants?"

Infants will respond to toys they can track with their eyes, gum in their mouths, grasp, shake, bang, and drop. Look for toys that support infants' active exploration.

Mobiles. Infants like patterns, circles, and areas of high contrast, especially black against white. Think about hanging a mobile over a newborn's crib or changing table. Choose one that is black and white and has designs with movement in them, such as a spiral or a bull's eye. As infants mature, they prefer more complex designs, including faces. They also enjoy movement and rhythmic sounds.

Experts recommend that you hang a mobile at the point where an infant's eyes focus best. For infants under three months, a mobile should be about 14 inches from the child's eyes. As infants grow and their eyesight improves, you can gradually raise the mobile. Because infants will be lying on their backs, the design should be on the bottom of the figures. When an infant can reach the mobile, that's the time to remove it altogether, since most are not made to be mouthed.

Mirrors. From the age of about two months, children are captivated by mirrors. They laugh with glee as their image appears and disappears in the mirror. You can position stable, unbreakable mirrors on the sides of cribs, changing tables, and on the bottom of walls in play spaces where children like Julio can continually admire themselves.

Cuddly toys. Very young children love stuffed animals, hand puppets, and soft, washable, one-piece rag dolls. Bright colors, boldly contrasting patterns, painted-on faces, and sounds are more important at this early age than realistic features or correct anatomy.

Grasping toys. From about three months on, children love to grab, shake, mouth, drop, and explore objects like rattles and soft teething rings they can hold in their fists.

---

[1] For detailed information on selecting developmentally appropriate toys, see Martha B. Bronson, *The Right Stuff for Children Birth to 8: Selecting Play Materials to Supplement Development*. Washington, DC: National Association for the Education of Young Children, 1995.

"What toys are appropriate for mobile infants?"

Mobile infants still enjoy toys that they can explore with all of their senses. Willard, for example, finds that an oversized stuffed dinosaur offers more hugging opportunities than a small rubber one. He enjoys looking at his image in a large wall mirror. As Abby yanks on large pop-it beads or inserts a circle into a foamboard, she learns how to squeeze, twist, push, and pull. Often, puzzles, block towers, and large pegs in a peg board are great fun to take apart, though the mobile infant may not yet be able to put them together. Other popular toys for mobile infants include the following.

Balls. According to Dr. Burton White of Harvard University, the single best toy for a child between the ages of seven months and two years is a plastic, inflatable beach ball.[2] Mobile infants love to carry, throw, and retrieve balls. Clutch balls with indented surfaces can be easier to handle than smooth balls. Other good choices include balls with chimes and visible objects rolling inside, or weighted balls and oddly shaped ones, such as footballs, which roll in unpredictable ways, and yarn balls, hung from the ceiling for babies to bat.

Puzzles. Puzzles are actually grasping toys. By exploring the puzzle pieces and discovering how the shapes fit together, infants develop eye and hand coordination. For mobile infants, select puzzles that have only two or three pieces and can be held by knobs. (You can glue empty spools on puzzle pieces to serve as knobs if they do not come that way.) The puzzles themselves should be colorful and show objects, people, and animals familiar to the child.

Activity toys. Many toys for mobile infants provide practice in coordination and promote physical skill development. To illustrate, activity centers that can be attached to furniture or are free standing provide opportunities for children to open doors, turn dials, pull on knobs, and push buttons.

Other popular activity toys include stacking rings, nesting cups, foam boards, shape sorters, busy boxes that can be poked and pulled at, and surprise boxes that pop-up. Household items such as measuring spoons and plastic pitchers children can fill with objects are equal to any store-bought toy.

Push and pull toys. When infants learn to crawl, they also learn to move their toys as well as themselves. For example, sturdy carriages and shopping carts are especially appropriate for children beginning to walk because they offer much-needed balance. More experienced walkers enjoy push and pull toys, such as plastic lawnmowers or carpet sweepers. Toys that play music or make sounds as they move can enhance the play experience.

Transportation toys. These are, in many ways, a combination of grasping and pushing toys. They include one-piece molded replicas of cars (6 to 8 inches long), buses, trains, trucks, and airplanes attached to large wheels or rollers. Indoors, mobile infants like to lift and push these vehicles across the floor. Outdoors, they love to straddle "ride-on" toys and move about using their feet as the car's motor.

---

[2] Burton L. White. *The First Three Years of Life,* Revised Edition. New York: Prentice-Hall, 1986, p. 146.

Blocks. At this stage of development children who are not yet able to build with blocks can have fun and make discoveries as they carry, pile, knock down, and even throw blocks. For these reasons, foam, cloth, and washable blocks are best. Later on, you can introduce firmer blocks, made of lightweight wood for stacking. Stacking blocks should be cube shaped, brightly colored or patterned, and easily grasped (2 to 4 inches). A selection of 20 to 25 blocks for a mobile infant is sufficient.

Outdoor play equipment. Nearly all of the toys mentioned so far can be brought outside to provide new experiences. Non-walkers enjoy swings as well as crawling platforms made of foam and vinyl. In addition, mobile infants like play equipment that allows them to get up and down and that can be used as a slide. Sturdy equipment that several children can use at once and that can be used both indoors and outdoors is a good investment.

Mobile infants with more developed physical skills enjoy low, carpeted climbers, lofts with side rails, tunnels, and obstacle courses. Outdoor play equipment of this sort challenges children to climb, slide, twist, and roll.

"What toys are appropriate for toddlers?"

Toddlers continue to use all of the toys mobile infants use. However, toddlers use the toys in more sophisticated ways. Here are some examples.

Mirrors and dolls inspire toddlers to engage in pretend play. Free-standing mirrors allow toddlers like Matthew to admire his own "adult" look as he puts on a hat. Boys and girls alike enjoy washing, feeding, dressing, and undressing dolls. Toddlers seem to prefer dolls about 12 to 15 inches long that they can carry in one hand, cradle in their elbow, or tuck under their arm. Dolls should reflect the ethnic backgrounds of the children in your program.

Push and pull toys often enhance toddlers' pretend play. Leo, for example, spends some time every morning pushing a carriage full of dolls around the backyard at his center. He also likes to mop and sweep up after the dolls with child-sized tools, shop for doll food with a cart, and pull the baby dolls in a bright, red wagon.

Soft, fuzzy stuffed animals are popular with toddlers, as are rubber, wood, vinyl, and plastic figures. Leo and Matthew like to carry around and dramatize stories using farm animals, exotic species, and even imaginary monsters. They especially like to use animals as action toys that move and make sounds.

Puzzles and matching games provide opportunities for toddlers to develop and apply thinking skills. Most toddlers can handle 4- or 5-piece puzzles (with and without knobs, made out of rubber and wood). Older toddlers who enjoy puzzles may want the challenge of more complicated puzzles, with as many as 12 pieces. As older toddlers become more skilled in sorting and matching, they love playing games in which they put giant dominoes (2 to 4 inches in size) together or match picture pieces to lotto boards.

Activity toys encourage toddlers to work on many emerging skills. For example, more advanced shape boxes, nesting cups, and stacking rings (with 5 to 10 pieces) enable toddlers to learn about shapes, colors, cause and effect, and sequence. As they play with these toys, toddlers also improve their eye and hand coordination. Pegboards and magnetic boards provide toddlers with opportunities to use their improved fine motor skills for exploring concepts such as shape, size, and color.

Toddlers also enjoy the surprise of reaching into mystery bags and boxes to discover objects that must be identified by their shape, texture, or smell. Gena, who has a difficult time reaching into "feelie" bags, likes to close her eyes and have Ivan surprise her with an object he rubs against her skin or one that she can sniff and then identify.

Toddlers naturally gravitate to toys that promote their independence. Self-help boards, cards, or frames for practicing fastening and unfastening Velcro™ strips, snaps, buckles, hooks, and zippers are always favorites. Learning to lace and string large wooden or plastic beads also provides children with experiences doing things on their own.

Transportation toys continue to hold toddlers' interest, although children this age usually prefer smaller (2 to 4 inches) or larger (12 to 15 inches) models than do mobile infants. Toddlers especially like ride-on trucks that they can climb into and imitate their parents. With their increased fine motor skills, toddlers enjoy handling moveable accessories: steering wheels that turn; bulldozing shovels that pick up and dump; cherry pickers that reach high; and knobs, levers, buttons, and wheels of all sorts.

Blocks are popular with toddlers who begin to use them for construction, rather than just stacking. To build stable constructions with blocks, toddlers need heavier, sturdier blocks for stacking than those used by mobile infants. Hardwood unit blocks are the universal favorites because of their weight, durability, and the many ways they can be used. While toddlers don't need the specialized shapes (such as arches or triangles) that preschoolers enjoy, they should have at least 40 to 60 blocks per builder in a group. With a good supply of blocks handy, children can experiment fully with constructions.

Older toddlers like to build with hollow blocks, and those made of heavy cardboard or sturdy foam. Toddlers of all ages also enjoy putting together interlocking blocks. Younger toddlers seem to prefer bristle blocks which fasten together much like Velcro.™ More skilled older toddlers enjoy using Duplos,™ which are larger versions of the popular Legos.™ A selection of 20 to 30 blocks per child will give toddlers a rich building experience.

Outdoor toys and equipment for toddlers promote gross motor skill development. Tunnels, swings, riding toys, and climbers continue to provide physical challenges and excitement. Large cardboard boxes that toddlers can use as caves or hideaways, make wonderful climbing spaces. Balls of varying shapes, colors, textures, and sizes are great for kicking, batting, throwing, and (occasionally) catching. As toddlers get to be close to age three— as Jonisha and Valisha are—they can learn to manage pedals and try a beginner's tricycle.

"Are home-made toys just as appropriate as those I can purchase?"

As mentioned earlier, some of the most popular items are not in fact toys, but "beautiful junk." For example, you can use empty hosiery packaging (such as L'Eggs™ egg-shaped containers) as shakers, or empty freezer containers as nesting cubes. Here are a few "recipes" for homemade toys that you might want to add to your program for toddlers.

A bag collection. With the help of families, collect paper shopping bags from grocery stores, drug stores, and the like. Hang the bags on low hooks that children can reach. The toddlers can then take a bag to carry a toy around or to use in their pretend play.

Shape sorters. Cut out holes in the plastic lid of a wet baby wipes box or a coffee tin. Let toddlers fit empty spools, clothespins, cards, and other "stuff" through the holes.

Drop and dump toys. Put objects such as large hair curlers, bean bags, gelatin boxes, or squeeze toys into a plastic pitcher, small waste basket, or rubber pail. You can even tie a rope to a ceiling hook and suspend the pail in the air at a height that reaches the toddler's waist. Place a rubber wash basin under the pail and let toddlers dump the objects into the basin and then refill the pail.

Lotto games. Make matching games that feature people and objects from the child's world. Use photos, catalog pictures, post cards, and the like. To get duplicates of items (for the lotto card and the marker), make color photocopies. Paste the pictures on cardboard "lotto cards," then laminate them. Let toddlers begin with two or three squares to be matched; add items as the children's skills grow.

Cardboard blocks. Fill empty milk cartons with newspaper squares or crumpled paper grocery bags and cover with Contact™ paper. "Brick" paper makes these blocks look like the store-bought ones.

Old equipment. Broken telephones, old computer keyboards, and other adult-like items are especially appealing to toddlers, who love to imitate the grown-ups in their lives.

Infants and toddlers do learn through their play with toys. Because there are so many appropriate toys to choose from, you need only to match materials to children's developmental levels.

"What adaptations are needed for a child with a disability?"

Often, children with disabilities find it difficult to play with toys. Consequently, these children may spend large parts of their days observing the play of other children instead of actively joining in. Simple adaptations to toys can open a new world of play and exploration for children with varying types and degrees of disabilities. You may find, to your surprise, that toys chosen for the child with a disability also become the favorites for the typically developing children in your program!

Some easy-to-implement, low-tech modifications to materials and your environment can make all the difference. Here are some suggestions.[3]

Handles or built-up knobs. Glue wooden knobs or corks to puzzles and other toys to assist children with limited fine motor skills. Add foam curlers to build up the handles of spoons, brushes, crayons, and markers.

Activity frames. Activity frames are similar to the "Baby Gyms" that are used for infants. Hang toys from the frame so that the children have easy access to them. These devices allow children with severe motor impairments to use toys that would otherwise be out of reach or would be dropped. The frames can be placed on the floor, attached to a table, or attached to a wheelchair or stander.

Grasping aids. Velcro™ is a wonderful invention for children who have trouble grasping objects. You can construct a number of different grasping devices with this material.

❖ A **stick holder** is a small stick with a piece of soft Velcro™ wrapped around one end. Attach a piece of rough Velcro™ to toys, such as toy people or cards. The child will then be able to use the stick to manipulate and pick up the toys.

❖ A **palm holder** is a piece of terrycloth with Velcro™ attached to it. The holder is placed around the child's palm (for children who have little or no grasping skills).

❖ A **Velcro™ mitt** is a mitten with Velcro™ attached to it.

Playboards. You can attach toys to a firm surface (such as foam core, a pegboard, or indoor-outdoor carpet) with Velcro,™ string, or elastic. This creates a variety of playboards that allow children to participate in imaginative play. Examples of simple playboards include a purse (with keys, brush, wallet, etc.), a tea party, or a playhouse (with people, furniture, and so forth). The child can then use his or her hands or a grasping aid to move the pieces around without fear of dropping them. Other children can also participate in this play activity.

Often the best toys don't require any modifications at all. For instance, Gena has difficulty grasping small objects, such as crayons and pens. Even with large crayons, she is too weak to draw on paper effectively. One day Ivan found some special "animal markers" at a discount store. (These markers are egg-shaped with different animals on each cap.) They were the perfect size for Gena to grasp and use. She can also grasp the cap and work on getting it on and off the

[3] Assistive Technology Training Project Staff. *Infusing Assistive Technology into Early Childhood Classrooms*, Draft Version. Phoenix, AZ: Assistive Technology Training Project, Fall 1996.

marker. A funny thing happened when Ivan brought them to class for Gena to use—all the children gathered round and wanted to play with "Gena's markers." All of a sudden, Gena was the focal point of a play activity in which she could fully participate. Ivan also used these markers to teach the children about different animals, the sounds they make, and colors.

Other strategies to help children with special needs are to attach play materials to steady surfaces, to enlarge materials (such as large puzzle pieces) for visually impaired children, and to simplify the game or toy (for children with processing problems).

Remember that the child's family and therapists are great resources. If possible, invite the child's physical or occupational therapist to visit your program and suggest ways to adapt your space and toys to meet the child's unique abilities.

"Should I select different toys for boys and girls?"

For many decades now, researchers have been studying sex differences in children's play. In 1933, Mildred Parten observed that during free play time, boys tended to push trucks around the room while girls cooked and washed dishes for their dolls.[4] Does this seem much different from what occurs in an early childhood classroom today? Are these preferences inborn or are they due to the ways adults interact with boys and girls? From many years of research on this topic, it has become clear that preferences are due to social experiences rather than genes.

At about age 12 months, some families—and even child care professionals—become uncomfortable if a boy likes "feminine" toys and a girl prefers "masculine" ones. These adults steer children toward toys that they feel are more gender appropriate. If your goal, however, is to help children become comfortable with a variety of roles and to feel capable of having any career they choose, then it's up to you to discuss your views with parents and seek their ideas as well. When you put together your inventory, select toys without concern for gender. And then respect a child's decision to play with any and all of these toys.

"How can I be sure a toy is safe for the children?"

As noted in Chapter 7, safety must be a first consideration when you are selecting toys for children. Ask these questions about each and every toy.

❖ Is it solid, without breakable parts, any sharp or jagged edges, or exposed nails, wires, pins, or splinters?

❖ Is it made of washable nontoxic materials?

❖ Is it too large to be swallowed (at least 1½ inches in diameter) and free of parts that might break off and become lodged in noses, ears, or windpipes?

❖ Are stuffed toys light enough to prevent accidental suffocation?

---

[4] Mildred Parten. "Social Play Among Preschool Children." *Journal of Abnormal and Social Psychology*, 28:136-147, 1933.

❖ Are plastic toys flexible?

❖ Are dolls' heads and limbs secure? Are facial features molded in, rather than sewn on?

❖ Are cords that could become wound around a child's neck shorter than 12 inches?

❖ Is it stable and free of parts that could pinch or pierce children or trap their hair or clothing?

❖ Are hinges and joints covered?

❖ If made of cloth, is it nonflammable or flame retardant (not flame resistant)?

"How should I arrange the environment so children can play with toys?"

Toys should be a natural part of the environment. Children can play with toys either on the floor or standing at a child-sized table. Because younger children may find it difficult to build or balance a toy on carpeting, make sure you have enough hard surfaces on which the children's toys can rest. Also, try to carve out enough space so children can play with toys near one another. While children younger than three are still too young to play cooperatively, many like the experience of playing near or next to another child. Here are some suggestions for the arrangement of toys.

Place only a few toys out at a time. As children master these toys, you can rotate your inventory. However, don't remove all toys that children have mastered. Like a familiar book, children find comfort in a favorite toy.

Store toys on low shelving. If they are on the bottom ledge of a bookcase or room divider, children can take them out when they want to play with them. Leave ample space between stored toys to prevent a cluttered look and to aid children in distinguishing between toys. Avoid using toy chests. They are safety hazards as well as messy.

Make a picture label of each toy. Place the label either behind or underneath the storage spot so that children know where to return their toys. You can draw a picture of the toy, photograph it, or cut out a picture from a catalog. Store unit blocks on shelves where you have placed outlines of the blocks cut from solid-colored Contact™ paper. When children return blocks to the corresponding shapes on the shelf they begin to understand matching, an important math skill.

Group toys together by type. This helps children locate their favorite puzzles, transportation toys, push and pull toys, and so forth. Grouping by type also teaches children how to classify objects.

Have duplicates of popular toys. Riding cars or stuffed animals are always in demand. Children younger than three have a difficult time sharing any toy.

Promoting Children's Play with Toys

For infants and toddlers, much of your work is already done if you have set the stage appropriately. However, to make playing with toys meaningful, you'll need to observe what children actually do. Many times you may decide that your most valuable response is to step back and let them play without interruption. Here are some strategies you can use to guide children's learning as they play with toys.

Young Infants

Probably the most important thing you can do for infants is to let them explore toys on their own. Just as an infant will let you know when he's hungry, tired, or in need of changing, so too will he let you know by his actions when he's ready for play.

Let's focus on how this works by taking a peek at some infant play. Linda, for example, creates an environment in which Julio can play with a mobile when he's ready. She hangs one mobile over Julio's crib and another over the changing table. Julio focuses his attention on these mobiles at times when he's comfortable—and not hungry, thirsty, or sleepy. Linda observes that in his enthusiastic play, Julio is learning that banging the mobile causes it to move, and that he can follow its movement with his eyes.

Janet encourages Jasmine's play by placing a mirror near the floor. Now, when Jasmine and Janet play peek-a-boo while sitting on a blanket on the floor, Jasmine can watch the action in the mirror.

To help Julio, Jasmine, and other infants learn through their interactions with toys, there will be times you will want to talk with them about the activity.

- ❖ **Describe what they may be experiencing:** "Who's that in the mirror?"
- ❖ **Mirror their emotions as you observe them:** "You love that teddy bear, don't you?"
- ❖ **Explain the concepts that are being demonstrated:** "I can hear you making noises with the rattle."
- ❖ **Provide vocabulary as they explore:** "Here comes the alligator puppet."
- ❖ **Build their confidence:** "What a big squeeze you gave that rubber ducky!"

Mobile Infants

Mobile infants such as Willard and Abby, with their increased physical skills, can be introduced to a variety of toys that they can learn to use independently. For example, Grace can show Willard how to push a toy lawnmower so that it not only moves, but steadies his toddling walk. As he grows more confident in his steps, Willard will figure out on his own that the same handle he uses for pushing on the lawnmower can now be used to pull it.

Once you've introduced a toy, you do not need to provide mobile infants with ideas about how they should play with it. These will come naturally. Your role is to offer children appropriate materials and then build on their own play activities.

Here's how this works. Suppose Abby is playing with vinyl blocks. She attempts to stack them, but they keep falling over. Instead of building a tower for her as a model, Brooks works with Abby to help her figure out a solution. She encourages Abby to experiment with placing the cubes. Eventually, through trial and error, Abby learns that the more fully the top cube covers the bottom one, the steadier the tower will be.

Through your interactions with mobile infants, you help them grow and learn. Here are some ways you can talk with children to focus their learning.

- **Help children observe changes** (cause and effect): "What happened when you dropped the ball on the floor?"

- **Encourage children to solve problems:** "Let's give your car a big push to get it out of the mud."

- **Build concepts such as color, size, and shape:** "Where does the circle go?"

- **Develop children's feelings of competence:** "You got all those blocks in the bucket."

Toddlers

Matthew, Leo, Gena, and the twins are growing and developing at a rapid pace. They use toys to build their physical capacities, master concepts, apply thinking skills, explore the world of make-believe, and assert their independence. Here are some ways that you can interact with toddlers to support these learnings.

- **Build physical skills:** "Let's take these big blocks over to the tree."

- **Develop thinking skills:** "Can you find the picture on the shelf that matches the fire trucks?"

- **Promote social skills:** "Leo, why don't you and Rachel take the bristle blocks over to the rug."

- **Encourage make-believe:** "What are you cooking for your baby?"

- **Promote a sense of competence:** "Look how tall your tower is!"

Playing with toys is one of the many ways children learn about the world around them and gain skills. The pure joy on a child's face as she pushes a button and watches a clown pop up, or dumps a can of blocks on the floor for the fourth time is enough to convince any adult of the value of toys.

Sharing Thoughts About
Playing with Toys

Dear Families:

We all know that toys are fun. But if we take a closer look, we can appreciate how toys are also important tools for learning. When children play with toys, they learn how to move, think, communicate, and relate to others. Here are just a few of the ways that toys help your child grow and develop.

When your child does this . . .

bats an arm at a mobile to make it move
rolls a ball
puts pieces in a form board
pops plastic beads together
takes blocks off the shelf and builds

Your child is learning . . .

cause and effect
about movement
concepts such as shape, size, color
eye and hand coordination
independence

What You Can Do at Home

Here are some ideas that can help your child make the most of playing with toys at home.

❖ *Keep in mind that quantity doesn't always equal quality.* Your child doesn't need a great many toys. In fact, it's far better to have a few good toys that really challenge your child.

❖ *Choose simple toys at first.* Good toys for infants are those they can explore with all their senses—rubber animals and rattles they can grasp, squeeze, and mouth are especially good.

❖ *Select active toys as your infant grows.* Mobile infants enjoy playing with toys they can push or pull, such as plastic lawnmowers. They also like toys with parts they can move or handle—doors, knobs, big buttons, switches, and the like.

❖ *Pick toys that challenge your toddler.* Toddlers need toys that encourage development of specific skills and let them show their independence. Puzzles, blocks, lotto games, and riding toys are good choices for this group.

❖ *Find and make wonderful toys using things you already have at home.* An empty box, large empty thread spools, pots and pans, plastic food containers—there are just a few of the items that will delight your child and lead to many hours of joyful play.

No matter whether you buy or make your child's toys, what's most important is that you take pleasure in watching your child play, and that you respond with enthusiasm to each new discovery.

Sincerely,

Algunas ideas sobre los juguetes

Estimadas familias:

Si observamos con detenimiento los juguetes, podremos apreciar que, además de ser gratos, también son importantes instrumentos de aprendizaje. Cuando los niños juegan con juguetes aprenden a moverse, a pensar y a relacionarse con los demás. A continuación les mencionamos sólo unas cuantas formas en que los juguetes contribuyen al crecimiento y el desarrollo infantil.

Cuando su hijo(a):	**El/ella está aprendiendo:**
mueve un móvil con la mano	sobre la relación causa-efecto
hace rodar una pelota	sobre el movimiento
coloca piezas en un tablero de figuras	conceptos como forma, tamaño y color
ensarta cuentas	coordinación ojo-mano
toma bloques de un anaquel y construye con ellos	a ser independiente

Lo que ustedes pueden hacer en el hogar

Las siguientes son unas cuantas ideas que pueden ayudarle a sus hijos a aprovechar al máximo el juego en el hogar:

❖ *Mantengan presente que cantidad no siempre es igual a calidad.* Los niños no necesitan una gran cantidad de juguetes. De hecho, lo mejor es tener sólo unos cuantos juguetes que les ofrezcan retos.

❖ *Al principio, elijan juguetes sencillos.* Los mejores juguetes para los niños pequeños, son los que ellos puedan explorar con todos sus sentidos; los animales de caucho y los sonajeros que puedan agarrar, apretar y meterse en la boca son especialmente buenos.

❖ *A medida que los niños crezcan, elijan juguetes activos.* Los pequeños que ya se mueven por todos lados disfrutan enormemente los juguetes que pueden empujar o halar, como las cortadoras de pasto plásticas y les encantan los juguetes con partes que se muevan o se puedan manipular, como puertas, botones, manijas, etc.

❖ *Elijan juguetes que les ofrezcan retos a sus niños.* Los pequeños necesitan juguetes que estimulen el desarrollo de destrezas específicas y les permitan expresar su autonomía. Para este grupo, los rompecabezas, los bloques, los juegos de lotería y los juguetes para subirse en ellos constituyen una buena elección.

❖ *Encuentren y construyan juguetes maravillosos con objetos que tengan en su casa.* Una caja vacía, carretes de hilo grandes y vacíos, ollas y cacerolas, recipientes de plástico, etc., son sólo unos cuantos de los objetos que pueden conducir a muchas horas de juego placentero.

No importa si ustedes les compran o les construyen los juguetes a sus hijos, lo más importante es que, ustedes disfruten obervándolos jugar y que respondan con entusiasmo a cualquier nuevo descubrimiento.

Les saluda atentamente,

Dabbling in Art

— ◆ —

"Abby, come here please," calls out Brooks Peterson, as she lines up a bowl of flour along with plastic pitchers of salad oil and water on the child-sized table. "We're going to make some squishy Cloud Dough today." Brooks holds the bowl so Abby can use her hands to shovel the flour out of it. Brooks then guides Abby in pouring oil and water into the mound of flour. "Me do it," says Abby, as she pushes Brooks' arm away. Abby smiles broadly as she pats and pushes the flour mixture into a ball.

— ◆ —

When people think of children and art, many envision a child with crayons or a paint brush in hand. Coloring and painting, though, are just two ways young children enjoy art. In fact, art experiences begin long before children are even able to grasp a crayon or paint brush. They begin when a baby notices sunlight streaming through a window or the pattern in his mother's dress. If encouraged, art becomes another language for children—a way for them to express their ideas and feelings.

The art activities you offer infants and toddlers serve many purposes. First, of course, they are sensory experiences. Children explore by touching different textures, squeezing and poking playdough, or moving their fingers through slippery fingerpaint. Second, art experiences provide children with opportunities to experiment. For example, children begin to explore cause and effect when they see a blue crayon leave a blue mark on paper, or observe that painting water on a fence can change the fence's color when it is wet. They develop a sense of spatial relations when they cover a tray with fingerpaint. In addition, painting, coloring, molding, and other art activities help children refine their fine motor skills and develop eye-hand coordination. And, if you've ever noticed children's faces while painting, you'll see how proud they feel to be creative.

Setting the Stage for Art

When you provide art opportunities in your program, you must make some important decisions about what materials are appropriate for each age group and how to prepare the environment. The goal is to ensure a satisfying experience for the children and for you. If art activities become too messy and out-of-control, you will avoid them, thus depriving children of very valuable learning experiences.

"What art materials are appropriate for young infants?"

Young infants explore the world through their senses. When you talk about the feel of their soft blanket or the bright color of a stuffed animal, you confirm the importance of these experiences. You may also want to provide some materials specifically meant to extend the range of sensory experiences. Here are a few examples.

Cloth and other types of materials that have distinct textures, such as pieces of flannel, corduroy, satin, silk, taffeta, netting, knits, hosiery, denim, fleece, lace, fake fur, burlap, carpet remnants, vinyl, and the like. (Be sure materials are large enough that they can't be swallowed.)

Various types of nontoxic papers that infants can crumple, tear, shred, hold up to the light, and wave in the air, such as pieces of waxed paper, butcher paper, parchment, rice paper, and cellophane paper.

"Edible" fingerpaint such as cooked pudding. Infants can use this pudding paint directly on high chair trays or on a table top while sitting on your lap. You can substitute yogurt for the pudding.

"What art materials are appropriate for mobile infants?"

In addition to the materials you provide for young infants, mobile infants can begin to dabble in painting with their fingers and a brush, drawing with crayons, and molding with dough.

Fingerpaint for One

3 cups liquid starch such as Vano™
1 tablespoon powdered tempera (any color)

Use a tongue depressor to mix all ingredients together in a bowl. Transfer to a squeezable bottle.

For finger- and waterpainting:

❖ **Something to paint with:** Their hands are the best tools for fingerpainting. For painting with water, children can use stubby-handled brushes (5–6 inches long).

❖ **Something to paint on:** Table surfaces or trays are ideal for fingerpainting. Alternatively, you can cover a table with oilcloth or vinyl. Other surfaces for painting with water include the walls of buildings, sidewalks, blacktops, and tree trunks.

❖ **The paint:** Use fingerpaints or water.

For drawing:

❖ **Something to draw with:** Collect jumbo crayons, jumbo chalk, water-based markers, soap crayons, and scribble wafers. Children can help you make soap crayons and scribble wafers. (See recipes.)

❖ **Something to draw on:** Get a variety of papers in various sizes and shapes, wrinkled and smooth, dry and wet. Children can use chalk on blackboards, sidewalks, and blacktops outdoors. They can draw on construction paper, oatmeal paper, sandpaper, and Masonite squares.

For molding:

❖ **Something soft and squishy:** For younger mobile infants, introduce doughs that are oily and easily squeezed, such as Cloud Dough or Homemade Plasticine. (See recipes next page.) Older mobile infants enjoy experimenting with other materials which have firmer textures. There are a number of good recipes for making doughs that are safe for mobile infants, who often find chewing on dough or clay irresistible.

Soap Crayons

1 cup soap flakes such as Ivory Flakes™
⅛ cup water
3 drops food coloring of choice

Grease plastic ice cube tray or popsicle molds with shortening or Pam.™ Mix ingredients together in bowl. Pour into tray or molds. Allow time to harden. Pop out.

Scribble Wafers

Ingredients: Stubs of old crayons

1. Preheat oven to 350° and then turn off.
2. Sort crayon stubs by color.
3. Remove papers.
4. Place crayons by color in separate sections of a muffin tin.
5. Place muffin tin in oven.
6. When wax is completely melted, remove pan from oven and let cool.
7. Release shiny, waxed wafers.

"What art materials are appropriate for toddlers?"

In addition to art materials suitable for mobile infants, you can introduce toddlers to more sophisticated painting and drawing activities, as well as to a greater variety of sensory materials. Here are some suggestions.

For painting:

❖ **Something to paint with:** Children can use flat bristled brushes (5–6 inches long) with nylon hairs and thick, stubby handles; empty deodorant bottles with rollers; and additional tools such as squeeze bottles, dishwashing pompoms, rollers, spray bottles, and cotton swabs.

❖ **Something to paint on:** Get a variety of papers—about 24 inches by 36 inches or larger. Big paper allows toddlers to paint by making broad pumping motions. Papers might include newsprint, computer paper, paper grocery bags, paper towels, and butcher paper of various sizes and shapes, as well as wallpaper, paper plates, and plastic doilies. Try covering an entire table with butcher paper to give children a broad "canvas." Most toddlers prefer to paint on the floor or standing at a table, although some older toddlers are ready to paint at an easel.

Cloud Dough

6 cups flour
1 cup salad oil
water to bind (approximately 1 cup)

Knead ingredients together. Final product will feel oily and very smooth. Store in an airtight container.

Soft, Homemade Plasticine

2 cups flour
1 cup salt
1½ cups warm water
2 tablespoons vegetable oil

Mix all ingredients together. Form into balls. Store dough on an open shelf; it does not have to be kept in covered container.

Beginner's Playdough

3 cups flour
1 cup salt
1 cup water
1 tablespoon salad oil

Knead all ingredients together. Form into balls. Store in airtight container.

Tempera Paint for One

2½ ounces water
1 tablespoon powdered tempera (any color)
3 drops liquid dish detergent such as Ivory Snow™

Pour all ingredients into an empty juice can. Stir with tongue depressor.

For fingerpainting, toddlers can use cafeteria trays, mirrored surfaces with protected edges, and plastic wrap taped to table and floor surfaces. Of course, they can also fingerpaint directly on a table.

❖ **The paint:** Use fingerpaint and tempera paint in one or two colors. For fingerpainting, toddlers can also use whipped cream, nontoxic shaving cream or mud—either at room temperature or slightly warmed.

For drawing:

❖ **Something to draw with:** Toddlers can use all the materials already listed, plus water-based felt-tip markers.

❖ **Something to draw on:** At one time or another, you'll want to offer children a variety of textured and colored papers, both dry and wet.

For molding:

❖ **Doughs of many colors:** Children can use an eye-dropper filled with liquid food coloring to add color to the doughs, and then work the color in with their fingers and fists.

❖ **Something to vary the experience:** Offer children basic props such as wooden mallets, tongue depressors, plastic rods cut to six-inch lengths, and potato mashers for pounding, poking, rolling, and stamping the dough.

Recipes for molding materials are shown on this and the opposite page.

For printing:

❖ **Something to print with:** Include a variety of printing tools such as rubber stamps, butter molds, sponges, dominoes, corks, golf balls, old puzzle pieces, and the rubber soles of old shoes. Make ink pads by fastening a piece of firm foam rubber or a sponge onto a Styrofoam™ meat tray, then pouring tempera paint into the foam or sponge.

❖ **Something to print on:** Collect tissue paper, butcher paper, newsprint, and a variety of colored and textured papers.

For older toddlers or those with good fine motor skills, you may want to include these additional art materials.

For collages and assemblages:

- ❖ **Materials to work with:** Almost any material will do. Consider pipe cleaners, wooden dowels, yarn, ribbons, papers with assorted textures and colors, magazines and catalogs, scraps of material, leaves, dried flowers and weeds, photographs, and recycled gift wrapping, greeting cards, post cards, and business cards.
- ❖ **Tools for putting artwork together:** Children can use library paste and, if appropriate, small, blunt-nosed scissors (4 inches and 4½ inches).

"Should I use food for art activities?"

In any discussion of children's art, the topic of using food as part of the art experience almost always comes up. You'll notice that most of the recipes on these pages contain one or more food products. Some families and educators strongly believe that it is inappropriate to use food or food products for anything other than nutrition. Other family members and educators may think that using food as a learning aid is entirely appropriate. Still others may take a neutral stand.

Because this topic is entirely personal, we can offer you no right or wrong answer. We do suggest, though, that you discuss this issue with your colleagues and the children's families. In most cases, if anyone has an objection, it would be best to honor that person's views. Alternatively, if no one has an objection, food can play a unique role in children's art. It is especially useful with infants who are forever putting things in their mouths. Also, you should know that researchers have found that children who have used food for art have no problem distinguishing food from inedible art materials as they grow older.

Moist Modeling Clay

1½ cups flour
1½ cups warm water
1 cup salt
2 tablespoons salad oil

Mix all ingredients together. Form into ball. To prevent clay from turning sour in storage, wash plastic bag with water, shake out, and place clay inside. Place bag in plastic zippered pillow case. Gather top of case together and secure with rubber band. Store in cool place.

GOOP

3 cups corn starch
2 cups warm water

Gradually add water to corn starch. Mix ingredients together with hands. Goop is done when mass goes from lumpy to satiny texture.

Goop hardens in the air and turns to liquid when held. It resists punching, but a light touch causes a finger to sink in.

Baker's Clay

4 cups flour
1 cup salt
1½ cups warm water

Mix all ingredients together. Shape into a ball. Store in an airtight container.

Paintable Playdough

2 cups corn starch
1 cup baking soda
1 cup water

Mix all ingredients together and cook over medium heat. Stir constantly until mixture forms a ball. Allow to cool slightly and knead. Store in plastic wrap in the refrigerator.

"How should I arrange the environment for art experiences?"

Beginning art experiences are a part of everyday explorations for young infants. You don't really need a special place for art. Older infants and toddlers need no more than bare floor space and a child-sized table to draw, paint, print, mold, tear, cut, and paste.

Up until about age 2½, children have limited wrist control. As a result, they draw and paint using broad, up-and-down or side-to-side strokes. It is much easier for children to perform these pumplike motions on the floor or standing at a table than at an easel or while sitting at a table. On the other hand, older toddlers, who have more control over their wrist and hand motions, will enjoy working at an easel or drawing a wall mural. Therefore, as children develop new skills and you expand the variety of materials, you may want to create a special area.

Give some thought to storage of materials. You will want to place certain types of materials on higher shelves or in storage cabinets where children can't get to them. These items include materials that you need to set up (paints and collage items) and those that require close supervision (paste and scissors).

Other materials like modeling doughs, papers, crayons, and chalk can be displayed in containers on a low shelf. Then children can choose what they want. It's also a good idea to put a picture label on the shelf. Picture labels help children recognize materials by sight, provide an opportunity to match objects with symbols, and promote clean up and responsibility.

Here are some storage ideas you can try.

❖ Use egg cartons turned upside down to store scissors or paint brushes. (Tape the lids of the carton together so the cartons can be turned upside down.)

❖ Punch holes in the plastic lid of a coffee can and cover the edges of the holes with masking tape so children can't cut their fingers. Use the container to hold markers, scissors, or brushes.

❖ Use empty orange juice containers covered in different colors of bright Contact™ paper as paint containers. When filled half-way with the corresponding color of paint and placed in a six-pack cardboard container with a handle, you'll have a paint caddie.

❖ Keep modeling doughs and clays in covered plastic containers or margarine tubs. Store library glue in squeeze bottles like the ketchup and mustard containers found in diners.

❖ Use baskets or plastic containers to hold chalk and crayons.

❖ Keep felt tip markers upside down in their caps. Here's one idea you can use for more permanent storage. First, pour plaster of paris into an old jelly-roll pan or tray. When the plaster starts to set, place the marker caps upside down in it. Finally, after the plaster has hardened, return the markers to their caps. Another idea, for children who have difficulty fitting the markers into caps, is to store markers in color coordinated juice cans.

"How can I keep mess to a minimum?"

As much as possible, you want children to be able to use art materials on their own. This means preparing the environment to minimize messes.

To protect your art area from spills and drips, you can use an old shower curtain or a painter's drop cloth. Try to locate art activities near a water source, especially when children are fingerpainting or mixing modeling doughs. If no sink is available, you can bring buckets of water to your art area for cleaning up. It's a good idea to fill empty hand lotion or liquid soap dispensers with water for hand washing, too. Cleaning equipment such as mops, paper towels, a broom, and a dust pan should be within close reach. Scrapers of the sort used to wash windows are also helpful.

Children can wear smocks to protect themselves from messes. (Children can also wear them when cooking and doing water play activities.) You can buy smocks in a store or make them from old shirts or pieces of oilcloth.

"What should I do with children's work?"

Even though children are more interested in doing art than in finishing paintings or drawings, you'll want to save some of their work. It's a good idea to provide a special place for hanging paintings to dry. You might buy a drying rack or use a clothesline. When children see that you value their pictures, they gain confidence and take increasing pride in their abilities.

Families, too, love seeing their children's artwork displayed. Think about posting a brief explanation of what you did with the children and why for parents to read while admiring their children's creations.

It's also important to display pieces of art where children will see them—on the bottom part of a wall or room divider, protected by clear Contact™ paper. Making a construction paper frame makes the art even more "special." You can also use the children's art as wrapping paper, shelf paper on your room dividers, or as writing paper for letters to the children's families.

Keep samples of children's art work to put in their portfolios and send the rest home. Most parents really like to display their children's artwork. Some children may report back that their picture is on the wall or refrigerator at home.

Encouraging Children to Dabble in Art

For infants and toddlers, art activities are, first and foremost, sensory experiences that involve exploring and experimenting with textures and materials. These experiences are part of everyday life. As children grow and gain more skills, you can expand the type of materials and plan various activities for them.

Young Infants

Give infants uninterrupted time to explore materials. You probably already have many materials in your indoor and outdoor environments that infants can touch, smell, look at, and even chew on. When you hold an infant in your lap, let her feel the texture of your scarf and reach for the round cushion in the chair. Hang a mobile made of terrycloth cutouts across a crib so the infant can kick or wave at it. When infants begin crawling and standing, you can put swatches of material or soft plasticine on a bottom shelf of a room divider. This allows children to get at these materials on their own.

As children grow and develop, they continue to enjoy exploring with their senses. See what happens when you put a dab of pudding on a child's high chair tray. Before you know it, the pudding becomes fingerpaint that can be swirled and slid. Select cloths or papers with distinct colors, feels, and sounds. As you choose materials, be aware that children younger than three tend to be more interested in shapes than in size or color. They even seem to prefer certain shapes, particularly round ones.

To help young infants get the most from their art explorations, talk with them about what they're doing and mirror their reactions of pleasure, enthusiasm, and surprise. Here are some examples.

- ❖ **Describe the sensory experience:** "The satin feels so smooth on your cheek."
- ❖ **Describe their actions:** "You crumpled the paper into a big ball!"
- ❖ **Provide them with words for the objects they are exploring:** "See how rough the sandpaper feels."
- ❖ **Build their confidence:** "You found the red ball on the shelf."

Mobile Infants

Mobile infants like Willard and Abby enjoy the soothing effect of squeezing and poking oily dough. They can grasp a crayon or brush, and "paint" with water on a chalkboard or fence. You can begin by giving the child a jumbo crayon or a homemade scribble wafer. Older infants grasp these fat, stubby crayons with their whole hand. Don't expect a child to hold the crayon with thumb and fingers, or to be able to draw using wrist movements. At this stage of development, drawing is a whole body process.

Offer the child a crayon or let him select one. He will probably be as interested in the feel, smell, and possibly the taste of the wax as he is in the crayon's color. Tape a large piece of paper (at least 24 by 36 inches) to the floor. Then, gently show the child how to use the crayon on the paper by placing his hand on the paper so he can make a mark with the crayon. Because most children have been waving their hands around since early infancy in a type of "air writing," the transition to drawing on paper is a natural one.

You can introduce older infants to painting with water in much the same way, since children go through the same developmental steps in painting as they do in drawing. Because children use their entire arms and bodies to paint, they approach painting with bold arm movements.

For molding experiences, children need nothing more than the freedom to spend time poking, pounding, and batting at doughs. As is true for drawing and painting, children explore the doughs; they aren't trying to create master-pieces! Nonetheless, handling molding materials is both soothing and filled with learning opportunities.

As you conduct art activities with mobile infants, here are some ways to promote their learning.

- ❖ **Describe changes children can observe:** "The fingerpaint turned the white tray green."
- ❖ **Help children solve problems:** "Let's mop up the water that spilled and get some more."
- ❖ **Encourage children to appreciate beauty and design:** "You really like that bright red crayon."
- ❖ **Comment on their actions:** "Abby, you sure can squeeze that playdough hard."
- ❖ **Build children's sense of competence:** "You covered that whole piece of paper with bright paint."

Toddlers

Many of the same experiences are appropriate for toddlers. However, their fine motor skills are more highly developed. As a result, they can begin to paint and draw with a variety of tools. Some toddlers have the muscle control to use paste and scissors; they can now try their hand at collages (pasting objects on paper) and assemblages (making three-dimensional pieces of art). Matthew, for example, proudly makes collages—in his fashion. He tears magazine pages into tiny pieces, with great concentration. When he pastes the papers, he may also paste a nearby object or get his finger stuck in his creation. For Matthew, the enjoyment is in the creative process. It makes no difference to him that his collage turns out to be a three-dimensional gob of paste with objects and the popsicle stick he used for pasting attached to it.

If you make a few simple adjustments, toddlers like Gena, who are physically challenged, can also have fun with art activities. For example, because Gena cannot fully extend her arms to reach an easel, Ivan has attached a long-handled paint brush to a Velcro™ headband. This arrangement allows her to use her head to guide the paint onto the paper. (If the child is painting at a table, tape the drawing paper onto the table and make sure the paint containers are weighted so they won't tip over.) Because Gena is very verbal for her age, she can also make use of voice-activated computer technology which allows her to use words and sounds to scribble and draw on a computer screen.[1]

Many older toddlers have developed wrist control. Because they can control their scribblings, their lines give way to curves, spirals, ovals—and eventually, to circles. These toddlers may start making patterns, repeating them, and sometimes seeing designs in what they have made. While the designs may be totally unplanned, they are thrilling for a child to discover.

To tap into the toddler's natural enthusiasm for art, you'll want to set up art activities for success. Here are some tips.

Preparing for an activity. As a first step, you can involve toddlers in the preparation process—making their own clays, playdoughs, fingerpaint, and GOOP. (See recipes.) You can place materials for non-messy activities, such as drawing and tearing, where children can get to them and use them on their own. For special planned activities, gather the art supplies ahead of time so you don't have to leave the children to get something.

Give some thought to preparing the environment, if the activity will be messy. Floors, carpets, and children's clothing are likely to need protection. Have cleaning supplies nearby. Keep paper towels on a low, open shelf. When they are easy to find, children will readily clean up spills and splashes.

During an activity. It's fine to encourage children to draw, tear, and use molding materials on their own. However, you can work with an individual child or with groups of two or three children when they do activities that need supervision, such as painting, cutting, and pasting. Keeping groups small helps to limit confusion.

---

[1] Children and families who have been identified as eligible for receiving early intervention services under Part C of the special education law are also eligible to receive assistive technology and related services.

Interacting with children as they work. Describe the art process to help children understand what they are doing: "Leo, you tore the paper into so many pieces." Make open-ended comments to encourage them to reflect on their work: "Jonisha, tell me about the design you made with the fingerpaint."

Extending Toddler's Experiences with Art

One of the best ways to enrich drawing or painting is to give children different types of papers to paint or draw on. Each different kind of paper can provide a special experience. See how children respond to:

- ❖ poster paper of differing colors, sizes, and shapes
- ❖ tissue paper of differing colors, sizes, and shapes
- ❖ crepe paper of differing colors, sizes, and shapes
- ❖ corrugated cardboard of differing colors, sizes, and shapes
- ❖ Sunday newspaper comics (for painting with water)
- ❖ wet and dry papers of all types
- ❖ fingerpainting papers coated with buttermilk, liquid starch, and sugar water (great for chalk)
- ❖ butcher paper

You can also give children different objects and tools instead of paint brushes, such as those we described earlier. Some other painting tools might include:

- ❖ feathers
- ❖ twigs or leaves
- ❖ eyedroppers
- ❖ foam rubber paint brushes
- ❖ toothbrushes
- ❖ vegetable and pastry brushes

You expose children to many science concepts when you encourage them to use paints of various textures and smells. As you prepare tempera paint, try changing its quality by adding one or more of the following items.

Adding this . . .	Makes paint . . .
flour	lumpy
Karo™ syrup	shiny and sticky
sand or sawdust	rough and gritty
Epsom salt	sparkling
liquid soap	slimy

You can also vary the experience by taking art outdoors. Natural light enriches all art experiences. Children are bound to find that drawing, painting, and molding are quite different when done outside. Then, too, it's very exciting on a sunny day to "paint" the side of a building, a driveway, or a tree trunk with water, then watch the "paint" disappear before your very eyes.

As you can see, there are a great number of appropriate art activities for infants and toddlers at each stage of development. Any activities, however, that focus on a finished product rather than the creative process are inappropriate for infants and toddlers, since young children are not yet developmentally able to create representative art. We recommend that you avoid the following:

- ❖ using coloring books;
- ❖ using patterns (stencils, tracing paper, and so forth);
- ❖ telling a child what to draw, paint, or make;
- ❖ expecting that a child will produce anything recognizable; and
- ❖ "finishing" a child's work to make it "better."

For infants and toddlers, art is both exciting and a way to express themselves.

Sharing Thoughts About
Art Experiences

Dear Families:

When you think of art experiences do you imagine a child with crayons or a paint brush in hand? Painting and coloring, though, are just two of the many ways young children enjoy art. In fact, art experiences begin early in life as children notice the sunlight streaming through a window or the pattern on a mobile. As they get older, they enjoy scribbling with a crayon or squeezing playdough between their fingers. Art experiences allow children to have wonderful sensory experiences and to experiment with a variety of materials. They also help children develop thinking skills and physical abilities. Here are some examples.

When your child does this . . .	**Your child is learning . . .**
covers paper with paint	about spatial relationships
mixes water with dry paint	science concepts
pokes a hole in playdough	cause and effect
tears paper for a collage	eye and hand coordination
successfully learns to use paste	pride in an accomplishment

What You Can Do at Home

It's easy to provide opportunities for your child to have art experiences at home. Here are some ideas.

❖ *Keep in mind that art experiences are part of everyday life.* An art experience can be as simple as talking to your child about the color of the sky or the soft feel of the blanket.

❖ *Make art experiences fun.* Just putting some pudding on your child's highchair and letting him fingerpaint is an adventure in art.

❖ *Plan some special things to do.* You can make playdough your child can squeeze and pound, or GOOP for another wonderful sensory experience. We have several recipes we'd be glad to share with you.

❖ *Provide plenty of uninterrupted time for your child to experience art.* For young children, it is the process of creating that is important, not the finished product. They are not yet ready to draw or paint something you might recognize. They are, however, ready to express their ideas and feelings with bold strokes of crayon and splashes of paint.

Together, we can give your child the kinds of experiences that form a foundation for both appreciating and doing art.

Sincerely,

Algunas ideas sobre el juego artístico

Estimadas familias:

Cuando ustedes piensan en alguna experiencia artística, ¿se imaginan a un niño con unas crayolas o con un pincel en la mano? Pintar y colorear son sólo dos de las múltiples maneras en que sus hijos pueden disfrutar del arte. De hecho, las experiencias artísticas comienzan tempranísimo en la vida, a medida que los niños notan que la luz del sol pasa a través de una ventana, o reconocen el patrón de un móvil. A medida que crecen, ellos disfrutan al garabatear con crayolas o amasar plastilina con sus manos. El juego artístico les permite a los niños tener maravillosas experiencias sensoriales y experimentar con una diversidad de materiales. Además, les ayuda a desarrollar tanto destrezas del pensamiento como habilidades físicas. Los siguientes son unos cuantos ejemplos:

Cuando su niño(a):	**El /ella está aprendiendo:**
cubre papel con pintura	relaciones espaciales
mezcla agua con pintura seca	conceptos científicos
le hace un hoyo a la plastilina	causa-efecto
razga papel para un collage	coordinación ojo-mano
utiliza la pasta con éxito	a sentirse orgulloso por sus logros

Lo que ustedes pueden hacer en el hogar

Es sumamente fácil permitirles a sus hijos tener oportunidades artísticas en el hogar. Las siguientes son unas cuantas ideas útiles:

❖ *Mantengan presente que las experiencias artísticas hacen parte de la vida diaria.* Puede tratarse de algo tan sencillo como hablar con su niño(a) acerca del color del cielo o sobre la suavidad de una manta.

❖ *Hagan que las experiencias artísticas sean placenteras.* El mero hecho de proporcionarles a los pequeños un tazón y sentarlos en una silla alta para que "pinten" con los dedos, puede ser toda una aventura artística.

❖ *Planeen hacer algo especial.* Elaboren plastilina para que sus hijos la amasen y la golpeen y tengan una maravillosa experiencia sensorial. Si lo necesitan, contamos con varias recetas para elaborar plastilina que nos encantaría compartir con ustedes.

❖ *Ofrézcanles a sus niños suficiente tiempo para que experimenten el arte sin interrupción.* Para los pequeños, lo importante es el proceso de creación, no el producto terminado. Ellos no están listos aún para dibujar o pintar algo que ustedes puedan reconocer. Pero están listos para expresar sus percepciones, ideas y sentimientos mediante los trazos bruscos con las crayolas y la salpicadura de pintura.

Juntos, podremos ofrecerle a sus hijos las clases de experiencias que constituyen la base para apreciar y producir el arte.

Les saluda atentamente,

Imitating and Pretending

— ◆ —

Valisha bites her lip in concentration as she walks around the outside of the playhouse that Reggie, La Toya's husband, built in the backyard for the children. "Let's see here," she says placing one hand on her hip just as Reggie does when he is contemplating a new project. "I need a hammer." She picks up a small rock and "hammers" a spot under the window in the front. A few minutes later, she moves her hand back and forth across the same spot in a sawing motion as she makes a "chhhh, chhhh, chhhh" sound. Looking up, she sees Reggie walking out the back door. "Look," she calls to him. "I fixed it!"

— ◆ —

Pretend play—also called make-believe play, symbolic play, and dramatic play—is one of the ways that young children come to understand the world around them. While true pretend play emerges between ages one and two, its foundation is established during early infancy. As infants become increasingly aware of the world around them, they begin to imitate what they see. They actively explore objects to find out what they can do. As they interact with significant people in their lives, they build the understandings they will need to engage in pretend play. While examples of imitating and pretending are woven throughout *The Creative Curriculum*, pretend play is so essential to children's healthy development, it deserves a chapter unto itself.

When toddlers engage in pretend play, they use symbols and make believe to replay events or actions they have observed and experienced. Using symbols involves the ability to use one thing to represent or stand for something else. Children represent an object (when they use a rectangular block as a car), a person or living being (when they pretend to be a dog or a mother), or an event (when they crawl in a cardboard box and pretend to be driving a car).

Pretend play helps children become able to think abstractly. For example, to imagine that a block of wood is really a car, a child must be able to recall what a car looks like, how it moves, what sounds it might make, and then "infuse" these properties into a block of wood. This is the same skill the child will use one day to understand and use letters and numbers. For this reason, pretend play is critical to children's language and their cognitive development.

Research tells us that children who have good dramatic play skills—who know how to pretend about situations, use props in imaginative ways, and interact with peers in their play—are more likely to be successful learners than those who do not have these skills. The skills used in dramatic play prepare children to think logically, solve problems, and take turns.[1] The ability to pretend about events and experiences also helps children to cope with fears and uncertainties.

Setting the Stage for Imitation and Pretend Play

Although children engage in imitation and pretend play naturally, they will not develop high level dramatic play skills unless adults encourage this type of activity. You can begin building the foundation for dramatic play by setting up an environment that promotes exploration. Keep in mind that, of all the elements in the environment, you—and your relationships with each child—are the most important.

"Do I need to set up a special place for pretend play?"

Young and mobile infants don't require a separate space to engage in pretend play. Pretend play can take place at any time and in any place.

Toddlers, on the other hand, can benefit from having a special place for their pretend play, since they favor using objects and props to supplement their play. A small table and chairs, a doll bed, carriage, and perhaps a sink and stove create a "stage" that toddlers can use to replay scenes they know.

"What materials should I provide for young infants?"

Young infants do not require special materials. Your voice, your face, and your actions will intrigue and fascinate infants more than any toy or prop.

You can, however, provide soft dolls that infants can grasp and hold. Dolls should be washable and have simple facial features with no moveable pieces or detachable parts. Young infants are attracted to bright colors and particularly enjoy dolls and stuffed animals that have rattles inside and make noise when shaken.

Nonbreakable mirrors that are securely attached to a wall or crib are another good choice for young infants. They are amused by facial expressions—their own and those of others. Seeing themselves in a mirror increases their self-awareness.

---

[1] J.E. Johnson. "The Role of Play in Cognitive Development." In E. Klugman & S. Smilansky, Eds. *Children's Play and Learning: Perspectives and Policy Implications.* New York: Teachers College Press, 1990.

"What materials will encourage mobile infants to engage in imitation?"

The active exploration of mobile infants—pushing, pulling, emptying, filling, climbing in and out, around and on top of furniture—provide experiences that build the skills they will use later in pretend play. Therefore, any of the toys discussed in the previous chapter are also appropriate for promoting imitation and pretend play.

Realistic materials are good choices for this age group. Mobile infants show a preference for life-like dolls of vinyl or rubber that they can carry around, bathe, and "feed." Other objects related to real life include:

 ❖ carts to push, a baby carriage, and other wheeled toys;
 ❖ doll bottles, baby blankets, and a cradle;
 ❖ play telephones or real ones; and
 ❖ pots, pans, and plastic dishes.

Mobile infants like to put on hats and admire themselves in a full length mirror. Pocketbooks and baby carriages are ideal containers for their collections of pegs, pop beads, and small blocks.

Transportation toys like cars, buses, trucks, and trains need not be fancy or detailed. In fact, the simpler the design the better. Plastic, rubber, or wooden toys are safer than and preferable to those made of metal. Mobile infants enjoy pushing these toys across the floor and filling them with plastic animals and people.

These early explorations with representations of real objects and living things sometimes inspire mobile infants to pick up a cup and pretend to drink, or hold a toy telephone to their ear and imitate a parent on the phone.

"What materials will inspire pretend play in toddlers?"

Toddlers require a variety of props to extend their play. These may include:

 ❖ dress-up clothes such as jackets, hats, and dresses;
 ❖ work-related props such as boots, firefighter hats, work gloves, stethoscope;
 ❖ suitcases, pocketbooks, lunch boxes;
 ❖ cloth bags, small briefcases; and
 ❖ ride-on toys.

While details in toys and props are not important to infants, they are very important to toddlers. Toddlers are intrigued by small cars with doors that open and shut, trucks with moveable parts, and dolls with painted features. Jonisha and Valisha are especially fond of dolls that look like real babies with movable arms and legs, hair, and fine features. They can handle simple doll clothes, removing them and replacing them. (To promote acceptance of differences, select dolls that reflect cultural diversity.)

Toddlers are developing the small muscle coordination needed to set up play scenes and move objects around. Matthew, for example, can play for long periods of time arranging people and animal figures inside and outside of a toy barn, talking to them as he plays.

Remember to resist the urge to put out too many things at one time. Toddlers can easily become overwhelmed and play often disintegrates when there are too many choices.

Promoting Imitation and Pretend Play Through Relationships

The first steps in promoting pretend play involve developing relationships with children and providing opportunities for them to explore and learn about the world. As mobile infants begin to imitate events they have experienced, and toddlers begin to pretend, your role is to be a good observer and a willing partner. This means being ready to follow a child's lead, expanding on what a child says and does, and being sensitive about not taking over or overwhelming a child.

Some toddlers need more encouragement than others to participate in pretend play. This is especially true for children with developmental delays, who are also likely to have delayed language skills. Knowing what to look for at each stage of development can help you to pick up on children's cues and make good decisions about when to step in and when to hold back.

Young Infants

The roots of imitation and pretend play are nourished by the trusting relationships you develop with young infants. Their trust in you leads infants to engage with the world around them, a world that soon beckons them to explore. These explorations become increasingly purposeful. Julio, for example, will explore objects in his grasp by taking them directly into his mouth, while Jasmine, at nine months, is more directed in her explorations. She also picks up a rattle, but rather than mouth it, she looks at it carefully, turns it over to examine it from different angles, and then shakes it vigorously.

Because of the strong connection between pretend play and language development, it is important to talk with infants as you care for them each day.

Examples of What You Might Say:

You see a young infant lying on her back in her crib carefully examining her hands in front of her face. You say, "Look at your hands. You're moving your fingers."

An infant pulls a rubber cow off the bottom shelf and begins chewing on one of its legs. You say, "That's a cow you are chewing on. Cows say 'Moo'."

Holding an infant as his grandmother leaves, you say, "Wave bye-bye to Grandma."

During a neighborhood walk, an infant turns her head towards the sound of a car horn and you say, "You hear a horn honking."

Mobile Infants

If you observe how mobile infants explore objects, you can see that they have learned to distinguish different properties. For example, when Brooks hands Abby a wooden spoon, Abby smiles and bangs it on the table, knowing that it will make noise. When given a cloth doll, however, Abby strokes it gently. This prompts Brooks to say, "You're taking good care of your baby."

Mobile infants also begin using materials in playful ways. For example, a child may take a hat, put it on his foot, look at you with an impish grin and say, "Here?" With some encouragement, he will continue the game, putting the hat on different parts of his body and repeating, "Here?" until he finally puts it on his head.

Among the favorite games of mobile infants are those that have elements of pretend play. "Peek-a-boo" is a game of surprise that delights almost all young children. Once they learn the game, they will initiate it themselves by covering their own face and re-emerging with squeals of laughter. Playing "Hide-and-Seek" is another way of exploring how the world works. And how many times have you engaged in the game of "Drop-and-Fetch"? In this game infants learn the give and take of relationships by manipulating you into picking up everything they drop!

Have you ever noticed how mobile infants intently watch and then imitate your actions? Imitation is the first stage of real pretend play. Mobile infants imitate events they have experienced first hand. When you describe their actions, you help them become aware of what they are doing. This attention lets them know that you value imitation and encourages this behavior.

Examples of What You Might Say:

You see a child lying down on a pillow during play time and you say, "Are you taking a nap?"

A child picks up an empty cup and brings it to his lips. You say, "Hmm, I bet that tastes good."

A child crawls around barking and you say, "What a nice doggy. Are you barking because you are hungry? Here's a bone for you, little doggy."

A child pushes a doll in a plastic shopping cart. You say, "Are you taking your baby shopping? What are you going to buy for dinner?"

Toddlers

In contrast to mobile infants who imitate actions with real objects, toddlers are developing the ability to use objects for pretend. Matthew can transform a block into a car, a paper towel roll into a hose, or an empty carton into a bus. Jonisha and Valisha are able to pretend even without objects. For example, La Toya noticed Valisha holding her hand to her ear and pretending to talk on the phone. This shows a high level of ability to pretend.

Toddlers also begin planning their play episodes and combining different actions. For example, a toddler may gather together several items needed to "play baby," and then hold the doll, feed it, and put it to bed. Toddlers can transform themselves into different characters: a scary monster, a favorite person in a story they love, or an animal. Sometimes they get so immersed in the character, they won't respond when you call them by name. Gena tells Ivan, "I'm not Gena. I'm Pooh Bear." Recognizing the value of pretend play, Ivan responds, "OK, Pooh Bear. It's time to eat your honey."

In the play of young toddlers, you can see elements of both imitation and true pretend play. Here are some signs that true pretend play is taking place:[2]

- ❖ **Performing simple actions on people or toys.** A child combs a doll's hair or hands a toy phone to an adult.

- ❖ **Substituting a toy object for the real object**. A child uses a ring from a stacking toy as a doughnut or a cylinder block as a baby bottle to feed her doll. The object must bear some resemblance in size and shape to the one it represents.

- ❖ **Pretending to do things adults do**. A child pretends to put on lipstick or picks up a book and pretends to read.

- ❖ **Performing several actions in appropriate order.** A child replays familiar events such as lying down to sleep, getting up and dressing, or carrying a briefcase and going out to work.

- ❖ **Pretending to be another person.** A child replays the role of someone well-known such as a father or mother, copying that person's actions and words. This role play shows an increasing awareness of other people and the ability to recall their actions.

- ❖ **Giving dolls or stuffed animals an active role.** A child seats a doll in a high chair, places the doll's hand on a spoon, and moves it to the doll's mouth. Another common action is to place a toy animal in front of a bowl and say, "Eat!"

Older toddlers, whose pretend play has been encouraged, often show a higher level of skills than those with fewer play experiences. Here are some signs to look for if you work with children two-and-a-half to three years old.

- ❖ **Acting out less familiar scenes**. A child replays going to the doctor or grocery store, thus moving beyond the more familiar family themes.

---

[2] Based on Elaine Weitzman, *Learning Language and Loving It, A Guide to Promoting Children's Social and Language Development in Early Childhood Settings.* Toronto, Ontario: The Hanen Centre, 1992.

❖ **Pretending with an object that is not similar to the one it represents.** A child may put on a firefighter's hat, pick up a piece of string, pretend it is a hose and use it to squirt water on an imaginary fire, and then put the string on a chair, sit down and pretend to drive off. This is an important achievement and shows the child is able to imagine the object in his or her mind without relying on a concrete representation.

❖ **Using imaginary objects.** A child holds an imaginary doll and pretends to rock it, pets an imaginary dog, or holds her hand to her ear and talks on the phone. The ability to pretend without using concrete objects is another indication that a child is able to create symbols or pictures in his or her mind.

Pretend play is an excellent way to manage fears and angry feelings. As toddlers become increasingly aware of their world, they typically develop fears—of loud noises, big animals, being separated from their parents, and many other scary things. Pretend play is one way they gain a sense of control over these fears. A toddler who stamps around the room growling and swiping the air with his arms is assuming the role of the scary monster he most fears. By becoming the monster, he can control what the monster does, and therefore experience some power over that which he fears. Similarly, a child who plays the mother going off to work and leaving her "baby" at child care may be working through her own unhappy feelings about her own mother leaving her. When you see these kinds of play, you can help by putting into words what you think children are feeling.

Examples of What You Might Say:

"What a scary monster! I bet that monster is hungry. Do you need something to eat, Mr. Monster?"

"Are you going to work, Mommy? Don't forget to kiss your baby good-bye. She'll be waiting for you to pick her up."

By accepting this type of play, verbalizing what you think a child is feeling, and joining in, you can help toddlers work through fears that they cannot put into words. For this reason, pretend play is as important to a child's emotional development as it is to cognitive and social development.

Encouraging Pretend Play During Other Activities

Opportunities to promote pretend play can emerge during many activities and daily routines. Caregivers/teachers who are aware of these opportunities will use them to engage children in make-believe activities.

Examples of Ways to Interact:

> While rolling out some playdough, Leo says, "A apple." Barbara responds, "Wow, that apple looks so good. May I have a bite?" When Leo nods his head, Barbara picks up the piece of dough and pretends to take a bite and chew. "Mmm. What a good apple."

> Outside in the play yard, Willard climbs into a cardboard box. Grace sits next to him. "Are you driving your car?" she asks. He looks at her and smiles. She moves her hands as if she were steering a car and makes the sounds of the engine. Willard watches and laughs. He joins her in "beep, beep, beeping" the horn.

From across the room, Ivan sees Gena reaching out to touch the head
of another child who is pretending to be a horse. He stays where he
is and lets the children play without interruption.

As Brooks and Abby come indoors from a walk in the snow, Abby
pulls off her hat and Brooks says, "Hello, Abby's head." In a minute or
two, Brooks pulls off Abby's boot, looks down, and says, "Hello,
Abby's toes." Abby laughs with delight and wiggles her toes.

As Mercedes and Matthew prepare grilled cheese sandwiches for lunch,
they sing a silly song about taking crunchy bites of toasty, cheesy
bread. Between verses, they pretend to take big crunchy bites.

Young children are most likely to use real life experiences as the content of their
play. A book such as *Peekaboo, Baby!* (Denise Lewis Patrick, 1995), can encourage such
play. Favorite stories can also inspire pretend play, especially with your encouragement.
For example, books such as *I Am a Little Cat, I Am a Little Dog, I Am a Little Lion, I Am a
Little Elephant* (Helmut Spanner, 1983), *Moo, Baa, La-la-la* (Sandra Boynton, 1984), and
Have You Seen My Duckling? (Nancy Tafuri, 1984), can set the stage for children pretending to be animals. Books such as *I Can Build a House* (Shigeo Watanabe, 1982), *When We
Went to the Park* (Shirley Hughes, 1985), and *Happy Birthday, Sam* (Pat Hutchins, 1978)
can help stretch children's play beyond more common everyday events such as food
preparation, going to work, and shopping.

Using **prop boxes** also promotes children's play. A prop box is a collection of
various pretend play materials, usually organized around a theme. The props inspire
children to replay familiar scenes. For example, older toddlers may replay first-hand
experiences at the doctor's when they pull pencils and "prescription pads" out of the
medical box. A set of cardboard coins in your grocery store box can lead to discussions
about money as well as help children feel "grown-up."

Yet always remember that, while props can be very helpful in extending pretend
play, the most effective strategy for encouraging this skill is your understanding of its
value for children and enthusiastic participation in pretend play.

Sharing Thoughts About Imitating and Pretend Play

Dear Families:

Imitation and pretend play are among the most important ways that children learn about the world. The foundation for this type of play begins when young infants explore their surroundings and build relationships with the important people in their lives. Soon, they start to imitate those around them and to make believe with real items. For example, a child might feed a doll with a spoon, or rock a doll to sleep. As they become toddlers, children develop the ability to use objects to stand for real things. For example, when a child imagines that a block is a car, the child must be able to recall what a car looks like, how it moves, what sounds it might make—and then transfer these understandings to the block.

This ability to think abstractly is the same skill your child will need one day to understand and use letters and numbers. In fact, research shows that children who have developed pretend play skills are more likely to be successful learners than those who lack these skills.

Being able to pretend also helps children cope with fears and deal with uncertainties in their lives. For these reasons—and also because children enjoy imitating and pretending—we encourage these activities every day in our program.

What You Can Do at Home

Because imitation and pretend play are so important to every child's development and eventual success in school, we hope you will try some of these activities at home.

❖ *Encourage your child to explore.* The more children learn about objects and people in their world, the more information they have on which to base their pretend play.

❖ *Provide props that inspire pretend play.* Dolls, doll blankets, a cradle, telephones (play or real), pots, pans, and plastic dishes will inspire your child to replay the roles of important people. Other useful props include rubber people and animals, and transportation toys such as cars, trucks, and boats.

❖ *Let your child dress up.* You can encourage your child's ability to pretend by providing dress-up clothes, work-related props such as firefighter hats, work gloves, and a stethoscope, and various ride-on toys. Remember not to confuse your child by putting out too many things at once.

❖ *Play make-believe with your child.* This is one of the best ways to encourage your child to pretend. You can also encourage pretend play by asking questions, offering a new prop, and taking on a role yourself.

Together we can help your child use pretend play as an important way to learn.

Sincerely,

Algunas ideas sobre el juego de imitar y pretender

Estimadas familias:

Jugar a imitar y a representar se encuentra entre las maneras más importantes en que sus hijos aprenden acerca del mundo. La base de esta clase de juego comienza cuando los pequeños exploran sus alrededores y construyen relaciones con las personas importantes en sus vidas. Muy pronto, ellos comienzan a imitar a aquellos a su alrededor y a pretender que son alguien más, haciendo uso de objetos reales. Por ejemplo, una pequeña puede alimentar a su muñeca con una cuchara, o mecerla para que se duerma. A medida que crecen, los niños desarrollan la capacidad de emplear objetos para representar a otros.

Esta misma capacidad para pensar de manera abstracta, es la misma destreza que sus hijos necesitarán más adelante para comprender y utilizar las letras y los números. De hecho, los niños que desarrollan las destrezas del juego de pretender —o juego imaginario— muy proba blemente serán aprendices más exitosos que aquellos que carecen de tales destrezas. Pretender también les ayuda a los niños a enfrentar sus temores y a bregar con la incertidumbre en sus vidas. Por estas razones —y también porque los niños lo disfrutan— nosotros estimulamos estas actividades en nuestro programa diariamente.

Lo que ustedes pueden hacer en el hogar

Debido a que el juego de imitar y pretender es de gran importancia en el desarrollo infantil y para el eventual éxito escolar, esperamos que ustedes pongan en práctica en sus hogares, algunas de estas actividades.

* *Animen a sus hijos a explorar.* Entre más aprendan los niños sobre los objetos y las personas en su mundo, más información tendrán sobre la cual basar su juego imaginario.

* *Provéanles accesorios que los inspiren a jugar a pretender.* Las muñecas, mantas, cunas, teléfonos (de juguete o reales), ollas, cacerolas y platos de plástico, inpirarán a sus hijos a recrear los papeles de las personas importantes en sus vidas. Otros accesorios útiles incluyen gente y animales de plástico, y juguetes tales como autos, camiones y botes.

* *Permitan que los niños se disfracen.* Ustedes pueden estimular la capacidad de sus niños de pretender, ofreciéndoles ropa para disfrazarse, accesorios relacionados con ciertos trabajos, como gorras, guantes, estetoscopios y diversos juguetes para subirse y conducirlos. Mantengan presente no sacar demasiados a la vez, para no confundir a los pequeños.

* *Jueguen imaginariamente con sus hijos.* Esta es una de las mejores maneras de animar a sus hijos a jugar a pretender. Mediante la formulación de preguntas, ofreciéndoles un accesorio nuevo y —asumiendo ustedes mismos— un papel imaginario.

Juntos, podremos ayudar a sus hijos a hacer uso del juego de pretender —o juego imaginario— como una importante herramienta de aprendizaje.

Les saluda atentamente,

Enjoying Stories
and Books

— ◆ —

"It's time for us to go outside," Mercedes announces. With Kara in the baby carrier, Mercedes reaches out her left hand towards Matthew. No sooner has Matthew grabbed her hand than he drops it. "Books, my books," he says, with great urgency in his voice. "Of course you can take your books," Mercedes tells him. Matthew goes to the coffee table and picks up the photo album of his family. He also chooses two picture books of animals displayed on the bottom shelf of the room divider. "Let's go find a comfortable, shady spot where we can read your books together," Mercedes suggests. Matthew clutches the books tightly to his chest, grins broadly, and starts spinning in a circle, in obvious delight. "Let's go, Mr. Spinner," says Mercedes, reaching out for Matthew.

— ◆ —

Think about the many things that books do for children. When Janet reads Caroline Bauer's *My Mom Travels A Lot*, she helps Jasmine adjust to her mother's frequent absences. When Abby looks at *Someone Special Just Like You* (T. Brown), she begins learning that she's not the only one who is part of a multiracial family. Gena feels less isolated when Ivan reads Rochelle Bunnett's *Friends at School*, which features children of all abilities. And Jonisha and Valisha take great pleasure in knowing that the identical twins in Valerie Flournoy's *The Twins Strike Back* have had experiences similar to theirs.

Even young infants Julio's age, who don't yet understand the messages found in books, learn from exposure to them. Feeling the warmth of Linda's body as she nestles with him in a rocking chair and enthusiastically reads aloud from Margot Griego's *Tortillitas Para Mamma: And Other Spanish Nursery Rhymes* creates enjoyable associations with books and reading.

There is another significant reason for including books in the curriculum. During the first three years of life, the brain is especially receptive to acquiring language. The sounds of words fascinate babies, and in fact, "wire" their brains. Research shows that children who are read to often and from a very early age enter school with more advanced language and better listening skills than those who have not had these experiences.

Setting the Stage for Books

Including books in your program seems simple enough. Nonetheless, you'll need to decide which books to select, where to keep them, and what types of book-related experiences are appropriate for young children. These issues are discussed here.

"Which books should I be using with young infants?"

For very young infants, books are interesting objects to look at. Simple bold illustrations are stimulating to the infant who is just now learning about the world. The steady rhythm of a book's words can attract the young infant's attention.

You can give infants younger than three months their first exposure to books by reading to them as you cradle them in your arms. You can also stand a stiff cardboard book in their crib or on the floor. Once a baby can support his head (at about three months of age), lap reading becomes a warm, shared experience.

As babies grow and begin to coo and grasp, they become more active partners in reading and storytelling. For the four-to-six-month-old, reading is sometimes book chewing, shaking, banging, sniffing, and observing. Infants this age need durable books that they can explore freely—cloth books, books with soft vinyl or oilcloth covers, and books with cloth or laminated edges. These very young children seem to prefer books with large, clear, colorful illustrations.

Infants like Jasmine, who are between six and eight months are likely to enjoy turning a book's pages. To encourage this important first step in learning to read, select board books—those with thick cardboard pages infants can easily grasp. Look for books with coated pages. These are easy for infants to turn and allow you to wash off sticky fingerprints.

Books for young infants should focus on familiar things—bottles and food, clothes, toys, pets, and people. Books should represent the diversity of the world, so that every child can identify with what he or she sees. Stories should be simple, rhythmic, or even wordless.

Here are some titles to consider when choosing books for young infants.

❖ *Animal Sounds for Baby* (Cheryl Willis Hudson)
❖ *Babies; I See; I Touch* (Rachel Isadora)
❖ *Baby's First Picture Book* (George Ford)
❖ *Baby's Friends; Baby's Home; Grandma and Me; Grandpa and* Me; and *Mommy and Me* (Neil Ricklin)
❖ *Babytalk* (Erika Stone)
❖ *First Snow* (Emily Arnold McCully)
❖ *I'm a Baby* (Phoebe Dunn)
❖ *My Toys* (Dick Bruna)
❖ *The Pudgy Where Is Your Nose? Book* (Laura Rader)
❖ *What Is It?* (Tana Hoban)
❖ *Word Sign* (Debbie Slier)

"Which books are appropriate for mobile infants?"

As infants become more aware of language, their interest in books increases. Willard and other infants who are 9 to 12 months old enjoy the content of a book as much as playing with it. They especially enjoy books with pictures of objects they can recognize easily.

Older, mobile infants like Abby, who have more interaction with the world and the people in it, can begin to enjoy simple, to-the-point themes and messages in picture books. They also enjoy books with repetition, rhyming verses, and nonsense syllables.

Here are some suggested titles.

❖ *Baby Has a Boo-Boo* and *Happy Babies* (Wendy Lewison)
❖ *Big Friend, Little Friend* and *My Doll, Keshia* (Eloise Greenfield)
❖ *Brothers; Sisters; My Dad; My Mom; Shoes; Hats;* and *Clothes* (Debbie Bailey/Susan Huszar)
❖ *Busy People* and *Making Faces* (Nick Butterworth)
❖ *Clap Hands; Dressing; Family; Friends; I See* (Helen Oxenbury)
❖ *Goodnight Moon* (Margaret Wise Brown)
❖ *Max's Bath; Max's Bedtime; Max's First Word;* and *Max's Toys* (Rosemary Wells)
❖ *Spot At Play* (Eric Hill)
❖ *Trucks* (Donald Crews)

"What books should I read to toddlers?"

Toddlers like Leo, Gena, Jonisha, and Valisha love to follow the simple plots in story-books. They especially like to hear stories about children and animals whose daily lives are similar to their own. Toddlers easily identify with mice who have grandmothers, or with children who learn to use the potty. From books, children can begin to learn values, explore their feelings, and gain insight about growing up.

Toddlers enjoy the whole process of listening to a story read aloud. They like books with pages they can turn, illustrations they can point to as you ask questions, and phrases that sound silly and are repeated predictably. For toddlers, books open up the world.

Here are some recommended titles of books for the toddlers in your program.

❖ *All Fall Down; The Checkup; Tickle, Tickle* (Helen Oxenbury)
❖ *Best Word Book Ever* (Richard Scarry)
❖ *Bright Eyes, Brown Skin* (Cheryl Willis Hudson and Bernette G. Ford)
❖ *The Chocolate-Covered-Cookie Tantrum* (Deborah Blumenthal)
❖ *Fuzzy Yellow Ducklings* (Matthew Van Fleet)
❖ *Gobble, Growl, Grunt: A Book of Animal Sounds* (Peter Spier)
❖ *Holes and Peeks* and *When You Were A Baby* (Ann Jonas)
❖ *I Love You, Sun I Love You, Moon* (Karen Pandell)
❖ *Moonlight and Sunshine* (Jan Omerod)
❖ *My Very First Mother Goose* (Iona Opie/Rosemary Wells)
❖ *Once Upon a Potty* (Alona Frankel)
❖ *Owl Babies* and *When The Teddy Bears Come* (Martin Waddell)

- ❖ *Sheep in a Jeep* (Nancy Shaw)
- ❖ *The Tub People* (Pam Conrad)
- ❖ *Train Leaves the Station* and *You Be Good and I'll Be Night* (Eve Merriam)
- ❖ *Will You Come Back for Me?* (Ann Tompert)

How can you keep up with the constant flow of new books for infants and toddlers? One useful way is to check with your local children's librarian from time to time. You can also use annotated lists to guide you in selecting appropriate titles. Two fine resources are: *The New York Times Parent's Guide to the Best Books for Children* (Eden Ross Lipson); and *Books to Grow By* (Bob Keeshan).

"Should I make books for the children?"

Older infants and toddlers love books about themselves. Knowing this may inspire you to try your hand at making books that describe or show something about each child's life.

For infants, you can make a "feelie" book similar to *Pat The Bunny* (Dorothy Kunhardt). You can use real-life objects, such as a baby's rattle or a spoon.

Older infants and toddlers love listening to stories and looking at pictures of themselves and their families. You can title such books *Me and My Family* or *My Family Child Care Home*. To make books, take photos of the people and important objects in the children's lives, paste the photos on cardboard, then laminate each page or cover with clear Contact™ paper. Punch holes in the pages and tie the book together with yarn.

And why not ask parents to record their child's favorite books, nursery rhymes, and stories on tape? Children find it very comforting to hear a parent's voice. You can also work with parents to record favorite stories in languages other than English. This, too, provides a natural link between home and the program for children whose first language is not English.

"How should I display books?"

It isn't hard to make books a regular part of your program. All you need are the books themselves and a comfortable place for children to look at books and read with you. To begin, you'll probably want to display just a few books—about five to eight for young and mobile infants and eight to twelve for toddlers. While you don't want to overwhelm children with too many choices, you do want to expose them to several different titles. When you provide a variety, children have a chance to develop favorites.

For infants, one effective way to store books is in wall pockets made of heavy-duty fabric and clear vinyl. A book pocket looks something like a shoe bag with one book in each pocket. The clear vinyl pocket not only protects the books, but also allows children to see their covers. As a result, children can learn to connect a book cover with the story being read to them. You can buy book pockets commercially or make them yourself.

For infants to be able to explore the books up close, you can remove them from the pockets and stand them in the crib or on the floor. Thick, cardboard books work best.

While book pockets can also be used with older infants and toddlers, many people prefer to display books by simply fanning them out on low, open shelves. This arrangement allows children to identify and reach for their favorites. As noted earlier with Matthew, a free-standing display encourages children to pick up a book themselves whenever they are interested.

Looking at books is something children can do anywhere in your program. You'll want to encourage children to look at books in their cribs, on the floor, and in a shady area outdoors. In addition, near the book display, you'll want to have soft, welcoming places for reading. An overstuffed pillow, covered mattress, carpeted risers, or a rocking chair make cozy "book nooks." Your space should be appropriate for reading with a small group of children as well as reading with one child at a time. You'll also want to provide an inviting area where a child can sink into a pillow or rock on a child-sized rocker to read a book by himself. Solitary experiences such as gnawing on a vinyl book cover or "reading" out loud while holding a book upside down are important foundations for literacy.

Enjoying Stories and Books with Children

Many caregivers/teachers consider one-on-one reading experiences among the most treasured times in their day. The warmth and closeness of sharing a book with a child forges a special bond. Reading with an individual child offers a chance to become close to each other as you explore books together.

Shared (or paired) reading is a variation of one-on-one reading. Shared reading occurs when two children share a book, with one child reading to the other. If you have children of mixed ages in your group, you'll discover the benefits of having an older child "read" to a younger one. The older child usually is pleased and proud to take on your role; the younger child enjoys having the full attention of the older one.

Another variation of paired reading takes place when children "read" a book to a doll or puppet. In these situations, children are more likely to be retelling a story they have heard many times or making up a story based on a book's illustrations.

Group reading times often occur spontaneously when a child brings you a book to read or joins in to listen to a book you have been reading with another child. Books that have word play or repeated responses are especially good for these small group times. Older children love to shout out a predictable response together, or to hear how silly a funny word sounds when everyone says it at the same time. These noisy and happy reading experiences can provide lifetime associations between reading and pleasure.

Here are some suggestions for enjoying stories and books with the children in your program.

Young Infants

For young infants, the joy of language is their first association with books and stories. The rhythm, patterns, and tone of your voice pull babies into the fascinating world of communication. Even though they don't understand all that you say, they learn to value language and its importance when you read to them, sing songs, and tell stories and rhymes each day.

Allowing children to explore books is a good way to help infants become attracted to books. Infants who have learned grasping skills enjoy turning the thick, cardboard pages of board books. They need time to do this on their own and with you. When you sit down to read a book with a child, choose a time when you have the child's attention—but don't expect that attention to last! Jasmine will let you know when she's lost interest by fidgeting, slamming the book shut, or crawling down from your lap. A page or two may be as much reading as an infant feels like doing at one time. Yet, no matter how long it lasts, the time you spend together looking at words and pictures and pointing out familiar objects teaches children a lot about books and reading.

Mobile Infants

Older infants are developmentally able to follow simple stories. They also have the physical skills and maturity to listen as you read to them—at least for a few pages! You can even try reading to a few children in a group of two or three. These experiences will be successful as long as you have realistic expectations and don't demand more of the children than is developmentally appropriate. To make reading most effective, keep these pointers in mind.

❖ **Wait until you have the child's attention before starting:** "Let's look at this book together."

❖ **Encourage the child to follow the illustrations as you read the text:** "Can you find Spot in the picture? Point to the doggie."

❖ **Take communication cues from the child's gestures, sounds, or words:** "Yes, that is a baby—just like you."

❖ **Ask simple questions.** These can help the child reflect on what is being read. Even nonverbal children can respond by pointing to a picture or making a sound in response. "They're going bye-bye, aren't they? Can you wave bye-bye like the mommy in the story?"

❖ **Be prepared to stop at any point.** Lost interest is your cue that the reading activity needs to be concluded. You can pick up the book again when the child shows interest.

Toddlers

Reading with toddlers can take on much more structure, because toddlers have longer attention spans and more developed language skills. As a result, reading with toddlers goes beyond learning about books; it offers opportunities for children to become involved in the stories themselves.

Toddlers love to look at books on their own and make up stories as they turn the pages. Some toddlers can even recite word-for-word the texts of beloved books you and their parents have read and reread to them.

With toddlers, all kinds of reading experiences are valuable. You can make the most of the learning opportunities by following these simple tips.

- **Make sure that everyone is comfortable (including you).** Every child you are reading to should be able to see the book clearly.

- **Show the cover and discuss what you see.** Ask the children if they recognize the book as one you've read together before. What do they think the book is about?

- **Encourage children to use the illustrations to describe what is going on.** "Where are the children now?" "What do you think will happen to the little girl now that it's started to rain?"

- **Pause in the reading and allow children time to anticipate the next words.** This works especially well when you're reading familiar rhymes or stories with words and phrases that are used many times. Children love word play and being involved with the story.

- **Skip an expected phrase or part of a familiar story from time to time.** Toddlers love correcting you and making you read the story "right." You'll get the same reaction if you switch words or play with words in silly ways.

- **Respond to the children's verbal and nonverbal cues about the illustrations.** Ask questions such as: "What's that you're pointing to? What do you think their Mommy will have to say about the spaghetti in the baby's hair?"

- **Relate the story to the children's own lives.** "Valisha, do people have trouble telling you and Jonisha apart like the twins in this story?"

- **If children are responsive, try reading a book all the way through.** Children can become caught up in the rhythm of the words and the flow of the plot. You'll soon learn which books capture the children's attention and which children are ready to sit through an entire story.

- **Follow-up on the reading experience.** Encourage children to reflect on the story. "Did you ever see a monkey like George?" "Does everyone go to the potty?"

- **Be prepared to read the same story over and over again.** Children have favorites and they never tire of hearing those stories every day.

Connecting Books to Other Activities

There are a number of related activities you can do, especially with toddlers, to extend their experiences with books. For example, dramatic play is a natural outcome of story-telling. Children can recall favorite stories and act them out in their own way

Music and movement also tie in very easily with reading. *The Raffi Singable Songbook*, for example, encourages children to sing the songs that go with the pictures. Many familiar pieces of music have been recreated as books, such as *Ring Around the Rosie* or *Old MacDonald Had a Farm*.

Perhaps most of all, book experiences lend themselves to the daily routines in a child's life. If you are having difficulty settling a child down for a nap, you might recite goodnight messages to the objects in your environment, just as in Margaret Wise Brown's *Goodnight Moon*. If you want to help children feel more independent about dressing themselves, you might recall the advice given in *How Do I Put It On?* (Shigo Watanabe).

Reading books and helping children learn to enjoy stories is one of the most important things you can do for a child educationally. Children who are regularly read to gain a foundation for literacy that helps them in school and lasts throughout life. Hearing stories, rhymes, chants, and poems read aloud teaches children the importance of language. It also opens up worlds of adventure and excitement.

Sharing Thoughts About
Stories and Books

Dear Families:

Everyone agrees that books are a necessary part of a child's education. But do you realize that it's never too early to introduce a child to books? Long before children learn to read, they need to know what language sounds like, how a story flows, and how books "work."

Research tells us that even the youngest infants benefit from having stories read to them! Looking at books and hearing an adult read stimulates an infant's brain development in critically important ways. Children who learn to love books from an early age are more likely to become successful learners and lifelong readers. In our program, we offer your child a wide variety of good books and we read together every day.

What You Can Do at Home

The most important thing you can do is to read and tell stories together every day. The words are important. So, too, are a book's pictures. But most of all, spending time with you as you read and tell stories aloud lets your child know how much you value this activity. What's more, these times together—whether part of a bedtime ritual or a lazy weekend moment—can be treasured memories for both of you.

Here are some suggestions of things to do as you read.

❖ *Pick a story you yourself enjoy. Share rhymes, chants, songs, and stories from your childhood.* Your interest and enthusiasm will become contagious. Start by talking about the book's cover or simply reading. This helps you get your child's attention.

❖ *Encourage your child to follow the illustrations as you read. You can use the illustrations to ask questions:* "Where is the dog's bone?" You can also take cues from your child's gestures, sounds, or words: "Yes, that's the baby's Grandma—just like Nona Maria."

❖ *Be prepared to stop at any point.* You don't want to force a child to be still while you read. Sometimes, children would rather do something more active. Stop when your child seems no longer interested. Alternatively, be prepared to read a story over and over again.

❖ *We'd be glad to share with you the titles of the books your child enjoys here.* You can help us, too. Let us know your child's current favorite books, stories, and rhymes at home so we can get copies for our program. We'd also love to have you make a tape as you read your child's favorite story or nursery rhyme so we can play it for your child here. We'll be glad to help you with the taping.

Together, we can help prepare your child to be a lifelong reader.

Sincerely,

Algunas ideas sobre el placer
de las historias y los libros

Estimadas familias:

Todo el mundo está de acuerdo con que los libros son esenciales en la educación infantil. Pero, ¿saben ustedes que nunca es demasiado pronto para presentarles libros a los niños? Mucho antes de que ellos aprendan a leer, necesitan saber cómo son los sonidos del lenguaje, como se encadena una historia y cómo "funcionan" los libros.

¡Incluso los niños más pequeños se benefician a partir de las historias que se les leen! Los niños que aprenden a amar los libros desde temprana edad, muy probablemente se convertirán en aprendices exitosos y en ávidos lectores por el resto de sus vidas. En nuestro programa, tenemos libros maravillosos y leemos con ellos diariamente.

Lo que ustedes pueden hacer en el hogar

Lo más importante que ustedes puede hacer para que sus hijos desarrollen el gusto por los libros, es leer junto con ellos todos los días. Aunque las palabras que les lean sean importantes, tal como lo son la historia y las ilustraciones, lo más importante, es destinar tiempo a leerles en voz alta a sus hijos, pues les demuestra cuánto valoran ustedes esta actividad. Más aún, estos momentos juntos —o bien como parte de un ritual a la hora de dormir, o un momento de pereza el fin de semana— pueden constituir valiosos recuerdos para ambos.

Las siguientes son unas cuantas sugerencias de lo que podrían hacer cuando lean:

* *Esperen hasta captar la atención del niño para comenzar.* Así estimularán la concentración en las palabras y las ilustraciones.

* *Animen a los niños a seguir las imágenes a medida que les lean.* Ustedes pueden emplear las ilustraciones para formularles preguntas: "¿Adónde está el hueso del perro?" Además, podrían basarse en los gestos, sonidos y palabras de sus hijos: "Si, esa es la abuelita del bebé, como la nona María".

* *Estén preparados para detenerse en cualquier momento.* No se debe forzar a los niños a permanecer quietos mientras se les lee. A veces, los pequeños prefieren hacer algo más activo. Cuando los niños parezcan no estar interesados, es mejor detenerse.

A nosotros nos encantaría recomendarles algunos libros que sus hijos podrían disfrutar. (También podrían consultar en la biblioteca local para que les ayuden a escoger). Permítannos saber cuáles prefieren sus hijos para que podamos obtener copias. Y, nos encantaría que grabaran una cinta cuando les lean sus historias favoritas para que, después, ellos puedan escucharlas aquí. Déjennos saber si podemos ayudarles con la grabación.

Juntos, podremos ayudar a sus hijos para que se conviertan en ávidos lectores por el resto de su vida.

Les saluda atentamente,

Tasting and Preparing Food

— ◈ —

"We're going to having an exciting snack today," announces La Toya to the children in her family child care home. "We have carrots right from our garden! After we scrub them clean, we can taste our home-grown snack." La Toya asks Valisha to help her set out vegetable brushes and water bowls on the trays in front of each child. She then lets each child take two carrots to scrub. As Jonisha displays her carrot for all the children to see how clean it is, La Toya raises her hand to give Jonisha a "high five."

— ◈ —

Food experiences provide a wealth of sensory learning experiences for infants and toddlers. Think about the example above. In just this one instance, the children in La Toya's family child care home are learning where carrots come from, and about counting, developing fine motor skills, refining eye-hand coordination, and demonstrating pride in a task well done.

Tasting and preparing food are part of everyday living with infants and toddlers. Children become aware of the tastes and textures of different cereals, fruits, and vegetables as you and their families gradually introduce them to new foods. They begin to express their personal preferences and soon start to learn the names of different foods. At first, they are primarily interested in squishing, mashing, and smearing food. But before long, they become eager and able to help prepare some of the foods they eat. Whether it's scrubbing a carrot or dipping a slice of apple in melted cheese, children enjoy and feel proud to be given the opportunity to help with a necessary, adult-like task.

Setting the Stage for Tasting and Preparing Food

As you prepare for activities involving food, you'll need to consider issues related to ensuring children's health and safety. You may also want to make some adjustments to your environment to make food preparation activities successful, and take steps to minimize confusion when cooking with toddlers.

"What safety measures should I be taking?"

Food preparation experiences that involve using adult utensils, gadgets, and appliances require close supervision. Some preventive measures will, however, eliminate many potential problems. For example, by choosing nonbreakable materials, you guard against accidents becoming dangerous. A plastic bowl, for example, may make a mess if its contents fall on the floor. However, plastic will not cut a child or get in food the way glass and ceramic shards might. Storing adult items—egg beaters, or anything with an electrical plug—out of reach or in a locked cupboard also makes sense.

Another preventive measure is to "childproof" the area where you will be cooking, especially if it is a kitchen. Cover outlets when not in use, and cover or lock the controls on the stove. Hide or remove electrical wires. (Consult Chapter 8, Ensuring Children's Safety, for more detailed information on checking the environment for safety considerations.)

Finally, in any tasting and food preparation experience with children, there is always the possibility that despite every precaution, a child may suddenly gag or choke. Since it's often difficult to think clearly in an emergency, it makes sense to post the guidelines for giving first aid for choking in the area where you will be cooking with children.

"Are there health issues I need to consider?"

First of all, it's probably not wise to begin tasting experiences with children younger than four months, since their digestive tracts are not yet able to break down solid foods. Food experiences should then be introduced gradually, with the knowledge and approval of parents. Children need time (five days is usually recommended) to get used to the taste and feel of new foods and to be sure that they aren't showing signs of allergic reactions.

In introducing children to new foods, follow the guidelines in Chapter 13, Eating and Mealtimes. And last but not least, familiarize yourself with the health considerations outlined in Chapter 9, Promoting Children's Health. This information can guide you in your planning.

"What changes do I need to make to the environment to include food activities in my program?"

For tasting experiences, you shouldn't need to make any changes to your program's environment, since eating is already a part of your daily routines. For special food activities, you may wish to make some adjustments. However, you needn't be concerned if you don't have access to a kitchen. In many ways it's easier to create your own space for cooking, since you'll want everything to be safe and accessible to children. For example, if an oven is not available, a toaster oven, an electric frying pan, or a wok will do nicely. Here are some considerations for setting up your program for food activities.

Have available a child-sized table and chairs. To enjoy the food preparation experience fully, children need to be able to work, move about, and observe freely. A child-sized table can be used as a work station as well as for eating. Chairs enable children to sit while someone else is at work, thus making the activity more orderly. You can include infants by bringing their high chairs over to the table.

Select and use utensils that children can explore and use on their own. As much as possible, start children using real utensils and appliances rather than toy ones. Real gadgets and utensils not only make the experience more authentic, but are less frustrating to use than toy ones that are often not intended to do real work. For safety's sake, assemble plastic, rubber, and nonbreakable tools. Utensils that children can learn to use include wooden spoons, plastic measuring cups, vegetable brushes, and potato mashers. Any potentially dangerous utensils or appliances you might use in leading a special cooking project should be stored out of the children's reach.

Store the safe cooking gadgets and utensils in low cabinets. If materials are stored on low shelves, children can get what they need on their own. Picture labels can show children where these materials belong so that they can help clean up.

Keep duplicates of the utensils children use for preparing food available for pretend play. This avoids waiting and allows children to recreate and extend their cooking experiences.

Have smocks available for the cooks to use. In this way children are free to be creative without fear of getting themselves or their clothes stained. If you don't have smocks, you or a parent can easily make them from old shirts or pieces of oilcloth.

Store cleaning supplies nearby so you can reach them easily. Invite children to help you wipe up the spills that are sure to occur.

"How can I make food preparation with mobile infants and toddlers a successful experience?"

Mobile infants and toddlers are by definition active "hands-on" people. This can be challenging when you are trying to organize a food preparation activity. Here are some suggestions to help minimize confusion for children—and for you.

Limit the number of children. Keep the numbers at three or four to prevent confusion and give each child a chance to participate. If cooking is a regular activity, children will soon learn that if they don't cook today, they can do so tomorrow.

Have all the ingredients and utensils assembled ahead of time. This will free you to focus on the children, which is where your attention should be.

Keep waiting time as brief as possible. You can cut down on waiting time by making sure children always have a task. For instance, if one child is stirring, another child can hold the bowl steady.

Communicate rules clearly, in positive terms. For example, say, "Wooden spoons are for stirring." Gently but firmly remind a child of the rule when she uses her spoon to poke another child instead of stirring the zucchini muffin batter.

Make picture cards for older toddlers to use. To give children a beginning foundation for literacy, use pictures to demonstrate the cooking steps they are following. Pictures pasted on index cards or chart paper and laminated can help children visualize the one or two steps they will take during the cooking experience. For instance, one card might show a picture of hands being washed. The second card can show a butter knife spreading apple butter on a cracker. Children can also use these picture cards to review and relive the cooking experiences they've had.

Promoting Children's Learning Through Food Experiences

Food experiences are a natural part of life. With children younger than three, your role is to be responsive to the children's interests and capabilities.

Young Infants

Food experiences with young infants are primarily tasting experiences. To turn the activity into a learning experience, allow children to explore their food and talk with them about what is happening. Identify foods and utensils by name so that children learn new vocabulary words. You might say:

> "Let's taste this cereal. Open your mouth. Here comes the spoon."

> "You're having a hard time picking up the applesauce because it's so slippery."

> "You like the taste of that squishy banana, don't you?"

Young infants will also enjoy being included as you "cook" with older children. Depending on their age and skill level, they can enjoy the sights, smells, and sounds of food preparation activities from a back pack, your lap, or a highchair and may be able to begin to participate in some of the activities we have listed in the next section.

Mobile Infants

In addition to tasting experiences, mobile infants enjoy being involved in the preparation of their own snacks and meals. Appropriate experiences for this age group include *shaking, dabbing, dipping, stirring,* and *mashing.* Some examples include:

- shaking grated cheese on macaroni or vegetable purees (squash, green beans, peas, carrots, beets, cauliflower or zucchini)
- dropping cheese cubes onto rice or mashed potatoes
- dabbing apple butter on bread or toasted bagel
- shaking cinnamon on cottage cheese, yogurt, cooked cereal, or apple sauce
- dipping steamed asparagus (at room temperature) into melted cheese
- dipping banana chunks or steamed apple or pear wedges into yogurt
- using a masher to make vegetable, fruit or combination purees from everything from avocados to steamed yams
- mixing cottage cheese with macaroni; kasha (roasted buckwheat) with noodle bow ties; macaroni with diced ham
- dipping or spooning yogurt on cucumbers or kiwi slices
- mixing dips for snacks using grated cheese or spices (such as powdered cinnamon and nutmeg) with sour cream, yogurt, or mashed chick peas

To reinforce learning, talk with mobile infants about what they are experiencing and ask questions to challenge their thinking.

"See if you can stir the milk into the chocolate pudding mix so that everything looks wet."

"Let's see what happens to the avocado when we mash it. We're going to use the avocado to make a dip called guacamole. Remember when Tia brought us some to eat?"

"Abby, could you please hand me the potato masher so that we can make some mashed potatoes for lunch? Come here and I'll show you how it works."

Toddlers

Toddlers can take an active role in preparing their food. You can plan activities that involve *spreading, pouring, slicing, whisking, squeezing,* and *garnishing,* such as:

❖ preparing finger food snacks using cucumber slices, toast strips, or crackers for the base, and cheese, cottage cheese, or fruit wedges for toppings

❖ using a plastic knife or a small icing spatula to spread apple butter (or other fruit butters) on crackers, bread, or toast

❖ stirring together the ingredients for hot cereal, and pouring milk or maple syrup into the finished dish

❖ scrambling eggs in a bowl

❖ dipping bread slices in beaten eggs, cinnamon, and milk to make french toast

❖ scrubbing potatoes or yams; mashing the cooked potatoes or yams

❖ mixing gelatin in water to make gelatin jigglers and wigglers

❖ using cookie cutters to shape jigglers, gingerbread, and biscuits

❖ making bread: adding yeast to water; stirring dough ingredients, kneading dough, punching down dough, shaping loaves, brushing dough with water

❖ squeezing lemons, oranges, and limes for fruit drinks

❖ snapping ends off of green beans

❖ shelling peas

❖ stirring cream, sugar, and mashed bananas together to make banana ice cream, and then pouring the mixture into a freezer container

❖ spreading apricot, pear, papaya, or mango puree onto plastic wrap-covered cookie sheet to make fruit leathers

❖ arranging foods decoratively on a plate, tray, or table

You can extend toddlers' learning by asking questions that cause them to reflect on the process. Consider these examples.

"How does this mashed banana look different from this whole banana?"

"Can you remember what else we baked on this cookie sheet?"

"How do you think we can open this pea pod?"

"What was the best part about making snack?"

Getting Ideas for Cooking Activities

Where can you get ideas for food preparation activities? Start with the meals and snacks you serve the children. Then think about how you might involve the children in preparing them. Preparations that have a limited number of steps and require only beginning physical skills such as dipping, shaking or mashing are good starters. More complex skills such as pouring, spreading, and squeezing can be added as children's mastery of fine motor skills improves.

For special projects, you might want to consult some of the published books for cooking with children. Here are a few.

❖ *Cup Cooking: Individual Child-Portion Picture Recipes* (Barbara Johnson)
❖ *Learning Through Cooking* (Amy Houts)
❖ *Learning Through Cooking: A Cooking Program for Children Two to Ten* (N.J. Ferreira)

One word of caution, though. Most children's cookbooks on the market are intended for use with preschoolers and older children. Moreover, even some that claim to be for infants and toddlers are often too difficult for young cooks or include preparing foods that are nutritionally inappropriate. To use cookbooks effectively with infants and toddlers, you'll need to rethink the recipes in terms of children's skills and any special dietary requirements.

Families are also an ideal resource for cooking ideas. Invite parents to share recipes for foods they prepare for their children at home. By recreating these foods at meals and snacks, you strengthen the bond between home and the program. Including family recipes is one way for your program to acknowledge the cultural backgrounds of the children and families you serve.

You'll find that most children are eager to participate in experiences involving food. With some thoughtful planning, you can make these experiences ongoing learning opportunities.

Sharing Thoughts About Tasting and Preparing Food

Dear Families:

Perhaps the idea of children so young participating in food preparation activities seems strange to you. Yet one of the reasons preparing food appeals to children is that it is a grown-up activity. To participate in these activities—the ones your child observes you doing day in and day out—is both exciting and motivating.

In our program, we build on this natural interest in food experiences. There are so many concepts and skills children can learn. For example, what do you think your child might learn from doing a simple task such as snapping the ends off green beans? Did you include these things?

shape   eye and hand coordination
color   part and whole
cause and effect   fine motor skill development
pride in completing a task

As you can see, preparing food is educational as well as practical and fun!

What You Can Do at Home

The most natural laboratory for involving your child in food preparation activities is at home. Here are some ideas:

❖ *Let your child participate.* Because you probably already cook at home, it's easy for you to involve your child. You can even include a young infant. Let him or her sit in a high chair as you discuss what's going on. Older infants and toddlers can be active participants. When your child helps you prepare or serve foods, you're showing that you value his or her contributions to keeping your family healthy and happy.

❖ *Talk about what's going on.* Here are some topics you might discuss as you prepare and taste foods together.
  • the names of different foods, and how they look, smell, feel, and taste
  • what different utensils do and where you keep them in the kitchen
  • why you serve a variety of foods with each meal

❖ *Maybe you'd like to do some cooking activities with the children at our program.* We'd love you to supply a recipe or help the children make their snack. Also, please send us your ideas for food preparation activities. We especially welcome your own family favorites or recipes that reflect your family's heritage. We want your child to have wonderful food-related experiences both here and at home.

Sincerely,

Algunas ideas acerca de
preparar y probar los alimentos

Estimadas familias:

Quizá a algunos de ustedes les sorprenda que los niños tan pequeños participen en actividades culinarias. Sin embargo, una de las razones por las cuales a los pequeños les llama la atención la preparación de alimentos es porque es una actividad de los adultos. Para ellos, participar en en esta clase de actividad —que los han observado a ustedes llevando a cabo diariamente— les fascina y motiva.

En nuestro programa nosotros construimos sobre la base de este interés natural en las experiencias alimenticias. Existe una gran cantidad de conceptos y de destrezas que los niños pueden aprender a partir de actividades de esta naturaleza. Por ejemplo, ¿se imaginan qué podrían aprender sus niños a partir de una tarea tan sencilla como cortarle los extremos a las habichuelas verdes? ¿Incluyeron lo siguiente?

coordinación ojo-mano	parte y todo
forma	desarrollo de la motricidad fina
color	orgullo por completar una tarea
causa-efecto	

Como pueden ver, preparar alimentos es —además de educativo— algo práctico y placentero.

Lo que ustedes pueden hacer en el hogar

❖ *Permitan que sus hijos participen.* Dado que es probable que ustedes cocinen en su hogar, les será fácil involucrar en ello a sus hijos, incluso a los más pequeños. Permítanles sentarse en una silla alta y comenten lo que hacen. Cuando sus hijos les ayudan a preparar o a servir los alimentos, ustedes les demuestran que valoran sus contribuciones para mantener a la familia saludable y feliz.

❖ *Hablen con los niños sobre lo que sucede.* Los siguientes son unos cuantos temas que ustedes podrían comentar, a medida que preparen y prueben alimentos juntos.
  • los nombres de los diferentes alimentos, su apariencia, olor, sabor y textura
  • lo que se puede hacer con los diferentes utensilios y adónde se guardan en la cocina
  • por qué ustedes sirven una variedad de alimentos en cada comida

❖ *Es posible que estedes deseen llevar a cabo algunas actividades culinarias con los niños de nuestro programa.* Nos encantaría que ustedes prepararan alguna receta o que les ayudaran a los niños con la merienda. Especialmente, las recetas favoritas de su familia o una que refleje su herencia cultural. Ya que, deseamos que sus hijos tengan experiencias maravillosas relacionadas con los alimentos, tanto en nuestro programa, como en sus hogares.

Les saluda atentamente,

Exploring
Sand and Water

— ◈ —

"Your dinosaur is looking mighty clean, Willard," says Grace, as Willard waves the washed animal in front of her. "Look how shiny it is when it's wet." "Mmmm," says Willard in an insistent tone, as he climbs to a standing position. "I bet you want another animal to wash," says Grace to a beaming Willard.

— ◈ —

Infants and toddlers are naturally attracted to sand and water play. There's something about the cool splash of water and the magical sensation of sand sifting through fingers that almost everyone finds appealing. Even as an adult, there may be times when you crave a warm bath or a walk on a beach. Sand and water remain soothing and relaxing throughout life.

In addition to its calming nature, sand and water play allows children to begin building concepts of science and math while they explore the many uses of these materials. For example, when Leo adds water to sand to create a new substance—mud—he sees that materials can change form. As Abby dumps a measuring cup of sand into a bucket, she senses that objects have a shape and size. And as Matthew combs a flowing design in sand, he is an artist.

Exploration and learning are natural outcomes when you provide opportunities for children to play with sand and water. These materials provide appropriate and inexpensive ways to expand children's skills and promote all areas of development.

Setting the Stage for Exploring Sand and Water

Offering sand and water play as an activity requires some advance planning. The decisions to be made include how to ensure children's health and safety, ways to manage mess, and what props and supplies to select to enhance the experience.

"What safety and health considerations should I be concerned about?"

There are a few small precautions you need to take so children can play safely with sand and water. While you don't have to hover over the children's every move, you do need to be a constant supervisor.

For water play, begin with no more than a tray full of water for infants. As children grow, you can progress up to two to three inches. (However, children have been known to drown in less than an inch of water. As remote as it may seem, you need to know mouth to mouth resuscitation procedures should an incident occur.)

Remember to empty the water after each use. Standing water not only poses a drowning hazard, but is a growth medium for bacteria.

If you're using a sink for water play, you'll need to check that the water temperature has been adjusted and that faucets do not easily turn on when touched. You'll also want to be sure that if children use a step stool, it is protected by rubber slats. Remove all electrical appliances (such as hair dryers) and cover the outlets so that the children's wet hands won't accidentally come into contact with electricity.

For sand play, sterilized, fine grained sand (purchased from lumber yards) is best for health reasons and because it holds its shape. While not toxic, eating it (as babies often do) is hardly recommended. Therefore, sand play activities are best left for older infants and toddlers.

For a different texture experience, consider using rice, cornmeal, or oatmeal as an alternative to sand. (Keep in mind though, that for some individuals, using food in this way is offensive. For this reason, avoid using beans or macaroni. Avoid Styrofoam™ "peanuts" as they pose a choking hazard.)

For both sand and water play, use individual trays or tubs to reduce the spread of infections. Sanitize the tubs each day using a bleach solution. Remember to cover outdoor sand areas while not in use to prevent cats and dogs from leaving droppings in them.

Props, too, need daily cleaning with bleach solution. Sponges—although great fun to play with—should be avoided, since they are a breeding ground for germs.

"How can I keep mess to a minimum?"

If you feel that sand and water play are simply too messy to deal with, you are not alone. You may ask yourself, aren't there less difficult ways of providing children with meaningful learning experiences?

Of course there are less messy activities such as looking at books and playing with toys. However, because children learn in a variety of ways and through a variety of experiences, the broader the array of experiences you provide, the more opportunities there are for growth and learning.

With a little planning on your part, sand and water play can be an activity that is manageable and fun. Here are some suggestions.

Start doing sand and water play activities outdoors. The best place to start is outdoors, where making a mess is not really a concern. A bare spot of ground and a puddle are nature's sand and water "tubs." Sandboxes and wading pools are also ready starting points. You can bring out dish tubs, specially designed sand and water tables, or use an old tire or inner tube as a sandbox frame. In warm climates, many centers use sand as their outdoor ground cover. This makes the entire outdoor area a giant sandbox.

Choose your indoor spaces carefully. To keep messes in check indoors, think about where clean up will be easiest. For family child care providers, the bathroom or kitchen are likely choices. Each of these rooms has a sink where you can do water play, and floors that are designed to be mopped. In a center, an uncarpeted area is the logical choice. However, even if all your floors are carpeted, you can still conduct sand and water play successfully, if you spread an old plastic tablecloth, shower curtain, or crib sheet on the floor.

Prepare for spills. You can wipe up spills easily and carry the sand outdoors to be emptied if you use a dropcloth. For further protection, spread old towels or newspapers on top of the plastic. Some caregivers put individual tubs inside a plastic wading pool. The tubs catch the splashed water or spilled sand.

Protect children's clothing. Protecting the children is a matter of either covering or uncovering them. In warm weather, you might find it easiest to let children play with sand and water wearing just their diapers or pants. Clean up is a breeze when there are no outfits to protect. Smocks can be commercially purchased or fashioned from old shirts, aprons, or heavy duty trash bags (to make ponchos). Another option is to have children play with water dressed in their raincoats and boots. In any event, it's always wise to have a fresh change of clothes on hand for each child—just in case!

Keep group size small. Limit the group playing with sand and water to no more than three or four at a time, so supervision doesn't become a problem. Small groups are easier for children to handle and permit you to interact with each child.

Keep clean-up supplies handy. Keep supplies—paper towels and child-sized brooms, dust pans, and mops—close at hand so that the older children can assist you in clean up. When clean up becomes a part of the play experience rather than a chore you have to attend to afterwards, sand and water play is a more inviting experience for all of you.

Determine the best time for sand and water play. Plan to do sand and water play with children at a time when there will be few interruptions. If you can find a body of time for set up, play, and clean up, the activity will be more successful. The late morning is often a good time, since many of the morning routines have been completed and children's interests and energy tend to run high.

"What supplies and props do I need to encourage children to explore with sand and water?"

To hold the sand and water, you can make use of cafeteria-style trays or shallow dish tubs. Individual trays or tubs allow each child to play in a defined area. Toddlers, who enjoy the company of other children, will enjoy playing at a child-sized water or sand table.

Young infants do not need props for water play. They are satisfied in using their senses to splash and explore water.

Mobile infants can do many play-related activities such as washing dolls or rubber animals and sifting and shoveling sand. Props help them stretch their skills and imaginations. Here are some props to consider:

- rubber/plastic animals or people figures
- balls
- floating toys, such as boats
- small shovels and pails
- rakes
- nesting cups (plastic measuring cups)
- funnels
- colanders
- sprinkling/watering can

For toddlers, any of the props listed previously are appropriate. You may want to add some of the following:

- wire whisks
- sieves
- water/sand mills
- plastic cookie cutters
- slotted spoons
- squeeze bottles
- pie tins (with and without bottom holes)
- ladles
- scoops
- muffin tins
- straws
- bubble blowing supplies
- large shells

Props are best stored on low, open shelves where children can get at them on their own. Picture labels make it easy for children to know where the wire whisk or squeeze bottle should be returned. However, avoid storing props in the tub or on the table. This is not only messy and unsanitary, but discourages children from deciding what they want to play with.

Promoting Children's Learning with Sand and Water

For infants and toddlers exploring sand and water is a wonderful sensory experience that exposes them to math and science and promotes their creativity in natural ways. At the same time, sand and water explorations develop fine motor skills, eye and hand coordination, and balance. Here are some ways to help infants and toddlers learn from their play.

Young Infants

Infants love exploring water. The feel of water on their cheeks, tickling their feet, and dripping down their tummies makes them squeal with delight. As babies sit in your lap, allow them time to splash water in a plastic tub. Just watching water jump when it's hit and feeling its coolness when it splatters on their skin provides infants with many sensory experiences.

Holding a baby's hand under a faucet of running water offers another perspective. So, too, does sprinting through a sprinkler with an infant in your arms on a warm summer day.

Talk with infants about what they are experiencing.

❖ **Describe what is happening:** "I bet the water is tickling your toes."

❖ **Talk about their actions:** "You splashed the water!"

❖ **Mirror an infant's emotions:** "That splash on your cheek surprised you, didn't it?"

❖ **Build children's confidence as they explore:** "You splashed with both hands!"

Mobile Infants

Mobile infants, who are more likely to play with sand than to eat it, can enjoy exploring both sand and water. They like using their hands as well as simple props such as funnels and sifters. Introduce props gradually and one at a time. Measuring cups and colanders, for example, open up a whole new world of play. Floating toys add another dimension to water play, as do a shovel and pail to a sandbox. If children enjoy a particular prop, give them many opportunities to play with it. Children tend to extend their play furthest when they can explore materials at length on their own. At the same time, too many props can be distracting.

Sand and water play can also give infants a chance to see examples of cause and effect. For example, as Abby shovels sand into a milk carton, she sees that sand poured over the carton piles up inside the carton while the sand that misses the carton falls on the tray.

When you offer sand and water activities to mobile infants, here are some ways to interact with them to promote their learning.

❖ **Describe changes the child can observe:** "The sand turned wet and dark when we added water."

❖ **Encourage children to appreciate designs:** "You made all those wavy lines in the sand with the rake."

❖ **Help children become aware of their emotions:** "Playing in the water can be so relaxing."

❖ **Provide children with vocabulary for their explorations:** "If we turn on the faucet, the cold water will come out."

Toddlers

With their ever-developing thinking and physical skills, toddlers explore sand and water with zeal. Leo can now use a cookie press to squirt water at a target or a vegetable brush to scrub a rock. Valisha can "cook" mudpies to serve La Toya, and Jonisha can wash her own hands as well as those of her doll.

In exploring water and sand, toddlers may observe that some objects float on water and that sifted sand forms a mound. They notice how sand and water drift through holes in a colander, and can spend long periods of time filling and dumping containers. Toddlers find great enjoyment in burying their feet and making imprints in the sand. Sand and water are excellent laboratories for finding answers to the many "Why?" questions toddlers like to ask.

To tap into the toddler's natural enthusiasm for sand and water play, talk with them in ways that help them reflect on what they are doing.

- ❖ **Point out cause and effect relationships:** "What happened to the sand when you poured it in the colander?"

- ❖ **Encourage children to solve problems:** "How could we get the water in this tub into the bucket?"

- ❖ **Challenge children to make predictions:** "What will happen to this wash cloth if we put it in the water tub?"

- ❖ **Support pretend play:** "What is your baby doll going to do after you've finished giving her a bath?"

Props expand toddlers' thinking by helping them explore and experiment with sand and water in new ways. When Valisha uses a whisk in the water tray, she makes bubbles that look like those formed by adding soap to water. Likewise, she sees that a sieve and a colander act in the same way. Each interaction teaches her new concepts.

As with younger children, introduce props gradually, making sure that toddlers have ample time to test and try them out. One all-time favorite for many is blowing bubbles into the wind. (A recipe for making long-lasting bubbles is shown below.)

Bubble Solution

2/3 cup of liquid detergent
(Joy™ or Dawn™ work best)
1 quart of water
1/3 cup of glycerin

Dip empty frames into the solution to make large bubbles. To make foamy bubbles, use empty shampoo bottles.

Give toddlers a variety of frames to dip into the bubble solution and then blow or wave them through the air. Empty eyeglass frames or plastic berry baskets make wonderful bubbles. Show children that bubble blowing works best when their hands and the frames are both completely wet. (A dry surface causes bubbles to burst on contact.)

Other special activities you might wish to try with toddlers include:

❖ "painting" a building, sidewalk, or tree with water;

❖ playing mood music to set the tone for children's sand and water play; and

❖ telling stories and acting out sand and water adventures they've observed, such as pretending to jump in a puddle or telling a story about the bulldozer.

Though it requires planning and supervision, exploring sand and water is a wonderful learning experience for infants and toddlers.

Sharing Thoughts About
Exploring Sand and Water

Dear Families:

Sand and water play is messy, no doubt about that. But children love it, and they learn from it, too. When an infant splashes at water, he learns that swinging his arm makes the water move (cause and effect). When a toddler pours a cup of sand into a bucket, she begins to learn about size, shape, and quantity. At the same time, these children are developing muscle skills and are learning to express themselves.

Here at the program, the children play with sand and water both indoors and outdoors. Infants splash at water in a tray. Older infants wash dolls and rubber toys; they practice digging and pouring sand. Toddlers squirt water through basters and blow bubbles into the breeze; they make designs in the sand with combs and cookie cutters. We encourage all children to explore sand and water.

What You Can Do at Home

Because sand and water play offers your child many different kinds of experiences, you'll probably want to do some activities at home. Here are some suggestions to consider.

❖ *Fill a tray or plastic tub with an inch or so of water.* A small amount of water is all your child needs to have fun. Place the tub on the floor, on top of some towels, and then let your child just splash away! If you have an older infant or toddler, you can provide plastic measuring cups, squeeze bottles, a funnel, or a sieve.

❖ *Talk with your child while you bathe him or her.* Ask questions to encourage observation and thinking: "What do you think will happen if you drop your big rubber froggie in the water?"

❖ *Fill a dishpan with clean sand.* In this way your child can play with sand either indoors or out. The container forms the boundaries for the sand and allows your child to control the area of play. To vary the experience, add a shovel, funnel, scoop, small plastic animals, or a variety of kitchen utensils.

❖ *Add a bit of water to the sand to make mud.* Invite your child to make mudpies for a pretend party.

We have many more ideas for creative sand and water play. We'd love to share them with you. Even more importantly, we hope you'll give us your ideas for sand and water activities your child especially likes.

Sincerely,

Algunas ideas sobre el juego
con arena y agua

Estimadas familias:

Es indiscutible que el juego con arena y agua ocasiona suciedad. Pero, a los pequeños les fascina y pueden aprender del mismo. Cuando un(a) pequeño(a) chapotea agua, aprende que al mecer su mano ocasiona que el agua se mueva (causa-efecto) y cuando vierte una taza de arena en un balde aprende sobre los tamaños, formas y cantidades. Al mismo tiempo, estos niños están desarrollando sus destrezas musculares y aprendiendo a expresarse.

En nuestro programa, los niños juegan con arena y agua, tanto dentro como fuera del salón. Los pequeños chapotean agua en bandejas y los mayorcitos bañan a sus muñecas y juguetes de plástico. Excavan y vacian arena; filtran agua a través de cedazos y soplan burbujas al viento; hacen diseños en la arena con peines y con moldes para galletas. Nosotros animamos a todos los niños a explorar la arena y el agua.

Lo que ustedes pueden hacer en el hogar

Dado que el juego con arena y agua les ofrece a los niños una variedad de experiencias, es probable que ustedes deseen llevar a cabo algunas de estas actividades en sus hogares. Tengan en cuenta las siguientes recomendaciones:

❖ *Llenen una bañera o una bandeja plástica con una pulgada de agua.* Lo único que necesitan sus hijos para disfrutarlo es un poco de agua. Coloquen la bañera en el suelo, sobre unas cuantas toallas y permítanles chapotear el agua. Si tienen otro(a) hijo(a) mayorcito(a) provéanles tazas plásticas para medir, envases que se puedan apretar, un embudo o un tamiz.

❖ *Hablen con su hijo(a) mientras el/ella se baña.* Formulen preguntas con el fin de estimular la observación y el pensamiento: "Mira cómo salen burbujas con el champú".

❖ *Llenen un platón de arena.* Así los niños podrán jugar adentro o afuera. El recipiente le pone límites a la arena y les permite a los niños controlar el área de juego. Para variar la experiencia, añada una pala, un embudo, una cuchara, animales de plástico pequeños u otros utensilios de cocina.

❖ *Añádanle un poco de agua a la arena para producir lodo.* Inviten a sus hijos a hacer pasteles para una fiesta imaginaria.

Nosotros contamos con otra serie de ideas para el juego creativo con arena y agua y nos encantaría compartirlas con ustedes. Esperamos que nos ofrezcan sus ideas acerca de las actividades con arena y agua preferidas por su niño(a).

Les saluda atentamente,

Having Fun with
Music and Movement

— ◈ —

**After starting a tape for the older children to dance to, Janet notices Jasmine
sitting on the floor bouncing to the music. "It looks like you want to dance too,"
Janet says. Janet sits on the floor next to Jasmine and moves her head and body
to the beat. They smile at one another. Then Janet holds out her arms and asks,
"Do you want me to pick you up to dance?" When Jasmine reaches toward her,
Janet picks her up and begins dancing across the room holding Jasmine in her arms.
Jasmine smiles, then shrieks with pleasure.**

— ◈ —

Music and movement are a natural part of children's lives. As newborns, they can
often be comforted by the rhythmic sound of a parent's heartbeat as the parent
holds them close, or by being rocked or gently bounced to a steady beat. By the
time they can sit, they may bounce up and down or move their arms to music. Toddlers
often have favorite songs. They love making "music" by hitting a spoon on a pot and they
enjoy moving to different tempos and rhythms.

Music and movement also contribute to children's overall development. Indeed,
research has shown that listening to and making music in early childhood helps wire
children's brains in ways required for understanding mathematics, science, and engi-
neering. In addition, music and movement provide opportunities to explore feelings,
relationships, and various concepts. These experiences also promote the development of
listening and speaking skills, motor skills, creativity, and aesthetic appreciation. For example, when Abby does "The Itsy Bitsy Spider" with Brooks, she not only enjoys being
with Brooks, but learns about up and down, and sharpens her fine motor skills as her
fingers become the spider, rain, and sun. When Jonisha dances with other children to a
calypso tape she brought to La Toya's, she feels full of energy and connected to home. As
she moves in different ways to the music, she stretches both her body and her imagination.
And for Gena, learning the words to a new song makes her feel proud and able to participate in singing with other children.

Setting the Stage for Music and Movement

In providing music and movement activities, you'll have many decisions to make. These include how to set up the environment, what kinds of music to play, what kinds of instruments you need, what types of activities are most appropriate for infants and toddlers, and how accomplished you need to be as a singer or dancer. Each topic is discussed below.

"How should I set up the environment for music and movement activities?"

It is likely you have already done what you need to do. Simply be sure you have a safe open space for dancing and moving. The space should be big enough so that children won't bump into anything or each other. Of course, it's often a good idea to use a carpeted floor space. Young children like to fall down, and they may not be wearing shoes for movement activities.

If you have a radio, tape recorder, or compact disc player, be sure to locate it—and any wires used to connect it to an electric outlet—out of children's reach.

"What kinds of music do infants and toddlers enjoy?"

Young children seem to prefer music and songs that have a strong rhythm, repetition, and nonsense syllables; evoke a mood (such as calm or lively); suggest different movements; and tell a story.[1] You can make up simple songs about the children themselves and about familiar things and people in their lives. For example, Gena loves to hear Ivan sing "Here come Gena and Franklin" when she and Franklin, her stuffed lamb, arrive in the morning. Children also enjoy songs you make up about the sounds of things—such as bells that "ding," horns that "honk," and trains that go "choo choo." You can, of course, also have fun singing old favorites such as "Old MacDonald Had a Farm" and "Wheels on the Bus."

In addition, there are many good recordings for young children. Examples include *Let's Sing Fingerplays* and *Activity and Game Songs* (Tom Glazer), *This-a-Way, That-a-Way* (Ella Jenkins), *Singin' and Swingin'* (Sharon, Lois, and Bram) and *Singable Songs for the Very Young* and *More Singable Songs for the Very Young* (Raffi).

You don't have to limit your music choices to selections recorded for children. Look over your own collection for music to share with children. Like you, children enjoy listening and moving to a variety of sounds: folk songs, jazz, classical music, popular music, and music from different cultures. Many public libraries have selections of children's records as well as other types of music children enjoy. Families can also be a rich source of music that reflects their individual tastes and cultures.

---

[1] Joan P. Isenberg and Mary Renck Jalongo. *Creative Expression and Play in the Early Childhood Curriculum.* New York: Macmillan Publishing Company, 1993.

"Do I need instruments? If so, what kinds?"

Simple rhythm instruments such as drums, xylophones, bells, clackers, rattles and shakers, tambourines, maracas, cymbals, wood blocks, and pots and pans with wooden spoons will allow children to create and respond to music as they bang, ring, swish, and click. You can make many of these instruments as well as buy them. For example, you can make drums from oatmeal boxes, cymbals from pie pans, and rattles and shakers by filling containers with rice, macaroni, or buttons, and fastening them securely.

If you—or any parents—play instruments, bring them in and play for children. Don't be surprised if toddlers join you for a jam session by strumming on a cardboard block as you play your guitar, or blowing through a funnel or cardboard tube as you play your recorder.

"What types of music and movement experiences are most appropriate for infants and toddlers?"

Music and movement should be built into each day. They need not be considered as a special activity only. Here are five types of music and movement experiences that children under three will especially enjoy throughout the day

Listening to sounds and music. Sounds are everywhere. When you call children's attention to the "pop" of snaps as you change their clothes, the "crunch" of the apple in the fruit salad they helped prepare, and the "honking" of horns during a neighborhood walk, you help children become more aware of their world and promote the skill of listening.

Listening to music can occur any time during the day. You may already play soft music for children to listen to at naptime or sing to them during routines such as dressing, diapering, and toileting. In Janet's home, children have been listening to a waltz tape that one family brought in. You can promote children's concentration and listening skills when you play music selectively and invite a child or two to listen with you. By choosing to play music at certain times, you prevent it from becoming background sound and tell children it is something to pay attention to and enjoy.

Making sounds and singing. Older infants and toddlers enjoy making sounds—of animals, vehicles, and anything else in their environment. Encourage them to imitate repeated sounds in stories that you read or to make sounds during pretend play. As for singing, most children under three enjoy it. Don't emphasize learning the words or worry about how well the children or you carry a tune. Rather, focus on the fun of singing together. Children differ in their abilities to carry a tune and sing words. Over time, most will try to copy your rhythm, rhymes, gestures, and words—and join in.

Dancing and moving. Movement is a natural partner of music. Even the youngest infants enjoy being held in your arms as you dance. Mobile infants will bounce and sway to music. They may like to sit in your lap facing you and play musical games such as "Row, Row, Row Your Boat," while holding hands and rocking back and forth. As they grow more steady on their feet, many children enjoy "Ring Around the Rosie." Toddlers often like to imitate the movement of various animals such as an elephant, butterfly, wiggly worm, or a road runner. As they move, they explore various concepts, such as when you suggest "Let's wiggle our fingers *silently*," or "Let's stamp our feet as *loudly* as we can." Over time, children learn how they can move their legs, feet, arms, and hands quickly and slowly, up and down, in and out, and over and under. As they become more comfortable with moving to music, you may want to offer them simple props such as feathers, scarves, or ribbons.

Fingerplays. Adding finger movements to classics like "The Itsy Bitsy Spider," "Two Little Blackbirds," and "Open Shut Them" gives children the opportunity to practice fine motor skills and coordination as they sing familiar songs. While some children may be able to get their fingers moving while they sing, others will participate by doing one or the other. Fingerplays also provide times to enjoy being together as you sit face to face with one child or with a small group. An "Itsy Bitsy Spider" fingerplay can lead to conversations about spiders, rain, and waterspouts. A fingerplay to "Two Little Blackbirds" can end up in a conversation about hellos and good-byes as your fingers form blackbirds that fly away and come back again. You may enjoy browsing through books of fingerplays, such as *Fingerplays and Action Chants* (Tonja Weimer) and *Fingerfrolics* (Liz Cromwell and Dick Hibner).

Playing rhythm instruments. Mobile infants and toddlers enjoy the pleasure and satisfaction of creating their own music. You can encourage children to create rhythms by clapping or stomping quickly, slowly, softly, and loudly. Later, introduce some simple instruments. (Provide duplicates to avoid fights, and be ready to step in to prevent children from using instruments as weapons.) Allow plenty of time for children to explore instruments. As with singing, place your emphasis on the pleasure of creating sounds and being together rather than on performing.

"Do I need to be able to sing and dance to do music and movement experiences with children?"

While some adults are accomplished singers and dancers, most of us are not. Don't worry. You can share music and movement with young children even if you can't carry a tune or do the *Macarena*.

Much more important than any music or dance skills you may—or may not—have is your ability to share with children your pleasure in and appreciation of music and movement. This is an important way to encourage children's interest and participation.

Promoting Children's Enjoyment of Music and Movement

As with all activities, take time to observe the children carefully so you can respond in ways that make each experience fun and meaningful for them. No matter how much you may want to share the beauty and pleasure of music and movement with children, remember that the key idea is that these activities should be fun. At no time should you force children to listen to music or to move and dance. At the same time, you should be aware of children's interest in one or more of various musical experiences. When necessary, you can step in to prevent the over-stimulation that can turn a music or movement activity into noise and chaos.

Here are some strategies you can use to promote children's exploration and enjoyment of music and movement.

Young Infants

Young infants like Julio and Jasmine may respond to sounds and music by turning their heads, smiling, laughing, or moving an arm or leg. They are generally soothed and calmed by soft, rhythmic sounds, such as a lullaby and the voice of a familiar caregiver. They tend to respond in more lively ways when music is peppy. Some infants are more sensitive than others to sounds and may cry at an unexpected or loud sound. Others are curious and attentive but may show fear when they hear certain sounds, such as the vacuum cleaner or garbage disposal.

For infants, as with older children, movement is the natural extension of music. Infants tend to respond to music with their entire bodies. Jasmine, for instance, bounces up and down and sways back and forth when Janet plays the new tape her older son brought home last week.

One of the most important ways to encourage infants' enjoyment of music and movement is to highlight and build on experiences that occur naturally in the course of daily life. Let's see how this works by looking in on Julio and Jasmine with their caregivers.

Because Julio is fussy, Linda picks him up and sings softly to him as she rocks with him in the rocking chair. He quiets down and gazes at her. She smiles and says, "You are feeling better, aren't you? Do you want to sing some more?" As Linda continues rocking and singing, she gives Julio a positive experience with music and movement.

Each afternoon, Janet and the children she cares for go outside into her backyard. While some of the older children play, Janet sits on a blanket with Jasmine. "Listen," she says, "do you hear the birds singing in the trees?" After a pause so Jasmine can listen, she whistles, copying their song. "Can you sing like a bird?" she asks. Janet is helping Jasmine understand that listening is an important skill. Over time, Jasmine will learn to distinguish among different sounds, rhythms, and volumes.

To encourage children's exploration of music and movement, you can talk with them about what they are experiencing. Always be sure, as Janet was, not to talk so much that you interfere with the sound and flow of the music. Here are some examples of ways you might interact with children.

- ❖ **Describe what they may be experiencing:** "You are swaying back and forth to the music."

- ❖ **Mirror the infant's emotions,** as you observe him or her listening to music and moving: "You like to dance, don't you?"

- ❖ **Explain concepts** they will come to understand over time and with experience: "That music is loud, isn't it?"

- ❖ **Provide vocabulary** as they explore music and movement: "That's a tuba you hear playing."

- ❖ **Build their confidence and self-esteem:** "You are listening carefully."

Mobile Infants

Willard and Abby also enjoy the sounds and music that are part of their daily lives. For example, each morning Willard waits for Grace to push the button of the blender to mix orange juice and happily joins in the "whirring." Abby beams with pleasure when Brooks sings, 'Abby, Abby, where is little Abby?" to the tune of "Alouette."

To respond to children's increasing skills, you can introduce music and movement activities to individual children or to small groups. These activities may include singing, playing rhythm instruments, and dancing during daily routines and playtime. For example, sing a song when changing a child's diaper. Encourage children to take "giant" steps when taking a walk around the neighborhood or playing outdoors.

As their language skills improve, some mobile infants may join you in a song. Sometimes they may repeat a sound over and over again, such as "B-B-B-B" or "DADADADADADA." They may half-babble half-talk, and even sing through a familiar song such as "Happy Birthday." With their increasing physical coordination and body awareness, they also enjoy playing simple rhythm instruments and moving to the music.

As you interact with mobile infants, you can promote both their pleasure in and learning from music and movement. Here are some ideas of ways to help children focus on their experiences.

❖ **Describe what they are doing**: "You are singing a song to the teddy bear."

❖ **Encourage children to respond to music with their bodies**: "You are moving slowly to this slow music."

❖ **Ask children to identify familiar sounds**: "Do you hear the clock ticking?"

❖ **Point out differences between selections of music**: "The drum is beating in this marching music. It goes 'boom, boom, boom'."

❖ **Build social relationships** around music and movement: "Let's hold hands and stomp through the leaves together."

Toddlers

Over the years, Leo, Matthew, Gena, and the twins have had many experiences with music and movement. They have discovered songs that they particularly like. They have learned to discriminate among certain sounds, and like some toddlers, can identify the sound of a specific instrument. They sometimes hum and sing as they play. Their increased fine and gross motor skills give them more control as they do fingerplays and move their arms and legs. And their growing imaginations open the way for different kinds of movement. Here are some ways to interact with toddlers to support these new learnings.

❖ **Encourage toddlers' enjoyment of songs**: "Shall we play the animal song you like so much?"

❖ **Help them discriminate among different sounds**: "Listen carefully. Do you know what instrument this is that makes such high notes?"

❖ **Encourage toddlers to sing familiar songs**: "Is today your baby's birthday? Are you going to sing 'Happy Birthday' to him?"

❖ **Focus attention on how their bodies move**: "Can you move quickly like the beat of this drum?"

❖ **Stimulate toddlers' imaginations**: "Let's pretend we are pancakes 'flip flopping' in the pan."

Music and movement are all around us. By including them in your program each day, you are opening the door to experiences that children can enjoy for the rest of their lives.

❖   ❖   ❖

Sharing Thoughts About Music and Movement

Dear Families:

The pleasures of listening to music and moving their bodies are natural and important parts of children's lives. Newborns are naturally comforted when they are rocked or gently bounced to a steady rhythm. Older infants and toddlers may have favorite songs, or may even make music by banging a spoon on a pot. In addition to the pleasures of listening and moving to music, these activities are important to children's overall development. Here are some examples.

When your child does this . . .	Your child is learning . . .
holds hands and dances with another child	about relationships
plays a rhythm instrument	being a "music maker"
stomps around the room to a march	to respond to musical patterns
claps slowly, then quickly	concepts of slow and fast
enjoys singing and dancing with others	the pleasure of music and moving

What You Can Do at Home

It's easy and fun to make music and movement a part of your child's life. Here are some suggestions for things you can do at home.

❖ *Notice everyday sounds with your child.* Point out the clock ticking or the birds singing. Encourage your child to point out different sounds to you.

❖ *Sing with your child. You can make up songs about your child and familiar people and events.* To start, use a familiar tune and just substitute the name of a person or an event: "Sarah had a little doll, little doll, little doll . . ." We'll be happy to share songs we sing with you, and we'd love to learn some of your "home" songs.

❖ *Move and dance together.* It's fun to take giant steps, then tiny steps during a walk. You can even try to hop like a frog or wiggle like a worm!

❖ *Offer your child simple rhythm instruments.* You can make drums from oatmeal boxes, cymbals from pie pans, and shakers by filling containers with rice or buttons and fastening them securely.

It doesn't matter if you can't carry a tune or play an instrument. What does matter is that you share your enjoyment of music and movement with your child. With that thought in mind, we can open the door to experiences your child will enjoy for the rest of his or her life.

Sincerely,

Algunas ideas sobre el placer de la música y el movimiento

Estimadas familias:

Escuchar música y mover el cuerpo son aspectos naturales, placenteros e importantes en la vida de los niños. Los recién nacidos se sientes reconfortados cuando se les mece con delicadeza y a un ritmo continuo. Los mayorcitos pueden tener canciones favoritas o, incluso, producir música al golpear una olla con una cuchara. Además de los placeres de escuchar música y moverse al son de la misma, estas actividades son de gran importancia para el desarrollo general de los niños. Los siguientes son unos cuantos ejemplos:

Cuando su hijo(a):	El/ella aprende:
se toma de las manos y baila con otro(a) niño(a)	sobre las relaciones sociales
toca un instrumento rítmico	a ser un(a) "productor(a) de música"
aplaude lentamente y luego rápido	a responder a la música
disfruta el cantar y bailar con otros	los placeres de la música y el movimiento

Lo que ustedes pueden hacer en el hogar

Es sumamente fácil y grato convertir la música y el movimiento en parte de la vida de sus hijos. Las siguientes son unas cuantas sugerencias que podrían poner en práctica en su hogar.

❖ *Noten los sonidos diarios con sus hijos.* Hagan notar el sonido del reloj o el canto de los pájaros. Anímenlos a señalarles a ustedes los diferentes sonidos.

❖ *Canten con sus hijos.* Ustedes pueden inventar canciones sobre sus hijos, parientes y eventos familiares. Para comenzar, elijan una melodía conocida y sustituyan el nombre de una persona o de un evento: "María tiene una pequeña muñeca, pequeña muñeca, pequeña muñeca . . ." Nos encantaría compartir con ustedes nuestras canciones y aprender algunas de las "hogareñas".

❖ *Muévanse y bailen juntos.* Durante una salida a caminar, es muy agradable dar pasos gigantescos y, luego, pasos pequeños. Ustedes podrían tratar, incluso, de saltar como las ranas o de deslizarse como los gusanos.

❖ *Ofrézcanles a los niños instrumentos rítmicos sencillos.* Ustedes pueden construir tambores con tarros de avena, timbales con los moldes para hornear y maracas con recipientes llenos de arroz o de botones, sellados en forma segura.

No se preocupen si no pueden cantar ni tocar ningún instrumento. En realidad no importa. Lo importante es que compartan con sus niños su gusto por la música y el movimiento. Así, podremos brindarle a sus hijos la oportunidad de gozar experiencias que disfrutarán por el resto de sus vidas.

Les saluda atentamente,

Going Outdoors

— ❖ —

"Look Gena, our lettuce will be ready to eat in a few days," Ivan says as he and Gena study the first crop in the wheelbarrow garden. "Do you think our garden needs a little more sun?" "Yes," agrees Gena as she observes the garden from her adaptive stroller. She watches as Ivan pushes the portable garden into a sunny corner of the Crane School's play yard. Gena turns her attention to the grassy spot under the tree. There children are chasing bubbles a teacher is blowing. "Do you want to go over and help blow bubbles?" asks Ivan. Gena nods and Ivan pushes her over to join the other children.

— ❖ —

Going outdoors is fun for children. It gives them—and you—a chance to stretch large muscles, breathe fresh air, take in the sunshine (or the rain or snow), and enjoy the freedom of open spaces. Young infants like the touch of a soft, warm breeze on their cheeks or the sight of light filtering through the leaves as they look up from their carriage during a walk. By the time they are mobile, they enjoy splashing in a bin of water and crawling over a path you can create by adding blankets, tires, and floor mats to the natural textures that exist in your outdoor play space. As toddlers, they cannot resist the challenge of running in open space, climbing over tree trunks, chasing soap bubbles you blow, and propelling themselves on riding toys.

In addition, outdoor play can contribute to children's overall development by giving them a chance to explore with all their senses, practice fine and gross motor skills, develop social skills, and begin to appreciate and respect other living things. For example, when Jasmine touches and pulls on the grass in Janet's backyard, she is exploring with her senses and using fine motor skills. For Leo, being outdoors is a time to use his big muscles as he runs and climbs in the center's yard. Outdoor play also allows children to experience the bigger world in which people are going about their everyday lives. When Leo walks with Barbara, he loves to stop in at the grocery store to visit Ben, who is sometimes sweeping, or putting things on the shelves.

Infants and toddlers should go outdoors every day, unless the weather is extreme. Going outdoors is important for their mental and physical health—and for yours.

Setting the Stage for Outdoor Play

When you go outdoors with the children, you need to make several decisions. These include which health and safety factors to consider, how to make the most out of the space you have, and what types of activities are most appropriate for infants and toddlers.[1]

"How do I create a safe and healthy outdoor environment?"

Keeping children safe and healthy when outdoors requires your ongoing attention. Here are some important aspects to consider.

Adult supervision. An adult needs to be able to see the entire play area at all times. If you are in a setting with more than one adult, each person can supervise an area, always being sure someone has a picture of the whole scene. Of course, everyone needs to be flexible and ready to step in if help is needed.

Nontoxic landscape. Soil should be analyzed for lead content initially and for toxic chemicals or other substances where there is reason to believe a problem may exist. Be sure all vegetation is non-poisonous in case a curious child takes a taste. Be on the lookout for mushrooms which can sprout up overnight. Check with your Regional Poison Control Center or Cooperative Extension Service for complete information.

Preventing drowning. According to the *National Health and Safety Performance Standards*, drowning is the third leading cause of unintentional injury in children younger than five. In some states, it is the leading cause of death. To prevent drowning, outside play areas should not include unprotected swimming and wading pools, ditches, quarries, canals, excavations in which water can collect, fish ponds, and other bodies of water.

The layout. The layout of your play area can make it more manageable, interesting, and safe. Defined areas with clear pathways not only provide a traffic pattern, but also help children make choices about what they want to do. All fixed play equipment should be arranged so that children playing on one piece of equipment will not interfere with children playing on or running to another piece of equipment. Locating swings and riding toys away from areas where children run can help prevent children from accidentally wandering into them and getting hurt.

Preventing unnecessary conflicts and crowding. You can reduce hitting, pushing, and biting incidents by offering plenty of interesting things to do. Provide duplicates of favorite outdoor toys such as balls, buckets and shovels, and riding toys. Be alert and ready to step in when necessary.

---

[1] The section is based on Jim Greenman and Anne Stonehouse, *Prime Times: A Handbook for Excellence in Infant and Toddler Programs*. St. Paul, MN: Redleaf Press, 1996, pp. 226–233; American Public Health Association and the American Academy of Pediatrics, *National Health and Safety Standards: Guidelines for Out-of-Home Child Care Programs*. Arlington, VA: National Center for Education in Maternal and Child Health, 1992, pp. 183–192; and Karen Miller, *The Outside Play and Learning Book*. Beltsville, MD: Gryphon House, 1989, pp.13–19; 23–26; 156; 159; 212.

Developmentally appropriate equipment. Equipment should be designed to match the size and skills of infants and toddlers. Choose equipment based on what you know about children's developmental abilities. (See Chapter 7, Creating a Welcoming Environment.)

Safe equipment. All equipment must meet all Consumer Product Safety Standards in regard to exposed surfaces, spacing, design, and location. All playground equipment should be installed so that an average-sized adult cannot cause a structure to wobble or tip. (See the *Safety Checklist* in Appendix C.)

Daily monitoring and maintenance. Outdoor play areas should be checked daily for broken glass, trash, and other hazardous materials such as animal feces, garden chemicals, or housepaint.

Monthly monitoring and maintenance. Check for the following once a month:

- visible cracks, bending or warping, rusting or breakage of any equipment;
- faulty or broken open hooks, rings, links, etc.;
- worn swing hangers and chains;
- missing, damaged, or loose swing seats;
- broken supports or anchors;
- cement support footings that are exposed, cracked, or loose in the ground;
- accessible sharp edges or points;
- exposed ends of tubing that require covering with caps or plugs;
- protruding bolt ends that have lost caps or covers;
- loose bolts, nuts, and screws that require tightening;
- splintered, cracked, or otherwise deteriorating wood;
- lack of lubrication on moving parts;
- broken or missing rails, steps, rungs, or seats;
- worn or scattered surfacing material;
- hard surfaces, especially under swings and slides, where resilient materials have shifted;
- chipped or peeling paint; and
- pinch or crush points, exposed mechanisms, and moving parts.

You may want to use items from this list and the checklists in Appendix C to create a checklist for tracking ongoing monitoring and maintenance of your program's outdoor play space.

Shock-absorbent materials. Any surface higher than 18–24 inches should be on 8–12 inches of grass or other shock-absorbent material that meets *Consumer Product Safety Guidelines*. Avoid using rubber, sand, pea-gravel, or wood chips that might be swallowed.

Protection from exposure to the sun. Encourage families to supply sunhats, sunglasses, and sunscreen for their children. Offer children water on very hot days. If you do not have a naturally occurring shady spot where children can get out of the sun, you can create one. Drape a sheet from a fence, put up a tent, or use an awning.

"My outdoor space—and my budget—are limited. How can I make the most of what I have?"

Money and space for outdoor play areas are often in short supply. But don't despair. With thought and careful planning, you can offer children safe and valuable outdoor experiences. Here are some suggestions to help you make the most of your space.

Build on what nature has to offer. Take advantage of soft grass for sitting or moving, tree stumps for climbing, wildlife, and various textures and sounds. Though we do suggest bringing toys and activities outdoors, don't get so busy lugging things and planning games that you forget to take time to watch a squirrel climbing a tree or to roll down a grassy hill with the children.

Think in terms of flexibility. Your space and what children can do in it naturally change with changes in the weather and the seasons. In addition, you can transform your space and add variety to children's experiences with props such as planks, boxes, rubber tires, and balls.

Make going outdoors manageable. You'll most likely take children outdoors frequently and enthusiastically if you can reduce related hassles. For example, you may not look forward to putting on snowsuits or searching for missing boots, but it helps to understand that dressing is a valuable learning experience in itself. For days when you take a walk, pack a shoulder bag or backpack with sunblock, tissues, and a first aid kit that contains emergency phone numbers and money for a pay phone. Add a container of bubble-blowing solution, and you will always have an engaging activity at hand.

Adapt your environment as necessary for children with special needs. According to the Americans with Disabilities Act (ADA), your outdoor play space should ensure that children with special needs can have the same or an equivalent experience as other children. Many adaptations are simply a matter of common sense and easy to do. For example, a ramp can make getting strollers and/or a wheelchair in and out easier. Consider using wagons for going outdoors and on field trips. Take special care to remove equipment that is easily overturned if a child pulls herself up on it or leans heavily against it. If more extensive adaptations are necessary, look into options for funding sources, including civic organizations and local businesses. Some programs may be eligible for a tax credit or deduction under the ADA to make structural adaptations.

Visit and talk with colleagues for other ideas. You never know what you might learn. Ivan, for example, heard about wheelbarrow gardens at a conference he attended last spring.

"Should I divide my outdoor space into different areas?"

Ideally, outdoor play space for infants and toddlers should include three areas: a shaded, grassy area for infants, an area with something to climb on and swings, and an area for riding toys that also has a place to play with sand and water. These three areas allow for a variety of experiences that children under three will enjoy.

In addition, think of areas in your community where children can visit. For example, children may enjoy playing in a neighborhood park, taking "field trips" to the corner market, or walking down the street to the large tree to collect and run through the falling leaves.

"What kinds of outdoor experiences should I offer infants and toddlers?"

Outdoor play should be a regular part of your daily schedule. (When possible, plan outdoor times in the mornings and afternoons.) There are three types of outdoor experiences children under three will especially enjoy: sensory exploration; gross motor play; and fine motor play.

Sensory exploration

With the sounds of singing birds and honking horns, the varied textures of grass, tree bark, and sand, and brightly colored sky, flowers, and leaves, outdoors is perfect for sensory exploration. To build on what nature has to offer, consider the following ideas.

Create interesting patterns of light. Hang colored plexiglas or a crystal from a tree branch or a fence. You can also hang large pieces of bright fabric to let the sun shine through and to create temporary shade.

Make effects of the wind visible and audible. Hang fabrics, banners, parachutes, pie tins, and wind chimes on a fence. Encourage children to watch, listen, and reach for items.

Become aware of smells. With older infants and toddlers, you can plant flowers and herbs. Call children's attention to the smell of grass, dried leaves, and the rain.

Grow foods for snacks. Plant lettuce, peas, carrots, and herbs for children to taste.

Take a texture walk. Call the attention of older infants and toddlers to rough bark on a tree, prickly sticky pine cones, and a smooth hard rock. Children will enjoy collecting some of these items in buckets.

Eat outdoors. Spread out a blanket and enjoy a picnic together.

Take a magnifying glass outside. Older toddlers will enjoy looking at the magnified leaves and flowers under the glass.

Go out—even if it is raining or snowing lightly. Many older infants and toddlers love jumping in puddles. If warmly dressed, they often enjoy feeling snowflakes on their cheeks or making footprints in light snow. On days when the weather is too severe to go outdoors, bring some of the outdoors in. For example, invite children to poke and dig in bins of snow.

Gross Motor Play

Moving their bodies comes naturally to infants and toddlers. To promote gross motor play, consider some of these ideas.

Create safe places for young infants. A blanket spread out on the grass away from the traffic patterns of older children provides a safe place for an infant to stretch, reach for a toy, and practice rolling over. Some infants may enjoy spending some time on the grass, while others will protest and tell you they do not like the feel. You can place an infant on his tummy on a blanket and take him for a "ride" by pulling the blanket around.

Encourage crawlers to move by creating interesting places to go. You may, for example, decide to bring some equipment outdoors, such as cardboard boxes, cloth tunnels, covered ramps, or a table covered with a blanket to create places for children to go in, under, and through.

Give newly mobile infants something to hold on to. Show children how to hold on to a fence or low bench. Consider building a low rail 8–12 inches off the ground to encourage mobile infants to cruise.

Provide safe places for children to climb. A "climber" need be no higher than 18 inches off the ground. Low wide steps should lead to a platform large enough for two or three children at a time, with cushioning material underneath. There should be handholds for children to grab when they need to steady their balance.

Provide wheel toys for toddlers. Riding toys, wagons, wheelbarrows, and doll carriages give toddlers a variety of ways to move themselves, their dolls, and assorted objects from place to place.

Play movement games with older mobile infants and toddlers. Invite children to flutter like butterflies, wiggle like worms, or pretend to be baby birds who fly away and come home to the nest. Show children how to make their shadows move. Play "Follow the Leader" or "Can You Do What I Do?"

Invent games that promote the development of gross motor skills. You can create a "balancing path" by laying a scarf or piece of rope across the ground for children to walk on. Set up a bowling game where children try to knock down empty food boxes or plastic soda bottles using a beach ball. Challenge older toddlers to throw a beach ball into a laundry basket or large box. Invite mobile infants and toddlers to chase bubbles that you blow.

Fine Motor Play

Outdoor play gives children many opportunities to use their fine motor skills. Here are some examples.

Collecting small natural objects. Mobile infants and toddlers love collecting leaves, pine cones, maple seeds, or small sticks in wagons, buckets, or other containers with handles. They may want to keep their items for a time or may enjoy transporting them to a different place, then dumping them out.

Sand play. Many activities discussed in Chapter 21 can be done outside without worry about spilling sand on the floor. Remember to cover sand boxes (always popular with cats) when they are not in use.

Water play. Toddlers often enjoy painting a fence, sidewalk, or wall with water. On a hot day, most infants like to splash in a shallow bin of water, wearing only their diapers. Mobile infants and toddlers can have fun as they run through a sprinkler.

Art. For toddlers, painting and pounding on dough are different experiences in the great outdoors. Encourage children to create "nature sculptures" by adding natural items to their dough. Children can collect and paint with twigs, stones, and leaves.

Reading. Sit together under a tree and read books about the outdoors. Make a texture book by gluing leaves, moss, twigs, and small stones to pages made of cardboard.

Pretend play. Offer toddlers props such as toy rubber people and animals, and plastic vehicles for the sandbox. Encourage children to think where each toy may be going and what each is doing.

Promoting Children's Exploration and Enjoyment of the Outdoors

It can be tempting to equate going outdoors with taking a break. While a change of scene is usually refreshing, children need you to remain "on duty" observing, interacting, and sometimes playing with them. This doesn't mean you can't sit down for a moment or talk to a colleague. It does mean that children are depending on you outdoors— just as they do indoors— to keep them safe and to respond in ways that make their experience fun and meaningful. Here are some strategies you can use.

Young Infants

Young infants like Julio and Jasmine usually enjoy outdoor sights and sounds. For them, being outdoors is not only a change of scene, but an interesting experience in itself. While Julio may fall asleep, many infants Jasmine's age may enjoy watching other children, sitting and playing on a blanket, crawling through the grass, and joining an adult in reading a story or singing a song.

To enhance children's pleasure and exploration of the outdoors, talk with them about what they are experiencing. Here are some examples of ways you might interact with children.

❖ **Describe what they may be experiencing:** "Do you feel the breeze blowing your hair?"

❖ **Mirror an infant's emotions:** "You like to touch the grass, don't you?"

❖ **Explain concepts** they will come to understand over time: "The birds are flying high up in the sky."

❖ **Provide vocabulary as they explore the outdoors:** "Do you hear the wind chimes?"

❖ **Build their confidence and self-esteem:** "You are finding all sorts of interesting things in the grass to look at today."

Mobile Infants

Willard and Abby also enjoy being outdoors. Each morning, Willard looks up eagerly when Grace asks if he is ready to go outside. Abby sometimes asks Brooks, "Out?" and goes over to her stroller.

Mobile infants need little encouragement to take off crawling, cruising, and climbing. Some may join in simple movement games. Almost all enjoy digging in the sand, playing with water, pushing wheel toys, and dumping and filling.

As you interact with mobile infants, you can talk to them to enhance their fun and learning.

❖ **Encourage appreciation and respect for nature:** "Let's sit here and watch the squirrel climbing in the tree."

❖ **Promote feelings of competence:** "You popped all the bubbles!"

❖ **Describe and identify familiar sounds:** "Do you hear the wind blowing in the leaves?"

❖ **Note differences in the natural environment:** "It is colder today than yesterday. Maybe it will snow."

❖ **Promote positive social interactions:** "Let's roll the ball to Lianna now."

Toddlers

Leo, Matthew, Gena, and the twins have spent lots of time outdoors over the months and years. Through their experiences they have learned new vocabulary and concepts. Their developing gross and fine motor skills give them more control as they explore and play. Their growing imaginations open the door to more complex pretend play. Following are some ways to interact with toddlers to support these new learnings.

- ❖ **Encourage toddlers' growing vocabulary about the outdoors:** "These maple tree seeds remind me of little helicopters as they fall to the ground."

- ❖ **Explain new concepts:** "The ants are crawling into their home under the ground."

- ❖ **Encourage toddlers' moving and exploring:** "Can you jump like the grasshopper?"

- ❖ **Promote use of fine motor skills:** "Can you bury this pine cone in the pile of leaves?"

- ❖ **Stimulate toddlers' imaginations:** "What do you think the bird is saying to us when it goes, "chirp, chirp."

The outdoors offers unique opportunities for fun and learning. By making going outdoors part of daily life in your program, you are opening the door to a world children can enjoy for the rest of their lives.

Sharing Thoughts About
Going Outdoors

Dear Families:

Going outdoors is fun for children. It gives them—and you—a chance to stretch large muscles, breathe fresh air, take in the sunshine (or the rain or snow), and enjoy the freedom of space.

Going outdoors contributes to children's overall development:

When your child does this. . .	Your child is learning. . .
crawls through the grass	to explore with all senses
climbs over a tree stump	to use gross motor skills
picks up a pine cone to put in a bucket	to use fine motor skills
watches a squirrel climb a tree	to appreciate nature
rolls a ball to another child	social skills

What You Can Do at Home

Here are some activities you might want to try next time you go outdoors with your child. Some of these you probably do already. Others, we hope, will give you some new ideas:

❖ *Enjoy nature.* Talk about the breeze touching your cheeks. Roll down a grassy hill together. Plant a garden—in your yard, a window box, or in a wheelbarrow you can move into the sun. Take a bucket so your child can collect things such as pine cones, acorns, leaves.

❖ *Take a texture walk.* Call your child's attention to soft sand, pine cones, and a smooth, hard boulder.

❖ *Invent games to play.* Create a "balancing path" by laying a piece of rope across the ground for your child to walk on. Play "catch and toss." Set up a bowling game in which your child tries to knock down as many empty food boxes by rolling a beach ball.

❖ *Take some "inside" activities outdoors.* Sit together under a tree and read a book. Give your child a paintbrush and water to paint the side of your house.

By working together, we can introduce your child to the fun and the wonders of the outdoors.

Sincerely,

Algunas ideas sobre el juego al aire libre

Estimadas familias:

Estar al aire libre es sumamente agradable para los niños. Además, les brinda —tanto a ellos como a ustedes— la oportunidad de estirar los músculos, respirar aire fresco, recibir sol (o disfrutar de la lluvia o la nieve) y gozar de la libertad del espacio abierto.

Jugar al aire libre contribuye al crecimiento de los niños en varias formas:

Cuando él/ella:	**Su hijo(a) aprende:**
gatea sobre el pasto	a explorar con todos sus sentidos
se trepa sobre el tronco de un árbol cortado	a hacer uso de su motricidad gruesa
recoge una bellota y la coloca en una canasta	a hacer uso de su motricidad fina
observa a una ardilla que trepa a un árbol	a apreciar la naturaleza
hace rodar una pelota y la dirige a otro(a)	destrezas sociales niño(a)

Lo que ustedes pueden hacer en el hogar

Las siguientes son unas cuantas actividades que ustedes podrían poner en práctica la próxima vez que salgan con sus hijos. Probablemente, algunas ustedes ya las practican. Otras, esperamos que les sirvan de inspiración:

❖ *Disfruten de la naturaleza.* Hablen sobre la brisa que toca sus mejillas. Rueden juntos por una pendiente. Planten un jardín en su patio, en materas, o en una carreta que puedan mover y poner al sol. Lleven un balde para que los pequeños puedan recolectar bellotas, hojas, piedrecillas, etc.

❖ *Vayan a caminar y noten texturas.* Háganles notar a los niños la suavidad de la arena, la dureza de las bellotas y la suavidad y firmeza de algunas piedras.

❖ *Inventen juegos.* Creen un "sendero de equilibrio" mediante un lazo puesto sobre el terreno y sobre el que puedan caminar los niños. Jueguen a "lanzar y atrapar". Organicen un juego de "bolos" en el que los pequeños traten de derribar cajas vacías con una pelota.

❖ *Lleven al exterior, algunas de las actividades que siempre realizan adentro.* Lean un libro sentados bajo la sombra de un árbol. Permítanles "pintar" una pared exterior con una brocha y agua.

Trabajando juntos, podremos hacer que sus hijos disfruten de las maravillas del mundo al aire libre.

Les saluda atentamente,

Part V Appendices

Self-Assessment

Goals and Objectives for Caregivers/Teachers

Caregiver/Teacher: _____ **Date completed:** _____

Directions: Read each goal, its objectives, and the examples. To rate yourself on each objective, write **X** in the appropriately numbered box. On the lines following the word *Comments,* give examples that explain your rating or that describe how you can improve.

Goal 1: To build responsive relationships

Objective: **To form positive, trusting relationships with children**

RATING
5 HIGH
4
3
2
1 LOW

Examples:
❖ Feed, change, and offer naps to infants on demand
❖ Offer consistency in caregiving from day to day so each child forms social attachments
❖ Mirror children's emotions and feelings (e.g., show excitement when a child makes a discovery or accomplishes a task; respond sympathetically if a child is upset)

Comments: _____

_____

_____

_____

_____

Objective: **To form positive relationships with families to support children's growth and development**

RATING
5 HIGH
4
3
2
1 LOW

Examples:
❖ Interact daily with families in a positive manner, answering questions and discussing children's progress
❖ Recognize that parents' values must be addressed by the program (e.g., consult with parents about dietary concerns; discuss approach to handling challenging behaviors)
❖ Encourage parents to participate regularly in program activities, conferences/home visits, and to join in on field trips

Comments: _____

_____

_____

_____

Goal 1: To build responsive relationships (continued)

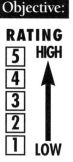

Objective: **To work with colleagues and community representatives to support children and families**

Examples:

❖ Collaborate with specialists and refer children with disabilities to community services

❖ Consult with colleagues and community representatives to develop procedures for reporting suspected child abuse

❖ Maintain a "yellow pages" of community resources and the services they provide, including contact persons and phone numbers

Comments:_____

_____

_____

_____

_____

Goal 2: To plan and manage a developmentally appropriate program

Objective: **To plan and evaluate a program that meets the needs of the children and families served**

Examples:

❖ Specify long-range and short-term goals and objectives for the program

❖ Develop a daily schedule that allows for individual and small group activities, balances quiet and active times, and is responsive to children's needs and interests

❖ Assess plans continually for effectiveness and make adjustments as indicated

Comments:_____

_____

_____

_____

Objective: **To observe children regularly and individualize the program based on these observations**

Examples:

❖ Observe children regularly to learn about their special characteristics, temperament, and learning styles

❖ Complete the *Individualizing Goals and Objectives for Children* form and the *Planning Form for Individualizing* on each child at least three times a year

❖ Specify curricular goals and objectives for each child based on the child's observed skills and needs

Comments:_____

_____

_____

_____

_____

Goal 2: To plan and manage a developmentally appropriate program
(continued)

Objective: **To create a warm and welcoming environment that supports children's growth and development**

Examples:

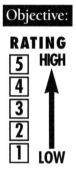

RATING

5 HIGH

4

3

2

1 LOW

- Create an environment that fosters trust and security (e.g., spaces for crawling and snuggling; soft, cuddly textures; safe and clean materials)
- Provide materials and toys that stimulate children's senses, build on developing skills, and are adaptable, if necessary, for a child with special needs
- Provide an outdoor environment in which children can safely play and explore

Comments: _____

_____

_____

_____

_____

Objective: **To ensure the safety of children in the program**

Examples:

RATING

5 HIGH

4

3

2

1 LOW

- Use the *Safety Checklist* form regularly to ensure that preventive measures are in place to reduce chances of accidents
- Have emergency procedures available in case of sudden accidents and natural disasters
- Balance children's need for safety with their need to explore

Comments: _____

_____

_____

_____

_____

Objective: **To ensure the health of children in the program**

Examples:

RATING

5 HIGH

4

3

2

1 LOW

- Have procedures in place for responding to health emergencies
- Follow proper sanitation and hygiene procedures to prevent the spread of disease
- Provide well-balanced meals and snacks that meet children's nutritional requirements

Comments: _____

_____

_____

_____

_____

Objective: **To guide children's behavior in positive ways**

Examples:

RATING

5 HIGH

4

3

2

1 LOW

- Set up the environment to eliminate potential behavior problems (e.g., provide duplicates of favorite toys, remove breakables, offer soothing activities)
- Work with families to provide children with consistent messages at home and at the program
- Develop strategies for helping children deal with frustration and anger in positive rather than negative ways (e.g., through words or pretend play rather than by hitting or biting)

Comments: _____

_____

_____

_____

_____

Goal 3: To promote children's development and learning

Objective: **To use routines as opportunities for growth and learning**

RATING

5 HIGH

4

3

2

1 LOW

Examples:

❖ Respond and repeat sounds infants make; talk, sing, and play word games while feeding, changing, and dressing children

❖ Offer toys to children to stimulate play during routines

❖ Explain what is being done during a routine and ask questions, even to nonverbal children

Comments: _____

_____

_____

_____

_____

Objective: **To provide activities that will facilitate children's growth and development**

RATING

5 HIGH

4

3

2

1 LOW

Examples:

❖ Offer children toys and materials that can be mouthed, shaken, cuddled, and explored with all the senses

❖ Plan daily activities for children—art, outdoor play, food experiences, and so forth—increasing activity periods as children mature

❖ Introduce activities as a natural part of the child's day

Comments: _____

_____

_____

_____

_____

Goal 4: To continue learning about children, families, and the field of early childhood education

Objective: **To participate in training to expand skills and knowledge**

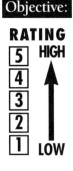

RATING

5 HIGH

4

3

2

1 LOW

Examples:

❖ Seek training opportunities offered by professional organizations

❖ Ask colleagues, supervisors, and families for assistance in acquiring new skills

❖ Identify areas where additional training would improve job performance

Comments: _____

_____

_____

_____

Objective: **To participate in professional early childhood education organizations**

RATING

5 HIGH

4

3

2

1 LOW

Examples:

❖ Read books and journals on young children published by professional organizations (e.g., *Young Children, Child Development, Child Care Information Exchange, Zero to Three*)

❖ Attend local, state, and national conferences sponsored by professional organizations

❖ Conduct workshops or present papers on topics of interest

Comments: _____

_____

_____

_____

Goal 4: To continue learning about children, families, and the field of early childhood education (continued)

Objective: To observe colleagues to learn new successful techniques and approaches

RATING

5 HIGH
4
3
2
1 LOW

Examples:

❖ Visit and observe colleagues and other programs

❖ Ask colleagues and/or supervisors to model particular teaching skills or interactions with children

❖ Work as a member of a team; develop a system of mutual support with colleagues

Comments: _____

_____

_____

_____

_____

Goal 5: To maintain professional standards

Objective: To be ethical in all dealings with children, families, and community representatives

RATING

5 HIGH
4
3
2
1 LOW

Examples:

❖ Be honest, reliable, and dependable; come to work each day and notify families of program policies (e.g., vacations, absences—yours and children's)

❖ Act conscientiously in performing routines (e.g., change children when they are wet; do not allow children to sit indoors with coats on; comfort crying children)

❖ Follow all regulations concerning health and safety standards, group size and ratios, and child abuse reporting procedures

Comments: _____

_____

_____

_____

_____

Objective: To respect the privacy and confidentiality of children and parents

RATING

5 HIGH
4
3
2
1 LOW

Examples:

❖ Share children's records only with their family and professionals who have a "need to know"

❖ Keep children's records—including observations—in a secure place

❖ Do not discuss children and families in public and/or with colleagues (unless there is a programming reason to do so)

Comments: _____

_____

_____

_____

_____

Goal 5: To maintain professional standards (continued)

Objective: **To demonstrate respect for all children and families**

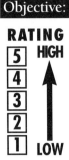

Examples:

* Learn ways to communicate successfully with all families (e.g., learn at least a few words in each family's home language, make home visits)
* Schedule meetings and conferences to meet an individual family's needs
* Seek input from families about home culture

Comments:_____

_____

_____

_____

_____

Goal 6: To be an advocate in support of children and families

Objective: **To educate others about the need for high standards and quality programs**

Examples:

* Introduce families to *The Creative Curriculum for Infants & Toddlers*; distribute and discuss *Letters to Families*
* Use meetings and workshops with parents and colleagues to stress the importance of a quality program for infants and toddlers
* Provide research and evaluation reports to program policy makers and parents

Comments:_____

_____

_____

_____

_____

Objective: **To work with community agencies in support of children and families**

Examples:

* Support organizations working to improve salaries and benefits for early childhood educators
* Campaign to elect public officials who support child and family issues; lobby elected officials to pass laws supportive of child and family issues
* Invite representatives of the community to visit the program to observe what is being done in support of children and families

Comments:_____

_____

_____

_____

_____

Appendix
B

Planning and Individualizing Forms

The following blank forms to help you plan your program and individualize for children and families are included in this Appendix:

Weekly Planning Form

Target goals/objectives: _____

Week of: _____

Changes to the Environment

Changes to Play/Activity Areas

Activities for the Week

	Monday	Tuesday	Wednesday	Thursday	Friday
Indoor Activities Planned					
Outdoor Activities Planned					

Changes to Daily Routines

Working with Families

Responsibilities

Individualizing Goals and Objectives for Young Infants

Name of child:_____   **Caregiver/Teacher:**_____

Date of birth:_____   **Date completed:**_____

Goal 1: To learn about themselves

Progress	Objectives	Evidence
☐ Not Yet/ Rarely ☐ Sometimes ☐ Consistently	**To feel valued and attached to others** **Examples:** ❖ smiles and shows pleasure when talked to ❖ moves body towards caregiver when she approaches ❖ enjoys games with others like "Where Is Your Nose?"	
☐ Not Yet/ Rarely ☐ Sometimes ☐ Consistently	**To feel competent and proud about what they can do** **Examples:** ❖ kicks a mobile and smiles ❖ squeezes a rubber toy and shows pleasure at its squeak ❖ drops a ball and laughs as it bounces	
☐ Not Yet/ Rarely ☐ Sometimes ☐ Consistently	**To assert their independence** **Examples:** ❖ pushes away bottle ❖ pulls at diaper when being changed ❖ grabs for spoon when being fed	

Goal 2: To learn about their feelings

Progress	Objectives	Evidence
☐ Not Yet/ Rarely ☐ Sometimes ☐ Consistently	**To communicate a broad range of emotions through gestures, sounds, and—eventually—words** **Examples:** ❖ cries when hears sudden loud noises ❖ coos and smiles when being rocked and sung to ❖ laughs aloud when playing peek-a-boo	
☐ Not Yet/ Rarely ☐ Sometimes ☐ Consistently	**To express their feelings in appropriate ways** **Examples:** ❖ while crying, lifts arms up to indicate need to be picked up and comforted ❖ bounces to get adult to continue a knee ride ❖ looks to familiar adult when a stranger approaches	

Goal 3: To learn about others

Progress	Objectives	Evidence
☐ Not Yet/ Rarely ☐ Sometimes ☐ Consistently	**To develop trusting relationships with nurturing adults** **Examples:** ❖ listens attentively to adult when being fed or changed ❖ kicks legs and squeals when familiar adult appears ❖ looks to adult for attention or help	
☐ Not Yet/ Rarely ☐ Sometimes ☐ Consistently	**To show interest in peers** **Examples:** ❖ watches other children ❖ reaches out to touch another infant's face ❖ grabs for toy another infant is holding	
☐ Not Yet/ Rarely ☐ Sometimes ☐ Consistently	**To demonstrate caring and cooperation** **Examples:** ❖ hugs doll ❖ pats adult on back when being held ❖ lifts bottom, in response to caregiver's actions, when being changed	
☐ Not Yet/ Rarely ☐ Sometimes ☐ Consistently	**To try out roles and relationships through imitation and pretend play** **Examples:** ❖ smiles at self in the mirror ❖ plays peek-a-boo ❖ pretends to feed familiar adult	

Goal 4: To learn about communicating

Progress	Objectives	Evidence
☐ Not Yet/ Rarely ☐ Sometimes ☐ Consistently	**To express needs and thoughts without using words** **Examples:** ❖ smiles to invite an adult to interact ❖ fidgets or cries when uncomfortable or bored ❖ holds rattle up for adult to shake	
☐ Not Yet/ Rarely ☐ Sometimes ☐ Consistently	**To identify with a home language** **Examples:** ❖ listens to conversations ❖ recognizes and begins imitating sounds of home language ❖ understands names of familiar objects in home language	

Goal 4: To learn about communicating (continued)

Progress	Objectives	Evidence
☐ Not Yet/ Rarely ☐ Sometimes ☐ Consistently	**To respond to verbal and nonverbal commands** **Examples:** ❖ looks up when called by name ❖ opens mouth as adult opens her mouth and offers a spoonful of food ❖ touches mirror when adult asks, "Where's the baby?"	
☐ Not Yet/ Rarely ☐ Sometimes ☐ Consistently	**To communicate through language** **Examples:** ❖ vocalizes to self and others ❖ begins babbling ❖ imitates tones and inflection	

Goal 5: To learn about moving and doing

Progress	Objectives	Evidence
☐ Not Yet/ Rarely ☐ Sometimes ☐ Consistently	**To develop gross motor skills** **Examples:** ❖ holds head up without support ❖ rolls over and sits alone ❖ begins creeping and crawling	
☐ Not Yet/ Rarely ☐ Sometimes ☐ Consistently	**To develop fine motor skills** **Examples:** ❖ scoops up piece of banana and eats it ❖ pulls large pegs out of pegboard ❖ transfers objects from hand to hand	
☐ Not Yet/ Rarely ☐ Sometimes ☐ Consistently	**To coordinate eye and hand movements** **Examples:** ❖ follows toy with eyes as adult slowly moves it ❖ looks at hand ❖ reaches for and grasps a rattle	
☐ Not Yet/ Rarely ☐ Sometimes ☐ Consistently	**To develop self-help skills** **Examples:** ❖ begins to hold own bottle ❖ begins to feed self finger foods ❖ sucks thumb or pacifier to comfort self	

Goal 6: To acquire thinking skills

Progress	Objectives	Evidence
☐ Not Yet/ Rarely ☐ Sometimes ☐ Consistently	**To gain an understanding of basic concepts and relationships** **Examples:** ❖ picks up pacifier and sucks on it ❖ drops spoon and watches it fall to the floor ❖ closes eyes as adult pulls shirt over his head	
☐ Not Yet/ Rarely ☐ Sometimes ☐ Consistently	**To apply knowledge to new situations** **Examples:** ❖ shakes stuffed animal in same way as rattle to hear noise ❖ kicks new crib toy to see if it will move ❖ squeezes and tastes new finger food	
☐ Not Yet/ Rarely ☐ Sometimes ☐ Consistently	**To develop strategies for solving problems** **Examples:** ❖ uses hand to steady self when sitting up ❖ reaches for a toy that has rolled away ❖ raises bottle as level of milk drops	

Individualizing Goals and Objectives for Mobile Infants

Name of child:_____   Caregiver/Teacher:_____

Date of birth:_____   Date completed:_____

Goal 1: To learn about themselves

Progress	Objectives	Evidence
☐ Not Yet/ Rarely ☐ Sometimes ☐ Consistently	**To feel valued and attached to others** **Examples:** ❖ looks at, goes over to touch familiar adults while playing ❖ imitates parent(s) and caregiver(s) ❖ clings to leg of program volunteer	
☐ Not Yet/ Rarely ☐ Sometimes ☐ Consistently	**To feel competent and proud about what they can do** **Examples:** ❖ fits a triangle into shape box and claps ❖ climbs up the slide and proudly looks around for caregiver ❖ chooses slice of pear at snacktime and smiles as she takes a bite	
☐ Not Yet/ Rarely ☐ Sometimes ☐ Consistently	**To assert their independence** **Examples:** ❖ moves away the hand of an adult who is helping with a puzzle ❖ insists on choosing what shirt to wear ❖ says "Me do!" when adult offers help in dressing	

Goal 2: To learn about their feelings

Progress	Objectives	Evidence
☐ Not Yet/ Rarely ☐ Sometimes ☐ Consistently	**To communicate a broad range of emotions through gestures, sounds, and—eventually—words** **Examples:** ❖ watches self making "happy, sad, or angry" faces in the mirror ❖ pushes aside unwanted food ❖ clings to parents as they say "good-bye"	
☐ Not Yet/ Rarely ☐ Sometimes ☐ Consistently	**To express their feelings in appropriate ways** **Examples:** ❖ helps caregiver comfort a crying child ❖ says "No!" when another child takes his toy instead of hitting ❖ looks to an adult for help when frustrated	

Goal 3: To learn about others

Progress	Objectives	Evidence
☐ Not Yet/ Rarely ☐ Sometimes ☐ Consistently	**To develop trusting relationships with nurturing adults** **Examples:** ❖ brings adult a book to read ❖ enjoys helping with chores such as carrying paper towels into the bathroom ❖ grabs onto caregiver's hand or leg when frightened	
☐ Not Yet/ Rarely ☐ Sometimes ☐ Consistently	**To show interest in peers** **Examples:** ❖ identifies the family members and possessions of other children ❖ joins other children in rocking wooden rowboat ❖ knows names of other children	
☐ Not Yet/ Rarely ☐ Sometimes ☐ Consistently	**To demonstrate caring and cooperation** **Examples:** ❖ helps caregiver hold young infant's bottle ❖ joins in search for a child's missing sweater ❖ gives adult a big hug	
☐ Not Yet/ Rarely ☐ Sometimes ☐ Consistently	**To try out roles and relationships through imitation and pretend play** **Examples:** ❖ enacts familiar events (e.g., puts on hat and looks in the mirror) ❖ scribbles on a shopping list adult is writing and says "Milk" ❖ pretends to call parents on the phone	

Goal 4: To learn about communicating

Progress	Objectives	Evidence
☐ Not Yet/ Rarely ☐ Sometimes ☐ Consistently	**To express needs and thoughts without using words** **Examples:** ❖ points to ask for an out-of-reach toy ❖ shakes head "No" when asked if hungry ❖ catches eye of an adult to ask for help	
☐ Not Yet/ Rarely ☐ Sometimes ☐ Consistently	**To identify with a home language** **Examples:** ❖ looks at a doll on hearing the word *doll* in the home language ❖ uses same sounds and intonations as parents do ❖ says several words in home language clearly	

Goal 4: To learn about communicating (continued)

Progress	Objectives	Evidence
☐ Not Yet/ Rarely ☐ Sometimes ☐ Consistently	**To respond to verbal and nonverbal commands** **Examples:** ❖ reacts to facial expressions of adult ❖ follows simple directions such as, "Will you carry these napkins to the table, please?" ❖ pushes foot into boot as adult pulls it up	
☐ Not Yet/ Rarely ☐ Sometimes ☐ Consistently	**To communicate through language** **Examples:** ❖ creates long babble sentences ❖ repeats familiar words ❖ calls caregiver by name	

Goal 5: To learn about moving and doing

Progress	Objectives	Evidence
☐ Not Yet/ Rarely ☐ Sometimes ☐ Consistently	**To develop gross motor skills** **Examples:** ❖ pulls self up and cruises around furniture ❖ walks ❖ seats self in small chair	
☐ Not Yet/ Rarely ☐ Sometimes ☐ Consistently	**To develop fine motor skills** **Examples:** ❖ scribbles with a crayon ❖ turns pages of a book, often two or three at a time ❖ stacks several blocks, one on top of the other	
☐ Not Yet/ Rarely ☐ Sometimes ☐ Consistently	**To coordinate eye and hand movements** **Examples:** ❖ stirs ingredients when helping to make playdough ❖ puts toy in a bucket ❖ peels a half of a banana	
☐ Not Yet/ Rarely ☐ Sometimes ☐ Consistently	**To develop self-help skills** **Examples:** ❖ uses spoon and cup, but may spill ❖ pushes arm through jacket sleeve ❖ undresses self	

Goal 6: To acquire thinking skills

Progress	Objectives	Evidence
☐ Not Yet/ Rarely ☐ Sometimes ☐ Consistently	**To gain an understanding of basic concepts and relationships** **Examples:** ❖ fills bucket with pop beads and dumps them out repeatedly ❖ asks for wooden spoon to bang on homemade drum ❖ pretends to open door using a toy key	
☐ Not Yet/ Rarely ☐ Sometimes ☐ Consistently	**To apply knowledge to new situations** **Examples:** ❖ blows on noodles when adult explains they are hot ❖ spots cat and says "dog" ❖ uses hammer instead of hand to flatten playdough	
☐ Not Yet/ Rarely ☐ Sometimes ☐ Consistently	**To develop strategies for solving problems** **Examples:** ❖ points to picture in a storybook and looks to adult for name of that object ❖ brings over a stool to help reach a toy ❖ tries various pieces in shape-sorting box until one fits	

Individualizing Goals and Objectives for Toddlers

Name of child:_____   Caregiver/Teacher:_____

Date of birth:_____   Date completed:_____

Goal 1: To learn about themselves

Progress	Objectives	Evidence
☐ Not Yet/ Rarely ☐ Sometimes ☐ Consistently	**To feel valued and attached to others** **Examples:** ❖ points out family picture in a scrapbook ❖ knows which child is out for the day after seeing who is there ❖ looks to caregivers for comfort and at times may comfort caregiver	
☐ Not Yet/ Rarely ☐ Sometimes ☐ Consistently	**To feel competent and proud about what they can do** **Examples:** ❖ pours own juice at snack time and says, "I did it!" ❖ helps another child find the crayons ❖ stands on one foot and calls, "Look at me!"	
☐ Not Yet/ Rarely ☐ Sometimes ☐ Consistently	**To assert their independence** **Examples:** ❖ insists on putting on own jacket ❖ refuses to wear diapers ❖ cheerfully says "Good-bye" to parents and goes to play	

Goal 2: To learn about their feelings

Progress	Objectives	Evidence
☐ Not Yet/ Rarely ☐ Sometimes ☐ Consistently	**To communicate a broad range of emotions through gestures, sounds, and—eventually—words** **Examples:** ❖ says "I did it!" after using the potty successfully ❖ hugs a doll and lovingly feeds it a bottle ❖ raises hand to make a "high five"	
☐ Not Yet/ Rarely ☐ Sometimes ☐ Consistently	**To express their feelings in appropriate ways** **Examples:** ❖ roars like a lion when angry instead of biting ❖ recognizes feelings in others (e.g., "Camilo sad.") ❖ bites on a bagel when has urge to bite	

Goal 3: To learn about others

Progress	Objectives	Evidence
☐ Not Yet/ Rarely ☐ Sometimes ☐ Consistently	**To develop trusting relationships with nurturing adults** **Examples:** ❖ imitates adult activities (e.g., reading a newspaper, setting the table) ❖ eager to help with chores (e.g., preparing meals, feeding the fish) ❖ calls adult over to show an accomplishment (e.g., a painting, block structure)	
☐ Not Yet/ Rarely ☐ Sometimes ☐ Consistently	**To show interest in peers** **Examples:** ❖ enjoys including other children in pretend play (e.g., driving in a car or going food shopping) ❖ refers to other children by name ❖ comments on who is a girl and who is a boy	
☐ Not Yet/ Rarely ☐ Sometimes ☐ Consistently	**To demonstrate caring and cooperation** **Examples:** ❖ responds to emotions of other children (e.g., helps adult pat a crying child) ❖ works with another child to complete a task (e.g., putting away a puzzle) ❖ feeds and puts doll to bed	
☐ Not Yet/ Rarely ☐ Sometimes ☐ Consistently	**To try out roles and relationships through imitation and pretend play** **Examples:** ❖ acts out simple life scenes (e.g., making dinner, going to the doctor) ❖ puts hat on and says, "I'm going to work" ❖ uses object to represent something else (e.g., box as car, block as phone)	

Goal 4: To learn about communicating

Progress	Objectives	Evidence
☐ Not Yet/ Rarely ☐ Sometimes ☐ Consistently	**To express needs and thoughts without using words** **Examples:** ❖ uses facial expressions to show excitement ❖ catches adult's eye for attention and reassurance when needed ❖ tugs on pants to indicate need to go to bathroom	
☐ Not Yet/ Rarely ☐ Sometimes ☐ Consistently	**To identify with a home language** **Examples:** ❖ speaks in home language with family members and others ❖ uses main language spoken in child care with those who don't speak home language ❖ recognizes tapes of stories and songs from home culture	

Goal 4: To learn about communicating (continued)

Progress	Objectives	Evidence
☐ Not Yet/ Rarely ☐ Sometimes ☐ Consistently	**To respond to verbal and nonverbal commands** **Examples:** ❖ follows directions such as "Bring the book to me, please" ❖ responds to adult's facial expression (e.g., stops throwing blocks after a stern look) ❖ goes over to cot when lights are dimmed for naptime	
☐ Not Yet/ Rarely ☐ Sometimes ☐ Consistently	**To communicate through language** **Examples:** ❖ tells a story ❖ tells about what happened over the weekend ❖ talks with other children while playing together	

Goal 5: To learn about moving and doing

Progress	Objectives	Evidence
☐ Not Yet/ Rarely ☐ Sometimes ☐ Consistently	**To develop gross motor skills** **Examples:** ❖ walks up stairs ❖ throws a ball ❖ runs	
☐ Not Yet/ Rarely ☐ Sometimes ☐ Consistently	**To develop fine motor skills** **Examples:** ❖ threads large beads ❖ scribbles with marker or crayons ❖ pastes papers together	
☐ Not Yet/ Rarely ☐ Sometimes ☐ Consistently	**To coordinate eye and hand movements** **Examples:** ❖ places pieces in a simple puzzle ❖ closes Velcro™ fasteners on shoes ❖ stirs ingredients in bowl when helping to cook	
☐ Not Yet/ Rarely ☐ Sometimes ☐ Consistently	**To develop self-help skills** **Examples:** ❖ uses the potty and washes hands ❖ pours own milk and juice from small plastic pitcher ❖ puts on own jacket and hat when going outside	

Goal 6: To acquire thinking skills

Progress	Objectives	Evidence
☐ Not Yet/ Rarely ☐ Sometimes ☐ Consistently	**To gain an understanding of basic concepts and relationships** **Examples:** ❖ experiments with mixing colors when painting ❖ tells another child, "Your mommy comes back after nap" ❖ runs to the tree and says, "I run fast"	
☐ Not Yet/ Rarely ☐ Sometimes ☐ Consistently	**To apply knowledge to new situations** **Examples:** ❖ sees a picture of a zebra and calls it a horse ❖ paints on side of building with water after painting at easel ❖ completes new puzzle using familiar strategy of turning pieces until they fit	
☐ Not Yet/ Rarely ☐ Sometimes ☐ Consistently	**To develop strategies for solving problems** **Examples:** ❖ cooperates with others in implementing a plan (e.g., carries a large pillow across the room for a jumping game) ❖ asks "Why?" questions ❖ dips paintbrush in water to clean it	

Planning Form for Individualizing

Name of child:_____   **Caregiver/Teacher:**_____

Date of birth:_____   **Date completed:**_____

This child's family background (use background information and observations):

This child can (use the *Individualizing the Goals and Objectives for Children* form):

This child is learning to (use the *Individualizing the Goals and Objectives for Children* form):

This child likes (use observations):

This child's temperament is (use observations):

This child learns best by (use observations):

This child's special needs are (use observations and the *Individualizing the Goals and Objectives for Children* form):

Sometimes this child has these behavioral challenges (use observations):

To individualize for this child, I intend to make these changes:

To the environment:

To materials and equipment:

To routines, transitions, and planned activities:

To the daily schedule:

To interactions:

Goals for Working with Families

Name of family:_____   Name of child:_____

Completed by:_____

Goal 1: To build a partnership with families		
Objectives	Documentation of What Was Done	Date
To involve families in the program's planning and evaluation process		
To listen to and discuss families' questions, concerns, observations, and insights about their children		
To communicate regularly with families at arrival and departure times about how things are going for their children at home and at the program		
To schedule regular conferences and/or home visits		
To discuss with families ways to handle children's challenging behaviors		
To resolve differences with families in a respectful way		
To help families gain access to community resources		

Next steps:

_____

_____

_____

_____

Goal 2: To support families in their parenting role

Objectives	Documentation of What Was Done	Date
To demonstrate respect for a family's approach to childrearing and their feelings about sharing the care of their child		
To celebrate with families each new milestone in their child's development		
To incorporate family rituals and preferences into the daily life of the program		
To offer workshops/training on child development and other topics of interest to families		
To help families network with one another for information and support		

Next steps:

_____

_____

_____

_____

Goal 3: To support families in their role as primary educators of their child

Objectives	Documentation of What Was Done	Date
To encourage family involvement and participation in program activities		
To provide families with strategies to support children's learning at home		

Next steps:

_____

_____

_____

_____

Goal 4: To ensure that the home cultures of the children's families are reflected in the program

Objectives	Documentation of What Was Done	Date
To support children's use of their home language		
To encourage children's awareness of and interest in home languages spoken at the program		
To seek the families' assistance in learning about the children's home culture		
To include objects and customs from the children's home culture in the program's environment, routines, and activities		
To interact with children in a style that is respectful of their home culture		

Next steps:

_____

_____

_____

_____

Appendix C

Safety and Health Checklists

Safety

This checklist identifies potential problems and describes safety measures that will reduce the chances of accidents occurring. Duplicate copies of this form and use it to identify problems in your program and note when they were corrected.

Safety Problem: Falls, Physical Injury		
Safety Measures	**Looks OK/Not Applicable**	**Problems Identified and Date Corrected**
Furniture is in good repair, with sharp edges protected by corner or edge bumpers.		
Safety straps are used on changing tables, in high chairs, strollers, swings, and car seats.		
Sides of cribs are kept in a raised position; latches and locks on the drop side are fastened.		
Windows open only from the top and are kept locked when closed. Furniture children can climb up on is positioned away from windows.		
Stairs and hallways are kept free of clutter.		
Locked safety gates are placed at tops and bottoms of stairs. Gates should be at least three-fourths of children's height.		
Riding toys are used on flat surfaces only.		
Steps and walks are kept free of snow and ice.		

 ©1997, Teaching Strategies, Inc., Washington, DC. Permission granted to reprint, for non-commercial uses only, by programs implementing *The Creative Curriculum for Infants & Toddlers.*

Safety Problem: Choking, Strangulation, or Suffocation

Safety Measures	Looks OK/ Not Applicable	Problems Identified and Date Corrected
Infants are held while fed. Toddlers eat meals and snacks seated and supervised.		
Rattles and/or pacifiers are not hung around children's necks.		
Toys are not tied to cribs.		
Venetian blind cords are secured out of children's reach or replaced with plastic rods.		
Batteries are stored and disposed of in areas out of children's reach.		
Pillows, heavy blankets, and large stuffed animals are kept out of cribs.		
Rattles and squeeze toys are removed from cribs when babies are sleeping.		
Children do not wear long scarves when climbing or jumping.		

Safety Problem: Fire, Burns, Scalding, Electrical Shock

Smoke alarm batteries are checked monthly.		
Emergency exits are marked, kept clear, and unlocked from the inside. Fire drills are conducted monthly.		
Heating and cooling systems are inspected regularly. Water temperature does not exceed 110°F.		
Water temperature in bathtubs and swimming and wading pools is between 82°F and 93°F.		
Unused electrical outlets are covered with caps.		
Small appliances are unplugged when not in use. Electrical cords are kept out of children's reach.		

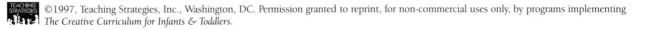

Safety Problem: Fire, Burns, Scalding, Electrical Shock

Safety Measures	Looks OK/ Not Applicable	Problems Identified and Date Corrected
Matches, lighters, gasoline, and cleaning fluids are stored in locked cabinets.		
Heaters, fireplaces, and radiators have screens or safety guards; pipes are covered or insulated.		
Outdoor metal slides and other play equipment are covered in hot weather when not in use so they don't overheat.		
Temperature of infant formula and children's food and drink is checked before being offered. Microwave ovens are not used to heat baby bottles (heating is uneven).		
Only back burners on a stove are used; pot handles are turned inward and to the back.		
Cooking or warming foods is not done while holding an infant.		
Adults do not drink hot beverages while holding an infant or standing near children.		

Safety Problem: Poisoning

Cleaning supplies, insecticides, weed killers, and paint supplies are stored in locked cabinets.		
Medicine is kept in child-proof containers and placed in locked cabinets or the refrigerator, as indicated on labels.		
Adult handbags and briefcases (which may contain unsafe objects or materials) are stored out of children's reach.		
Empty cleaning product bottles are rinsed before being thrown away.		

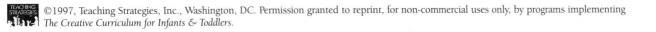

Safety Problem: Cuts, Eye Injuries

Safety Measures	Looks OK/ Not Applicable	Problems Identified and Date Corrected
Sharp objects (pins, needles, knives, adult scissors) are stored out of children's reach.		
Toys and outdoor playthings are regularly checked to see that they have not developed sharp edges and are splinter-free.		
Toys are stored on open shelves, with the heavier items placed at the bottom.		
Drawers are secured by locks.		
Wastebaskets are kept out of children's reach.		
Outdoor play area is kept free of glass, nails, and debris.		

Safety Problem: Security

Children are supervised at all times, both indoors and outside.		
Children do not enter or leave the program on their own.		
Children in all areas of the program are always in view.		
Accident/incident reports are completed promptly. Families are notified immediately, if appropriate.		
Vehicles used to transport children are kept locked when not in use.		

Safety Problem: Transportation

Adults wear seat belts and never hold any children in their laps in a moving vehicle.		
Children weighing less than 20 pounds are strapped in an infant carrier when being transported in a vehicle. They ride backwards in a semi-reclining position in the back seat.		

The Creative Curriculum for Infants & Toddlers

First Aid Kit (continued)

Items	Date Checked	Date Checked	Date Checked
ible gauze bandages (one box each of 2" and 4")			
n" (the most commonly used size) and 25 assorted smaller dages			
iangular muslin bandages			
ndage tape			
up of ipecac (1-ounce bottle) *Before administering, check* h child's pediatrician or Poison Control Center. The vomiting uced by syrup of ipecac can cause serious harm to the ophagus if child has swallowed a poison such as lye or drain aner.			
ect sting ointment			
stic bags (for ice packs)			
cohol-based wipes			
afety pins			
dditional supplies for specific health needs of children in are (e.g., antihistamine for child with severe allergies, glucose blets for diabetic child who might experience low blood ugar)			

Safety Problem: Transportation (continued)

Safety Measures	Looks OK/ Not Applicable	Problems Identified and Date Corrected
Children weighing 20 pounds or more (who can sit by themselves) are secured in a toddler safety seat. The seat is attached to the car with a seat belt. Children ride in the back seat, facing forward.		
Children enter and leave vehicles only on the curb side of the road or in a driveway.		
Only adults are permitted to buckle and unbuckle children at pick-up and drop-off.		
Children are kept from sticking their heads, hands, or objects out of the vehicle windows.		
Emergency evacuation procedures are practiced with children.		
Children wear identification tags when being transported (and when away from the program site).		
Children hold adult's hand when walking across streets.		

Safety Problem: Drowning

Safety Measures	Looks OK/ Not Applicable	Problems Identified and Date Corrected
Children play in or near water only with an adult standing directly beside the water, not at a distance from it.		
Children play in water no deeper than two inches.		
Wading pools and water tubs are emptied daily and turned upside down when not in use.		
Swimming pools and/or built-in wading pools are fenced in with a locked gate.		
Children do not use toilets and other bathroom facilities unsupervised.		

Emergency Procedures

A list of procedures can be helpful when emergencies happen. Below is a chart that may be copied. We recommend that you display it where adults can see and use it.

Emergency Procedures List

1. **Find out what happened.** Discover who was injured, if the scene is safe, and if there are bystanders who might be of assistance.

2. **Check for life-threatening problems.** These are known as the ABC's:
   A = open the airway;
   B = check for breathing;
   C = check for circulation (pulse and bleeding).

3. **Call your local emergency medical services—911 or an ambulance—if you have any doubts about the seriousness of the problem.** In situations that are life-threatening, it may be advisable to call the emergency medical service before administering any first aid, so that the ambulance can be dispatched and on its way while you are tending to the child. Use your judgment and good common sense to decide if the child has a better chance of survival if you call for an ambulance before or after you administer emergency first aid.

4. **Check for injuries, starting at the head and working down.** You will need to give this information to medical personnel.

5. **Regroup.** Calm the other children. If the injured child needs your attention, ask a co-worker or back-up provider for assistance.

6. **Contact the child's parents or guardian** as soon as possible.

7. **Follow local procedures for filing an accident report.** Be sure families get a copy.

Above all:

- **Do not move a child,** unless it is to save the child's life. Movement may make injuries worse; and,

- **Do no harm.** Harm means both failing to do anything and making things worse.

First Aid

A first aid kit should contain everything you need should an emergency arise. Make a point to ch
kits several times a year to ensure that they are fully stocked. You can use the checklist below for t

First Aid Kit

Items	Date Checked	Date Checke
Roll of quarters (for calling doctors or children's families from a pay phone)		
Copy of each child's emergency contacts form; *Emergency Telephone Guide*		
Index cards and pens (for writing down instructions or keeping notes to give medical staff)		
A quick reference manual (for example, *A Sigh of Relief—The First Aid Handbook for Childhood Emergencies* by M. Green)		
Water		
Clean washcloth and antibacterial soap		
Small plastic cup		
Disposable latex gloves		
Flashlight with working batteries		
Thermometer		
Blunt tip scissors		
Tweezers		
Small plastic or metal splints		
3-ounce rubber bulb syringe (for rinsing out wounds and eyes)		
Gauze pads (one box each of nonstick, sterile 2x2 and 4x4)		

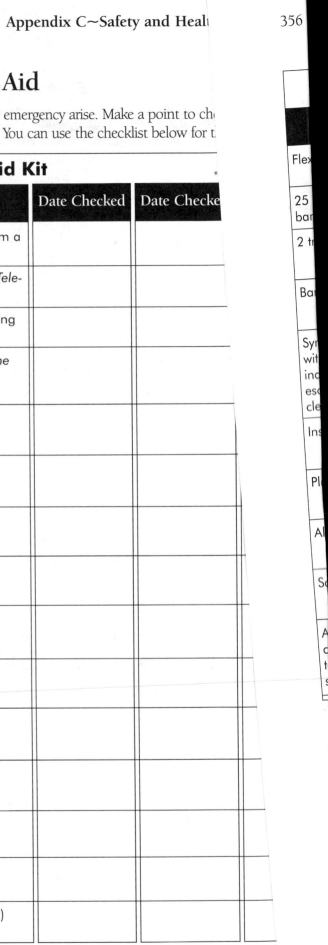

Good Health Practices in Your Program

Keeping infants and toddlers healthy requires ongoing monitoring of your environment and practices. Use the checklist below to ensure that your program promotes good health and to identify practices that need your attention.

Area of Concern: Environment		
Practices	Yes, we do this regularly	No, we don't practice this
Clean all surfaces daily with fresh bleach solution made by mixing ¼ cup bleach with 1 gallon of water (or 1 tablespoon bleach per quart of water).		
In programs without central air conditioning, open windows every day.		
Keep air temperature between 65° and 72°F.		
If air is dry, use a humidifier or cool air vaporizer. Clean these with bleach solution, change water, and add a mold inhibitor every day. (Steam vaporizers may be dangerous to children who get too close and should not be used.)		
If you use air conditioners, clean them weekly to remove dust and mold.		
Take children outdoors daily.		
Avoid using aerosol products.		
Place garbage in lined metal containers or in plastic containers with lids.		
Use the food preparation area only for food.		
Locate the refrigerator near the food preparation area. Check daily to make sure the refrigerator is working.		
Locate the food preparation area near a water source.		
Locate the diapering/toileting areas near a second water source.		
Separate sleeping areas from other activities.		
Keep each child's clothes and personal belongings separate to avoid contamination.		
Don't use cribs for storage when children are not asleep.		
Wear indoor slippers or shoe coverings when walking in infant play areas.		

Area of Concern: Toys and Play Equipment

Practices	Yes, we do this regularly	No, we don't practice this
Clean rubber, plastic, and wooden toys, infant seats and feeding tables, changing tables, and eating utensils every day with fresh bleach solution (¼ cup bleach to 1 gallon of water).		
Wash stuffed toys weekly in a washing machine; wash them more frequently if soiled.		
Cover outdoor sand play areas at night to protect from animal feces.		

Area of Concern: Diapering and Toileting

Practices	Yes, we do this regularly	No, we don't practice this
Use diapering area exclusively for diapering.		
Be sure changing surface is at least 3 feet above the floor (to prevent spread of infectious diseases).		
Check that the diapering surface is non-porous (e.g., plastic with no tears or cracks).		
Clean diapering surface with fresh bleach solution after each use.		
Use disposable plastic gloves in accordance with program policy.		
Place a fresh, clean piece of paper beneath the child's buttocks so that the child's body does not directly touch the diapering surface.		
Use disposable diapers (rather than cloth) to reduce skin irritations.		
Seal soiled diapers in plastic bags and place them in plastic-lined containers that are equipped with a cover and foot pedal.		
Place soiled outer clothing in plastic bags, stored away from child's other belongings; send bag home with parents at the end of the day.		
Clean the child's urinary and anal areas with disposable wipes. Wipe child front to back once with each wipe until clean, to reduce chances of urinary tract infections. If a child is allergic to disposable wipes, use paper towels with antibacterial soap and water.		
Apply creams and lotions only with parental permission. Label products with child's name and use only with that child. Avoid using talcum powder because of danger to children's lungs.		

continued on next page

Area of Concern: Diapering and Toileting (continued)

Practices	Yes, we do this regularly	No, we don't practice this
Wash the child's and your hands after each changing.		
Keep written records of each child's diapering times and bowel movements.		
Locate toilets in rooms separate from cooking, eating, or play areas.		
Accompany children who are being trained. If toileting area is on another floor or outside of the program's space, be sure to accompany all children to and from the bathroom.		
Check that there is a minimum of one sink and one toilet available for every 10 toddlers. In centers, be sure that fixtures are child-sized (i.e., a maximum of 11" for toilets and 22" for sinks). If child-sized equipment is not available, use modified toilet seats and step aids.		
Use bleach solution to sanitize the bathroom daily and as needed, if contaminated by feces or vomit. Keep bathroom well stocked with disposable wipes, toilet paper, paper towels, and liquid antibacterial soaps.		
If your program uses potty chairs, flush contents down toilet, rinse chair in a utility sink not used for any other purpose, wash with soap and water twice using paper towels (empty rinse water into the toilet), spray with bleach solution, and allow it to air dry.		
Be sure that there is at least one container with a pedal-operated lid in the toileting area. Empty the containers daily and sanitize them with bleach solution.		
Be sure you wash your hands after you use the toilet or change children's diapers. Toddlers should wash their hands after using the toilet. Use paper towels to dry hands. Turn water off with the towel. Use hand lotion to prevent drying and cracking skin.		

Area of Concern: Personal Hygiene

	Yes, we do this regularly	No, we don't practice this
Wash your hands and apply hand lotion before and after each task e.g., before and after handling food; toileting and diaper changing; assisting a sick child; upon arrival; before giving a child medication or taking temperature; after sneezing, coughing, or blowing your nose; after touching your face or hair; and after handling money or a pet.		
Use disposable towels to dry your hands. Don't reuse towels.		

continued on next page

Area of Concern: Personal Hygiene (continued)

Practices	Yes, we do this regularly	No, we don't practice this
Don't use wash cloths and sponges because you can't sanitize them after each use.		
Drape a clean towel, diaper, or pad across your shoulder when you hold an infant. Don't reuse shoulder drapes.		
Wipe infants' mouths with gauze daily.		
Label children's toothbrushes and do not permit sharing. Store brushes with bristles up. Replace brushes every three months.		
Store each child's brushes, combs, and personal items separately from those of other children.		

Area of Concern: Sleeping and Resting

	Yes, we do this regularly	No, we don't practice this
Assign each child who spends more than 4 hours a day in care his or her own crib, bed, mat, or cot.		
Locate cribs away from heaters, drafts, window blinds, and hanging cords.		
Separate cribs and cots by at least 3 feet of space to discourage the spread of germs (unless cribs have solid headboards and footboards or you use plexiglass partitions).		
Use nonabsorbent, washable covers on mats and cots.		
At rest time, place children head to foot to reduce spread of germs.		
Place infants on sides or backs in cribs to help prevent Sudden Infant Death Syndrome (SIDS).		
Have each child use own linens. Change linens daily for infants. Send toddler's linens home each week for laundering—or sooner if the linens are soiled.		
Clean crib mattresses and cots weekly and when soiled or used by another child.		
Avoid using substances of animal origin other than wool bedding. Some substances (such as feathers) may cause allergic reactions.		
Avoid using pillows, fluffy blankets, and bumper guards to reduce the chances of suffocation or SIDS.		

Area of Concern: Feeding and Eating

Practices	Yes, we do this regularly	No, we don't practice this
Be sure that individual feeding supplies are available and that children use their own bottles and utensils.		
Post information on children's food allergies and special nutritional needs in the food preparation area and eating areas.		
Label and date food brought from home. Store perishable foods (such as expressed milk) in the refrigerator or freezer.		
Prepare formula according to written instructions from parent or health professional and store it in refrigerator until used. Discard any unused portion within 48 hours. Once a child has stopped drinking at feeding time, do not save the bottle to give to the child later in the day.		
Hold infants being bottle fed; do not prop bottles.		
Introduce semi-solid foods (such as rice cereal) when infants are between 4 and 6 months old, or as directed by a health care professional. Observe a 5-day "watch and see" period before introducing another food.		
Introduce solid foods such as fruits and vegetables when infants are between 6 and 8 months, or as directed by a health care professional. Observe a 5-day "watch and see" period before introducing another food. Introduce wheat products only after children are at least 7 months old because many younger infants are allergic to them.		
Introduce food with lumps, such as mashed potatoes, at 8 to 9 months, or as directed by a health care professional. Introduce these foods one at a time. Observe a 5-day "watch and see" period before introducing another food.		
Serve a complete meal to children who eat finger food and table foods. Encourage children to eat foods of their own choosing.		
Introduce cow's milk when children are 6-12 months old, or as directed by a health care professional. Don't introduce skim milk until 18-24 months (or later, if so directed), because children need the extra calories and contents of whole milk for nerve and brain development.		
Keep records for each child of the time, type of feeding, and, for young infants, amount of food consumed.		

Area of Concern: Management of Illness

Practices	Yes, we do this regularly	No, we don't practice this
Verify that policies regarding exclusion of children and staff, isolation requirements, administration of medicine, emergency contacts, and long-term care are in place.		
Make daily health checks of each child for the following signs of illness: severe coughing, difficulty in breathing, sore throat, yellowish skin or eyes, pinkeye (tearing, red or pus-filled eyes), infected skin patches, nausea or vomiting, diarrhea, loss of appetite, rashes, lice, oozing insect bites or sores, bruises, and unusual behavior.		
Exclude children with communicable symptoms/conditions from the group until such time as they are no longer considered contagious.		
When sick children need to be sent home, provide a comfortable, quiet area to rest until a parent or guardian arrives.		
Wash your hands after assisting a sick child.		
Wash and disinfect a crib or cot used by a sick child; launder bed linens.		
Send written notes to notify families of children exposed to communicable diseases as soon as possible, so families can watch for symptoms.		
Administer both prescription and nonprescription drugs only following training and with written approval of a parent or health care professional. Keep all drugs in the original medication dispensers. Maintain documentation of the time and amount given.		
Take universal precautions for blood. These include using nonporous disposable gloves when in contact with blood, body fluids, or tissue discharges containing blood. Following exposure, discard gloves immediately and wash hands with antibacterial soap. Use bleach solution to disinfect blood-contaminated surfaces and mops used in cleaning.		

Immunization Schedule

Infection	Vaccine Name	Ages When Vaccine Should Be Administered
Diphtheria	DTP (4 doses)[1]	Dose #1: 2 months Dose #2: 4 months Dose #3: 6 months Dose #4: 12-18 months (6 months must separate dose #3 and dose #4)
Tetanus	The DTP shot combines diphtheria, tetanus, and pertussis vaccines.	See schedule for diphtheria vaccine.
Pertussis (whooping cough)	The DTP shot combines diphtheria, tetanus, and pertussis vaccines.	See schedule for diphtheria vaccine.
Polio	OPV (3 doses)	Dose #1: 2 months Dose #2: 4 months Dose #3: 6-18 months
Measles	MMR	12-15 months
Mumps	The MMR shot combines measles, mumps, and rubella vaccines.	See schedule for measles vaccine.
Rubella (German measles)	The MMR shot combines measles, mumps, and rubella vaccines.	See schedule for measles vaccine.

Haemophilius influenzae type B (Influenza)	Hib
	(3 or 4 doses, depending on type of vaccine)
		For PRP-OMP type vaccine:
		    Dose #1: 2 months
		    Dose #2: 4 months
		    Dose #3: 12-15 months
		For other types of vaccine:
		    Dose #1: 2 months
		    Dose #2: 4 months
		    Dose #3: 6 months
		    Dose #4: 12-15 months

Hepatitis B	HB
	(3 doses)
		For children born to mothers negative for the disease:
		    Dose #1: birth-1 month
		    Dose #2: 1-4 months (1 month must separate dose #1 and dose #2)
		    Dose #3: 6-18 months
		For children born to mothers positive for the disease:
		    Dose #1: within 12 hours of birth
		    Dose #2: 1 month
		    Dose #3: 6 months

[1] Many diseases require follow-up immunizations later in a child's life. The number of doses noted here are for the years 0–3 only.

Free Immunization Charts in English and Spanish Available

To help educate parents about the importance of having their children immunized against diseases that can cause blindness, hearing loss, and other serious disabilities, Healthtex, a manufacturer of children's playwear, is distributing free, pocket-sized pull-charts that list the immunization schedule required for children from birth to age 16.

For a free copy of the Healthtex Immunization chart, send a self-addressed, stamped, business envelope to: Kids Chart – English version or Kids Chart – Spanish version, Healthtex, P.O. Box 21488, Greensboro, NC 27420-1488. Indicate language preference on the envelope.

Intervention Resources

Contact Information for the Central Directory of Early Intervention Services, Resources, and Experts

Available in the States and Jurisdictions
Participating in the Part C Program*

Alabama
Department of Rehabilitation Services
Division of Early Intervention
2129 East South Boulevard
P.O. Box 11586
Montgomery, AL 36111-0586
(800) 543-3098 (TDD)

Alaska
Healthy Baby Hotline
Division of Vocational Rehabilitation
Assistive Technologies of Alaska
2217 East Tudor Road, Suite 5
Anchorage, AK 99507-1068
(907) 563-0138 (Voice/TDD) or
(800) 770-0138 (Voice/TDD)
WWW: http://www.corcom.net

American Samoa
Part H Program
Department of Health
Government of American Samoa
Pago Pago, AS 96799
(684) 633-4929 or 2697

Arizona
Children's Information Center
Department of Health Services
1740 W Avenue, Room 200
Phoenix, AZ 85008
(800) 232-1676 (Voice/TDD, AZ only)

Arkansas
Arkansas Children's Directory of Organizations and Resources (ARCDOOR)
P.O. Box 251712
Little Rock, AR 72225
(800) 752-2160 (Voice)

California
Department of Developmental Services
Prevention and Children Services
Branch/Early Start Program
1600 9th Street, Room 310
Sacramento, CA 95814
(800) 515-BABY (Voice)
(916) 654-2054 (TTY)
WWW: http://www.birth23.org

Colorado
Special Education Division
Department of Education
201 East Colfax, Room 301
Denver, CO 80203
(800) 288-3444

Commonwealth of Northern Mariana Islands
Early Childhood/Special Education Programs
CNMI Public School System
P.O. Box 1370 CK
Saipan, MP 96950
(670) 664-3754

Connecticut
Birth to Three INFO LINE
United Way of Connecticut
1344 Silas Deane Highway
Rocky Hill, CT 06067
(800) 505-7000 (Voice/TDD, CT only)

Delaware
Department of Health and Social Services
1901 North DuPont Highway
New Castle, DE 19720
(For print directory): (302) 577-5710
(800) 752-9393 (Voice, Kent and Sussex Counties)
(800) 671-0050 (Voice, New Castle County)
(800) 464-4357 (Voice, Helpline)

District of Columbia
DC EIP Services
Office of Early Childhood Development
609 H Street NE
Washington, DC 20002
(202) 727-8300 (Voice, Child Find)
(202) 727-2114 (TDD)

Florida
Directory of Early Childhood Services
259 East Seventh Avenue
Tallahassee, FL 32303
(800) 654-4440 (Voice)
(904) 921-5444 (Voice)

---

* Compiled by the National Early Childhood Technical Assistance System (NEC*TAS). Because this information changes frequently, readers are encouraged to refer to the NEC*TAS site on the World Wide Web for current information: http://www.nectas.unc.edu/. NEC*TAS is supported through cooperative agreement number H024A60001 with the Office of Special Education Programs of the U.S. Department of Education. For more information about NEC*TAS and the resources it offers, please contact NEC*TAS at: 137 East Franklin Street, Suite 500, Chapel Hill, NC 27514; (919) 962-2001 (voice); (919) 966-4041 (TDD); (919) 966-7463 (fax); E-mail: nectasta.nectas@mhs.unc.edu; World Wide Web: http://www.nectas.unc.edu/.

Georgia
Parent-to-Parent of Georgia, Inc.
2900 Woodcock Boulevard, Suite 240
Atlanta, GA 30341
(800) 229-2038 (Voice/TDD, GA only)

Guam
Department of Education
Division of Special Education
P.O. Box DE
Agana, GU 96910
(671) 475-0549 or 0554

Hawaii
H-KISS
Zero to Three Hawaii Project
1600 Kapiolani Boulevard, Suite 1401
Honolulu, HI 96814
(808) 955-7273 (Voice/TDD, Oahu)
(800) 235-5477 (Voice/TDD, Other islands)

Idaho
Idaho CareLine
Idaho Infant/Toddler Program
450 West State Street
P.O. Box 83720
Boise, ID 83720-0036
(800) 926-2588 (Voice, ID only)
(800) 677-1848 (Spanish)
(208) 332-7205 (TDD)

Illinois
Help Me Grow Hotline
535 West Jefferson Street
Department of Health
Springfield, IL 62761
(800) 323-4769 (IL only)
(800) 547-0466 (TDD, IL only)

Indiana
Indiana Parent Information Network
4755 Kingsway Drive, Suite 105
Indianapolis, IN 46205
(800) 964-4746 (Voice/TDD, IN only)

Iowa
Iowa COMPASS
Information and Referral for Iowans with Disabilities and Their Families
University Hospital School
100 Hawkins Drive, Room S277
Iowa City, IA 52242-1011
(800) 779-2001 (Voice/TDD)
(319) 353-8777 (Voice/TDD)
E-mail: IOWA-COMPASS@uiowa.edu
WWW: http://www.uiowa.edu/uhs/compass.html

Kansas
Make a Difference Information Network
Department of Health and Environment
900 Southwest Jackson, LSOB,10th Floor
Topeka, KS 66612-1290
(800) 332-6262 (Voice/TDD, KS only)

Kentucky
First Steps
3717 Taylorsville Road
Louisville, KY 40220
(800) 442-0087 (Voice)
(502) 564-4448 (TDD)

Louisiana
Disabilities Information Access Line (DIAL)
Developmental Disabilities Council
P.O. Box 3455
Baton Rouge, LA 70821-3455
(800) 256-1633 (TDD)
(800) 922-DIAL (Voice)
(504) 342-7700 (Voice, Baton Rouge)
(504) 342-5704 (TDD, Baton Rouge)

Maine
Child Development Services
State House Station #146
Augusta, ME 04333
(207) 278-3272 (Voice)
(207) 287-2550 (TDD)

Maryland
Governor's Office for Children, Youth, and Families
Maryland Infants and Toddlers Program
301 West Preston Street, 15th Floor
Baltimore, MD 21201
(800) 535-0182 (Voice, MD only)
(410) 333-8177 (TDD)

Massachusetts
Information Center for Persons with Disabilities
29 Stanhope Street
Boston, MA 02116
(800) 462-5015 (Voice/TDD, MA only)

Michigan
Early On
Michigan 4C Association
2875 Northwind Drive, Suite 200
East Lansing, MI 48823
(800) EARLY-ON (Voice/TDD, MI only)

Minnesota
Children with Special Health Needs
Department of Health
717 Southeast Delaware
P.O. Box 9441
Minneapolis, MN 55440-9441
(800) 728-5420 (Voice/TDD)

Mississippi
First Steps Early Intervention System
Department of Health
2423 North State Street
P.O. Box 1700
Jackson, MS 39215-1700
(800) 451-3903 (Voice, MS only)
(601) 960-7629 (TDD)

Missouri
INFORM
Information Network for Missouri's Children with Special Needs
Central Missouri State University
204 Humphrey's Building
Warrensburg, MO 64093
(800) 873-6623 (Voice/TDD)

Montana
Parents Let's Unite for Kids (PLUK)
1500 North 30th Street
Billings, MT 59101-0298
(800) 222-7585 (Voice/TDD, MT only)

Nebraska
Hotline for Disability Services
301 Centennial Mall South
P.O. Box 94987
Lincoln, NE 68509
(800) 742-7594 (Voice/TDD, NE only)

Nevada
Project ASSIST
P.O. Box 70247
Reno, NV 89570-0247
(800) 522-0066 (Voice, NV only)

New Hampshire
Infants and Toddlers Program
Division of Mental Health and Developmental Services, Department of Health and Human Services
105 Pleasant Street
Concord, NH 03301
(800) 298-4321 (Voice/TDD, NH only)

New Jersey
Resources
Developmental Disabilities Council
CN 700
Trenton, NJ 08625-0700
(800) 792-8858 (Voice)
(609) 777-3238 (TDD)

New Mexico
Information Center for New Mexicans with Disabilities/Babynet
435 Saint Michael's Drive, Building D
Santa Fe, NM 87505
(800) 552-8195 (Voice/TDD, NM only)

New York
Office of Advocate for Persons with Disablities
One Empire State Plaza, Suite 1001
Albany, NY 12223-1150
(800) 522-4369 (Voice/TDD, NY only)

North Carolina
Family Support Network of North Carolina
University of North Carolina
CB#7340
Chapel Hill, NC 27599-7340
(800) 852-0042 (Voice/TDD)
E-mail: cdr@med.unc.edu
WWW: http://www.med.unc.edu/wrkunits/1dean/commedu/familysu/

North Dakota
Developmental Disabilities Division
Department of Human Services
600 South Second Street, Suite 1A
Bismarck, ND 58504-5729
755-8529 (Voice)
(701) 328-8968 (TDD)

Ohio
Ohio Coalition for the Education of Children with Disabilities
Bank One Building
165 West Center Street, Suite 302
Marion, OH 43302
(800) 374-2806 (Voice/TDD, OH only)

Oklahoma
Oklahoma Areawide Services Information System (OASIS)
Oklahoma University Health Sciences Center
4545 North Lincoln, Suite 281
Oklahoma City, OK 73105
(800) 426-2747 (Voice/TDD)

Oregon
Department of Education
700 Pringle Parkway SE
Salem, OR 97310
(503) 378-3598

Republic of Palau
Special Education
Department of Education
P.O. Box 189
Koror, PW 96940
(670) 664-3754

Pennsylvania
CONNECT Information Service
150 South Progress Avenue
Harrisburg, PA 17109
(800) 692-7288 (Voice/TDD, PA only)

Puerto Rico
Primeros Pasos
Programa de Infantes con Impedimentos
Division de Servicios de Habilitacion
Secretaria Auxiliar de Medicina
Preventiva y Salud Familier
Departamento de Salud de Puerto Rico
P.O. Box 70184
San Juan, PR 00936-8184
(800) 981-8492
(809) 250-4552

Rhode Island
Rhode Island Parent Information Network (RIPIN)
500 Prospect Street
Pawtucket, RI 02860-6260
(800) 464-3399 (Voice, RI only)
(401) 727-4151 (TDD)

South Carolina
BabyNet Central Directory
South Carolina Services Information System (SCSIS)
Center for Developmental Disabilities
University of South Carolina School of Medicine
Columbia, SC 29208
(800) 922-1107 (Voice/TDD)

South Dakota
Midco Communications
410 South Phillips
Sioux Falls, SD 57102
(800) 529-5000 (Voice/TDD, SD only)

Tennessee
Tennessee's Early Intervention System
East Tennessee State University
P.O. Box 70434
Johnson City, TN 37614
(800) 852-7157 (Voice/TDD, TN only)

Texas
Early Childhood Intervention (ECI) Program
ECI Care Line
4900 North Lamar
Austin, TX 78751-2399
(800) 250-2246 (Voice)
(512) 502-4996 (TDD)

Utah
Access Utah Network
555 East 300 South, Suite 201
Salt Lake City, UT 84102
(800) 333-UTAH (Voice/TDD)

Vermont
Agency of Human Service
Department of Health
Children with Special Health Needs
P.O. Box 70
Burlington, VT 05402
(800) 660-4427 (Voice/TDD, VT only)
(802) 863-7338 (Voice/TDD)

Virgin Islands
Guide to Services for the Disabled in the USVI
Infant and Toddler Program
Department of Health
Elaine Co Complex
St. Thomas, VI 00803
(809) 777-8804 (Voice)

Virginia
First Steps
Department of Rights of Virginians with Disabilities
James Monroe Building
101 North 14th Street, 17th Floor
Richmond, VA 23219
(800) 234-1448 (Voice/TDD)

Washington
Healthy Mothers, Healthy Babies Coalition of Washington
300 Elliott Avenue West, Suite 300
Seattle, WA 98119-4118
(800) 322-2588 (Voice/TDD; WA, ID, OR only)

West Virginia
Family Matters
P.O. Box 1831
Clarksburg, WV 26302-1831
(800) 734-2319 (Voice/TDD, WV only)

Wisconsin
First Step
Lutheran Hospital-Lacrosse
1910 South Avenue
Lacrosse, WI 54601
(800) 642-7837 (Voice/TDD)

Wyoming
Governor's Planning Council on Developmental Disabilities
122 West 25th Street
Herschler Building, 1st Floor West
Cheyenne, WY 82002
(800) 438-5791 (Voice/TDD)

Supplemental Resources

General References

The following resources offer additional insight about developing quality programs for infants and toddlers. Write or phone for further information.

Caring for Infants & Toddlers in Groups: Developmentally Appropriate Practice
J. Ronald Lally, Abbey Griffin, Emily Fenichel, Marilyn Segal, Eleanor Szanton, and Bernice Weissbourd (1995). This book is a guide to the special knowledge and program design necessary to address the unique developmental characteristics of children in the first three years of life. (Available from ZERO TO THREE: National Center for Infants, Toddlers and Families, 734 15th Street NW, Suite 1000, Washington, DC 20005-1013.)

Developmentally Appropriate Practice in Early Childhood Programs
Sue Bredekamp and Carol Copple (Eds.) (1997). This revised edition of the industry standard on appropriate practices devotes a chapter to exploring the needs and appropriate caregiving responses to children from birth through age three. (Available from NAEYC, 1509 16th Street NW, Washington, DC 20036-1426, 800-424-2460.)

Infants, Toddlers and Caregivers
Janet Gonzalez-Mena and Dianne Widmeyer Eyer (1997). This book gives a wonderful overview of infant-toddler development and quality infant-toddler child care. It emphasizes respect for the individual child and helps caregivers focus on the relationships they build with children. It addresses multicultural issues facing caregivers, such as bilingual communication and culturally appropriate curriculum. (Available from Mayfield Publishing Company, 1280 Villa Street, Mountain View, CA 94041.)

PrimeTimes: A Handbook for Excellence in Infant and Toddler Programs
Jim Greenman and Anne Stonehouse (1996). This book helps readers understand the needs of children under three, and their families and caregivers, and how to use this information to create a quality program. (Available from Redleaf Press, 450 N. Syndicate, Suite 5, St. Paul, MN 55104-4125, 800-423-8309.)

Trusting Toddlers
Anne Stonehouse (Ed.) (1990). This is an insightful look at how to build relationships and create a program that addresses the special needs of those "exhausting, demanding, and wonderful" toddlers. (Available from Redleaf Press, 450 N. Syndicate, Suite 5, St. Paul, MN 55104-4125, 800-423-8309.)

1,2,3...The Toddler Years: A Practical Guide for Parents and Caregivers
Irene Van der Zande (1990). Written with the staff of the Santa Cruz Toddler Care Center, this easy-to-read, practical book gives readers a clear picture of the characteristics of toddlers and strategies for ways to live and work with them. (Available from Santa Cruz Toddler Care Center, 1738 16th Avenue, Santa Cruz, CA 95062.)

Topic-Related References

The following resources are recommended to readers who wish to know more about specific topics explored in *The Creative Curriculum for Infants & Toddlers*.

Knowing Children's Families

Getting Men Involved: Strategies for Early Childhood Programs
James A. Levine, Dennis T. Murphy, and Sherill Wilson (1993). This book offers practical suggestions for ways to welcome and involve the men in the lives of the children in your program. (Available from Scholastic, Inc., 555 Broadway, New York, NY 10012.)

Six Stages of Parenthood
Ellen Galinsky (1987). As it describes the stages of parenthood, this book reminds readers that parents are growing and developing too. (Available from Addison-Wesley Longman Publishing Company, One Jacob Way, Reading, MA 08167.)

Communities: Building a Network of Support

Community Mobilization: Strategies to Support Young Children and Their Families
Amy Laura Dombro, Nina Sazer O'Donnell, Ellen Galinsky, Sarah Gilkeson Melcher, and Abby Farber (1996). This guide includes detailed descriptions of hundreds of community collaborations throughout the country that have as their goal improving the lives of young children and their families. It takes the reader through the practical steps of creating change and offers tips and lessons learned, thus allowing communities to build on what others have done. (Available from Families and Work Institute, 330 Seventh Avenue, 14th Floor, New York, NY 10001.)

Promoting Health and Safety

American Red Cross Child Care Course: Health and Safety Units
The American National Red Cross and the American Academy of Pediatrics (1990). This multi-media package provides in-depth training for caregivers on infant and child care first aid, as well as preventing childhood injuries. (Available from American Red Cross National Headquarters, 2025 E Street NW, Washington, DC 20006.)

The Consumer Reports Guide to Baby Products (Fifth Edition, 1997.)
This report provides ratings of thoroughly tested childproofing products and child gates. It includes warnings on products judged not acceptable. (Available from Consumer Reports Books, 101 Truman Avenue, New York, NY 10703, 515-237-4903, reference # P664.)

First Aid for Children Fast

The Johns Hopkins Children's Center (1995). This user-friendly manual gives step by step instructions that are easy to understand and follow. Color photographs illustrate each step. This book is an excellent resource for preparing emergency plans. (Available from Dorling Kindersley Publishing, 95 Madison Avenue, New York, NY 10016.) Additional information on the Johns Hopkins Children's Center may be obtained from their Office for Public Affairs at 410-955-8662.

Healthy Young Children

Abby Shapiro Kendrick, Roxanne Kaufmann, and Katherine P. Messinger (Eds.) (1995). This resource focuses on ways to promote the health and well-being of young children in group programs. The research-based information covers safety, first aid, emergency procedures, and other topics. The manual represents a cooperative effort by the following groups: the Administration for Children, Youth and Families (ACYF); the Division of Maternal and Child Health, U.S. Department of Health and Human Services (HHS); Georgetown University Child Development Center; the Massachusetts Department of Public Health; and the National Association for the Education of Young Children (NAEYC). (Available from NAEYC, 1509 16th Street NW, Washington, DC 20036-1426, 800-424-2460.)

National Health and Safety Performance Standards. Guidelines for Out-of-Home Child Care Programs

American Public Health Association and the American Academy of Pediatrics (1992). This definitive statement on safety standards can serve well as a reference in every infant and toddler program. (Available from the Maternal and Child Health Bureau, 200 15th Street North, Suite 701, Arlington, VA 22201-2617.)

Starting Point: How To Open Your Program (and Your Heart) to Children with Special Health Needs

Division of Maternal and Child Health, Graduate School of Public Health, San Diego State University (1993). This helpful manual provides guidance on providing services for children with health and/or physical challenges, developing culturally competent services, ensuring confidentiality, preventing childhood injuries, preventing the spread of communicable diseases, providing play experiences, and dealing with challenging behaviors. A Spanish version, *Punto de Partido*, is available. (Available from National Maternal and Child Health Clearinghouse, 2070 Chain Bridge Road, Suite 450, Vienna, VA 22182-2536.)

Creating a Welcoming Environment

Caring Spaces, Learning Places: Children's Environments That Work

Jim Greenman (1988). This excellent book shows how to create environments that make use of space creatively, with attention to children's developmental needs. A separate chapter on infant and toddler environments includes wonderful ideas illustrated with photographs and diagrams of indoor and outdoor spaces. (Available from Exchange Press, Inc., PO Box 2890, Redmond, WA 98073.)

Landscapes for Learning: Designing Group Care Environments for Infants, Toddlers and Two Year Olds
Louis Torelli and Charles Durrett (1996). This excellent handbook on designing developmentally appropriate learning environments for infants and toddlers merges the principles of child development with architectural design. (Available from Torelli-Durrett, 1250 Addison Street, Suite 113, Berkeley, CA 94702.)

Learning Through Routines and Activities

Anti-Bias Curriculum: Tools for Empowerment
Louise Derman-Sparks and the A.B.C. Task Force (1989). This classic on the subject of multiculturalism provides guidance on selecting materials for children that eliminate barriers based on race, culture, gender, age, or ability. (Available from NAEYC, 1509 16th Street NW, Washington, DC 20036-1426, 800-424-2460.)

Behavior Guidance for Infants and Toddlers
Alice S. Honig (1996). In simple and vivid language, this book offers caregivers and parents positive discipline techniques that are appropriate for infants and toddlers. Tips for thinking about fusses and "disobedience" will be useful for adults puzzled by such behaviors. (Available from Southern Early Childhood Association, P.O. Box 56130, Little Rock, AR 72215-6130, 501-663-0353.)

Creative Art for the Developing Child
Clare Cherry (1990). This useful text takes a developmental approach to children's explorations with art. The book is filled with teaching suggestions and strategies. (Available from Fearon Teacher Aids, 500 Harbor Boulevard, Belmont, CA 94002.)

Creative Expression and Play in the Early Childhood Curriculum
Joan P. Isenberg and Mary Renck Jalongo (1993). Grounded in the authors' experiences teaching teachers, this book offers strategies and activities to stimulate readers' ideas of ways to promote the play and creativity of young children. (Available from Macmillan Publishing Company, 366 Third Avenue, New York, NY 10022.)

Emerging Literacy: Linking Social Competence and Learning
Derry Koralek for Aspen Systems Corporation (1997). This excellent guide, targeted to teachers and other educators, provides background information and training ideas on making children partners in conversation, the magic world of reading, and setting the stage for literacy. (Available from the Head Start Bureau, Administration for Children and Families, U.S. Department of Health and Human Services, Washington, DC 20447.)

More Than ABCs: The Early Stages of Reading and Writing
Judith A. Schickendanz (1986). This standard in the field traces the development of literacy skills which begin at birth. It describes ways to maximize the reading experience for children throughout the early childhood years. (Available from NAEYC, 1509 16th Street NW, Washington, DC 20036-1426, 800-424-2460.)

The Outside Play and Learning Book
> Karen Miller (1988). This comprehensive and extremely creative collection of outdoor activities includes a separate chapter on "Infants and Toddlers Outside." In addition, many of the ideas in other sections of the book are appropriate or can be adapted for infants and toddlers. (Available from Gryphon House, PO Box 207, Beltsville, MD 20704, 800-638-0928.)

Play Is a Child's World: A Lekotek Resource Guide on Play for Children with Disabilities for Families, Friends, and Professionals
> The National Lekotek Center (n.d.) The 51 Lekotek Centers throughout the United States provide support, resources, and toys to families of children with disabilities. This guide, and the companion manual *Lekotek Play Guide for Children with Disabilities,* focus on using appropriate adaptive toys for children with disabilities. (Available from National Lekotek Center, 2100 Ridge Avenue, Evanston, IL 60201, 800-366-7529.)

The Right Stuff for Children Birth to 8: Selecting Play Materials to Support Development
> Martha B. Bronson (1995). This comprehensive manual is an excellent resource for selecting toys to match the developmental skills of children. Careful consideration is given to safety issues. (Available from NAEYC, 1509 16th Street NW, Washington, DC 20036-1426, 800-424-2460.)

Talking with Your Baby: Family as the First School
> Alice S. Honig and Harriet E. Brophy (1996). Caregivers and parents will appreciate the ideas for using "turn-talking-talk" to enhance their daily interactions with very young children. Many photos illustrate how tuned-in talk can enrich affectionate relationships and promote early learning. Diapering, bath time, shopping trips, and other ordinary routines become opportunities to increase language power. (Available from Syracuse University Press, 1600 Jamesville Avenue, Syracuse, NY 13244, 315-443-5541.)

Index

Teaching Strategies, Inc. strives to improve the quality of early childhood programs by producing comprehensive and practical curriculum and training materials. Our products and staff development services are making a difference in preschools, elementary schools, Head Start, school-age programs, and child care programs worldwide.

Curriculum Resources

The Creative Curriculum® for Infants & Toddlers

A comprehensive yet easy-to-use framework for planning and implementing infant and toddler programs in center-based and family child care settings. Focusing on routines and activities, this book recognizes that relationships form the basis of curriculum for very young children.
#CB0052, $34.95

A Journal for Using The Creative Curriculum® for Infants & Toddlers

A companion to *The Creative Curriculum® for Infants & Toddlers* for use as a personal guidebook for understanding and applying the Curriculum. A perfect tool for ongoing staff development, group meetings, and personal reflection.
#CB0053, $25.00 (set of 5)

The Creative Curriculum® for Early Childhood, 3rd Ed.

Shows how teachers build curriculum for preschool and kindergarten children around the environment using ten interest areas: Blocks, House Corner, Table Toys, Art, Sand and Water, Library, Music and Movement, Cooking, Computers, and Outdoors.
#CB0071, $39.95
Also available in Spanish: #CB0074, $39.95

The Creative Curriculum® for Family Child Care

Helps you design a developmentally appropriate program in your home for each age group—infants, toddlers, preschoolers, and school-age children.
#CB0084, $29.95

Resources for Parents

A Parent's Guide to Early Childhood Education

Also available in Spanish and Chinese. Explains what happens in a developmentally appropriate early childhood program and the important role parents play in helping their children succeed in school and in life.
#CB0075, $22.50 (set of 10)

A Parent's Guide to Infant/Toddler Programs

Also available in Spanish. Shows parents how warm and responsive care helps shape the development of infants and toddlers and their ability to learn.
#CB0033, $22.50 (set of 10)

Competency-Based Training Materials

The "Caring for . . ." series:
- **Caring for Infants and Toddlers**
- **Caring for Preschool Children, 2nd Ed.**
- **Caring for Children in Family Child Care**
- **Caring for Children in School-Age Programs**

Each of the four sets in the *"Caring for . . ."* series is comprised of 13 modules in two volumes which correspond to the Child Development Associate (CDA) functional areas. Volume I covers Safe, Healthy, Learning Environment (Program Environment in the School-Age set), Physical, Cognitive, and Communication. Volume II includes Creative, Self, Social, Guidance, Families, Program Management, and Professionalism.
$34.95 each volume

Videos

The Creative Curriculum®

A 37-minute, award-winning videotape that shows how children learn in each interest area and how teachers set the stage and encourage their learning.
#CB0072, $99.50
Also available with Spanish subtitles: #CB0014, $99.50

Observing Young Children: Learning to Look, Looking to Learn

This 30-minute videotape illustrates how staff can use ongoing observation to learn about each child, measure children's progress, and evaluate their program.
#CB0054, $55.00

The NEW Room Arrangement as a Teaching Strategy

A 15-minute slide/videotape. Presents concrete ideas for arranging early childhood classrooms to support positive behavior and learning.
#CB0076, $35.00
Also available in Spanish: #CB0010, $35.00

Caring and Learning

This 23-minute, award-winning videotape shows four exceptional family child care providers in action using the activity areas described in *The Creative Curriculum® for Family Child Care.*
#CB0087, $42.00

Order Form

Please type or print clearly.

SHIP TO:

Name_____

Organization_____

Street_____

City_____ State_____ Zip_____

Phone (_____)_____ Fax (_____)_____

Mailing Label Code_____

BILL TO:

Name_____

Organization_____

Street_____

City_____ State_____ Zip_____

Phone (_____)_____ Fax (_____)_____

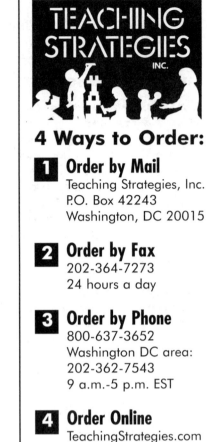

4 Ways to Order:

1 **Order by Mail**
Teaching Strategies, Inc.
P.O. Box 42243
Washington, DC 20015

2 **Order by Fax**
202-364-7273
24 hours a day

3 **Order by Phone**
800-637-3652
Washington DC area:
202-362-7543
9 a.m.-5 p.m. EST

4 **Order Online**
TeachingStrategies.com
24 hours a day

ORDER:

Item #	Qty	Description	Unit Price	Total

Please call for information on quantity discounts.

Subtotal	
DC residents add 5.75% sales tax	
Shipping/handling: 8% of net order ($5 minimum)	
Rush Delivery ☐next day ☐second day	
TOTAL	

PAYMENT METHOD:

All orders must be accompanied by payment, purchase order number, or credit card information. Customers with an established credit history are welcome to use P.O. numbers. First-time customers please pre-pay orders.

☐ Check Enclosed

☐ Authorized Purchase Order #_____

☐ Please charge my credit card: ☐VISA ☐MasterCard

Card #_____ Expiration Date_____

Signature_____

Teaching Strategies has an ongoing commitment to donate a portion of our annual revenues to organizations—such as the Center for the Child Care Workforce (formerly NCECW)—that work to assure high-quality, affordable child care by upgrading the training and compensation of early childhood educators.

☐ Please send me more information about the Center for the Child Care Workforce (CCW) and its Worthy Wage Campaign.

SHIPPING & HANDLING CHARGES
(Applies to U.S. Mainland only) 8% of net order ($5 minimum)

ALASKA, HAWAII and INTERNATIONAL DELIVERY Call for shipping charge.

RUSH DELIVERY
Place your order before 12:00 noon EST and receive it by next day or second day delivery. You will be billed actual UPS charges plus a $10 handling fee.

VIDEO RENTAL
All videotapes are available for a 2-week rental for $20 per tape plus $5 shipping and handling. If you wish to rent a tape to preview, we will gladly credit the rental fee toward the purchase price if the tape is purchased within 2 weeks of rental.

GUARANTEE
Teaching Strategies guarantees your satisfaction. If you are not thoroughly delighted with the printed materials you order, return the item(s) in saleable condition within 30 days for a full refund. All videotape sales are final. However, please see "video rental" above for information on how you may preview the videos.

QUESTIONS/COMMENTS
If you would like assistance in selecting materials, feel free to call. Or, e-mail us at custserv@TeachingStrategies.com. We welcome your questions and suggestions.

Prices subject to change without notice. Infant/Toddler CB

Thank you for your order.